MW01401244

The Magnolia Plantation

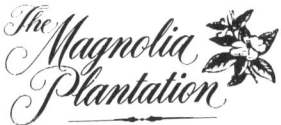

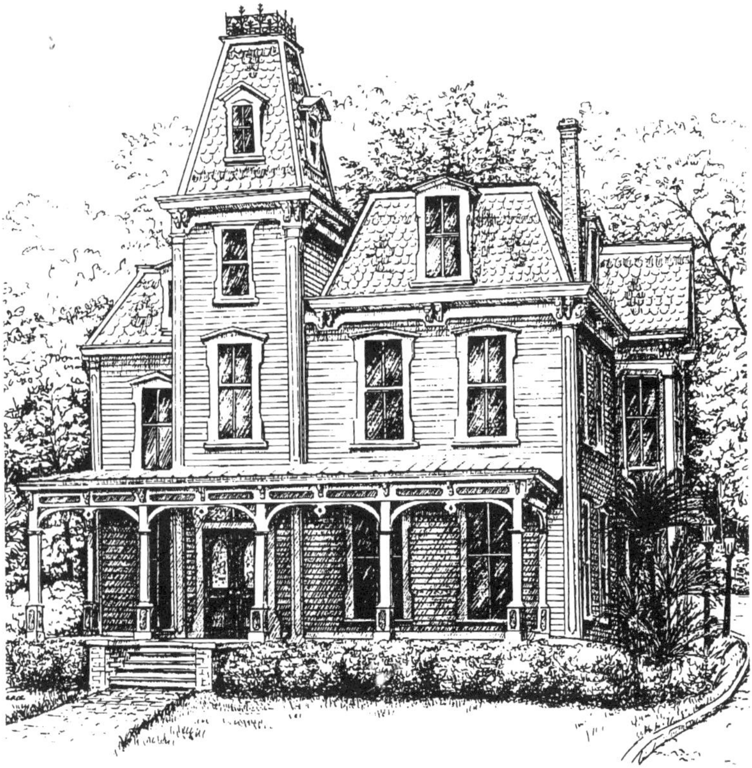

Experience Victorian Romance With Southern Hospitality

CIRCA 1885

Joe and Cindy Montalto, Proprietors *Gainesville, Florida*

Cover Photograph Credits:

Front Cover: *Cliffside Inn Bed and Breakfast*, Newport, Rhode Island by permission of owner Mr. Win Baker, photographed by George Gardner, Hillsdale, New York

Back Cover: *The Captain Lord Mansion*, Kennebunkport, Maine by permission of Rich Litchfield, photographed by Warren Jagger

Cover Design: Childers & Associates and Henry Lewis Design, Memphis Tennessee

The information contained in this publication is prepared as accurately as possible from material provided by the innkeepers for the most part and is subject to change. Therefore, it is necessary to contact each property listed to confirm all of the information before making a reservation. All references to ratings or approvals of the properties by any agency is based upon information provided by the innkeeper and is not guaranteed by the author and publisher.

The responsibility for making a reservation rests solely between the guest or agent and innkeeper in terms agreeable to all parties regardless of any and all representations made in this publication. We declare and disclaim any liability for errors or omissions and our liability for any loss or damage to any party that might occur through the use of this publication.

© 1995 Marie Baiunco-Brindza, Editor/Publisher
All rights reserved. No part of this book may be reproduced in any manner whatsoever without written permission of the author other than brief excerpts for review purposes.

Ninth Edition, 1995
Published 1987, 1988, 1989, 1990, 1991, 1992, 1993, 1994

Published by:

BED & BREAKFAST Guest Houses & Inns of America®

PO Box 38929 Memphis Tennessee 38183-0929 Tel 901-755-9613

ISSN: 1056-8069   ISBN: 0-9629885-4-5 9.95   SAN: 1056-8069

$9.95

West Coast Edition

Contents

Preface	1-4
Introduction	5-8
Innkeeper Travel Articles	9-18
Alaska	19-29
Arizona	30-47
California	48-165
Colorado	166-198
Hawaii	199-203
Idaho	204-208
Montana	209-216
Nevada	217-220
New Mexico	221-236
Oregon	237-256
Utah	257-263
Washington	264-287
Wyoming	288-293
Canada	294-308
Display Ads	Final

PREFACE

Bed & Breakfast accommodations are thriving in the United States more than ever .... as American travelers discover the excitement of European-style Bed and Breakfast, Guest Houses and Country Inns, right in their own backyard!! Long the **accommodation of choice** for Europeans, Bed and Breakfast accommodations are experiencing a phenomenal growth in the United States - beginning in the late 1980's and continuing today - offering travelers exciting lodging choices at every stop.

If you're unfamiliar with Bed & Breakfast accommodations - you have a whole new experience awaiting you by selecting a different inn for each trip if you like, whether your trip is business, a family vacation or a near-by weekend get-away or for a *special occasion!* B&Bs are smaller and more intimate compared to commercial hotels. Guests feel like they're staying at a friend's or relative's home -rather than a motel. The typical property listed in this publication has five to seven guest rooms which means you truly become a family member - from the moment you arrive until you return. You'll meet all of the guests and the innkeepers, who jealously see to your every comfort. After-all, they are truly people who enjoy meeting each guest, swapping tales, exchanging stories and trading ideas. They are well-travelled too and understand the meaning of comfort while traveling. So a Bed & Breakfast is not just the warmth of a cozy evening fireplace in a friend's home or a complimentary sherry upon arrival ... but a feel of being home at every stop during your trip.

And what a variety of homes, castles, tepees and entire private islands from which to choose!! Bed and Breakfasts are generally a home with one or two "extra" bedrooms located anywhere from traditional suburban neighborhoods to rural farms. Guest Houses would be similar to "tourist homes" offering five to nine guest rooms and generally more extensively furnished and decorated, including more guest amenities, while a Country Inn, for our purposes, provides more personalized service in an intimate setting with fewer than thirty guest rooms. Just as each family is unique - so it each Bed and Breakfast - which is looked after with the loving attention of the owner/innkeeper - insuring each guest feels at home. Each innkeepers' interests are reflected in their Bed & Breakfast and you might meet a former olympic skier, politician, artists, dancers, sailing enthusiasts, antique buffs who will lead you to the "best buys", authors, writers, well-known photographers, museum curators ... along with doctors, lawyers and indian chiefs .... and even Clint Eastwood, if he's in, at his *Eastwood Ranch* in Carmel California is a Bed & Breakfast.

Each Bed & Breakfast represents a new adventure - as close as around the corner. Travelers choose from an endless array of accommodations - allowing your imagination to run rampant. Spend a night in a tepee on a true Indian Reservation (offering a honeymoon special), all of San Francisco's night lights are outside your windows in a Francisco Bay lighthouse or choose the bedroom where celebrities such as Clark Gable and Carole Lombard and Jack and Jackie Kennedy honeymooned. Choose a luxury 100 foot yacht for a night or your own island off the Georgia Coast! For the adventuresome, a frontier cabin in Alaska without running water, phone or electricity - to the world's only underwater lodge off Key West Florida offering four guest rooms twenty fathoms below the sea - are ready for guests! Today you can stay in the family estates of famous families such as Bigelow, Palmolive, Stanley (Stanley steamer auto fame), William Wrigley and Barnum of the famous Barnum and Bailey Circus fame. If you're looking for a romantic oceanfront with candlelight dining - there are many along with TV and movie sets of leading programs and/or movies such as *On Golden Pond* (Holderness, New Hampshire listings), Alan Alda's *Four Seasons* (Edson Hill Manor, Stowe, Vermont), *Matlock* (Tranquil House, Maneto, North Carolina), *Knotts Landing* (The Cotten House in California) - or a great adventure for an exciting family vacation, new adventures await within this ninth edition.

The Mansions (Barbara Streisand's a frequent guest) in San Francisco offers it's own certified ghost, a night of magic before dining and a five million dollar art and sculpture collection - to an Inn in Santa Fe, New Mexico called *Lightening Fields*, where guests spend the night in the center of a desert field surrounded with steel rods, designed to attract lightening strikes - providing an enlightening experience! For **"kids of all ages"**, The Hugging Bear Bed & Breakfast offers over four thousand teddy bears throughout the Inn. You'll find over 10,000 choices and innkeepers anxious to greet you .... providing years of enjoyable memories and adventures to share with friends.

One of the B's in Bed and Breakfast represents the guest rooms where the innkeepers make every effort to see to your comfort. Canopy beds abound, four posters, brilliant brass, wicker and gorgeous antique heirlooms appear almost everywhere - while fitted with a handmade quilt or down comforters. In addition, many inns offer jacuzzi, evening turn-down service, complimentary evening sherry at bedside and a late night chocolate upon your pillow.

The second B in Bed and Breakfast is important to travelers too - and that represents breakfast, normally included in your room rate. Breakfast ranges from a continental or light breakfast to a sumptuous gourmet, four course meal featuring local specialties of grits in the South, fresh-picked strawberries or blue berries for your cereal or maple syrup you made the day before. You can frequently choose to have "breakfast in bed", before a winter's fire or on the veranda in spring and summer - often overlooking a flowering patio garden or a lush rolling meadow. And if you find a particular recipe to your liking -- your innkeeper will be thrilled to share it.

You'll find **best-selling cookbook author** Julee Rosso-Miller (*The Silver Palate, The Silver Palate Good Times Cookbook*) selecting and perhaps preparing your breakfast at the *Wickwood Country Inn* in Saugatuck, Michigan while in the beautiful Northwestern Montana mountains at *Huckleberry Hanna's Montana Bed and Breakfast*, you'll find famous cookbook author Deanna Hansen-Doying busily preparing breakfast in between her next book for her *Huckleberry Hanna Series* of cookbooks.

Why are Bed and Breakfast's increasing in popularity? Because they are economical - an important factor to every traveler today. As commercial hotel room rates soar, travelers are learning B&Bs offer the **best value today**. Business travelers save the most because Bed and Breakfast's offer weekday discounts -- just when business travelers need the savings. Weekday rates at Bed and Breakfasts offer the best values - with many offering 50% discounts during the week.

Who should consider a Bed and Breakfast for their lodging needs? Easily everyone who travels! More than fifty percent of all Europeans stay only at Bed and Breakfasts for a good reason. Business travelers tired of the **same old hotel room** and suffering with the *same old hotel blues*. Even the *Wall Street Journal* in 1989 reported the trend of business travelers changing to Bed and Breakfast accommodations. Family vacationers can choose a waterfront, mountain top wooded log cabin or a farm with all the animals where their children can feed the chickens, geese and other animals while gathering fresh eggs for their breakfast; women traveling alone love the security and comfort B&Bs offer; honeymooners, family relocations, retirees, antique collectors, the parents of college-bound children .... just about every traveler will find a lodging to meet their needs in this directory.

Once you've decided to try a Bed and Breakfast ... you face the most difficult portion of the trip ... that of finding "just the right one". Since B&Bs have small advertising budgets they are not easily found and frequently their names are *highly guarded secrets passed on only to the best of acquaintances*. Therefore, guidebooks have developed into the leading source of information on B&Bs and probably offer the only means of maintaining your sanity during your search. Your choice of guidebooks is not easy since there are literally thousands of choices. Since you chose this directory, we'll be the first to let you know you have the most comprehensive, complete and accurate directory available. We can easily say that because our primary subscribers for years have been travel agents. Published since 1987, our directory has earned the reputation as the **most complete reference available"** from subscribers and book reviewers alike. This means you have the largest reference available of Bed and Breakfasts - with over 10,000 listings in the Index Section, compared to other national guides with two hundred to a several thousands listings. Secondly, you will find more extensive descriptions .... **so you'll know all of the details even before contacting the Bed and Breakfast** to make your reservation. Phone numbers change, fax numbers are added, 800 numbers become available --- continuous changes you need to have to make finding *just the right Bed & Breakfast* an enjoyable part of your trip ... or job if you're a travel agent.

This ninth edition includes changes to help you enjoy your Bed and Breakfast experiences even more. More photographs and line drawings are included. This edition introduces a new feature - regional groupings rather than one large national listing. We've divided the United States into four regions, with Canada as the fifth region making it easier to use. This edition introduces innkeepers to readers. Innkeepers across the USA have contributed articles about their town, state or area which appear at the beginning of each region. Their articles offer ideas, suggestions and points of interest. Just as each Bed and Breakfast and town is different .... you'll find thousands innkeepers with a common thread of hospitality, goodwill and a sincere interest in welcoming travelers to their communities. We know you will enjoy their articles and we hope you will stop and personally meet them.

One comment pertaining to a travel industry issue regarding descriptive information on properties appearing in Bed and Breakfast publications. Member-innkeepers prepare their own listing descriptions for a number of reasons. Due to the large numbers, it's impossible to visit and review each property and still publish a national publication. Secondly, innkeepers know their Bed & Breakfast, nearby activities and sights and their town better than anyone else - therefore, they have the best knowledge. How objective are they going to be? We have found them to be very objective - after all, unlike a reviewer or rating organization, they face each guest upon arrival and have to justify their glowing description if it is not deserved. Even professional travel writers and reviewers are subject to over and/or under statement - but they depart the following day and don't face arriving guests to justify a review to the guest. This publication is a directory and not a guidebook (we do not review Bed & Breakfasts) containing a listing of accommodations following traditional European Bed & Breakfast style of properties across the United States and Canada. This information, we feel, benefits travelers by learning about the thousands of wonderful and beautiful Bed & Breakfasts overlooked by many guidebooks.

Thank you for using this directory as a reference source for your many new adventures, acquaintances and friendships that develop during your travels. If you are pleased with the book, we would appreciate your telling friends and innkeepers you visit about us. It helps innkeepers to know which books are used by guests and travel agents. More importantly, it helps you too because more Bed and Breakfasts will include descriptions in future editions providing a wider choice of lodgings for your next trip. If you know of a Bed & Breakfast, Guest House or Country Inn that is not included in our directory, we would appreciate your letting us know about them or letting the innkeeper know. Perhaps you'll find your favorite Bed and Breakfast listed in future editions, allowing other travelers to experience the same enjoyment they'll treasure in the years to come and share with others.

INTRODUCTION

The purpose of this directory is to provide travelers with the most comprehensive, single reference source of current, accurate and complete information on Bed and Breakfast-type of accommodations throughout the United States and Canada and to promote Bed and Breakfast accommodations to the traveling public. The properties listed meet our criteria of the traditional European B&Bs, limited to a maximum of thirty guest rooms; are host-owner operated in the daily operation of the inn and provide period, unique, antique, unusual or non-commercial decor and furnishings. This directory had been prepared exclusively for travel agents for the past eight years and the content has been designed to provide complete booking information about the properties listed before calling. Because this material has been prepared for professionals, important information is included you won't find in other books; information such as *toll-free 800 numbers, discount periods, money-saving packages, airport distances* and much more. Published annually, the information is accurate and complete compared to books published every two years.

Making a reservation at a Bed and Breakfast is the same as any hotel, the difference is that **each property is different**, so a full understanding and description of the property is essential for a pleasant and enjoyable trip. Reputable innkeepers are just as interested as the guest in making sure there aren't any mis-understandings and that the Bed and Breakfast will exceed the guests' expectations. For the sake of clarity and a common understanding, the terms utilized throughout this directory are listed below.

BED & BREAKFAST RESERVATIONS

In only a few minutes, you'll find *"just the right B&B"* anywhere in the USA by following a few steps. Since each Bed & Breakfast is unique, a complete description and understanding of the property is essential and time permitting when you call to make your reservation, we suggest your requesting the innkeeper to provide you with brochures for you to review before arriving. The brochures are beautifully prepared and the innkeepers are pleased to send one to you.

1. First, look in the ***Index Section*** which is an alphabetical list by state, city and Bed & Breakfast names.

2. If the B&B's name is **bolded**, look in the **Descriptive Section** for the Bed & Breakfast's name. This section is arranged alphabetically by state, city and Bed & Breakfast name.

3. Call the Bed and Breakfast you select to confirm the information listed and to make your reservation. Request that a brochure and reservation confirmation is sent to you.

4. You will find some listings without descriptions and the notation *"Refer to the same listing name under_____ city for a complete description."* **Cross-City Listings** indicate B&Bs in nearby towns.

One last note about reservations .... *MAKE THEM EARLY!* You've taken an excellent step in preparing yourself for your Bed and Breakfast adventures by purchasing a directory. Don't miss an opportunity to stay at your favorite Bed and Breakfast or in a favorite room. Innkeepers are booked weeks, months and even years in advance for traditional holidays, weekends, vacation periods. Weekday periods are less hectic and you'll find better availability on shorter notice. But ... that may not be the case. Since you've taken the first step in planning your trip - don't forget to call early.

INTERPRETING THE DESCRIPTIVE LISTINGS

RES TIME This is the best time to call for making a reservation. When a time is not listed you can't go wrong calling between 8am and 8 pm.

SEASONAL This indicates any period when the B&B is closed to guests. If NO is listed, this usually means guests are accepted year round. Some listings indicate RATES VARY which means the room rates vary by season and it is necessary to obtain more information from the innkeeper regarding their seasonal period rates.

ROOMS The number of private and shared bath guest rooms are listed here. Listed beneath each category are the Single and Double occupancy rates for that room type. Usually a range of rates are quoted and the type of room and the appropriate rate needs to be confirmed with the innkeeper. The room rate will depend upon the amenities, size, decor and location of the room. So if you're looking for a pool side or ocean front room with a canopy bed, jacuzzi and fire place and so forth, the room will be priced accordingly.

PHONES/FAX Phone numbers are listed (including 800's when available) along with fax numbers

PAYMENT *Cash, check, travelers check* and specific credit cards accepted; confirm what credit cards are accepted since this frequently changes.

MEALS The second "B" in B&B is breakfast which is usually (but not always) included in your room rate. Information concerning breakfast is included in the descriptive information. This information should be confirmed as well since innkeepers change the type and style of breakfast served. The definition of the various meals are understood to be:

Breakfast

* Continental: Juice, hot beverage and pastry or breads
* Continental Plus: The same as above but also includes choices of several breads, pastries and cold cereals
   * Full: The same as above plus eggs, meats, pancakes, waffles or other main entree
   * Gourmet: An unusual or different means of preparing a food dish, often a specialty of the innkeeper

EP European Plan indicates **NO** meals are included
MAP Modified European Plan includes breakfast and dinner
AP American Plan includes all three meals
FAM Family Style Dining Service pertains to how meals are served

DESCRIPTIVE SECTION

The listings in this section have been prepared by the innkeeper to describe their property, furnishings, decor, proximity to points of interest, local activities, their background, complimentary breakfast description and is intended to provide you with a flavor of the Bed and Breakfast. All B&Bs are not museums filled with antique furnishings and not all travelers are interested in staying in museums. Hopefully the descriptions will convey the uniqueness of each Bed & Breakfast.

*/** Notation At The B&B's Name
This notation is published for professional travel agents and indicates the innkeepers are agreeable to paying a 10% commission fee for their reservation services. This amount is not added to to the guest's rate but rather paid by by innkeeper. A single * indicates the property normally pays commissions; a double ** indicates we guarantee the commission payment to the travel agent. To be eligible to participate in the guaranteed commission program, travel agents must purchase their publications directly from the publisher.

Permitted Children, pets, smoking and drinking have been listed **when they are permitted** by your hosts. When one of the categories is not listed, it means the hosts do not permit that activity. Staying at a Bed and Breakfast is like staying at a friend's home .... so you should always ask the host if they permit the particular activity if you're not sure.

Reservations Check the reservation requirements before calling and confirm them with the innkeeper when calling because they are subject to change. Ask for a **written confirmation from the innkeeper** to eliminate possible errors.

Airport The name and distance/s to nearby airports is listed for guest's convenience.

Packages Types of packages available are listed when available and provide excellent savings for travelers.

Discounts Since each Bed and Breakfast has their own discount policies, check when calling.

Brochure Each innkeeper has brochures, write-ups, news articles, maps and other material they gladly provide guests. Request this information when making your reservation.

West Coast

The Southwest

The Southwest is wide open spaces with multi-hued red rock formations; snow-capped mountains with pine, spruce and shimmering aspen; the first mesa, second mesa and the plateau with endless desert. We are isolated ranches, small villages, reservations, towns and large cities. Wherever you travel, the scenic beauty and complexity of the Southwest changes faster than the shadows of the clouds, but we have one thing in common - *The Hoo Hoo Kam* - *"The people who have gone before"*. That is how the Pima-Maricopa Indians of Arizona describe their ancestors.

Yes, this is Indian Country. It is home to the largest number of Native Americans in North America. On their reservations they are sovereign nations .... a very private, independent people. But the *Hoo Hoo Kam* knew of no barriers nor borders. This land belonged to no man, no tribe, no nation. The land, the mountain, the tree, the stream, the river, the rock .... like the wind, the thunder and the rain; like the bird, the deer and the snake, belong to all people .... are one with the people.

The *Hoo Hoo Kam* marked this land; and there is no appreciation of its wonder, its beauty or its awesome danger other than as they knew it and have loved it. It is a sacred land, an enchanted land. When you travel the Southwest, travel in this spirit.

- Paul Kelley, Innkeeper, **Maricopa Manor** Phoenix, Arizona

Mendocino County

As I grew up in Ukiah, California, Mendocino County, I never realized the beauty and unique experiences this valley had to offer for the body and soul. It was not until I returned home from my first year at college that I realized what drew so many people here to live and an increasing number to play. This valley holds some of the finest wineries in the world, home to the largest supplier of environmentally aware products, a museum full of paintings and artifacts from the Pomo Indians, and of course, The Redwood Forests on the way to Mendocino Coast. It was not until I returned home from the traditions and heritage of my east coast college and surroundings did I see the traditions and heritage that make Mendocino County what it is today.

The thirty-five wineries to which I refer are sprinkled throughout Mendocino County, with Ukiah being home to eight of them. Some of these

 wineries are world-renown, with others being hidden jewels, nestled in their vineyards awaiting discovery. Mendocino County is also home to two of the world's best brandy distilleries, Jepson Vineyards and Germaine-Robin, whose brandies have won awards and both have been served in the White House. Ukiah, the county seat, is home to the innovative company *Real Goods*, an environmentally-centered mail order catalog with its showroom open to the public. A visitor can learn about solar power and hydro power while shopping for energy saving products for their home and office. The store also offers alternatives to the run of the mill toys with is educational toys and books.

The Sun House Museum is another one of Ukiah's unique experiences because of the Pomo Indians who live here. The museum consists of the original redwood house built by Dr. and Mrs. Hudson. Mrs. Hudson was well know internationally as an artist who painted incredible oil paintings of these Native Americans before they changed to modern clothing. The portraits of babies and families glow with the beauty of these people, their culture and her appreciation of their way of life. These paintings are displayed in the new art museum located behind the original house and is filled with her paintings, artifacts from the tribe and touring exhibits related to the Native Americans in this region.

The city of Ukiah is also a perfect starting point from which to explore the nearby California Redwoods either by car or via the town of Willit's famous *Skunk Train* that winds its way over to the coast. The Mendocino Coast, one of the most popular stops in Northern California, is a scenic drive and a perfect day trip or weekend getaway. This quaint town is featured on *CBS* every Sunday night on *Murder She Wrote* as Angelia Lansbury's hometown in Maine, Cabbot Cove. The town itself offers a host of incredible art galleries, shops and restaurants. It is also home to Cafe Beaujolais, owned and operated by gourmet chef Margaret Fox.

For those who would like outdoor recreation, there are several lakes, including Mendocino County's own Lake Mendocino, and the appropriately named Lake County with Blue Lakes and Clear Lake, California's largest natural lake, for water skiing, fishing, canoeing and boating. The Russian River runs through Mendocino County, offering fishing and tubing, while the Eel River is know for its steelhead and salmon fishing. Ukiah is located in a long valley 600 feet above sea level and is surrounded by mountains that are up to 4,500 feet in elevations with trails for mountain biking, motorcycling and hiking.

Mendocino County and its surrounding areas offer guests the opportunity to explore Northern California to the fullest. Located only two hours north of San Francisco, this area offers the classic beauty of the world famous Mendocino Coast, the traditions of the wine country, and the timeless beauty of the outdoors. I invite you to come and see why people want to save the old growth forests, stop offshore oil drilling and preserve the beauty that draws people, life myself, back to Mendocino County.

- Annelies Ashoff, Innkeeper **Vichy Springs Resort** Ukiah, California

Destination: Durango

Durango has come a long way since 1846, when Daniel Webster described this mountain outpost as *"a vast, worthless area, a region of savages and wild beasts, of deserts, of shifting sands and endless mountain ranges impenetrable, and covered with eternal snow."*

Even after Durango was established as a railroad town in 1880 -- servicing the many local gold, silver, and coal mines in the vicinity -- it was far from *"civilized."* Saloons and brothels dominated the downtown area; hangings and shoot-outs were not uncommon.

Although, today, Durango has settled down some, it still retains much of its frontier flavor. Moreover, Durango is one of the few funky cowboy towns with a functioning, self-supporting downtown area still intact.

Friendly folks here, now, and a good mix -- cowboys and Indians (of course), but also professionals and working-class folks, and a lot of young outdoor types -- hikers, bikers, and skiers. In fact, Durango is one of the most engaging towns left in the Old West -- kind of a throwback to the gentle 60's -- no doubt due to the influence of Ft. Lewis College, founded here in 1956. Good book stores (Maria's on Main), music stores (Southwest Sound, right next to Maria's), even poetry -- the most unique event being the annual Cowboy Poetry Festival in the fall.

What To Do

There is so much to do in and around Durango you really need to stay more than just a couple of days. Durango is truly a *"destination"* resort. Here are just a few suggestions:

Have a great time power-shopping downtown Durango. Hit all the shops and galleries -- including many new factory outlets.

Take a walk along the Animas River (cross the footbridge at the base of Twelfth Street). Or take a hike up to the top of the mesa on "The Nature Trail" (east end of Tenth Street) to Ft. Lewis College -- great views of Durango and the surrounding La Plata Mountains. Also check out the Victorian homes on historic Third Avenue.

Go rafting, kayaking and fishing on the Animas River. During the summer, the local rafting and kayaking companies have their booths set up on both sides of Main.

Although the downtown stretch of the Animas River is pretty gentle, there are a couple of good Class II rapids downstream. The kayak course north and south of town has been the site of Olympic trails. Fly fishing is also good right downtown (some catch and release) and elsewhere in La Plata County, rivers, alpine lakes and streams abound. World-class fly fishing for trophy-size trout can be found here all-year-round. Fishing, boating, water-skiing and swimming are available at nearby Vallecito and Navajo reservoirs. Or if it's warmer waters you seek, go for a soak in the pools at Trimble Hot Springs just north of town (the site of the summer jazz festival).

Attend the bi-weekly P.R.C.A. Rodeo at the County Fairgrounds. Picture this:

Ext. Rodeo Arena - - Night

CAMERA focuses on dust of rodeo in progress.

Then, as dust clears, CAMERA sees bronc rider mounted on wild-looking bronc.

Roar of crowd momentarily rises to deafening level on AUDIO.

DISSOLVE TO shot off bronc rider being violently bucked off bronc and sent head over heels to dusty floor of arena.

Crowd becomes suddenly hushed.

Voice of announcer comes up in AUDIO background.

ANNOUNCER

Boy, that'll jerk the puddin' out of ya'.

CUT TO ANGLE ON head of snorting bronc.

CUT TO shot of bronc rider on all fours - dazed, struggling to get up.

Have you seen this movie yet? Just another night at the Durango P.R.C.A. Rodeo.

Take the Durango-Silverton Narrow Gauge Railroad. Without a doubt, the centerpiece of Durango's thriving tourist industry is this classic narrow gauge train ride through the rugged Animas Canyon. This old coal-fired train has become highly recognizable as a result of being used as a famous prop in the many Western movies filmed in and around the Durango area -- *Viva Zapata, How The West Was Won, Butch Cassidy And The Sundance Kid*, to name a few. The ride itself is well worth the cinders and smoke. Tickets are available at the train station at the south end of Main Avenue.

Vista Mesa Verde National Park. One of the most magical places in the Four Corners area is the Mesa Verde National Park -- one hour west of Durango on Route 160. Established in 1906 (the second oldest park in the National Park system), Mesa Verde was the home of the ancient Anasazi Indians, who inhabited this site for five hundred years before mysteriously disappearing in the early 1300's. Spend some time at the Chapin Mesa Museum and be sure to walk to Spruce Tree House -- probably the most well-known cliff dwelling in North America. If you have time, drive the rim trail -- where you can view some of the hundreds of other cliff dwellings in this magnificent natural setting. Although the park is open year-round, lodging and camping facilities are seasonal.

Ski at Purgatory. In the wintertime, of course, the most popular attraction is the Durango-Purgatory Ski Resort -- twenty minutes north of Durango on Highway 550. Especially suited for families, the resort offers over 600 acres of maintained ski terrain, 150 acres of it groomed, and nine chair lifts. Regular shuttle service is provided from Durango. While there, dine at The Sow's Ear down the hill or at The Cascades down the highway -- one of the finest gourmet restaurants in the Four Corners area. After skiing, relax at Farquharts; the bar faces the slopes. Across the road, you can also cross-country ski at the Nordic Center (lessons available).

One of my favorite things to do is to take a drive through the surrounding countryside -- north, south, east or west -- some of the most spectacular drives in the Southwest.

There are many fine restaurants downtown. These are some of my favorites:

For Sunday brunch, try The Red Lion (they have a patio right over the river) or Francisco's (the best place to catch the game on weekends -- four TV screens in the lounge). The best brunch by far, though, is served at The Palace Grill -- right next to the train station.

During weekdays, get your basic breakfast at the local greasy spoon, The Durango Diner on Main.

For lunch, go to Lola's Place, just one block up from Main on Second Avenue. This unique restaurant -- located in the newly-restored Victorian "painted Lady" just two doors north of The Leland House -- offers a gourmet menu featuring delicious and healthy daily specials, including soups and salads. Bright, colorful atmosphere!

Back on Main Street, you might try Carver's Bakery and Brew Pub Cafe --

your minimum daily required foodstuffs here -- fresh-baked bread and home-made beer. My favorite entrees: the veggie ruben and the grilled veggie sandwiches, the garden Swiss burger (the veggie burger), and the chicken stew in a bread bowl (reminds me of Mon's chicken-and-dumplings). Eat at the pub in the back -- or order at the counter and eat by the windows in front.

Another good place is the Olde Tymer's Cafe. Formerly the 100-year-old Wall Drugstore, Olde Tymer's still retains the original ornate Victorian mouldings and ceiling. Artifacts, sundries from the period line the walls. Books, bottles, vintage vending machines, packaged medicines and potions fill the upstairs balconies. These days, Olde Tymer's is the unofficial headquarters of the local mountain bikers. Old Tymer's is known for its American cuisine (especially the burgers) and the inexpensive menu. Full bar. Patio out back.

One of my favorite places for the atmosphere is Father Murphy's -- which has all the ambience of an Irish pub. I always get the club sandwich or the BLT here, though their specialty is beer-battered cod. Father Murhpy's also has a patio out back. Friendly waitresses here (*"Go and sin no more,"* inscribed on their T-shirts).

For genuine Northern New Mexico cuisine, go to Gazpacho. Try the veggie combo plates. The tamales are especially good.

After lunch (or earlier if you like) visit the Durango Coffee Company -- simply the best cappuccino place in Durango -- friendly service, a number of well-lighted tables, jazz on the stereo.

For evening hors d'oeuvres, the fresh oysters at The Red Snapper are excellent -- delivered fresh on Tuesdays and Fridays. The hot oyster appetizers are only $3.95 during "Oyster Hour" -- 5:00 to 6:00 p.m., seven days a week.

For dinner I would recommend Ariano's, Randy's, or the Ore House -- all corners of a triangle in the middle of Sixth Street, between Main and Second Avenues. Ariano's features northern Italian specialties. I like the chicken in parchment paper, the linguine in clam sauce (red or white), the beef, the fish -- everything is good (though sometimes a bit rich). Pasta comes on the side with every dish. Randy's, same side of the street, is known for veal chops, chicken, and escular -- when available (a delicate, white fish from Mexico). Randy's serves food at the bar -- making it another good place to watch the game. The Ore House, directly across the street, is a great steak and lobster place -- with salad bar. The fresh Colorado mountain trout is always excellent -- pan-fried, grilled, almandine, or Sonora style.

Another consistently good restaurant is The Palace Grill (next to the train station). I remember the baby-back pork ribs, the honey duck and the goulash (simmered with mushrooms and onions in a red wine sauce).

After dinner entertainment might include rock and roll at Farquahrts, honky-tonk piano at The Diamond Belle, or jazz at The Pelican. Do the two-step at The Sundance, where all the cowboys hang out. Or tour the local saloons.

The Old Muldoon, up from The Palace on Main Avenue, is my regular hangout: Victorian setting -- flower print wallpaper, wainscotted walls, lots of mirrors, paintings of reclining nudes, velveteen-covered love seats, high-backed chairs, marble-topped coffee tables -- two barber chairs in the back (where the dart boards are located) -- Tiffany lamps, stained-glass everywhere, brass rails, ornate, hand-carved wood-back bar. Older group here, but a good mix -- local businessmen, hat-maker who owns the shop across the street (O'Farrel's), owner of the leather shop next door (The Apaloosa Trading Company) -- assorted cowboys -- construction crews -- occasional Indians (Lone Eagle, a Sioux from South Dakota who was mixing it up with a Navajo last time I was here). Local character, calls himself Little Beaver, comes in looking for cigarettes -- loose change in cracks of the overstuffed couches. Little Beaver wearing headband and feather, or bandanna wrapped around his head, or one time a Mexican sombrero -- serape -- pants too short -- hair cut in spiky short butch, or mohawk, or shaved bald -- Little Beaver carrying on long discussion with himself.

The Diamond Belle (next block up Main) is another interesting place -- Victorian decor -- part of the Strater Hotel (the oldest hotel in town). At the Diamond Belle, I run into a young guy from back east who has quit his office job and set out to conquer the highest peaks in every state in the west -- just did Wheeler Peak in New Mexico -- now headed for Humphrey's Peak in Arizona. After a few beers, though, I find out that there is also a lost love behind this enterprise.

And further up the street is Farquharts -- typical, low key college dance place -- your usual poster-flecked falls -- brick and wood decor -- main floor crammed with tables -- full bar and pretty good pizza -- and your usual young lovelies drifting in -- college coeds. But in Durango, there's always a good mix -- working class guys in for the happy-hour pitcher specials -- young professionals -- but no cowboys ("Bouncer ushers them right out of here", one of the locals tells me -- "they just don't mix with the hippie-types, I guess -- don't like the music maybe.") "Leftover Salmon" is playing tonight.

The most colorful saloon in town is The El Rancho at the Central Hotel -- local dive and pool hall (seven tables) -- also known at "Ol' Rauncho." I am sitting at the bar the El Rancho when I am tapped on the shoulder -- and turn around to greet Larry Harjo, Medicine Man from Oklahoma -- Seminole, he tells me. Larry apologizes, thinking I'm someone else, chats with me about a spirit gathering in Kansas that he's about to attend -- tells me he's in town to exorcise bad medicine from house of local Ute man -- says he hears spirits, but none he can identify -- but he'll try once more tonight -- says he does bad medicine too. We shake left hands (Indian style) and he blesses me -- gives me good medicine -- for me and my family.

©*Bed & Breakfast Guest Houses & Inns of America, Memphis TN*

I wish him luck and apologize for having to leave -- not sure what to make of all this medicine, his holy words, his generous incantation.

But you might just say it's just another day in Durango -- a true vacation destination.

- Fred Wildfang, **Leland House B&B Suites**, Durango, Colorado

The Valley of the Sun - Arizona

We offer the rugged excitement and natural beauty of the Old Southwest blended with all the sophistication of the *New* Southwest. We also offer wonderful experiences you'll remember for a lifetime. Because when it comes to the things you want most in a destination, the Valley has all of them. No matter how long you plan on staying, you'll find our Bed and Breakfast accommodations and Southwestern hospitality will make you want to stay longer. You can pamper yourself. Phoenix and the Valley of the Sun will make you feel right at home, no matter how far from home.

Our name, Valley of the Sun, just about says it all. Phoenix has over 300 days of sunshine a year, very low humidity and an average yearly temperature of 72 degrees. To go along with our comfortable weather, we also have a very comfortable dress code. Other than several restaurants which require jacket and tie for dinner, the dress is casual year round. Shorts in summer are perfect. Be sure to pack swim suits anytime of the year. Jeans and western wear are always in style. And when the rest of the country is wrapped in parkas, a sweater or jacket is all you'll need.

Fresh Atlantic lobster grilled over Southwestern mesquite. Savory cowboy steaks charbroiled under a Southwestern sunset. From unforgettable down-home cooking to sophisticated continental cuisine to a traditional Mexican fiesta, memorable dining experiences await you in the Valley of the Sun. Comedy clubs, jazz, rock, big band music ... there are so many things to do in the Valley.

Life may not be all fun and games but in the Valley it certainly comes close. We're home of the NFL Phoenix Cardinals, NBA Phoenix Suns, Arizona State Sun Devils and the Arizona Rattlers. We're the annual site of the Fiesta Bowl, PGA Phoenix Open, LPGA Standard Register Turquoise Classic, PGA Seniors Tradition Tournament, Checker 500 NASCAR Winston Cup and CART Indy Car races. We also host polo matches, Arabian horse shows, dog racing, thoroughbred racing - even authentic western rodeos. And, as much as there is to see, there's even more to do. Water skiing, swimming, tubing down the Salt River, glider flying, hot-air ballooning, horseback riding, mountain climbing, jeep touring, trail hiking and endless hours of camera clicking. Sports fans are sure to become devoted farms of the Valley of the Sun.

If variety is the spice of life, wait until you get a taste of our golf and tennis. In the Valley of the Sun, golfers can tee-off on over one hundred courses. Choose a desert course, stadium course, traditional course - even a choice of challenging designs by Jack Nicklaus and Tom Weiskopf ... and that's just half of it! For tennis, the Valley offers a thousand courts of clay, laykoid, grass and stadium play. Obviously, if you love golf or tennis, don't miss Phoenix and the Valley of the Sun.

For visitors who love the arts, Phoenix can easily become a first love. You can see the culture of the American Indian come to life at the world-renown Heard Museum. See the acclaimed permanent collection, the national and international traveling exhibits at the Phoenix Art Museum. Enjoy the sights and sounds of symphonies, ballets, opera and live theatre. You can walk into the past at an Old West town, walk through the timeless architecture of Frank Lloyd Wright, take in the natural beauty of the Desert Botanical Garden and naturally, don't miss the Phoenix Zoo.

Shop hop ... mall crawl ... seek a boutique ... if you're serious about shopping, we've got fun for you! The art galleries, Western shops and international boutiques in the Valley of the Sun are legendary ... Italian leather, French lingerie, dusty antique, sparkling diamonds, American Indian sculpture and good-old American bargains abound. Even if you have the energy, you're bound to wear-out your credit card before the day is over.

Centrally located in Arizona and the heart of the Sonora Desert, Phoenix is the perfect getaway to the beauty of one of the nation's most diverse states. Towering pines, a forest of majestic cactus, the red rock country of Sedona, the man-made wonder of Lake Powell, nature's greatest wonder ... the Grand Canyon - even the experimental world of Biosphere II are within easy reach! Whether your plans allow you the opportunity of just a few days or an extended stay, you'll discover for yourself why we're the number one visitor destination of the Southwest USA! Arizona, **One Grand Adventure After Another.**

- Darrell Trapp, Keeper of the Inn **Westways** Phoenix, Arizona
Bed & Breakfasts Inn Arizona/Arizona Accommodation Reservations

The Mendocino Coast

Do you dream about serene coutryside, azure blue seas, dramatic cliffs, endless beaches, billowy clouds, misty mornings, redwood forests? It's real and you will find it all on the Mendocino Coast. Driving scenic Pacific Coast Highway One, you will discover the villages and towns of Gualala, Anchor Bay, Point Arena, Manchester, Irish Beach, Elk, Albion, Little River, Mendocino, Caspar, Fort Bragg, Cleone, Westport and Rockport.

The Mendocino Coast is a mecca for multi-talented people. Old-timers and newcomers pool their experiences to share with the community. Whether it's a pancake breakfast at the Grange, symphony concert, musical theater at Cotton Auditorium, or benefit art show and wine tasting, you can count on the folks from all walks of life to Be There. Our celebrations include: **Whale Festivals**, Mendocino, Fort Bragg and Gualala - last three weekends in March; **Heritage Days**, Mendocino - First week of May; **World's Largest Salmon BBQ**, Noyo Harbor - July 4th weekend; **Paul Bunyan Days**, honoring the Logging Industry, Fort Bragg - Labor Day Weekend; **Great Day in Elk**, Parade, BBQ, dancing - mid-July; **Hometown Christmas**, Fort Bragg - First weekend in December.

Romance ... music ... theatre ... fine arts ... crafts ... great food ... towering Pacific breakers ... deep secret forests ... meandering peaceful rivers ... All on the Mendocino Coast!

- Colette M Bailey, Innkeeper **The Grey Whale Inn** Fort Bragg, California

Central Coast of California

The Central Coast of California welcomes you with the distinct Pacific breeze that freshens the hillsides golden with poppies, tempers the heat of the summer sun and warms the sands during afternoon strolls on winter beaches. Sounds unique to the region will entice you at each stop along your travel route -- the bark of seals and otters in Monterey Bay, the clatter of the *Giant Dipper* on the Santa Cruz Beach Boardwalk, the cable car clang on San Francisco hills and the gull cries over Point Reyes. The silent redwood giants harbor peaceful glens. Complementing the serenity of these natural wonders, the large cities and small towns offer informative museums, enriching art centers and lively theatre faire. The richness of the ethnic diversity of this area is reflected in an array of food palaces offering the finest cuisines of the world. At each destination you innkeeper-host will help you fully experience the gifts of the region whether you are the vigorous hiker looking for spectacular views from coastal peaks, the determined shopper seeking treasure or trinket of local beauty or the wine connoisseur pursuing a great chardonnay. Like the first discoverers of California, when you reach the Central Coast you'll exclaim *"Eureka! I've found it"*.

- Patricia O'Brien, Innkeeper **Blue Spruce Inn** Soquel California

Alaska

*Grandview Gardens B&B — Anchorage AK

4424 Campus St #2 99507-1578
907-277-REST

Rates:	Pvt Bath 2	Shared Bath 2	Payment Terms:
Single	$ 75.00	$ 55.00	Check
Double	$ 85.00	$ 65.00	

Enjoy the Northern "Frontier" in this elegant log cabin lodge setting that includes all the "creature comforts" you'd find anywhere much less here! Three different theme rooms are available along with elegant guest services to assure romantic evenings during your stay. There's a hot tub, flowers, comp wine, bikes and car rentals available along with a continental breakfast included with your room. **BROCHURE:** Yes **PERMITTED:** Smoking & drinking. [E11ACAK-20]

**Lilac House — Anchorage AK

Cathy Kerr
907-272-3553

950 P St 99501

Rates:	Pvt Bath 1	Shared Bath 2	Payment Terms:
Single	$ 65.00	$ 55.00	Check
Double	$ 85.00	$ 65.00	MC/V

Built in 1989, this second story addition to a lovely old Anchorage home is perfectly located in a quiet tree-filled neighborhood for the vacationer and business traveler. Guest rooms are light and airy and include original artwork, stimulating books and tasteful furnishings selected by the owner, an interior decorator. Tree-shaded Denali View Guest Room features lovely vistas of Mount Denali and the Chugach Mountains, two single beds, dining table and chairs and writing desk. Facing west, the Sun Room fills with glorious Alaska sun light when the insulated shades are lifted. Laura Ashley linens grace the two single beds with a writing desk, chairs and a chest complete the comfortable decor. Each room has a private phone for free local calls and the Denali View and Sun Room have a deck with a beautiful view of the Chugach Mountains. Complimentary tempting, fresh-baked breakfasts served in guest room. Located adjacent to Delaney Park, guests are just a ten minute walk to downtown Anchorage shops, restaurants, offices and courthouses and the Coastal Trail, a walking, bicycling and skiing trail is just a few minutes walk

Alaska

away. Fishing gear for everyone interested in trying their luck. **AIRPORT:** Anchorage-15 min; Alaska Railroad Depot-3 min drive **RESERVATIONS:** One night's deposit, 48 cancel policy in season, 7 day policy low season (Oct-Apr). $10 up-charge for one night's stay, 11am check-out **BROCHURE:** Yes **PERMITTED:** Children, drinking, smoking outdoors **LANGUAGES:** Some French [R05DPAK-12222]

Mc Carthy B&B		Anchorage AK
Babbie Jacobs		PO Box 111241 99511
907-277-6867		**Res Times** 24 Hrs
Rates:	**Shared Bath** 4	**Payment Terms:**
Single	$ 50.00	Check
Double	$ 70.00	

In the heart of the Wrangell - Saint Elias National Park, *McCarthy* has changed little since the early 1900s. Mail is delivered by bush plane weekly - no phones, electricity, running water. Water is hauled from a crystal clear spring, bathing is done in a wood-fired log-sauna bath house, reading by kerosene lamps and plumbing is outdoors! The cabins were once the Territorial Commissioner's Cabin and the other was the Mother Lode Powerhouse (on the *National Historic Register*). Groups can occupy the Commissioner's Cabin while there are three bedrooms in the Powerhouse. Both cabins offer a perfect & intimate retreat from the "fast life" and a unique opportunity to sample the frontier life of Alaska. Your host offers guided tours & trips to Historic Kennicott, White Water Rafting, Exploring Root Glacier along with a multi-day venture which includes mountaineering, glacial skiing, backpacking & rafting. A hearty full breakfast is included to begin each daily adventure. **RESERVATIONS:** Deposit of 50% of length of stay required. **BROCHURE:** Yes **PERMITTED:** Children, drinking [E07BCAK-24]

Favorite Bay Inn		Angoon AK
Roberta & Dick Powers		On Favorite Bay 99820
907-788-3123		
Rates:	**Shared Bath** 4	**Payment Terms:**
Single	$ 65.00	Check
Double	$ 75.00	

Located on Admiralty Island overlooking the Angoon Boat Harbor, you're in the heart of wildlife with whales, bald eagles, sea lions and drumming grouse that frequently serenade guests. The rambling home was built in 1937 and enlarged to serve as a general store. Your hosts are familiar with all the points of interest and where to go, depending on your

Alaska

interests. The island is accessible by daily ferry and sea plane service from Juneau and Sitka. A continental breakfast is included, with other meals available at added cost. **RESERVATIONS:** Deposit of $25 per days stay required at booking time. **BROCHURE:** Yes **PERMITTED:** Children, drinking (bring your own, the island is dry) [E02BCAK-25]

Porter House B&B		Bethel AK
Rose Porter		624 First Ave 99559
907-543-3552		
Rates:	**Shared Bath** 4	**Payment Terms:**
Single	$ 60.00	Check
Double	$ 80.00	MC/V

Over look the Kuskokwim River in this comfortable combination of country and contemporary living accommodations while exploring Alaska. All the comforts of home away from home but with the frontier atmosphere. Breakfast is a real treat served on china and silver that includes imported jams, homemade croissants, omelettes and reindeer sausage. Airport pick-ups available. **BROCHURE:** Yes **PERMITTED:** Children, limited pets [E11ACAK-26]

** *7 Gables Inn*			Fairbanks AK
Paul & Leicha Welton			4312 Birch Lane 99708
907-479-0751			**Res Times** 8am-10pm
			Fax 907-479-2229
Rates:	**Pvt Bath** 8	**Shared Bath** 4	**Payment Terms:**
Single	$ 60-95.00	$ 45-70.00	Check
Double	$ 60-120.00	$ 50-80.00	AE/DC/MC/V

Historically, *7 Gables Inn* was a fraternity house within walking distance to the UAF campus, yet across the road from the Chena River. Our spacious Tudor home offers 10,000 sq ft of unique custom-energy efficient design. Guests enter through the floral solarium into the antique stained-glass decorated foyer with an indoor waterfall - just part of the unique architecture. Other features include cathedral ceilings, a wedding chapel, wine cellar and rooms with dormers, giving a quiet elegance to the premises. A gourmet breakfast is served daily, ranging from a variety of crepes, quiches and specialty egg dishes, as well as fresh fruit, muffins,

©*Bed & Breakfast Guest Houses & Inns of America, Memphis TN*

Alaska

sweetbreads, coffee cakes, fruit juices, coffee and tea. The area offers: Univ of Alaska Fairbanks campus and Museum, Riverboat Discovery, Alaskaland, Pumphouse Restaurant, Cripple Creek Resort, Alaska Pipeline "permafrost house", Gold Dredge #8, Public Lands Info Center, fishing, skiing, dog mushing and the Santa Claus House. Laundry facilities are available, jacuzzi, bikes, luggage and/or game storage and a library collection. Each room includes cable TV, VCR, phone. Comp canoes are available for river rides down to the historic Pumphouse Restaurant. **DISCOUNT:** Fall, Winter, Spring **AIRPORT:** Fairbanks Intl-2 mi **RESERVATIONS:** 1/3rd deposit of entire stay, 48 hr cancel notice for refund **SEASONAL:** Rates vary **BROCHURE:** Yes **PERMITTED:** Children, drinking, limited pets, limited smoking **CONFERENCES:** Wedding chapel used for dancing, business meetings, rehearsal dinners **LANGUAGES:** Spanish, German [I07GPAK2-11978]

Glacier Bay Country Inn			Gustavus AK
Al & Annie Unrein			PO Box 5 99826
907-697-2288			**Res Times** 9am-5pm
			Fax 907-697-2289
Rates:	**Pvt Bath** 6	**Shared Bath** 1	**Payment Terms:**
Single	$ 99.00 AP	$ 84.00 AP	Check
Double	$ 184.00 AP		

Experience **Real Alaskan Country-style of life** - away from the crowds - surrounded by the lush, green rainforests in a wilderness setting with a majestic mountain backdrop. The Inn is constructed of lumber logged and milled right on the homestead. With accommodations for just eighteen guests, your hosts see to your every need, Furnished for comfort with warm flannel sheets, cozy comforters and fluffy towels, guest become members of the family. Dining is a superb treat with vegetables, herbs and fruits from the large garden on the premises. You'll also find homemade breads & deserts with local seafood entrees of crab, halibut and salmon. Your hosts will make sure you experience every Alaskan event including charter fishing & flying, boat & kayak rentals and whatever. *Special tour package rates available. **RESERVATIONS:** 50% deposit to confirm reservation with a 45 day cancel policy for refunds less $25 service fee **BROCHURE:** Yes **PERMITTED:** Children, drinking [E01BCAK-6082]

Magic Canyon Ranch			Homer AK
Carrie Reed			HCR 40015 Waterman Rd 99603
907-235-6077			**Res Times** 8-5pm
Rates:	**Pvt Bath** 1	**Shared Bath** 2	**Payment Terms:**
Single	$ 58-65.00	$ 52-58.00	Check

Alaska

Double $ 65-75.00 $ 57-67.00

Just outside of town you'll enjoy this *raw country setting* with all the comforts of home though! Deluxe rooms with all modern amenities but furnished with frontier Alaska antiques offering tremendous views of Kachemak Bay & Glaciers. Full breakfast **BROCHURE:** Yes **PERMITTED:** Children, limited drinking [C11ACAK-50]

**B&B Inn Juneau			**Juneau AK**
Ronda Flores			1801 Old Glacier Hwy 99801
907-463-5855			**Res Times** 7am-10pm
			Fax 907-463-5259
Rates:	**Pvt Bath** 1	**Shared Bath** 6	**Payment Terms:**
Single	$ 65.00	$ 48.00	Check
Double		$ 55.00	AE//MC/V

Located on the outskirts of town, *Bed & Breakfast Inn Juneau* offers six rooms with shared baths and one room with a private bath, along with an apartment for family groups or large parties. There is a large comfortable lounge area with cable TV and laundry facilities. The whole Inn is decorated with artwork by some of Alaska's most popular artists and may be purchased if desired. The grounds are landscaped and picnic tables and barbecues are available. Bicycles are also available for those wishing to see the area in a relaxed fashion. Bus service to town is readily available or assistance with rental cars can be provided if needed. The full breakfast includes specialties of crepes, Alaskan sourdough hotcakes, fresh fruit, syrups and jams from berries grown on the grounds and occasionally fresh salmon. Assistance with sightseeing activities, fishing charters or other travel arrangements can be provided. We look forward to providing further information on our accommodations. **RESERVATIONS:** Deposit required **BROCHURE:** Yes **PERMITTED:** Children, No handicap facilities [Z11DPAK-6306]

**Wintels B&B			**Kodiak AK**
Willie & Betty Heinrich			PO Box 2812 99615
907-486-6935			**Res Times** 8am-10pm
Rates:	**Pvt Bath** 1	**Shared Bath** 4	**Payment Terms:**
Single	$ 90.00	$ 55-80.00	Check
Double	$ 90.00	$ 55-80.00	

Whether you're traveling for business or pleasure, *Wintels* has everything needed to make your stay in Kodiak more enjoyable and relaxing. You're located within walking distance of shops, beaches, jogging paths, hiking trails and the boat harbor, home of the world-famous fishing fleet.

Alaska

Guests can choose a pleasant and comfortably furnished single or double guest room, each with a complimentary fruit basket. You can enjoy one of the many books and videos your hosts have available for guests to use in the separate den area or enjoy the soothing jacuzzi. You'll be treated to a delicious full Alaskan breakfast each morning - with your hosts ready to prepare box lunches and evening dinners upon request. This great location offers spectacular views from the inn of eagles, sea birds, sea lions or a beautiful channel view. Nearby you can browse the many specialty shops or even shop at the gift shop in the Inn and choose from the many Alaskan gift items, jewelry, basketry and artwork created by some of Alaska's famous artists. Fishing is spoken here! Try your favorite rod and reel in some of Kodiak's legend fishing scenic rivers or your hosts can help with arrangements for ocean and air charters. **DISCOUNTS:** Off season **AIRPORT:** Kodiak State Airport-5 mi **PACKAGES:** Yes, Individually planned & money-saving for interested activities **RESERVATIONS:** $50 deposit to hold reservation **BROCHURE:** Yes **PERMITTED:** Limited children, smoking outdoors only **LANGUAGES:** Spanish, some German [Z03FPAK2-12173]

Totem Inn	**Valdez AK**
	Mile .02 Richardson Hwy 99686
907-835-4443	**Res Times** 8am-10pm

Rates:	**Pvt Bath** 24	**Payment Terms:**
Single	$ 80-up	Check
Double	$ 95-up	MC/V

In the center of frontier Alaska and convenient to everything outdoors, guests can experience all the excitement and atmosphere while having modern amenities available including cable TV. Enjoy the hot tub or wildlife displays during your visit. **MEALS:** Full breakfast daily with other meals available at added cost. **BROCHURE:** Yes **PERMITTED:** Children, smoking, drinking and pets. [E11ACAK-2900]

Alaska

Anchorage
42ND AVENUE
ANNEX
907-561-8895

ALASKA
SOURDOUGH
907-563-6244

ALL THE COMFORTS
OF HOME
907-345-4279

ANCHORAGE B&B
907-333-1425

ANCHORAGE EAGLE
NEST HOTEL
907-243-3433

ARCTIC LOON
907-345-4935

B&B AT RASPBERRY
MEADOWS
907-278-9275

BED & BREAKFAST
INN
907-276-1902

CAMAI B&B
907-333-2219

COASTAL TRAIL B&B
907-243-5809

COPPER WHALE INN
907-258-7999

COUNTRY GARDEN
907-344-0636

COUNTRY STYLE
B&B
907-243-6746

DARBYSHIRE HOUSE
907-279-0703

DOWN HOME B&B
907-243-4443

FAIRBANKS B&B

FAYS B&B
907-243-0139

FORGET-ME-NOT
B&B
907-243-1638

GALLERY B&B
907-274-2567

*GRANDVIEW
GARDENS B&B
907-277-REST

HEAVENLY VIEW
B&B
907-346-1130

HILLCREST HAVEN
907-276-8411

HOSPITALITY PLUS
907-333-8504

LAKESIDE B&B
907-334-1662

**LILAC HOUSE
907-272-3553

LOG HOME
907-276-8527

LYNNS PINE POINT
B&B
907-333-3244

*MC CARTHY B&B

907-277-6867

PILOTS ROW B&B
907-274-3305

SIEGFRIEDS B&B
907-346-3152

SIX-BAR-E RANCH
B&B
907-279-9907

SIXTH & B B&B
907-279-5293

VALLEY OF THE
MOON B&B
907-279-7755

WALKABOUT TOWN
B&B
907-279-2918

WRIGHTS B&B
907-561-1990

Angoon
*FAVORITE BAY INN
907-788-3123

Bethel
*PORTER HOUSE
B&B
907-543-3552

Big Lake
JEANIES ON BIG
LAKE

Cantwell
ADVENTURES
UNLIMITED LODGE

Central
ARCTIC CIRCLE HOT
SPRINGS
907-520-5113

©*Bed & Breakfast Guest Houses & Inns of America, Memphis TN*   25

Alaska

Coffman Cove
BAYVIEW BED & MEALS
907-747-3111

Cordova
OYSTERCATCHER B&B
907-424-5154

RELUCTANT FISHERMAN
907-474-3272

Denali Natl Park
CAMP DENALI
907-683-2290

CARLO CREEK LODGE
907-683-2512

DENALI CROWS NEST
907-683-2321

KANTISHNA ROADHOUSE
907-345-1160

Douglas
WINDSOCK INN
907-364-2431

Fairbanks
AH ROSE MARIE B&B
907-456-2040

** **7 GABLES B&B**
907-479-0751

BEAVER BEND B&B
907-452-3240

BETTY'S B&B
907-479-5016

BLUE GOOSE B&B
907-479-6973

BOREALIS HOTEL

CHENA RIVER B&B
907-479-2532

DAYBREAK B&B
907-479-2753

ELEANORS NORTHERN LIGHTS B&B
907-452-2598

FAIRBANKS B&B
907-452-4967

FAIRBANKS DOWNTOWN B&B
907-452-7700

GOLDSTREAM B&B
907-455-6550

HILLSIDE B&B
907-457-2664

INIAKEEK LAKE LODGE
907-479-6354

JOANS B&B
907-479-6918

KAREN'S B&B
907-456-3146

PIONEER B&B
907-452-5393

SOPHIE STATION HOTEL
907-479-3650

SUMMIT LAKE LODGE
907-822-3969

WILD IRIS INN
907-474-IRIS

Gakona
CHISTOCHINA TRADING POST LODGE
907-822-3366

Gustavus
*****GLACIER BAY COUNTRY INN**
907-697-2288

GOOD RIVER B&B
907-697-2241

GUSTAVUS INN
907-698-2254

PUFFIN B&B
907-679-2260

Haines
CACHE INN LODGE
907-697-2254

FORT WILLIAM SEWARD
907-766-2856

OFFICERS B&B
800-542-6363

SUMMER INN B&B
907-766-2970

Halibut Cove
QUIET PLACE LODGE
907-296-2212

Homer
B&B/Seekins
907-235-8996

BEACH HOUSE

Alaska

907-235-5945

BRASS RING B&B
907-235-5450

DRIFTWOOD INN
907-235-8019

HALCYON HTS B&B
907-235-2148

HALIBUT COVE
CABINS
907-296-2214

KACHEMAK BAY
WILDERNESS LODGE
907-235-8910

*MAGIC CANYON
RANCH
907-235-6077

PIONEER BNB
907-235-5670

RIDGETOP B&B
907-235-7590

SADIE COVE
WILDERNESS LODGE
907-235-7766

SEASIDE FARM

STARDUST RETREAT
907-235-6820

TUTKA BAY LODGE
907-235-3905

WILD ROSE B&B
907-235-8780

WILLARDS MOOSE
LODGE
907-235-8830

Juneau
ADMIRALTY INN
907-789-3263

B&B INN JUNEAU
907-463-5855

BLUEBERRY LODGE
907-463-5886

DAWSONS B&B
907-586-9708

GRANDMA'S
FEATHER BED
COUNTRY INN
907-789-5005

INN AT THE
WATERFRONT
907-586-3800

JAN'S VIEW B&B
907-463-5897

LARSON'S LANDING
907-789-7871

LOST CHORD B&B
907-789-7296

LOUIES PLACE ELFIN
COVE
907-586-2032

MULLINS HOUSE
907-586-2959

POT BELLY B&B
907-586-1279

SILVERBOW INN
907-586-4146

TENAKEE INN
907-586-1000

Kenai
CHINULNA POINT
LODGE
907-283-7799

DANIELS LAKE
LODGE
907-776-5578

HAHTNU B&B
907-283-7152

Ketchikan
GREAT ALASKA
CEDAR WORKS
907-247-8287

HIDDEN INLET
LODGE
907-225-4656

KETCHIKAN B&B

MAIN STREET B&B
907-225-8484

Kodiak
BARANOF MUSEUM
ERSKINE HOUSE
907-486-5920

WINTELS B&B
907-486-6935

Lake Louise
EVERGREEN LODGE
907-822-3250

Manley Hot Springs
MANLEY LODGE
907-672-3161

Matanuska
YUKON DANS B&B
907-376-7472

Palmer

©*Bed & Breakfast Guest Houses & Inns of America, Memphis TN*   27

Alaska

HATCHER PASS LODGE
907-754-5897

NORTH COUNTRY B&B
907-822-3670

OCEANVIEW MANOR
907-443-2133

POLLENS B&B
907-745-8920

RUSSELLS BED & BOARD
907-376-7662

TERN INN BY THE LAKE B&B
907-745-1984

Paxson
PAXSON LODGE
907-822-3330

Petersburg
BEACHCOMBER INN
907-772-3888

JEWELLS BY THE SEA B&B
907-772-3620

LITTLE NORWAY INN

SCANDIA HAUS
907-772-4281

Port Graham
FEDORA'S BNB N SKIFFS
907-284-2239

Seldovia
CROW HILL B&B
907-234-7410

MCKENZIE BOARDWALK HOTEL
907-234-7816

SELDOVIA ROWING CLUB INN
907-234-7614

Seward
MOM CLOCKS B&B
907-224-5563

SEWARD WATERFRONT LODGING
907-224-5563

STONEY CREEK INN
907-224-3940

SWISS CHALET B&B
907-224-3939

VAN GILDER HOTEL
907-224-3079

WHITE HOUSE B&B
907-224-3614

Sitka
BIORKA B&B
907-747-3111

HANNAH'S B&B FISHING CHARTER
907-747-8309

HELGA'S B&B
907-747-5479

KARRAS B&B
907-747-3978

MOUNTAIN VIEW B&B
907-747-8966

PUFFIN B&B

907-747-3912

SITKA HOUSE B&B
907-747-4935

Skagway
GOLDEN NORTH HOTEL
907-983-2294

IRENES INN
907-983-2520

SGT PRESTONS LODGE

SKAGWAY INN
907-983-2294

WIND VALLEY LODGE
907-983-2236

Skwentna
SKWENTNA ROADHOUSE

Soldotna
ARCTIC TERN B&B
907-262-5720

BRUMLEYS B&B
907-262-6252

BUNK HOUSE INN
907-262-4584

EAGLES NEST B&B
907-262-5396

HONEYMOON COVE B&B
907-262-4286

POSEYS KENAI RIVER HIDEAWAY
907-262-7430

Alaska

RIVERSIDE INN
907-262-4451

SOLDOTNA B&B
907-262-4779

Sterling
SUNRISE B&B
907-262-4951

Talkeetna
FAIRVIEW INN
907-733-2423

RIVER BEAUTY B&B
907-733-2741

TWISTER CREEK UNION
907-258-1717

Tok
STAGE STOP
907-883-5338

Trapper Creek
REFLECTION POND
907-733-2457

TRAPPER CREEK B&B
907-733-2220

Valdez
ALPINE MOUNTAIN INN 907-835-2624

B&B OF VALDEZ
907-835-4211

BEST OF ALL B&B
907-835-4524

CHALET ALPINE VIEW 907-835-5223

CHRISTIAN B&B
907-835-2609

FORGET-ME-NOT B&B
907-835-2717

FRANCE INN B&B
907-835-4295

JOHNSON HOUSE B&B
907-835-5289

LAKE HOUSE B&B
907-835-4752

MINERAL CREEK B&B
907-835-4205

RAINBOW LODGE

*TOTEM INN
907-835-4443

Ward Cove
NORTH TONGASS B&B
907-247-0879

Wasilla
EDE DEN B&B
907-376-2162

WASILLA LAKE B&B
907-375-5985

Whittier
SPORTMANS INN

Wrangell
CLARKE B&B
907-874-2125

Arizona

Managers House Inn	Ajo AZ
Jean & Micheline Fournier	#1 Greenway Dr 85321
602-387-6505	**Res Times** 7am-10pm
	Fax 602-387-6508

Rates:	**Pvt Bath** 5	**Payment Terms:**
Single	$ 69.00	Check
Double	$ 69.00	MC/V

Situated atop the highest hill in Ajo and built in 1919, the *Manager's House* was the former residence of the New Cornilia Company Mine manager. Today, much remains the same with each room offering a different decor with comfortable furnishings. There are spacious common rooms suitable for business and social events along with beautifully maintained grounds which provide a quiet and serene setting. Ajo and the surrounding area offer natural sights such as Organ Pipe Cactus Natl Park with over 300,000 acres of nature trails, rare organ pipe and senita cacti, Kitt Peak Observatory and Cabez Prieta National Wildlife Refuge. While relaxing at the inn, guests can enjoy the Library/Sunroom, Spa, TV & VCR and a small gift shop. A lavish country breakfast is included along with a decanter of brandy on your nightstand for guests desiring a nightcap before retiring in this peaceful desert setting. **RESERVATIONS:** Credit card to hold reservation, same as *AAA*. A pet B&B is available off-site to board your pet during your stay **BROCHURE:** Yes **PERMITTED:** Drinking, limited smoking **CONFERENCES:** Yes for groups to 16 persons, including patio area [E08BCAZ-8370]

Bisbee Inn	Bisbee AZ
Gail Wade/Bill Thomas	PO Box 1855 85603
800-421-1909 602-432-5131	

Rates:	**Shared Bath** 18	**Payment Terms:**
Single	$ 39.00	Check
Double	$ 44.00	AE/MC/V

A certified historic restoration, the *Bisbee Inn* dates from 1917, when it was known as the LaMore Hotel. Overlooking Brewery Gulch, once one of the Southwest's wildest boomtowns! Like many of Bisbee's buildings, the Inn is a mixture of architectural styles set in a charming Victorian mining town era and atmosphere. The guest rooms are attractively furnished with large, comfortable beds and beautiful oak antique pieces.

Arizona

Each room has its own sink and guests share seven toilets and five heated tiled showers. A hearty western breakfast is served. Visit such famous sites as Tombstone or the ghost towns of Gleeson and Courtland. **RESERVATIONS:** Deposit at res time to guarantee room **BROCHURE:** Yes **PERMITTED:** Children, limited pets [E02BCAZ-2]

<u>**Inn At Castle Rock**</u>   **Bisbee AZ**
Jim Babcock   112 Tombstone Canyon 85603
800-566-4449 602-432-4449

Rates: Pvt Bath 15   **Payment Terms:**
Single $ 40.00   Check
Double $ 50-60.00   MC/V

Driving into Bisbee though Mule Pass Tunnel brings travelers to another era - a unique setting of an early Western mining town set in the Mule Mountains. The Inn, built in 1890 as a miner's boarding house, is centrally located on the Main Street of Old Bisbee at the edge of the business district and across from Castle Rock. The Inn was built over a mine shaft that later filled with water (guests will find goldfish swimming in the well) which is now a centerpiece of the dining area, with natural rock walls, Mexican tile work and antique furniture. Each of the fifteen guest rooms and suites has a private bath and its own unique decor and furnishings, including Victorian antiques and original art. The one acre hillside garden at the back of the Inn has fruit trees, wild flowers and ramadas and many little trails to explore. A glass-walled upper sitting room has a fireplace, books and lovely views of the town. A ground floor parlor features Mexican tile and a sacred Indian spring while the art gallery is located in the top floor parlor. A full breakfast is included with complimentary evening wine served around the fireplace. Local sights include Lavender Open Pit Mine, Mining Museum, historic houses, art galleries, shops, an underground mine tour and excellent restaurants. If we were to describe ourselves, we might say *"personable, a bit off-beat, and a fine alternative to impersonal hotels"*. **RESERVATIONS:** One nigh deposit to guarantee, cancel noon, day of arrival for full refund **PERMITTED:** Children, drinking **BROCHURE:** Yes **LANGUAGES:** Spanish **CONFERENCES:** Two meeting rooms for groups to thirty R08GPAZ2-69]

<u>**Cochise Stronghold Lodge*</u>   **Cochise AZ**
Rita Wilburn & Al Okemah   RD #1 Box 51 85606
602-862-3442   **Res Times** 8-5pm

Rates: Pvt Bath 1   **Shared Bath** 2   **Payment Terms:**
Single $ 50.00 $ 32.00   Check
Double $ 41.00

Arizona

Snuggled in the Dragoon Mountains at 4500 feet is this complete guest cottage providing spectacular views surrounding the entire home. All amenities including a wood-burning fireplace for chilly evenings plus a/c for any humid nights that might occur. A continental breakfast is included. **RESERVATIONS:** $5.00 surcharge for just one night's stay **BROCHURE:** Yes **PERMITTED:** Smoking, drinking [C11ACAZ-72]

**Inn At 410			**Flagstaff AZ**
Howard & Sally Krueger			410 N Leroux St 86001
800-774-2008 602-774-0088			**Res Times** 9am-8pm

Rates:	**Pvt Bath** 7	**Shared Bath** 2	**Payment Terms:**
Single	$ 80-110.00	$ 70-80.00	Check
Double	$ 80-110.00	$ 70-80.00	AE/MC/V

The Inn At 410 offers guests four seasons of hospitality in a charming 1907 Craftsman home, once the family residence of a wealthy banker and rancher. Now fully renovated, the Inn is elegantly furnished with antiques, stained glass and touches of the Southwest. Curl up with a book and hot cider in the spacious living room or sip an iced tea while relaxing in the lovely garden gazebo. Nine guest rooms are uniquely decorated from Victorian and Art Deco to contemporary Southwest. The innkeepers pamper each guest with a personal touch that includes oven-fresh cookies and scrumptious, healthy breakfasts. *The Inn At 410* is an easy jaunt to the Grand Canyon, volcanic and meteor craters, ancient Pueblo ruins, Hopi and Navajo villages, the Painted Desert, the red rocks of Sedona, Oak Creek Canyon and other attractions. The innkeepers are happy to recommend their favorite hiking and skiing trails in the San Francisco Peaks. Located two blocks from historic downtown Flagstaff, within walking distance of shops, galleries and restaurants; a short drive to Northern Arizona University, Lowell Observatory and Museum of Northern Arizona. Voted the *"Best Place for a Weekend Getaway in Flagstaff"* by *Arizona Republic*. **RESERVATIONS:** One night full deposit, more than one night-50%, 7 day cancel policy **PERMITTED:** Children, limited drinking **BROCHURE:** Yes **AIRPORT:** Phoenix Sky Harbor-140 mi **SEASONAL:** Rates vary [R07GPAZ2-18988]

**Maricopa Manor		**Phoenix AZ**
Mary Ellen & Paul Kelley		15 W Pasadena Ave 85013
602-274-6302		**Res Times** 24 Hrs
		Fax 602-266-3904

Rates:	**Pvt Bath** 5	**Payment Terms:**
Single	$ 79-129.00	Check
Double	$ 79-159.00	AE/DISC/MC/V

© *Bed & Breakfast Guest Houses & Inns of America, Memphis TN*

Arizona

Imagine yourself a privileged guest, among good friends, in the sumptuous atmosphere of a fine home ... enjoying all of the comforts of home while being catered to with the most attentive service ... and a home that reflects your finest sensibilities while fulfilling your personal and professional needs. Experience the *Maricopa Manor* ... in the very heart of North Central Phoenix, a few minutes from Central and Camelback, Uptown Plaza Shopping Center and restaurants. This beautiful Spanish-styled manor house was built in 1928 on what was then a quiet country road, five miles from downtown Phoenix. Today *Maricopa Manor* is at the crossroads of the Valley of the Sun, offering travelers intimate ambiance and an elegant urban lifestyle. The main house provides three unique guest rooms with various amenities such as canopied king beds, outside private entrances, beautiful antiques, a Franklin Stove while The Guest House offers two luxurious suites, Reflections Past & Reflections Future - each a spectacular experience. Surrounded by a forest of palms - evenings bring guests outdoors to relax and enjoy a patio fire with the hosts and other guests. A continental plus breakfast is served each morning. **AAA** ♦♦♦ **and Mobil** ★★★ **Award**; member of Arizona Association of B&B Inns **AIRPORT:** Sky Harbor Intl-3 mi **DISCOUNTS:** Yes, summers **CONFERENCES:** Yes, for small groups. **RESERVATIONS:** One night deposit, 7 day cancel notice for refund less $15 fee **SEASONAL:** Rates vary **BROCHURE:** Yes **PERMITTED:** Children, drinking, limited smoking [I07GAZ2-12115]

**Arrowzona "Private" Resort	Phoenix/Valley of the Sun, AZ
Darrell Trapp	PO Box 11253 85318
602-561-0335	**Res Times** 10am-4:30pm
	Fax 602-561-2300
Rates: Suite 2	**Payment Terms:**
Single $ 49-98.00	Check
Double $ 49-122.00	AE/MC/V

For a casual, sophisticated stay, this luxury Casita Townhouse is the Valley's best kept secret - located in the Northwest Phoenix-Arrowhead Ranch area and convenient to I-17 and 101 Loop. Operated as a "private" facility (not available to the general public), by advance reservation only. *Arrowhead Casita* is operated by the former innkeeper of Westways Resort Inn which enjoyed the highest number of awards each consecutive year of operation throughout the state of Arizona. From arrival to departure as a friend - your stay is fashioned after 5 Star Resorts, offering courtesy

Arizona

bath robes, bath toiletries, turn down service, daily morning paper, private phone and etc ... to numerous to mention all of the pleasant surprises. Overlooking the 10th hole and the 11th green on Arrowhead's Arnold Palmer-designed Championship Course, each suite includes private bath, Southwestern decor, color CATV, in-room mini fridge and microwave, private petite patio and private parking. A full hardy breakfast is included daily except during summer when a deluxe continental plus breakfast is served. Complete use of Arrowhead Country Club facilities, just a short stroll, are included. Ideal for a couple or individual traveler offering low-key graciousness and style, created to serve the special guest who deserves comfort, luxury and warmth from their *"home away from home."* Your host is a former travel agent and can help you find the *who, what, where of attractions, sightseeing, dining and shopping*. **RESERVATIONS:** One night's deposit at res time **BROCHURE:** Yes **PERMITTED:** Drinking, smoking limited [R07GPAZ2-85]

Mount Vernon Inn **Prescott AZ
John & Sybil Nelson   204 N Mount Vernon Ave 86301
800-754-7284   602-778-0886   **Res Times** 8am-9pm

Rates: Pvt Bath 7   **Payment Terms:**
Single $ 80.00   Check
Double $ 110.00   AE/DC/MC/V

Step back in time to the genteel hospitality of another era. This grand Victorian home has the charm of yesterday and all of the amenities of today. Stay in a main house guest room or one of our completely private cottages, each unique and special. Our guest rooms all have a private bath and queen bed and are tastefully decorated and furnished with antiques. Cottage guests may enjoy privacy and flexibility with a breakfast basket delivered to the door, join the other guests in the main house or prepare breakfast in the fully-equipped kitchen. All cottages are furnished with televisions. The quiet relaxing atmosphere of the *Mount Vernon Inn* will give you the feeling of being an invited guest to a private home, yet with the proper concern for privacy. For your day's adventure, stroll downtown to antique shops and unique boutiques, wonderful restaurants, exciting galleries and museums, or take a walking or driving tour of historical sites. Enjoy a host of artistic events scheduled year-round on the beautiful tree-lined Courthouse Square, including evening entertainment during the warmer months. Other activities in the area are thoroughbred and quarter horse racing, golf, tennis, hiking, backpacking, fishing and picnicking. A full complimentary breakfast and afternoon refreshments included. **RESERVATIONS:** One night's deposit, 7 day cancel policy, check in 3-8pm, later arrival only with prior arrangements on a case-by-case basis **PERMITTED:** Children, pets, limited drinking, limited smoking **SEASONAL:** No **BROCHURE:** Yes **DISCOUNTS:** Mid-week

Arizona

October through April; Sixth night free when staying five nights **AIRPORT:** Phoenix-97 mi **PACKAGES:** *Two-For-One*, Sunday-Thursday, Oct-April; *15% Second Night*, Monday-Thursdays, May-September. [R03GP-AZ2-18200]

**Inn At The Citadel	**Scottsdale AZ**
	8700 E Pinnacle Peak Rd 85255
800-927-8367 602-585-6133	

Rates:	**Pvt Bath** 11	**Payment Terms:**
Single	$ 150-265.00	Check
Double	$ 150-265.00	AE/DC/MC/V

Let the splendor of the Sonoran Desert enchant you at the Inn. Eleven private, intimate suites are appointed with antiques and original art work. Fireplaces, terraces and spectacular views woven together into a tapestry of unequalled ambiance. Fine dining, shopping and salons await you at the *Citadel*. A deluxe continental breakfast is included with your stay, which is served in the Market or delivered to your room. Room service is available from 7:00 am to 10:00 pm, Complimentary robes are in each suite, cable TV with HBO and a Service Bar is located inside the armoire. Massages, facials and manicures are also available in rooms. For business, our Board Room is available; VIP Lounge, complete with up-to-the-minute stock quotes and national newspapers; computer and fax facilities; full-service banking services and conference room capacity of thirty with banquet and catering service. **RESERVATIONS:** Deposit required to guarantee reservation, 7 day cancel policy for refund **SEASONAL:** Rates vary **PERMITTED:** Children **BROCHURE:** Yes **CONFERENCES:** Yes **AIRPORT:** Phoenix Sky Harbor Airport-30 mi **PACKAGES:** Yes, inquire at reservation time [Z07GPAZ2-14081]

**Westways "Private" Resort	**Scottsdale AZ**
Darrell Trapp	
800-266-STAY 602-582-3868	**Res Times** 10am-4:30pm

Rates:	**Pvt Bath** 6	**Payment Terms:**
Single	$ 49-98.00	Check
Double	$ 49-122.00	AE/MC/V

Refer to the same listing located under Phoenix AZ for a complete description. [M11BCAZ-6545]

**A Casalea B&B	**Sedona AZ**
Lea Pace/Vincent Mollan	PO Box 552 86339

©*Bed & Breakfast Guest Houses & Inns of America, Memphis TN*

Arizona

602-282-2833   **Res Times** 7am-10pm

Rates:	**Pvt Bath** 10	**Payment Terms:**
Single	$ 107-206.00	Check
Double	$ 119-229.00	

A *Casalea* was designed and built to showcase Sedona's history and its native beauty while taking advantage of commanding views of majestic red rocks. A *Casalea -to Lea's house*, is located next to Tlaquepaque Market Place in the heart of old town Sedona. Expect something out of the ordinary; sunken kiva, library, balconies, fireplaces, whirlpool tubs, sauna, outdoor hot tub, handicapped facilities. In our old Pueblo, we feature a collection of museum-quality regional artifacts and memorabilia. Full gourmet Arizona breakfast and evening refreshments. **Opening Spring 1994 RESERVATIONS:** One night's deposit within 7 days of booking, 48 hr cancel policy for refund, min stay on selected holidays **BROCHURE:** Yes **PERMITTED:** Drinking, limited smoking **CONFERENCES:** Yes, when renting entire home [Z04FPAZ1-8843]

**Briar Patch Inn	**Sedona AZ**
Jo Ann & Ike Olson	Star Rt 3 Box 1002 86336
602-282-2342	

Rates:	**Pvt Bath** 15	**Payment Terms:**
Single	$ 110-165.00	Check
Double	$ 110-165.00	MC/V

As your hosts, we look forward to sharing with you our love of the Red Rock Country of Sedona. The *Briar Patch* is not a resort of typical amenities but a Bed and Breakfast Inn whose desire is to create a quiet, soothing atmosphere that will give you the opportunity to create your own discovery experience. Private cottages are furnished in an Arizona Indian and Mexican decor - designed for those whose sensitivities ask for rustic ambiance with comfort. Fireplaces, shaded patios and privacy lead to the reading of a good book or the pure enjoyment of a private moment. Nestled at the base of the Mogollon Rim, the mountains invite guests to nurture a relationship with nature whether it is hiking, exploring Indian caves or quietly watching the sun ease its way out of the canyon. The spring fed waters of Oak Creek create a magical oasis for guests and peacocks, squirrels, Goldie the goat and a caring staff. The eight and one-half acres provide fishing for German Browns, bird watching and visits from bald eagles alighting in spring. Noted as one of five major centers for experiencing the *Vortex Energy* in this area, guests from around the world are drawn to Oak Creek Canyon. Activities at selected times throughout the year include small workshops in creative arts of painting, Navajo weaving, Indian arts, photography and music apprecia

Arizona

tion. Also available are Astrology, Philosophy and Self-Healing through spiritual, emotional and physical awareness. We welcome you to experience the sparkling music of the cool and refreshing Oak Creek - whiling your time as your private moment. Complimentary breakfast included. **AIRPORT:** Phoenix Sky Harbor-115 mi **RESERVATIONS:** One night deposit within one week of booking, 10 day cancel policy less $10 service fee **BROCHURE:** Yes **PERMITTED:** Children, drinking **CONFERENCES:** Groups to sixteen **LANGUAGES:** Spanish, French [R12EPAZ2-89]

Cozy Cactus B&B	Sedona AZ
Bob & Lynne Gillman	80 Canyon Circle Dr 86351-8673
800-788-2082 602-284-0082	**Res Times** 9am-9pm

Rates:	**Pvt Bath** 5	**Payment Terms:**
Single	$ 70-85.00	Check
Double	$ 75-90.00	DISC/MC/V

Cozy Cactus weaves magical red rock vistas and breath-taking sunsets playing across the nearby red cliffs with healthy doses of old-fashioned hospitality into a memorable experience. Located at the foot of Castle Rock and overlooking the valley between Sedona's red rock cliffs and Wild Horse Mesa, one of John Wayne's favorite movie locations, is this ranch-style home, comfortably furnished with family heirlooms and theatrical memorabilia from Lynne & Bob's diverse professional careers. All of the cozy bedrooms are uniquely furnished and include the Wyeth Room (Andrew Wyeth's simple style is reflected in the decor), the Country French Room, and the Nutcracker Room, (showcasing Bob's extensive collection of nutcrackers from around the world) and the American Room (featuring a queen-size bed with handmade quilt) and Music Box Room. Each room has large windows and private baths; each pair of bedrooms share a sitting room featuring a fireplace and small kitchen. Full breakfasts are served in the great room where guests can watch the morning sun begin to warm the face of Bell Rock. Relaxing afternoon sunsets are enjoyed with complimentary beverages on the patio while the sun slips behind Castle Rock. Nearby sights include Coconino National Forest for hiking, bird watching and photography, Jerome, an historic old copper mining town, Montezuma's Castle, Walnut Canyon and Sunset Crater. Your hosts are delighted to help arrange golf at two excellent courses, jeep and horseback trips in the back-country, tours, or dinner in nearby Sedona. **DISCOUNTS:** Yes for weekly stays. **AIRPORT:** Phoenix Sky Harbor-120 mi **RESERVATIONS:** One night's deposit, 7 day cancel policy; check-in 4-6pm, later by arrangement, two night min weekends; three night min holiday weekends **BROCHURE:** Yes **PERMITTED:** Children, drinking, smoking on outdoor patio **LANGUAGES:** Italian [Z07GPAZ2-14572]

Arizona

Greyfire Farm — Sedona AZ

David Payne/Elaine Ross
602-284-2340
1240 Jacks Canyon Rd 86336

Rates: **Pvt Bath** 2
Single $ 75.00
Double $ 80.00

Payment Terms:
Check
MC/V

You are welcome to join us at *Greyfire Farm*, a 2-1/3 acre farm nestled amidst pine trees in the rural valley between Sedona's red rocks and Wild Horse Mesa, one of John Wayne's favorite Western movie sites. The views of both are exceptional. The nearby National Forest Service Land has beautiful bridle paths suitable for horseback riding or hiking - offering heavily-wooded areas by the dry creek beds and panoramic views from the higher ridges. The comfortable ranch home, furnished mainly with antiques and quilts, provides just two guest rooms: The Canyon Suite (a spacious room with private full bath attached) which offers spectacular sunrise views of Jacks Canyon with Lee Mountain on one side and Wild Horse Mesa on the other; and Red Rock Vista with a large picture-window framing Courthouse Butte, a well-known Sedona landmark. It has a private, full bath with skylight directly across the hall. Both rooms have queen size beds. A full hearty breakfast is served which features waffles, homemade muffins, or buttermilk blueberry pancakes with fresh seasonal fruits. A quiet peaceful setting, just 1.8 miles from the shopping and restaurants in the Village of Oak Creek and 8 miles from downtown Sedona, guests can easily visit the many art galleries and shops, including Tlaquepaque, the beautiful and famous replica of an old Mexican village. **PACKAGES:** Seven nights for the price of six **AIRPORT:** Phoenix Sky Harbor-2 hrs **RESERVATIONS:** One night or 50% deposit (which ever is greater), 14 day cancel policy (less $10 fee) check-in 4-6 pm or other with prior arrangement, two night min weekends, 3 night min holiday weekends **BROCHURE:** Yes **PERMITTED:** Children, drinking, limited pets, limited smoking. Horses boarded, $6.00 night extra [R11DPAZ-14338]

**Rose Tree Inn — Sedona AZ

Rachel M Gillespie
602-282-2065
376 Cedar St 86336
Res Times 8am-8pm

Rates: **Pvt Bath** 4
Single $ 82.00
Double $ 116.00

Payment Terms:
Check
MC/V

Touted as the **best kept secret in Sedona**, *The Rose Tree Inn* is located right in the heart of "Old Town" and one block off the highway. Guests are within walking distance to shops, restaurants and art galleries. *The*

Arizona

Rose Tree Inn is a beautiful property situated in a lovely English Garden environment. Inviting patios, whirlpool, gas BBQ grill brings everyone together to enjoy the beauty of Sedona. Three of the four units have fully equipped kitchenettes. Complimentary coffee and tea is in each room. A great setting, just 2 hours north of Phoenix and 2-1/2 hours south of the Grand Canyon - there's golf, tennis and horseback riding nearby. Reservations are a must. **PACKAGE-DISCOUNT:** Five night rate (Sun-Thursday) available. **AIRPORT:** 100 mi-Phoenix. **RESERVATIONS:** One night's deposit, 50% for extended stays, cancel policy: one night - 48 hrs, weekly - 14 days, entire property - 30 days, check-in 2pm, check-out 11am **SEASONAL:** Rates vary **BROCHURE:** Yes **PERMITTED:** Children, social drinking, limited smoking [Z07GPAZ2-94]

Sipapau Lodge B&B			**Sedona AZ**
Lea Pace/Vincent Mollan			PO Box 552 86336
602-282-2833			**Res Times** 7am-10pm
Rates:	**Pvt Bath** 3	**Shared Bath** 2	**Payment Terms:**
Single	$ 65-75.00	$ 50.00	Check
Double	$ 70-80.00	$ 55.00	

Sipapau Lodge is our private home in West Sedona. The Sipapau is the opening in a Hopi kiva through which enlightened beings enter this dimension. As guests enter *Sipapau Lodge*, they too, can come into another dimension of renewed energy in a unique retreat. This ranch-style home is constructed of local red rock and is surrounded by natural vegetation and herb gardens. Anasazi Indian culture is evident in decor throughout the home. Your hosts are knowledgeable about the history and geography of the area. Unique recipes from Lea's kitchen are a specialty at each full buffet-style breakfast. Vincent is a massage technician, craftsman and potter. Many of his original pieces are on display in each spacious room along with Indian artifacts. True southwestern hospitality makes it easy to enjoy the special Red Rock experiences of Sedona. **RESERVATIONS:** One nights deposit within 7 days of booking, 48 hr cancel policy for refund. Min stay on selected holidays **BROCHURE:** Yes **PERMITTED:** Children, pets, drinking, limited smoking **CONFERENCES:** Yes, when renting entire home [S09CPAZ-8843]

Copper Bell B&B			**Tucson AZ**
Hans Herbert/Gertrude Kraus			25 N Westmoreland Ave 85745
602-629-9229			**Res Times** 7am-10pm
Rates:	**Pvt Bath** 6	**Shared Bath** 2	**Payment Terms:**
Single	$ 65.00	$ 60.00	Check
Double	$ 75.00	$ 70.00	

©*Bed & Breakfast Guest Houses & Inns of America, Memphis TN*

Arizona

Copper Bell is a unique turn of the century lava stone home which was built from 1902 to 1920 providing a unique blend of architectural styles, including art nouveau. The current owners relocated here from their native border town between Germany, France and Luxembourg. They brought heirloom furnishings from Germany along with German doors, windows and building materials not normally seen in the USA and created an Inn that combines the old world with the new. A lovely arched porch on the house front provides great shade for relaxing with an afternoon tea and socializing with your charming hosts and guests. The beautiful copper bell hung in a place of honor is another treasure brought from a German church. A lovely honeymoon suite including a waterbed is available too. You'll enjoy the homemade full breakfasts, included in your room rate, where Gertrude creates either a German, French or American-style meal - including homemade marmalade and jam! Conveniently located, your hosts will help you find the sights of Tucson including downtown, shops and restaurants, Old Tucson, Sabino Canyon, Sonora Desert Museum, San Xavier Mission, Titan Missile Museum, Pima Air Museum and local colleges. While you're staying here, you can learn about gem carving and sculpting from their son or goldsmithing from their daughter, a well-known gold craftsperson. **AIRPORT:** Tucson Intl- 10 mi **RESERVATIONS:** Deposit required to guarantee reservation; 4-6pm check-in (late arrival upon arrangement) check-out 11am. Extended stay discounts. **BROCHURE:** Yes **PERMITTED:** Limited smoking, children 10-up **LANGUAGES:** Fluent German, French [J05FPAZ2-12116]

**El Presidio B&B Inn	**Tucson AZ**
Patti Toci	297 N Main Ave 85701
602-623-6151	**Res Times** 7am-9pm

Rates:		**Payment Terms:**
Single	Pvt Bath 3	Check
	$ 75.00	
Double	$ 110.00	

A luxury Inn in **an award-winning Victorian Adobe Mansion** situated

Arizona

in *El Presidio Historic District*, close to downtown Tucson. Listed in the *National Register*, circa 1879. Romantic, lush garden courtyards filled with old Mexico ambiance. Fountains and cobblestones surround the richly-appointed guest house and suites. Gourmet full breakfast, complimentary beverages and fruit, private baths and entrances, TV, phone, his and her robes, individual designer-decor with antiques. Walk two blocks to fine dining, Southwestern cuisine, Mexican or Continental, museums, shopping and the *Arts District*. Carriage House Suite, a guest house, has a living room, kitchenette, bath with shower, bedroom with one queen size bed - $110.00. *Gate House Suite* offers a combined bed and sitting room, kitchenette, full bath (one queen size bed) - $90.00. *Victorian Suite* has one bedroom (queen size bed), full bath, parlor - $100.00. Featured in numerous national magazines; *Gourmet, Travel & Leisure, Glamour, Innsider* and the book *The Desert Southwest*. **Mobil ★★★ Rated** Excellent location for pleasure and business travelers alike. **RESERVATIONS:** One night deposit, 50% for extended stays with 2 week cancel policy for refund, late arrival only with prior arrangements **PERMITTED:** Drinking **BROCHURE:** Yes **CONFERENCES:** Yes, groups of 6-12 persons **DISCOUNTS:** Yes, business and extended stays **AIRPORT:** Tucson Intl-6 mi **PACKAGES: *Honeymoon, Weddings, Family Reunions*** [I07GPAZ2-67]

Hacienda del Sol Ranch			**Tucson AZ**
		5601 N Hacienda Del Sol 85718	
602-299-1501		**Res Times** 7am-11pm	
Rates;	**Pvt Bath** 14	**Shared Bath** 3	**Payment Terms:**
Single	$ 60.00	$ 40.00	Check
Double	$ 90.00	$ 85.00	AE/MC/V

The *Hacienda del Sol Guest Ranch Resort*, one of the few authentic ranches in Southwest Arizona is located in the Catalina Foothills. Built by the well-known Josias T Joesler in 1929, it was converted into a historic resort overlooking the city and the Foothills. The *Hacienda* prides itself on offering guests an *"Understated Elegance Time Honored"* with an ambience representing original Tucson hospitality. Stroll where many famous guests relaxed such as Clark Gable, Spencer Tracy and the Westinghouses and enjoy the mountain panoramas, exciting scenery and the restful southwestern climate. All of the guest rooms include private patios with facilities for swimming, jacuzzi, tennis, shuffle board,

Arizona

volleyball and horseback riding. **RESERVATIONS:** One night's deposit required at booking, one week cancel policy **BROCHURE:** Yes **PERMITTED:** Children, pets, smoking, drinking **CONFERENCES:** Yes to 100 persons **LANGUAGES:** Spanish [R03BCAZ-6812]

La Posada del Valle B&B	Tucson AZ
Tom & Karen Dennen	1640 N Campbell Ave 85719
602-795-3840	**Res Times** 9am-7pm
	Fax 602-795-3840

Rates:	**Pvt Bath** 5	**Payment Terms:**
Single	$ 90-120.00	Check
Double	$ 90-120.00	MC/V

An elegant Southwest adobe home built in 1929 that greets guests through a courtyard surrounded by gardens and orange trees that perfume the air each spring. The guest rooms, each with private bath & outside entrance, are tastefully decorated with antique furnishings & pieces from the 1920's and 30's. Each room is named after women from that same period: for example Sophie's Room is named after Sophie Tucker, Pola's Room after Pola Negri and Claudette's Room after Claudette Colbert. A large book-lined living room offers guests a warm retreat as they end their busy days and gather for tea each afternoon. A basket of menus from some of Tucson's finest restaurants is waiting for their perusal. Turndown service is included each evening. Breakfast is always a sumptuous array of freshly-baked breads and pastries, homemade granola, fresh fruit juices, and on weekends, surprises like cream cheese blintzes with fresh raspberry sauce or banana buckwheat pancakes and mesquite-smoked bacon. **MEALS:** Other meals available upon request. **DISCOUNTS:** Yes, inquire at res time **AIRPORT:** Tucson Intl-20 min **RESERVATIONS:** 50% of stay required as deposit by check or credit card within 5 days of booking **BROCHURE:** Yes **PERMITTED:** Children, drinking **CONFERENCES:** Great setting for business retreats for groups to 15-20 **LANGUAGES:** German [Z07GPAZ2-101]

**Lodge On The Desert*	Tucson AZ
Schuyler Lininger	306 N Alvernon 85711
800-456-5634 602-325-3366	

Rates:	**Pvt Bath** 40	**Payment Terms:**
Single	$ 50-up	Check
Double	$ 54-up	AE/DC/MC/V

A rare example of a vanishing tradition of personal hospitality and individual service - *Lodge On The Desert* is one of the few remaining owner-operated resorts in the country and is one of the select few resorts

Arizona

in Arizona listed in the prestigious *Country Inn and Back Roads*. For more than fifty years, this unique garden resort has been a haven of quiet and seclusion for knowledgeable travelers from around the world. Here they find the old-world charm of a Spanish hacienda with adobe-styled casitas and ocotillo-shaded verandas overlooking spacious lawns and colorful, flower-filled gardens. The *Lodge* provides a tranquil retreat for vacationers and small business and professional groups. Most of the spacious guestrooms are on the ground floor, many offering mesquite log-burning fireplaces - one even includes an indoor pool! Room decor is enhanced with beamed ceilings, hand-painted Mexican tile accents and authentic Monterey furniture. Semi-private patios, surrounded with the fragrant scent of fresh flowers and blossoming fruit trees, overlook vistas of distant mountains. The tradition of fine dining, which made famed restaurant critic *Duncan Hines* a frequent visitor still continues at the *Lodge* today. A continental breakfast is included in your room rate while a full breakfast and other meals are available. **RESERVATIONS:** Cash deposit or credit card number to guarantee reservation, 10 day or 48 hr cancel policy **PERMITTED:** Children, pets, drinking, smoking **BROCHURE:** Yes **CONFERENCES:** Yes, for groups to 25 persons **LANGUAGES:** Spanish, some French **DISCOUNTS:** Yes, inquire at res time **PACKAGES:** *The Twelve Days of Christmas* (Dec 22- Jan 2), American and European Plans **AIRPORT:** Tucson Intl-8 mi [R05FPAZ1-102]

Peppertrees B&B **Tucson AZ
Marjorie G Martin CTC   724 E University Blvd 85719
800-348-5763 602-622-7167   **Res Times** 8am-7pm

Rates:	**Pvt Bath** 3	**Shared Bath** 4	**Payment Terms:**
Single	$ 68.00*	$ 68.00*	Check
Double	$ 78.00	$ 78.00	DISC/MC/V

Your charming English hostess greets guests to a warm and charming Victorian home built at the turn-of-the-century. The old house, filled with wonderful antique furniture is complimented by guest houses having a modern western decor, making for a house-full of surprises. Marjorie, a travel agent and CTC for 20 years knows what guests look for when traveling and she makes sure they are spoilt while here. The location is absolutely unique since it's within walking distance of the Univ of Ariz campus with it's museums, theaters & entertainment. A full choice of restaurants and shopping areas is within an easy stroll or else guests

Arizona

can hop aboard the old trolley that passes the door and go to the 4th Avenue shopping district with boutiques, antique shops, thrift stores or else continue onto downtown to the convention center, historic and art districts and city offices. Or else they can explore the Arizona Sonora Desert Museum, Tucson Valley or the attractions in southern Arizona by car. A full gourmet breakfast with homemade breads, scones, a variety of entrees, jams, jellies & fresh fruit. The professional chefs in the family trade their expertise and secret recipes in preparing the likes of Scottish Shortbread for high tea. Picnic lunch/private dinners are available by special arrangement. Meals are served family-style in the dining room or outdoors in the cool, quiet, fountain patio. Complimentary non-alcoholic beverage upon arrival. **DISCOUNTS:** Yes, 15% June-Sept **AIRPORT:** Tucson Intl-20 min **RESERVATIONS:** One night's deposit, 7 day cancel policy for refund. *Winter PST (Summer). *There are two, 2 bedroom guesthouses with 1-1/2 bath in each guesthouse for private or shared accommodations, depending upon occupancy and preferences. **BROCHURE:** Yes **PERMITTED:** Limited children, limited smoking **CONFERENCES:** Yes for groups to 8 persons **LANGUAGES:** French, Spanish [I07GPAZ2-8347]

SunCatcher	Tucson AZ
Dave Williams	105 N Avenida Javalina 85748
800-835-8012 602-885-0883	**Res Times** 24 Hrs

Rates:	**Pvt Bath** 4	**Payment Terms:**
Single	$ 110-130.00	Check
Double	$ 110-130.00	AE/MC/V

Guest rooms at *The SunCatcher* bear homage to four of the world's great hotels - The *Connaught* in London; The *Regent* in Hong Kong; The *Oriental* in Bangkok; and The *Four Seasons* in Chicago. Each of these four rooms is furnished in the style of its namesake. All the desired amenities are provided - from luxurious bath soaps and fine linens, to the convenience of a video player in every room. Days begin with unhurried conversations over a complimentary full breakfast. Guests have their choice of a cold breakfast with fresh fruit and cereal or a hot breakfast which changes daily. After using our pool, guests can hike in the adjacent Sahuaro National Monument East, use our pass to a nearby tennis or athletic club, or simply sit in our large outdoor jacuzzi. At the eastern edge of Tucson, *The SunCatcher* offers uncompromising views of both the Catalina and Rincon Mountains. Our four acres of rolling hills and cactus will provide the greatest degree of privacy and *"quiet"*. **DISCOUNTS:** Travel agents **AIRPORT:** Tucson Intl-20 mi **RESERVATIONS:** Two night minimum stay, two night deposit required **BROCHURE:** Yes **PERMITTED:** Children, drinking, limited smoking **CONFERENCES:** Yes for small groups **LANGUAGES:** Spanish [R09EPAZ2-15783]

Arizona

Ajo
*GUEST HOUSE INN
602-387-6133

MANAGERS HOUSE INN
602-387-6505

Bisbee
BISBEE INN
800-421-1909

COPPER QUEEN HOTEL
602-432-2216

GREENWAY HOUSE
602-432-7170

INN AT CASTLE ROCK
602-432-7195

JUDGE ROSS HOUSE
602-432-4100

MILE HIGH COURT
602-432-4636

PARK PLACE B&B
800-388-4388

Chandler
CONES TOURIST HOME
602-839-0369

Cochise
COCHISE HOTEL
602-384-3156

COCHISE STRONGHOLD LODGE
602-862-3442

Cornville

PUMPKINSHELL RANCH
602-634-4797

Flagstaff
ARIZONA MOUNTAIN INN
602-774-8959

*BIRCH TREE INN
602-774-1042

CEDAR B&B
602-774-1636

****INN AT 410****
800-774-2008

DIERKER HOUSE
602-774-3249

*WALKING L RANCH
602-779-2219

Fountain Hills
VILLA GALLERIA B&B
602-837-1400

Grand Canyon
PHANTOM RANCH

Grand Canyon Village
EL TOVAR HOTEL

Greer
GREER LODGE

MOLLY BUTLER LODGE

WHITE MOUNTAIN LODGE

Hereford
RAMSEY CANYON INN
602-378-3010

Jerome
MINERS ROOST

Kingman
ARCADIA LODGE

Lakeside
*BARTRAMS B&B
602-367-1408

Litchfield Park
WIGWAM RESORT
602-935-3811

Oracle
*TRIANGLE L RANCH
800-266-2804

*VILLA CARDINALE
800-266-2660

Patagonia
LITTLE HOUSE
602-394-2493

Payson
KOHLS RANCH

Pearce
GRAPEVINE CANYON RANCH
602-826-3185

Phoenix
HILLSIDE B&B
602-997-8826

HOTEL SAN CARLOS

****MARICOPA MANOR****
602-274-6302

TALBOTS STOP OVER
602-840-3254

Arizona

Phoenix/Valley Of The Sun
**ARROWZONA "PRIVATE" RESORT
602-561-0335

Prescott
BENSONS B&B
602-772-8358

HOTEL VENDOME
602-776-0900

LYNX CREEK FARM
602-778-9573

*MARKS HOUSE INN
602-778-4632

**MOUNT VERNON INN
800-754-7284

*PRESCOTT COUNTRY INN
800-362-4759

*PRESCOTT PINES INN
800-541-5374

VICTORIAN INN OF PRESCOTT
602-778-2642

Sasabe
RANCHO DE LA OSSA
602-823-4257

Scottsdale
AZURA EAST

CASA DE MARIPOSA
602-947-9704

**INN AT THE CITADEL

800-927-8367

VALLEY O'THE SUN
602-941-1281

WESTWAYS "PRIVATE" RESORT
800-266-STAY

Sedona
**A CASALEA B&B
602-282-2833

**BRIAR PATCH INN
602-282-2342

CANYON VILLA INN
800-453-1166

CATHEDRAL ROCK LODGE
602-282-7608

**COZY CACTUS B&B
800-788-2082

GARLANDS OAK CREEK LODGE
602-282-3343

GRAHAMS B&B INN
602-284-1425

GREYFIRE FARM
602-284-2340

KEYES B&B
602-282-6008

L'AUBERGE DE SEDONA RESORT
800-272-6777

LANTERN LIGHT INN
602-282-3419

LEDUC'S B&B

602-282-6241

LODGE AT SEDONA
800-619-4467

**ROSE TREE INN
602-282-2065

*SADDLE ROCK RANCH
602-282-7640

SLIDE ROCK LODGE
602-282-3531

SIPAPAU LODGE B&B
602-282-2833

*TOUCH OF SEDONA
602-282-6462

Sierra Vista
BROWN FAMILY
602-458-6678

Strawberry
STRAWBERRY LODGE

Tempe
FIESTA INN

Tombstone
BUFORD HOUSE
602-457-3168

Tucson
ARIZONA INN
800-933-1093

BIRD IN HAND B&B
602-622-5428

BRIMSTONE BUTTERFLY
800-323-9157

Arizona

CASA ALERGE
602-628-1800

CASA SUECIA B&B

CASA TIERRA
602-578-3058

COPPER BELL B&B
602-629-9229

DESERT DREAM
602-297-1220

DESERT NEEDLE-
WORK RANCH

DESERT YANKEE
602-795-8295

**EL PRESIDIO B&B INN
602-623-6151

FORD'S EASTSIDE
B&B
602-885-1202

HACIENDA DEL SOL RANCH
602-299-1501

JUNES HOME
602-578-0857

LA MADERA RANCH
& RESORT
602-749-2773

*LA POSADA DEL VALLE B&B
602-795-3840

**LODGE ON THE DESERT
800-456-5634

MYERS BLUE CORN
HOUSE
602-327-4663

**PEPPERTREES B&B
800-348-5763

REDBUD HOUSE
B&B
602-721-0218

SPRINGVIEW
602-790-0664

**SUNCATCHER
800-835-8012

TANQUE VERDE
RANCH
602-296-6275

WHITE STALLION
RANCH
602-297-0252

Wickenburg
FLYING E RANCH

*KAY EL BAR RANCH
602-684-7593

RANCHO DE LOS
CABALLEROS
602-684-5484

WICKENBURG INN

Williams
CANYON COUNTRY
INN
602-635-2349

JOHNSTONIAN B&B
602-635-2178

California

Fensalden Inn	Albion CA
Scott & Francis Brazil	33810 Navarro Ridge Rd 94510
707-937-4042	**Res Times** 8am-8pm
Rates: **Pvt Bath** 8	**Payment Terms:**
Single $ 80-135.00	Check
Double $ 80-135.00	MC/V

The panoramic view of the ocean, cypress trees, deer feeding in the meadow - the symphony of frogs after the rain - the whales spouting and playfully tending their calves - the quietness gently accented by the buoys bobbing in the ocean - the cozy crackle and warmth of the fireplace as the day fades into evening. These are some of the memorabilia of guests at Fensalden Inn. Overlooking the Pacific Ocean from twenty tree-lined pastoral acres, *Fensalden Inn* offers a quiet respite for the perfect get-away. A Stagecoach Way Station during the 1860's, the Inn has been completely restored and now offers a restful, yet interesting stay for the traveler. There are eight guest quarters, some are suites with fireplaces and kitchens, most have beautiful ocean views and all are furnished with antiques and have private baths with tiled showers or tubs. Come and whale watch, glimpse the deer during a stroll through our meadow, or just relax and enjoy! **DISCOUNTS:** Yes, weekly rates **AIRPORT:** San Francisco or Oakland-100 mi **PACKAGES:** Yes, inquire at res time **RESERVATIONS:** 50% deposit of entire stay with check or credit card **BROCHURE:** Yes **PERMITTED:** Drinking, limited children **CONFERENCES:** Full meeting rooms and catering [R03FPCA2-168]

Anaheim Country Inn	Anaheim CA
Lois Ramont/Marilyn Watson	856 S Walnut St 92802
800-755-7801 714-778-0150	**Res Times** 7am-6:30pm
Rates: **Pvt Bath** 6	**Payment Terms:**
Single $ 60-75.00	Check
Double $ 65-80.00	AE/DIS/MC/V

This darling Princess Anne, c1910, is on nearly an acre in a charming residential neighborhood and has been restored to *just-as-new condition*. The residence of a former mayor of Anaheim, it is furnished with antique period furnishings and heirlooms. Beveled leaded glass windows, log-cabin antique pattern floors and turn-of-the-century country

California

furnishings are reminiscent of another era. Guests can relax in the quiet upstairs reading room or on one of the airy porches, wander through the garden beneath the many avocado trees on the grounds. Scrumptious gourmet breakfasts include quiches, casseroles, homemade muffins and fresh seasonal fruits. Close to everything: Disneyland, Knotts Berry Farm, Universal Studio. **RESERVATIONS:** One night's deposit at res time, late arrival only with prior notice **BROCHURE:** Yes **PERMITTED:** Limited children, limited drinking **CONFERENCES:** Yes for groups to 30 persons for small conferences and planning seminars, etc [Z04FPCA1-173]

Apple Lane Inn			**Aptos CA**
Doug & Diana Groom			6265 Soquel Drive 95003
408-475-6868			**Res Times** 8am-8pm

Rates:	**Pvt Bath** 3	**Shared Bath** 2	**Payment Terms:**
Single	$ 70.00		$ 60.00 Check
Double	$ 125.00	$ 85.00	DC/MC/V

Minutes south of Santa Cruz, this fully restored historic Victorian farmhouse offers charm and tranquility of another era. Nestled on four acres of vineyards and apple orchards, its a peaceful oasis for weekend guests to get-away and a great location for mid-week travelers. Guests enjoy the afternoon sun on the brick patio with blooming wisteria, roses and trailing vines. A Victorian gazebo perched amid trim lawns and flowering gardens - where weddings are frequently held - is another favorite spot for guests. Your hosts have decorated each guest room in different themes ranging from the Blossom Room with mauve & white decor, lace queen canopy bed, to the Pineapple Room in blue & white, antique pine furniture with a four-poster queen bed. The old Wine Cellar with large wicker casks of wine, exposed floor joists and redwood plank floor finds guests enjoying darts, table games or just socializing. An elegant full complimentary breakfast includes a platter-full of fresh fruit, coffee, fresh-squeezed juices, hot spicy apple and a trayful of warm Danish coffee-cakes - followed by a fluffy omelette-souffle, Eggs Christy or Morning Monte Cristo. Activities range from visiting the horses & chickens, picking apples or vegetables, playing horseshoes & croquet, to borrowing a novel from the library. Nearby is Cabrillo College with a Saturday farmer's market, New Brighton State Beach, Nisene Marks State Park, golf, antiquing, wine tasting , sailing & deep sea fishing and all of Santa Cruz sights within 10 miles. **AIRPORT:** San Jose-35 mi **DISCOUNTS:** $15 off weekdays, Sun-Thursday. **RESERVATIONS:** One night's deposit in advance with 5 day cancel policy less $15 service fee. Check-in 3-6pm, check-out by 11am **BROCHURE:** Yes **PERMITTED:** Limited children, pets, drinking **CONFERENCES:** Lovely wine cellar setting for groups to 30 persons, outdoor receptions and weddings to 150 persons [S05FPCA2-175]

California

Bayview Hotel B&B	Aptos CA
Barry & Sue Hooper	8041 Soquel Drive 95003
408-688-8654	**Res Times** 3-6pm

Rates:	**Pvt Bath** 8	**Payment Terms:**
Single	$ 75.00	Check
Double	$ 80.00	MC/V

This Santa Cruz County vintage California Victorian was built in 1878 and soon became famous for its warmth, hospitality and culinary excellence. It also functioned as a community center, housing the area's first post office and general store. The village of Aptos was alive with activity during the late 1800s. Next door to the hotel, trains left daily from the Aptos Station, loaded with lumber and produce from the surrounding area and returned with thousands of tourists from around the world. The guest list the *Bayview's Golden Era* included Lillian Russell, King Kalakaua of Hawaii and many distinguished European visitors. Today, the *Bayview* remains the focal point of the modern-day Aptos, an affluent residential community 90 miles south of San Francisco and 35 miles from San Jose. Our comfortable accommodations are in a convenient location near golf, tennis, fishing, state beaches, antique shops and restaurants, only a block from the entrance to the 10,000 acre Nisene Marks State Park. All rooms have private baths and are furnished with antiques. Our buffet-style breakfast includes fresh squeezed orange juice, seasonal fruit, pastries, muesli, savory egg dish and gourmet coffee. If you wish, guests may also enjoy lunch or dinner in the fine restaurant. Special Bridal and family suite available. **DISCOUNTS:** Mid-week business, extended stays **AIRPORT:** San Jose-35 mi **PACKAGES:** *Dinner Package at Verandas*, a fine restaurant on the premises **RESERVATIONS:** One night's deposit or 50% if longer must be received within 7 days of booking to hold room; 7 day cancel policy, less $10 service fee, check-in 3-6pm, later by prior notice **BROCHURE:** Yes **PERMITTED:** Children 5-up **LANGUAGES:** French, Italian [Z11DPCA-176]

Arroyo Village Inn	Arroyo Grande CA
John & Gina Glass	407 El Camino Real 93420
805-489-5926	**Res Times** Until 10pm

Rates:	**Pvt Bath** 7	**Payment Terms:**
Single	$ 75-110.00	Check
Double	$ 95-165.00	AE/DC/MC/V

This award-winning, country Victorian Inn provides a delightful blend of yesterday's charm and hospitality with today's comfort and conveniences. Featuring seven unique garden-theme suites decorated in Laura Ashley prints with antique furnishings and special touches of window seats, sky-

California

lights and balconies. A full gourmet breakfast is served in the parlor or in bed and teas and cordials are served in the late afternoon. Located half-way between Los Angeles and San Francisco in the heart of California's beautiful Central Coast, you're near Hearst Castle, San Luis Obispo, Pismo Beach, mineral spas, beaches and horseback riding on the beach and wineries. **DISCOUNTS:** 20% mid-week **AIRPORT:** San Luis Obispo-15 mi **RESERVATIONS:** Full payment prior to arrival, late arrivals ok **BROCHURE:** Yes **PERMITTED:** Children, drinking; this is a non-smoking Inn **CONFERENCES:** Yes for groups 15-20 persons **LANGUAGES:** Italian, some Spanish [Z04FPCA2-182]

**Baywood B&B Inn	**Baywood Park CA**
*Pat & Alex Benson	1370 2nd St 93402
805-528-8888	**Res Times** 7am-8pm

Rates:	**Pvt Bath** 15	**Payment Terms:**
Single	$ 80-160.00	Check
Double	$ 80-160.00	MC/V

Nestled in a tranquil neighborhood overlooking beautiful south Morro Bay, this charming Inn offers travelers fifteen different reasons to return because each of the fifteen rooms is unique - - each with its own personality. Whether you're planning a romantic or an adventurous vacation, *Baywood B&B Inn* has a room that's just right for you that will bring you back again. While each room has a distinctive theme, all rooms provide a beautiful view of the bay, a woodburning fireplace, private bath with tub and shower, phone, outside entrance, sitting area, kitchenette with microwave and queen beds. In-addition, suites have separate sleeping areas and some include sleeper sofas and dining areas. Two bedroom suites and a handicapped fitted suite are available. From Americana to Santa Fe, Wiliamsburg, Queen Victoria, California Beach, Manhattan, Granny's Attic, Emerald Bay, Kensington, Avonlea to Appalachian - choose the one you want to suite your mood! During your stay, you'll be treated to a tour of all of the rooms not occupied so you can choose the one you want to try on your next trip. Unlike many bed & breakfasts, *Baywood B&B Inn* allows for the privacy and convenience of a larger inn. Your stay at the inn includes evening wine and hors d'oeuvres on the mezzanine overlooking the bay. A continental breakfast is served in your room each morning by the La Patisserie restaurant located within the inn. Breakfast varies but typically includes a large fruit-filled croissant, fresh-squeezed juice and a selection of fine coffees or teas. Conveniently located near shops, restaurants, boating, golf, hiking, biking and picnicking - beautiful Montano De Oro State Park, San Luis Obispo and Hearst Castle are just minutes away. **AIRPORT:** Los Angeles-200 mi; San Luis Obispo-12 mi. **RESERVATIONS:** One night's deposit required, two night min stay on weekends and holidays, check-in

California

2-6pm, please call to arrange arrivals after 8pm **BROCHURE:** Yes **PERMITTED:** Children, drinking [R02EPCA-12483]

**Gold Mountain Manor	**Big Bear CA**
John & Conny Ridgway	1117 Anita 92314
909-585-6997	**Res Times** 8am-8pm

Rates:	**Pvt Bath** 3	**Payment Terms:**
Single	$ 75-180.00	Check
Double	$ 75-180.00	MC/V

Breath-taking experience in this lavish and historic Gold Mining Log Mansion used as a commercial location for *Ralph Lauren, Eddie Bauer* and *Vogue* magazine. Recommended in *The Best Places To Kiss* and *Fifty Most Romantic Places In Southern California*. History abounds everywhere in this Inn where the wealthy original owner planned to make this Manor the **"wealthiest and most beautiful resort in all of the West"!!** Antique furnished, gorgeous verandas, beamed ceilings, handhewn staircase and wait until you see the guestrooms, each named for a different event and with individual decor. Three-star and AAA rated you can journey back in time to the days of extravagant Wild West!! State Historic Monument on prestigious North Shore. **RESERVATIONS:** 7 day cancel policy, check-in 2-9pm, later by arrangement, two night weekend minimum **SEASONAL:** Rates vary **DISCOUNTS:** Yes, inquire at res time **BROCHURE:** Yes **PERMITTED:** Limited children, smoking outdoors only, drinking, pets **CONFERENCES:** Perfect setting for privacy with luxury. Up to groups of 40 persons **LANGUAGES:** French, German, Dutch **AIRPORT:** Ontario CA-50 mi; Los Angeles-100 mi [A07GPCA2-202]

***Matlick House**	**Bishop CA**
Ray & Barbara Showalter	1313 Rowan Lane 93514
800-898-3133 619-873-3133	**Res Times** 7am-9pm

Rates:	**Pvt Bath** 5	**Payment Terms:**
Single	$ 69-79.00	Check
Double	$ 79-89.00	AE/MC/V

Nestled at the base of the Eastern Sierra Nevada Mountains, Bishop is close to year-round fishing, hiking, backpacking, skiing, trail-riding and just plain relaxing. Completely renovated, this 1906 ranch home once housed the Alan Matlick Family, pioneers to Owens Valley. All rooms are individually decorated and complete with handmade quilts and curtains with authentic antique furnishings throughout. Wine and hors d'oeuvres are served nightly in the parlor and a full gourmet breakfast of ranch fresh eggs, mahogany smoked bacon & sausage, country fries, fresh

California

squeezed juice, homemade biscuits and bread starts your day right. Located mid-way between Los Angeles & Reno-Tahoe, you have the perfect stopping-off place for spending an enjoyable and restful night. Other meals available with prior notice including picnic lunches. **RESERVATIONS:** Full payment within 7 days of booking, two night min on weekends, 7 day cancel policy. **BROCHURE:** Yes **PERMITTED:** Limited children, smoking, drinking **CONFERENCES:** Business and social meetings to 14 persons including dining [Z08GPCA2-206]

**Cain House	**Bridgeport CA**
Chris & Marachal Gohlich	340 Main St 93517
800-433-CAIN 619-932-7040	**Res Times** 10am-9:30pm

Rates:	**Pvt Bath** 6	**Payment Terms:**
Single	$ 80-135.00	Check
Double	$ 80-135.00	AE/DC/MC/V

The *Cain House*, a successful blend of European elegance with a relaxing Western atmosphere is nestled in a country setting where mornings bring the beauty of crystalize trees set against the deep blue sky while the air sparkles with the morning frost. At a 6500 ft elevation - summer evenings cool perfectly, spring valleys become alive with green meadows, meandering streams and wildflowers while aspens turn fiery red, gold and orange with the beginning of fall's crisp air. The culmination of years of experience and travel throughout Europe where your hosts gathered ideas for interior design and food preparation - the *Cain House* is *"the perfect place to spend a few nights or a few weeks"*, says Meta Cheryl Coffey, *The Review-Herald*. Guest rooms are furnished with antiques and include queen size beds, quilts, down comforters, TV's discretely tucked away in armoires, thick towels, plush comforters and feature their own unique decor. A gourmet/country full breakfast is served at your convenience between 8-10 am offering a daily changing menu that makes it tempting enough to stay another day just for breakfast! In the middle of a valley with the rugged beauty of the Eastern Sierra Mountain range as a backdrop - valleys, streams and lakes await you for hiking, boating, fishing, hunting and x-country skiing. Nearby is a ghost town, Bodie; Yosemite Valley, a two hour drive and downhill skiing and Nevada gaming. *Cain House* is **Rated AAA ♦♦♦, Mobil ★★★, ABBA 3-Crown approved**. **RESERVATIONS:** One night deposit or credit card number, 48 hr cancel policy **SEASONAL:** 4/30-11/1 **PERMITTED:** Children, drinking **BROCHURE:** Yes **AIRPORT:** Reno/Cannon-113 mi [Z07GPCA2-10050]

Brannan Cottage Inn	**Calistoga CA**
Jack & Pamela Osborn	109 Wapoo Ave 94515
707-942-4200	**Res Times** 8am-10pm

©*Bed & Breakfast Guest Houses & Inns of America, Memphis TN*

California

Rates:	Pvt Bath 6	Payment Terms:
Single	$ 80-95.00	Check
Double	$ 100-110.00	

Perfect setting for this Victorian cottage from the turn-of-the-century in the wine country nestled on lovely grounds; and furnished in period antiques and details. You're close to wineries, world-famous spas, shops, antique stalls, and all the Valley sights. Full breakfast included with complimentary bikes and beverages. **RESERVATIONS:** Deposit at res time, 10 day cancel policy **BROCHURE:** Yes **PERMITTED:** Children, pets, smoking, drinking. Handicap access available. **LANGUAGES:** French, Spanish [E11ACCA-221]

Christopher's Inn — Calistoga CA
Christopher Layton — 1010 Foothill Blvd 94515
707-942-5755 — **Res Times** 8am-8pm

Rates:	Pvt Bath 10	Payment Terms:
Single	$ 120-170.00	Check
Double	$ 120-170.00	AE/MC/V

Christopher's Inn is a recent arrival to the Napa Valley offering guests elegance, intimacy, and, located in Calistoga, close proximity to all the wine country has to offer. The owner, Christopher Layton, a San Francisco architect and landscape designer, turned three buildings built fifty years ago as a summer visitor's hideaway into a traditional English Country Inn with Georgian elegance. The ten gracious rooms each feature different Laura Ashley decor and exquisite antiques. Five rooms offer the romance of wood-burning fireplaces and some have private patio gardens. All guest rooms include private bath. Each room inspires its own mood from the Chinois Suite - the largest room, featuring a sleigh bed, fireplace, and antiques with an exotic Far Eastern flavor - - to the cozy Blue Room which features delicate Wedgewood Blue figurines and it's own small jasmine-covered porch. There is also a two-

California

room suite with fireplace and private patio, and the Secret Garden Room which provides a spacious, gated garden patio with an umbrella shaded table for enjoying a glass of Napa Valley wine or a morning coffee <u>alfresco</u>. Breakfast is a country basket filled with fresh-baked croissants, muffins, fresh fruit and yogurt or hot fruit cobbler, coffee and juice - delivered to your door each morning. *Christopher's Inn* offers a complete concierge service to help you plan a perfect stay in the wine country. Calistoga is the home of the world-famous hot springs and more than a dozen spas offering a multitude of treatments - from mud baths and massages to aromatherapy and seaweed wraps - are within walking distance from the *Inn*. The newly opened Lavender Hill Spa, which specializes in a spa experience for couples is just across the street. When you call, ask about our special *Spa Packages*. **RESERVATIONS:** Full payment 2 days or less, 50% if longer within 5 days of booking, 7 day cancel policy less $15 service fee; commissionable only weekdays; two night min weekends and holidays **PERMITTED:** Limited children, drinking **BROCHURE:** Yes **CONFERENCES:** Yes, groups to ten persons **DISCOUNTS:** Midweek Nov 1- May 1, (excluding holidays and special Valley events) **AIRPORT:** San Francisco Intl-2 hrs; Santa Rosa-45 mins **PACKAGES:** *Spa, Bicycle, Balloon, Wine Train* [J11FPCA2-17608]

Quail Mountain B&B	Calistoga CA
Alma & Don Swiers	4455 N St Helena Hwy 94515
707-942-0316	**Res Times** 10am-9pm

Rates:	**Pvt Bath** 3	**Payment Terms:**
Single	$ 90-115.00	Check
Double	$ 100-120.00	MC/V

Quail Mountain is our home offering luxurious guest accommodations while visiting the beautiful Napa Valley. Located on 26 acres and 300 feet above Napa Valley, this secluded hide-away is on a heavily forested mountain range. Traveling along Hwy 29, guests drive into Quail Mountain Lane, our private road, alongside our vineyard and orchard. Passing through a wrought iron gate, you begin your ascent to *Quail Mountain B&B* - passing red woods, madrona, oak and Douglas fir trees. During your trip and stay, you will find this pristine location filled with deer, raccoons, squirrels, hummingbirds and our beloved quail. Numerous windows in this contemporary style home brings the surrounding forest into every room. Furnished with antiques and works of

California

art, your hosts enjoy sharing their home and making each guest part of their family. Guest rooms feature king size bed fitted with goose down comforters and pillows, a private bath and outdoor deck. A delicious full breakfast is served in the sunny solarium, outdoors on one of the many decks or before a blazing fire in the formal dining room. Breakfast consists of fruit juices, fresh bread and/or pastries, a hot entree and beverage which varies each day. Guests can begin or end their day with a refreshing dip in the pool or hot tub. Your hosts will help plan a memorable trip to Napa Valley by providing directions and information on the activities ranging from winery visits to an afternoon at a nearby spa. Upon request, they will also help with reservations at one of the fine Napa Valley restaurants. **DISCOUNTS:** Yes, travel agents **AIRPORT:** Oakland & San Francisco-75 mi; Santa Rosa-20 mi; Calistoga-1-1/2 mi. **RESERVATIONS:** Deposit at res time to hold, 5 day cancellation policy for refund, less 10% handling fee. Check-in 4-6pm, 11:30 am check-out. Two night min on weekends and holidays **BROCHURE:** Yes [I02FPCA2-236]

**The Elms B&B Inn	**Calistoga CA**
Elaine Bryant	1300 Cedar St 94515
800-235-4316 707-942-9476	

Rates:	**Pvt Bath** 7	**Payment Terms:**
Single	$ 100-165.00	Check
Double	$ 110-175.00	AE/MC/V

The last of Calistoga's **Great Eight Homes** *and the only example of the Second Empire Style still standing today, it is listed in the National Register of Historic Places.* A tribute to preservation commemorating the finest chapter of the last century's heritage, *The Elms* was completed in 1871 when the first European Elm seedlings were planted, which stand today as the largest elm trees in the Napa Valley. Guests receive royal treatment beginning with immaculate rooms many with personal touches, antique furnishings, private baths, robes, coffee and tea in your room plus a decanter of port for your nightcap, queen or king size feather beds, down comforters, lots of pillows and reading lights. Your thoughtful hostess hasn't overlooked anything - from the full multi-course gourmet breakfast served in the dining room or outside on the patio to nighttime chocolates ... guests find intimacy, romance and step into the past where life was quieter and the pace relaxed. Located on the Napa River, you'll relax outdoors among gardens, huge elm trees, brick patios and comfortable lawn chairs. The city park next door has a gazebo that's perfect for afternoon picnics - and the gentle, lovable, laid-back German Shepherd "Boomer" is available for petting and walks. Located just a half-block off Calistoga's Main Street, you are within easy walking distance to shops, fine restaurants, spas, tennis, golf, bike rentals, glider rides and hot air ballooning. Fifteen of Napa Valley's wineries are within biking distance.

California

Your hostess is delighted to assist in making all of your reservations. **RESERVATIONS:** Full payment for length of stay at reservation time, 7 day cancel policy for refund, gift certificates available **PERMITTED:** Drinking **BROCHURE:** Yes **CONFERENCES:** Yes, for groups to 14 persons **DISCOUNTS:** Off-season, Midweek **AIRPORT:** San Francisco-1-1/2 hr [R05FPCA1-6257]

**The Pink Mansion	**Calistoga CA**
Jeff Seyfried	1415 Foothill Blvd 94515
800-238-7465 707-942-0558	**Res Times** 24 Hrs
Rates: **Pvt Bath** 5	**Payment Terms:**
Single $ 105.00	Check
Double $ 115.00	MC/V

Turn-of-the-century elegance with modern amenities are combined in *The Pink Mansion* - offering wine-country travellers "*old-fashioned comforts*". Built in Calistoga's heyday, the crystal-chandeliered grand parlor treated numerous visiting dignitaries and townspeople to enjoyable evenings. Built in the 1870s on land given by Calistoga's founder, Sam Brannan, William F Fisher cleared the steep mountainside for vineyards and dug the wine caves for the Schramsberg and Beringer operations. A pioneer and adventurer, Fisher also established Calistoga's first stage line. linking the town with mining sites on Mount Saint Helena. Today guests are treated to individually decorated guest rooms in keeping with your innkeeper's aunt, Alma Simic, *The Pink Mansion's* last and longest owner. An ardent collector, many of the rooms are adorned with her angels, cherubs, Victorian and Oriental treasures. Each guest room includes queen size beds, valley or forest view and private bath. Guests are invited to share the large Victorian parlour, drawing room, dining room and to enjoy the lavish full breakfast in the breakfast room. Less than a 1/4 mile from downtown, all of Calistogas' shops, restaurants, spas and much more are readily available. Calistoga is ideally situated among the famous wine districts of Napa and Sonoma, a little more than one hour to the Pacific Ocean, the magnificent Redwoods and the city of San Francisco. **RESERVATIONS:** One night's deposit required within 7 days of booking to confirm reservation; 72 hr cancel policy for refund less $10 service fee **PERMITTED:** Limited children, limited pets, no smoking **BROCHURE:** Yes **CONFERENCES:** Yes, for guests, groups to 16 persons **LANGUAGES:** Spanish **DISCOUNTS:** Yes, inquire at res time **AIRPORT:** Santa Rosa-15 mi [R01FPCA2-235]

**Wishing Well Inn	**Calistoga CA**
Marina & Keith Dinsmoor	2653 Foothill Blvd Hy 128 94515
707-942-5534	

©*Bed & Breakfast Guest Houses & Inns of America, Memphis TN*

California

Rates:	Pvt Bath 3	Payment Terms:
Single	$ 100.00	Check
Double	$ 120-150.00	AE/MC/V

A long chapter of California's history was written at the *Wishing Well Inn*, formerly known as the Cyrus Ranch and dating from the 1840s. John Cyrus married one of the survivors of the 1846 Donner Party tragedy and his family originally settled most of the western part of Calistoga. Many of Calistoga's early travelers were welcomed at the Cyrus Ranch, and the original Bear Flag, the forerunner of the current California state flag, was sewn here. Today the white three-story home is reminiscent of visiting your grandmother - the grounds are filled with grape vines, fig, mulberry and walnut trees along with a friendly poodle named Misha who frequently is the first to greet guests. This picturesque setting next to a wooded hillside offers spectacular views, resident squirrels, beautiful flowering gardens and amenities such as an inground swimming pool and spa. There are two guest rooms in the main house, or guests can choose the private carriage house, furnished in an old fashioned country-style including a clawfoot tub with a fireplace in the sitting room that offers extra space for family travelers. Ever ready to greet guests, your gracious hosts provide complimentary hors d'oeuvres and wine outdoors (weather permitting) or before the warmth of the large stone fireplace. The summer garden brings fresh veggies with dip or Marina's wonderful homemade salsa or pesto pizza for guests to enjoy too. A full country breakfast is standard fare and varies from Marina's delicious baked pears, breads and egg frittati or Keith's special banana blintzes accompanied with homemade plum syrup and preserves. The *Wishing Well Inn* provides a quiet rural setting for enjoying all that the Valley and Calistoga has to offer. **DISCOUNTS:** Off-season, extended (5 day-up) stays **AIRPORT:** San Francisco or Oakland 90 mi **RESERVATIONS:** Deposit required, 5 day cancel policy less $10 service fee for any cancellations **BROCHURE:** Yes **PERMITTED:** Children, drinking [R11EPCA2-241]

Cobblestone Inn	Carmel CA
Ms Charlie Aldinger	Junipero & 7th 93921
800-833-8236 408-625-5222	**Res Times** 7am-11pm

Rates:	Pvt Bath 24	Payment Terms:
Single	$ 102-200.00	Check
Double	$ 105-200.00	AE/MC/V

French doors greet each guest to this charming stone, two-story Inn located in the heart of Carmel-by-the-Sea. The Inn offers a fresh country atmosphere with a large stone fireplace in the main living room that's furnished with country antiques, overstuffed chairs and sofas, fresh flowers and a myriad of colorful green plantings. Guest rooms are

California

individually decorated with print wallpapers of teal, pink or yellow and feature pine furniture, fresh fruit, fireplace, refrigerator stocked with soft drinks, TV, phone, carpeting, private bath in dove gray and chalk white complete with robes and toiletries. Concierge service is available for planning dinner reservations, plays, concerts, golf, tennis, tours, sights and for an afternoon picnic lunch near the ocean. Your charming hosts spoil each guest with nightly turn-down service, shoe shine and morning newspapers. A full complimentary breakfast buffet and afternoon wine with hors d'oeuvres are included. This country inn offers an unforgettable experience in warmth and comfort, hospitality and grace and is *the perfect retreat for your special occasion or birthday* **RESERVATIONS:** One night's deposit at res time, 48 hr cancel policy for refund. Less than 48 hrs, refund only if room is re-rented. **BROCHURE:** Yes **PERMITTED:** Children and limited smoking, drinking **CONFERENCES:** Yes, groups to 10 persons [E09BCCA-252]

**Holiday House				**Carmel CA**
Dieter & Ruth Back			Camino Real At 7th 93921	
408-624-6267				**Res Times** 7am-9pm

Rates:	**Pvt Bath** 4	**Shared Bath** 2	**Payment Terms:**
Single	$ 95.00	$ 90.00	Check
Double	$ 100.00	$ 95.00	

This comfortable wood-shingled home is located on a hillside amidst a colorful, well-maintained garden. Built in 1905 as a summer retreat, it still reflects the congenial and slightly Bohemian side of Carmel, that attracted so many artists to this part of the coast. All bedrooms look out to the ocean or onto the beautiful garden. The sloping roof with its protruding dormer-windows adds charm that is irresistible. Sunset can be observed from the sunporch while enjoying a glass of sherry. It is ideally located three blocks from the beach and one block from the main street. Pebble Beach and Monterey's proximity as well as the rugged Big Sur coast make it a perfect area to explore. A full breakfast is offered, buffet style. Choice of cereals, orange juice, coffee, tea, pastries, fresh fruits and a variety of casseroles, adding a spicy accent to breakfast. **RESERVATIONS:** One night's deposit to hold reservation, two night min on weekends, 5 day notice of cancellation for refund less $10 handling fee, 2:00 pm check-in time **BROCHURE:** Yes **PERMITTED:** Drinking **LANGUAGES:** German [A05FPCA2-257]

Sandpiper B&B At The Beach	**Carmel CA**
The MacKenzies	2408 Bay View Ave 93923
800-633-6433 408-624-6433	**Res Times** 9am-9pm

©*Bed & Breakfast Guest Houses & Inns of America, Memphis TN*

California

Rates:	Pvt Bath 16	Payment Terms:
Single	$ 80-180.00	AE/MC/V
Double	$ 80-180.00	

An intimate European-style Country Inn since 1929 in a quiet and beautiful residential area just sixty yards from Carmel Beach. Sixteen charmingly furnished rooms and cottages filled with antiques and fresh flowers, all with private bathrooms and queen and king size beds. Some rooms have glorious ocean views along one mile of the beach, others have fireplaces. Complimentary continental breakfast is served beside the fireplace in the comfortable lounge and library. The atmosphere is informal and relaxed and there are lots of paths along the beach for walking or jogging. Ample 24 hour parking is provided. **RESERVATIONS:** Advance deposit required, minimum stay on weekends, holidays and special events **PERMITTED:** Children 13-up, drinking, limited smoking **BROCHURE:** Yes **DISCOUNTS:** Value Season Rates 11/15-4/15, midweek periods (Sun-Thur), excluding holidays and special events **AIRPORT:** San Francisco-90 mi; San Jose-60 mi; Monterey Peninsula-3 mi **CONFERENCES:** Sun-Thur, groups to 20 persons **LANGUAGES:** German, French **PACKAGES:** *Honeymoon, Monterey Aquarium* [Z07GPCA2-264]

**Robles del Rio Lodge*	**Carmel Valley CA**
Glen Gurries	200 Punta del Monte 93924
800-883-0843 408-659-3705	**Res Times** 8am-10pm

Rates:	Pvt Bath 31	Payment Terms:
Single	$ 69-149.00	Check
Double	$ 69-149.00	MC/V

Built in the 1920's, the oldest operating Lodge in Carmel Valley, this rustic Inn is perched on top of a mountain with spectacular views and nestled into the mountainside forests. Completely refurbished, you can choose guest rooms from a board-and-battened countryside look to a Laura Ashley motif, with color TV's hidden into armories, or you can choose from among the guest cottages that include private fireplace and kitchenettes. Gourmet dining at the award winning Ridge Restaurant is available. Continental plus breakfast is enjoyed in the Lodge living room offering guests a warm fireplace setting from which to enjoy the panoramic views of the mountain scenery. Olympic-size pool, hot tub, sauna and tennis courts on the premises. **RESERVATIONS:** One night's deposit or credit card guarantee; 48 hr cancel policy. **BROCHURE:** Yes **PERMITTED:** Children, drinking **CONFERENCES:** Yes, groups to 40 persons **LANGUAGES:** Spanish, French [Z11CPCA-271]

California

Inn On Mount Ada	Catalina Island CA
Marlene McAdam/Susie Griffin	398 Wrigley Rd 90704
213-510-2030	**Res Times** 8-10pm

Rates:	**Pvt Bath** 6	**Payment Terms:**
Single	$ 150.00	Check
Double	$ 250-350.00	AE/MC/V

Georgian colonial mansion built c1921 for William Wrigley Jr, chewing gum multi-millionaire with nothing spared. Completely restored by the island residents at a cost of over one million, this is the perfect spot for a special occasion. Spectacular views of the ocean town and bay with antique furnishings throughout. Full breakfast included & evening wine and hors d'oeuvres. Free pick-up at ferry or airport and comp shuttle for riding around the island. **RESERVATIONS:** Make them early, six months or more!! **BROCHURE:** Yes **SEASONAL:** Closed Christmas **PERMITTED:** Children 13 and over limited smoking. [C11ACCA-188]

****Ye Olde Shelford House*	Cloverdale CA
Ina & Al Sauder	29955 River Rd 95425
800-833-6479 707-894-5956	

Rates:	**Pvt Bath** 6	**Payment Terms:**
Single	$ 85-110.00	Check
Double	$ 85-110.00	DC/MC/V

Ye Olde' Shelford House, c1885, is a stately Victorian charmer built on property given to Eurastus M Shelford which was formerly part of Rancho Musalacon. Completely restored with beautifully decorated rooms - guests are reminded of the pleasures of the Victorian days. There are three cozy bedrooms with lots of windows and window seats for viewing the surrounding vineyards. Each room has authentic family antiques, home made quilts, plants and fresh flowers from our own flower gardens. A Carriage House offers three beautiful rooms of antique furnishings. A game room offers fun and entertainment while the wrap-around porch provides a relaxing swing where you can enjoy a glass of wine or reading a book. Since *Ye Olde' Shelford House* borders acres of vineyard - the view is exceptional. You'll relax and enjoy the detail and the crisp, clean - light and airy atmosphere of our Inn. Three additional beautiful guest rooms full of antique furnishings are located in the

California

Carriage House. Each morning you awaken to the aroma of fresh oven baked goods wafting through the hallowed halls. In-addition, you'll find fresh squeezed orange juice, fresh fruit, jams, jellies, quiches, coffee, tea or milk. Complimentary beverages and homemade cookies are always ready in our homey kitchen. Complimentary ten-speed bikes or a bike built-for-two take guests on vineyard tours - while a hot tub offers a romantic dip under the clear & star-filled evening. There's also a pool for the guests to enjoy. Guests shouldn't miss the ***Surrey & Sip Tour*** *in an authentic "surrey with a fringe on top"* and a sip of wine in a barrel gazebo. **DISCOUNTS:** Yes **RESERVATIONS:** One night deposit to guarantee reservation; 14 day cancel policy for refund. Check-in 3-6pm; Check-out 11am **BROCHURE:** Yes **PERMITTED:** Limited children, drinking, smoking outdoors only. **CONFERENCES:** Yes, for groups to twenty persons [I03FPCA2-282]

Vineyard House			Coloma CA
Paul & Cindy Savage			Cold Spring Rd 95613-0176
916-622-2217			**Res Times** 8am-10pm
			Fax 916-933-1031
Rates:	**Pvt Bath** 1	**Shared Bath** 6	**Payment Terms:**
Single	$ 99.00	$ 80-99.00	Check
Double	$ 99.00	$ 89-99.00	AE/MC/V

Built in 1878 by Robert & Louisa Chalmers, vintners of some of the finest wines of the period, today guests can enjoy their lovely 9400 sq ft mansion. Once the social and political center of California, visiting guests included the then former President Ulysses S Grant. The decor is much the same when Louisa roamed the halls - providing seven guest rooms with period furnishings, all with beautiful views of the surrounding area. A renowned restaurant occupies the main floor providing exquisite dining indoors and out during summer, while the old wine cellar and "jail cell" downstairs, house a Wild West saloon and gift shop. Guests awake to the aroma of fresh brewed coffee or tea, complemented with a full country breakfast served between 8-10am. Relive the exciting Gold Rush Era on the grounds where governors, local politicians and James Marshall, who first discovered gold in California, were patrons. Gold Rush State Park is just a hundred feet away and has a wonderful museum, shops and the ruins of the original *Vineyard House* winery. The nearby American River has some of the finest white-water rafting available and the historic town of Coloma is an easy half-mile stroll. **BROCHURE:** Yes **PERMITTED:** Children, drinking and limited smoking. **RESERVATIONS:** Full payment in advance, late arrival with prior arrangements. **CONFERENCES:** Yes, including banquet facilities for unforgettable business and social meetings. **DISCOUNTS:** Sun-Thur, corporate rates **AIRPORT:** Placerville-20 mins; Sacramento-40 mins **PACKAGES:** *Hot Air Ballooning, White-water Rafting* [R05EPCA2-286]

California

Columbia City Hotel	**Columbia CA**
Tom Bender	Main St 95310
209-532-1479	**Res Times** 8am-10pm
	Fax 209-532-7027

Rates:	**Pvt Bath** *10	**Payment Terms:**
Single	$ 65-85.00	Check
Double	$ 65-85.00	AE/MC/V

Footsteps on the boardwalk ... Live Theater ... Panning for gold ... Fine Dining ... Tall Tales ... Catching the next stage, some things haven't changed in Columbia for over 130 years. Relive the frontier days in a small, intimate hotel which remains much the same as when the gold miners strolled the streets. Each room is individually appointed with antiques to convey a genuine feeling of the gold rush era but with modern plumbing, heating and a/c. Balcony rooms overlook the tree-lined main street while Parlor Rooms open onto the main sitting parlor. The tradition of a fine country inn begins with a generous continental breakfast of California quiche, fresh baked breads, muffins, cereal, orange juice and our own houseblend of coffee. Dining is unforgettable, offering cuisine incorporating the fundamentals of French cooking with the influence of contemporary flavors. A seasonally changing menu is based exclusively upon the availability of fresh ingredients - with emphasis on locally grown and produced items. The hotel's wine list is regarded as one of the finest in California. Located in Columbia State Historic Park, activities include Fallon House Theater, built in 1875 and home of Columbia Actors Repertory, *Hidden Treasures* offers gold mining tours and gold panning, visiting the 1855 *Columbia Gazette* and enjoying a thirst-quenching sasparilla at the *Douglass Saloon* before boarding the stage coach for a ride around town. Nearby attractions include Yosemite National Park, caverns, wine tasting & tours and winter skiing. **AIRPORT:** Columbia Airport-1 mi; Stockton-50 mi **PACKAGES:** *Dinner, Theater & Lodging* **RESERVATIONS:** Advance deposit, 72 hr cancel policy for refund. **BROCHURE:** Yes **PERMITTED:** Children, drinking no smoking **CONFERENCES:** Inn has two meetings rooms (25 & 50 person capacity) and nearby hall for 150-200 [I07GPCA2-288]

Victorian House 1894 - Dance Studio	**Coronado CA**
Bonnie Marie Kinosian	1000 Eighth St 92118
619-435-2200	**Res Times** 7am-9pm

©*Bed & Breakfast Guest Houses & Inns of America, Memphis TN*

California

Rates:	Pvt Bath 4	Shared Bath 2	Payment Terms:
Single	$ 200-250.00	$	Tvlrs Check
Double	$ 200-250.00	$ *200-250.00	

A truly unique accommodation & experience is waiting guests in beautiful Coronado, sister city to San Diego. This charming 1894 Victorian home welcomes guests to a fascinating get-away with an **added bonus, a vacation and dance package!** Owner/host/dance teacher, Bonnie Marie, showers her guests with personal attention. You are treated to a full menu of Armenian & Lebanese hospitality & health foods including fresh fruits, juices, rolls, and baklava pastry served on the outdoor patio. Guest rooms are furnished with period antiques and family heirlooms, oriental rugs, brass beds or pre-Civil War Sleigh beds and stained glass doors & windows throughout. This three-story home is located in the very center of Coronado's activities: one block from the central business district for great shopping, galleries, restaurants, theater, parks and entertainment. With great weather year round, you can fill your days with walks on miles of Pacific beaches, biking tennis, golf, trolley rides & ferry boat trips into San Diego to find the largest zoo in the world, Sea World, Wild Animal Park and Old Town. Add to all this, your choice of dance lessons. Choose social, ballroom, ballet, jazz, tap, Hawaiian, belly dancing or low-impact aerobics and stretching! Enjoy meeting this pleasant hostess and her warm and welcoming Victorian which has been featured in many articles in *San Diego, Bridge & Bay Magazines, San Diego Union* newspaper. **RESERVATIONS:** Full payment in advance for entire stay, two week cancel policy less 15% service fee. 2-day min on weekends & 3-day min for holidays. *Two Bedroom Suite **BROCHURE:** Yes **PERMITTED:** Children, limited drinking, smoking outdoors **CONFERENCES:** Yes, to 35 persons [R02BCCA-6554]

**A Weavers Inn			Eureka CA
Dorothy & Bob Swendeman			1440 B St 95501
707-443-8119			

Rates:	Pvt Bath 2	Shared Bath 2	Payment Terms:
Single	$ 85-105.00	$ 55.00	Check
Double	$ 95-115.00	$ 70-80.00	AE/DC/MC/V

A Weaver's Inn, home and studio of a fiber artist and her husband, is a stately Queen Anne/Colonial Revival home built in 1883 and remodeled in 1907. Placed in a spacious fenced garden, it is airy and light but cozy and warm when veiled by wisps of fog. Arriving early, you might visit the studio, try the spinning wheel before the fire or weave on the antique loom, before having refreshments. Each guest room is uniquely furnished with special names like the Pamela Suite which offers two romantic rooms with sliding door, fireplace, bath with tiled shower, queen bed, sofa bed

California

in sitting room and the Cynthia Room with a sunny bay window and wicker furnishings, fireplace, king bed and a shared bath with clawfoot tub. A complimentary delectable full breakfast may include treats from the garden and is served in the gracious dining room. After breakfast, play croquet surrounded by colorful flowers or contemplate the Japanese garden before exploring the ambience of the Victorian Era in Old Town, playing golf, fishing or combing a beach. Elegant relaxing is always in style in the Victorian Parlor with its piano. Your hosts will pamper you, the weather will refresh you and the visit delight you. Come visit us soon. **DISCOUNTS:** Weekly rate **AIRPORT:** Eureka-Arcata-10 mi **PACKAGES:** *Weaving Instruction & Lodging* **RESERVATIONS:** One night's deposit or credit card number to guarantee within seven days of booking reservation, 72 hr cancel policy for refund **BROCHURE:** Yes **PERMITTED:** Children, pets, drinking, smoking outdoors only [Z07GPCA2-12280]

**Elegant Victorian Mansion			**Eureka CA**
Lily & Doug Vieyra			1406 "C" Street 95501
800-386-1888 707-444-3144			**Res Times** 10am-6pm
Rates:	**Pvt Bath** 2	**Shared Bath** 2	**Payment Terms:**
Single	$ 85-115.00	$ 75.00	Check
Double	$ 95-125.00	$ 85-95.00	MC/V

This elegantly restored *National Historic Landmark* is Eureka's most prestigious and luxurious accommodation. Spectacular Victorian architecture outside - authentically restored and furnished opulence inside. Both **AAA & Mobil ★★★ Recommended**, the Inn is exclusively for the non-smoker. Spirited and eclectic InnKeepers serve lavish hospitality in the regal splendor of a meticulously restored 1888 Victorian masterpiece; complete with original family antique furnishings. Each room is individually decorated with elegance and comfort in mind. Guests enjoy gourmet breakfasts and a heavenly night's sleep on world-famous custom mattresses. Tranquil setting on a park-like estate with colourful victorian flower gardens, croquet field with bicycles, sauna and tennis. Secured garage parking, complimentary laundry service. Butler, fireplaces, cable TV, VCR with a library of silent film classics. Impeccable style, grace, charm and unrivaled quality lead to an unforgettable Bed and Breakfast Experience. Located in a quiet, historic residential neighborhood overlooking the city and Humboldt Bay. Near "Old Town", carriage rides, Bay Cruises, museums, antique shops, theatre, dining. Just minutes from Giant Redwood National Park, coastal beaches, ocean charters, horseback riding, golf and fishing. The Inn has been featured in the *New York Times, Los Angeles Times, San Francisco Chronicle, Focus, Sunset* and *Country* magazines, among others. **RESERVATIONS:** Full payment at time of reservation, 3-6pm check-in, 11am check-out, 7 day cancel notice required for refund **PERMITTED:** Drinking **BROCHURE:** Yes

California

CONFERENCES: Yes, for groups to 15 persons **LANGUAGES:** French, Dutch **DISCOUNTS:** 10% for cash **AIRPORT:** San Francisco-300 mi; Arcata Commuter Airport-25 mi **PACKAGES:** *Dinner, Bay Cruise, Carriage Ride & lodging $160.00*; *Museums, Art Gallery Tour, Theatre, Bay Cruise & Lodging $160.00* [Z07GPCA2-12481]

Hotel Carter			Eureka CA
Mark & Christi Carter			301 L Street 95501
707-444-8062			

Rates:	**Pvt Bath** 24	**Shared Bath** 3	**Payment Terms:**
Single	$ 79-99.00	$ 79-89.00	Check
Double	$ 79-119.00	$ 89-109.00	AE/MC/V

The *Hotel Carter* is a replica of a circa 1880 Eureka hotel which was known as The Old Town Cario Hotel. Original art, oriental rugs and antique appointments highlight the guest rooms and the public areas. Comp wine & appetizers every afternoon; bedtime cookies, tea and cordials, with a full exquisite breakfast in the morning. Other meals are available at the gourmet restaurant on the premises which has received favorable reviews in *Bon Appetit* and other national publications. Their famous five course dinner - which shouldn't be missed - include vegetables, herbs and edible flowers grown in the hotel's own garden. **RESERVATIONS:** Deposit required at res time to guarantee reservation **BROCHURE:** Yes **PERMITTED:** Children,drinking, limited smoking **CONFERENCES:** Yes **LANGUAGES:** Spanish [E09BCCA-8835]

**Gingerbread Mansion*		Ferndale CA
Ken Torbert		400 Berding St 95536-0040
800-952-4136 707-786-4000		**Res Times** 8:30-8pm

Rates:	**Pvt Bath** 9	**Payment Terms:**
Single	$ 100.00	Check
Double	$ 185.00	AE/MC/V

California's most photogenic example of Victorian architecture - the exquisite turrets, carved and gabled details are beautifully trimmed in peach and yellow - while spectacular English Gardens surround the home. Built in 1898 as a doctor's residence, in 1981 Ken began his extensive "Victorianization". Inside guests will find Victorian elegance at it's best! The nine guest rooms are large, beautifully appointed with antique furnishings and include private baths - several of which are spectacular! Just for fun, old-fashioned clawfooted bathtubs have been placed in several of the rooms, with **two such tubs in some suites**. The luxurious Fountain Suite bath offers **two tubs** and fireside bathing where

66   ©*Bed & Breakfast Guest Houses & Inns of America, Memphis TN*

California

mirrored walls reflect the flames of a beautiful, floral-tiled fireplace and a Victorian fainting couch provides fireside reading. The Gingerbread Suite tubs are on a raised platform surrounded by a Victorian railing and face each other for soaking and conversation - with reading lamps thoughtfully provided above each tub - and naturally, bubbles for luxurious soaking! Morning brings a tray of coffee or tea to take to your room while a generous full breakfast of muffins, cakes, granola, fresh fruits, locally made cheeses and baked egg dishes is prepared. Afternoon tea, coffee and a variety of cakes, cookies, pastries and confections is served in the four parlors where guests can enjoy fireside conversations, a book or magazine from the large selection available or contribute to the Inn's own 1000 piece jigsaw puzzle in various stages of completion. Amenities include neatly folded bathrobes, nightly turn-down service with hand-dipped chocolates, complimentary bikes painted to match the Inn and if it should rain, your thoughtful innkeeper has umbrellas to keep you dry. Located in Ferndale, a State Historical Landmark and listed in the *National Historic Register* because of all of the well-preserved Victorian homes, the three blocks of Main Street are filled with delightful shops and art galleries. Just 5 miles from the coast and nestled against the forested hills, Ferndale area has exciting coastal drives, redwood forests, river activities and little-known backroads to explore. **DISCOUNTS:** 10% travel agents **AIRPORT** Arcata-Eureka Airport-35 mi **RESERVATIONS:** Full payment within 7 days of booking, 3-6pm check-in **BROCHURE:** Yes **PERMITTED:** Children 10-up, drinking [I07GPCA2-315]

Karen's Yosemite Inn	Fish Camp CA
Karen Bergh & Lee Morse	PO Box 8 93623
800-346-1443 209-683-4550	**Res Times** 7am-10pm

Rates:	**Pvt Bath** 3	**Payment Terms:**
Single	$ 80.00	Check
Double	$ 85.00	

Towering pines and whispering cedars welcome guests to the quiet and warmth of this contemporary country home nestled high in the Sierras (5000 feet). The quiet of the front porch brings scurrying squirrels - scolding jays and wind sighs of the forest while evening produces millions of sequins splashed across a velvet sky. Indoors, your hosts have individually decorated and named each room. Choose the Rose Room (light and airy with wicker furniture and twin day beds), Blue Room with a queen

California

bed (its intimate coziness is a favorite for romantic getaways) or the Peach Room (cheery charm of soft curtains and brass appointments with a queen bed). Evening offers the warmth of an upstairs fireplace and a library or a crackling fire in the woodstove or a good movie or TV show in the living room. A bountiful full country breakfast in a romantic dining room setting begins each day. Tempting tidbits from Karen's kitchen and seasonal beverages are offered each afternoon (4-6pm). Regardless of the season, guests will enjoy the pristine beauty of winter or the challenge of summer. Winter brings crystal silence of a x-country ski trail or the delightful sounds of music from the outdoor skating rink. Summer offers rock climbing, back woods exploring by horseback or train through beautiful lush mountain meadows. Sights include Yosemite Park (3 mins), Mariposa Grove of Giant Sequoias (5 mins), Wawona Village (15 mins), Bass Lake, Badger Pass Ski area and Glacier Point. **AIRPORT:** Fresno-65 mi **DISCOUNTS:** 10%, 7 day stays or longer, $5 for multiple room bookings. **RESERVATIONS:** 50% deposit (one night's min), 7 day cancel policy except holidays (14 days) group bookings (2-3 rooms) 21 days. No refund for early departures. Late arrival (after 8pm) requires prior notice. **BROCHURE:** Yes **PERMITTED:** Children, **No** radios, TV, music or sound equipment is permitted in the upstairs guest areas unless booking all three guest rooms. **Quite Time** 10pm to 6am [K05FPCA2-6261]

**Narrow Gauge Inn	**Fish Camp CA**
Carol Donnell, GM	48571 Hwy 41 93623
209-683-7720	

Rates:	**Pvt Bath** 27	**Payment Terms:**
Single	$ 80-120.00	Check
Double	$ 80-120.00	AE/DC/MC/V

A cozy mountain lodge at the Southern Gateway to Yosemite National Park - relive the turn-of-the-century wild west! The buildings (including the Inn), offer a unique blend of Victorian and Western-style architecture with rich panelling, massive fireplaces and stain glass. The Dining Hall is lit with kerosene lamps and charmed by an oak fire - creating an intimate setting for your evening dinner. There's a swimming pool, hot bubbling pool, garden courtyard and miles of hiking trails to enjoy. The twenty-eight cozy rooms with patios provide guests with splendid views of the forest and mountains beyond and unrivaled sunrises. Fine food

California

and spirits and comfortable lodgings combine for a tradition of gracious hospitality. Breakfast and other meals are available at added cost from a full selection menu. The adjoining buildings include The Bull Moose Saloon for the high-spirited guest; the General Store, a den of delights offering books, handmade gifts and necessities for the mountain hiker and traveler. Next door to the Inn is the Logger, a narrow gauge steam powered railroad that relives old fashioned sights and sounds of a steam powered train while riding open logging cars through the forest to Lewis Creek Canyon. *For a memory that will last a lifetime - stay at the Narrow Gage Inn.* **AIRPORT:** Fresno-65 mi **DISCOUNTS:** Travel agents **RESERVATIONS:** One night's deposit by check or money order. Four day cancel notice for full refund **BROCHURE:** Yes **PERMITTED:** Children, drinking, smoking [R02FPCA2-317]

**Grey Whale Inn	Fort Bragg CA
Colette & John Bailey	615 N Main St 95437
800-382-7244 707-964-0640	**Res Times** 8am-8pm

Rates:	Pvt Bath 14	Payment Terms:
Single	$ 60-140.00	Check
Double	$ 80-160.00	AE/DIS/MC/V

A Mendocino Coast landmark since 1915, the *Grey Whale Inn* is celebrating its 15th anniversary as Fort Bragg's first Bed & Breakfast Inn. Stately, romantic, serene, the *Grey Whale Inn* is the perfect place to celebrate that special occasion, or to just bask in anonymous solitude. The Grey Whale Inn is exceptionally conducive to group parties - family reunions, weddings and birthdays. Whales can be seen from the Inn during their migration. And this Inn is conveniently located within strolling distance of the ocean, fine restaurants, unique gift shops, art galleries, antique stores, theatre and music performance houses. Beaches, hiking trails, dramatic coastal headlands are only minutes away by automobile. Each room has a special feeling, and provides spacious surroundings and the utmost in privacy. All rooms have baths and telephones. Some rooms feature TVs, fireplaces, kitchenettes. Sunrise Suite has a jacuzzi for two and private sun deck; Point Cabrillo is wheelchair accessible. Views vary: ocean, town & hillside, or garden. The recreation area has a pool table room, TV/VCR theater, fireplace lounge; an immense selection of books and board games is available. The buffet breakfast is lavish and includes a hot entree, prize-winning coffee

California

cakes, fresh fruit, juices, cereal, special blend *Grey Whale Inn* coffee, teas & cocoa. We're happy to assist you with dining, fishing, theatre and Skunk Train reservations. The *Grey Whale Inn*, gracious accommodations on the Mendocino Coast ..... a world away. **DISCOUNTS:** Yes, seasonal **AIRPORT:** San Francisco Intl-160 mi **PACKAGES:** Special promotions available, inquire at reservation time **RESERVATIONS:** One or more night's prepayment upon booking, 2-3 nite min on week-ends & holidays with full prepayment, 800 for reservations only **BROCHURE:** Yes **PERMITTED:** Children 12-up. No Smoking within the building **CONFERENCES:** Yes, for groups to 16 persons **LANGUAGES:** Spanish [K04FPCA4--324] *[Sunrise Suite photo, courtesy Leona Walden, Mendocino CA]*

**Pudding Creek Inn	**Fort Bragg CA**
G & C Anloff/Jacque Woltman	700 N Main St 95437
800-227-9529 707-964-9529	**Res Times** 8am-9pm
	Fax 707-961-0282
Rates: **Pvt Bath** 10	**Payment Terms:**
Single $ 50.00	Check
Double $ 125.00	AE/DC/MC/V

Intrigue, romance and adventure were the criteria for owners Gary and Carole Anloff in their search for a Bed & Breakfast Inn. At *Pudding Creek* they found it all. Built in 1894 by a Russian Count, who, according to legend, buried his mysteriously-acquired riches on the property. The Inn is a triumph of renovation. New features have been added but the historic past of the structures and property have been retained and cherished. Each room is romantically named and decorated in its own style and filled with antique furnishings. Travelers and romantics who choose to stay close to home will find much to occupy themselves at the Inn. A stroll through the garden full of award-winning flowers; a picnic with a basket of goodies, prepared upon request; snuggling before the fire with a good book or game in the parlor or in the new TV and recreation room. A full complimentary breakfast begins each day. Phone, fax and laundry facilities are available. For those venturing out, the delights of the Mendocino Coast and the fine restaurants of Fort Bragg are close-by. The overall experience of *Pudding Creek Inn* is nostalgic, founded on a tradition of fine innkeeping with emphasis on outstanding personal service. **AIRPORT:** San Francisco Intl-3 to 4 hrs **DISCOUNTS:** Yes, inquire at res time **RESERVATIONS:** Deposit required, 5 day cancel policy for full refund, check-in noon to 9pm, late arrivals only with prior arrangements **BROCHURE:** Yes **PERMITTED:** Children, drinking, limited smoking [R04FPCA2-328]

**Campbell Ranch Inn	**Geyserville CA**
Mary Jane & Jerry Campbell	1475 Canyon Rd 95441

California

800-959-3878 707-857-3476

Res Times 8am-10pm

Rates:	**Pvt Bath** 5
Single	$ 90-155.00
Double	$ 100-165.00

Payment Terms:
Check
MC/V

Spectacular views highlight a stay at this 35 acre ranch located in the heart of Sonoma County Wine Country. Surrounded by beautiful rolling vineyards and Mary Jane's abundant flower garden, a perfect setting is created for summer breakfast - while enjoying the wonderful view. A full complement of amenities for guests include a professional tennis court, 20x40 swimming pool, hot tub spa, bikes, horseshoes and ping pong. The Inn has four spacious guestrooms in the house and a separate cottage, all with king size beds. Most rooms have a balcony and there's a fireplace in the Cottage. Fresh flowers and fruit greet guests along with bathrobes, pool towels and back rests for reading in bed. A masseuse is available for an hour massage in your room. Guests gather in a lovely room with a large fireplace or in the comfortable family room offering music, TV with satellite dish and a VCR. A full breakfast selected from a menu offers choices of fruits, cereals, hot dishes, homemade breads, muffins and coffee cakes. Homemade pie or cake welcome guests upon their return from evening dinner while daytime ice tea or lemonade are readily served. All of Sonoma County wineries and sights are nearby along with water recreation, hiking, fishing, canoeing with short trips to visit historical sights, Redwood parks, Russian River area and the Mendocino Coast and Napa Valley. Come to the *Campbell Ranch* and enjoy the peaceful and serene 35 acre country estate. **AIRPORTS:** Santa Rosa Sonoma Airport-15 mi. **RESERVATIONS:** Credit card number for deposit guarantee; 72 hr cancel policy for refund, check-in 1:00pm, check-out 12 noon, two day min on weekends, 3 day min holidays **BROCHURE:** Yes **PERMITTED:** Drinking, limited children. **CONFERENCES:** Yes, for groups to 10-12 [Z07GPCA2-337]

Country Rose Inn   **Gilroy CA

Rose Hernandez
408-842-0441

PO Box 1804 95021
Res Times 6-8am/8-10pm

Rates:	**Pvt Bath** 5
Single	$ 79-169.00
Double	$ 79-169.00

Payment Terms:
Check
AE/MC/V

Featured in *Country Inns*, the *Country Rose Inn* is nestled in a grove of ancient trees at the base of Santa Clara Valley. The Manor is of the Dutch Colonial-style from the 1920s offering comfort and relaxation in rural grandeur. Surrounded by farmland - guests get a sense of Old California - in this natural and beautiful setting. Virgin rolling hills are feathered

California

in grass and oak - while an immense Magnolia and pines tower above the fertile valley floor. The spacious guest rooms include private baths - with a special bridal suite including a bathtub with jets and a steam shower. Each room is infused by this peaceful and serene rural setting and furnished in warm understated tones. A full breakfast of freshly-squeezed juice, coffee and granola is followed by a specially prepared California entree, served with fruit and dessert. There are spacious common areas for relaxing with a choice of the large parlor or by exercising the baby grand piano. Afternoon tea is served at 4 pm daily; turndown service nightly. Restaurant and local theater reservations made by your hosts. Nearby activities: wineries, hiking, hot air ballooning, outlet shopping, Hecker Pass Theme Park, Henry Coe State Park. A perfect locale for traveling to San Juan Bautista, the ocean, San Francisco and Silicon Valley. **RESERVATIONS:** First night's deposit, 7 day cancel policy for refund less $10 fee, late arrival by prior arrangement; add state hotel and sales taxes to above rates **BROCHURE:** Yes **PERMITTED:** Limited drinking. **CONFERENCES:** Yes, to twenty persons. **LANGUAGES:** Spanish **DISCOUNTS:** 10% mid-week (must request at reservation time) **AIRPORT:** San Jose Intl-30 mi [Z06FPCA1-6211]

**Groveland Hotel	**Groveland CA**
Peggy Mosley	18767 Main St 95321
800-273-3314 209-962-4000	**Res Times** 24 Hrs

Rates:	**Pvt Bath** 17	**Payment Terms:**
Single	$ 85-165.00	Check
Double	$ 85-165.00	AE/DC/MC/V

The recently restored 1849 Monterey Colonial Adobe and the 1914 Queen

◇ **THE GROVELAND HOTEL** ◇

Anne buildings are of major historical significance to the area. The *Groveland Hotel* was built to support the hundreds of miners from the *Gold Rush Era*. It provided lodging, food and pleasure - gambling and

California

ladies of the evening - and acquired recognition as the **best house on the hill!** The fourteen rooms and three suites are furnished with European antiques, with terry robes, down comforters, upscale linens and private baths. Some have private sitting rooms, fireplaces and jacuzzi tubs. A European continental breakfast and afternoon wine and cheese hour are included in the room rate. A gourmet restaurant on the premises presents California seasonal, fresh cuisine in a most exciting manner. The *Groveland Hotel* presents an outstanding calendar of events throughout the year including *Luau, Winemaker Dinners, Halloween Party, The Twelve Days of Christmas* and *Valentine Days. New Year's Puttin' On The Ritz Bash, Murder Mystery Weekends, Monte Carlo Carnival Night, '50s Night*, art shows and others. Call for a schedule. Nearby activities include Yosemite National Park, golf, tennis, hiking, world-class white water rafting, swimming, horseback riding and gold panning. **RESERVATIONS:** One night deposit or credit card number to guarantee reservation **PERMITTED:** Children, drinking, limited pets **BROCHURE:** Yes and video **CONFERENCES:** Groups to twenty five, private entrance and complete audio visual equipment **AIRPORT:** Sacramento-2 Hrs; San Francisco-3 Hrs **PACKAGES:** Mid-week Winter Specials, 3 nights lodging, one evening dinner with wine for two, Sun-Thursday [O08GPCA2-12488]

**North Coast Country Inn	**Gualala CA**
Loren & Nancy Flanagan	34591 S Hwy 1 95445
800-959-4537 707-884-4537	**Res Times** 8am-10pm

Rates:	**Pvt Bath** 4	**Payment Terms:**
Single	$ 135.00	Check
Double	$ 135.00	AE/MC/V

Nestled in the forest with the sound of barking sea lions in the distance is the *North Coast Country Inn*, an enchanting and rustic array of buildings on the coast of Northern California. The Inn is unique in many ways, with its foliaged privacy and ocean views. From the masses of flowering shrubs and bushes to the open beamed ceilings and wood-burning fireplaces, the owners have sought a romantic and private feeling throughout the complex. With a delicate balance of exquisite antiques, art treasures, potted greenery and authentic collectibles and memorabilia, this is country elegance at its very best. The four guest rooms each have a fireplace, spacious bathroom, kitchenette, a sitting

California

area and private deck. All have antiques and a queen size, four poster bed. On the shelves are books and games. Flower, candy and juice, plus a tray set with the makings for coffee/tea are but a few of the amenities. After a day of sightseeing or beach combing, an outdoor hot tub is ideal for relaxing and in the upper garden, the gazebo is perfect for lounging on a quiet afternoon. A full breakfast is served in the room, along with a hot entree and fresh bakery from the oven is a fruit dish and pot of special blend fresh ground coffee. The Inn's office boasts an antique shop with many unique country pieces for sale. The *North Coast Country Inn* is a perfect place for a vacation getaway, with great hospitality and comfort, all in an elegant country environment. **AIRPORT:** San Francisco-135 mi **RESERVATIONS:** One night's deposit, 5 day cancel policy for refund **BROCHURE:** Yes **PERMITTED:** Drinking, limited children [I05FPCA2-6187]

**Cypress Inn	**Half Moon Bay CA**
Victoria Platt	407 Miranda Rd 94019
800-83-BEACH 415-726-6002	**Res Times** 7am-9pm

Rates:	**Pvt Bath** 8	**Payment Terms:**
Single	$ 135-250.00	Check
Double	$ 135-250.00	AE/MC/V

Cypress Inn is located five miles north of Half-Moon Bay and twenty-six miles south of San Francisco and offers guests the essence of California beach-side living. The inn is on a 5-mile stretch of pristine white sand beach and each of the eight luxury rooms offers a private deck overlooking the ocean. The interior decor is Mexican Indian folk art with wonderful bright colors, carved animals and terra cotta tile floors. Each guest room includes a private bath and a fireplace for romantic evenings. Our in-house masseuse was a pioneer of the healing art of therapeutic massage since 1981 and was featured in a well-known pictorial book *A Day in the Life of California*. Partial to full massage while listening to the sound of waves are available or guests can learn the art of therapeutic massage by taking part in her classes. Breakfast is a specialty - with unexpected superb fare like peaches & cream french toast or eggs benedict - accompanied by homemade breads, luscious seasonal fruit, fresh-squeezed orange juice and cup after cup of fresh roasted coffee. All within 5 mins of the inn, guests can beach picnic (your hostess will gladly prepare your lunch), whale watch, sail, sport fish, tidepool, horseback ride, bike, hike, golf and wine taste. Jazz and classical music are just steps away each weekend along with fine restaurants and nightclubs. Your host is ready to make your stay unforgettable - all you have to do is ask! **DISCOUNTS:** Yes, inquire at res time **PACKAGES:** Yes, inquire **AIRPORT:** San Francisco Intl-25 mi **RESERVATIONS:** Deposit required within 10 days of booking. **BROCHURE:** Yes **PERMITTED:** Drinking,

California

limited children, limited smoking **CONFERENCES:** Yes for all special occasions [R01EPCA2-10039]

**Old Thyme Inn	**Half Moon Bay CA**
George & Marcia Dempsey	779 Main St 94019
415-726-1616	**Res Times** 7am-10pm

Rates:	**Pvt Bath** 7	**Payment Terms:**
Single	$ 70.00	Check
Double	$ 220.00	MC/V

Snuggled into a fragrant English herb and flower garden - *Olde Thyme Inn* is a beautifully-restored 1899 Queen Anne Victorian offering guest rooms appropriately named for familiar herbs. All of the rooms are unique with lovely antiques, whimsical stuffed animals, fresh-cut flowers and private baths. Cozy fireplaces and whirlpool tubs are available in four of the guest rooms while clawfoot tubs are feature in the others. The Inn provides a friendly informal atmosphere - where the center of daily activity begins with a delicious breakfast in the dining and ends with complimentary beverages served around the wood-burning stove each evening. Breakfast specialties may include homemade banana bread, quiche, cinnamon-raisin scones with raspberry jam, swedish egg cake with fresh fruit, blueberry muffins, frittata and baked croissants with cheeses and turkey. After breakfast and within a short walking distance are beaches, quaint shops, art galleries and restaurants in this historic seaside village. Be our guest at the *Old Thyme Inn* for a wonderful experience from a bygone era. **AIRPORT:** San Francisco Intl-22 mi; San Jose Intl-29 mi **RESERVATIONS:** One night's deposit or credit card number to guarantee reservation, 7 day cancel policy for refund less $10 service fee **BROCHURE:** Yes **PERMITTED:** Children 11-up, drinking; smoking not permitted **CONFERENCES:** Yes [R07FPCA2-366]

**Irwin Street Inn	**Hanford CA**
Bruce Evans	522 N Irwin St 93230
209-583-8791	**Res Times** 24 Hrs

Rates:	**Pvt Bath** 30	**Payment Terms:**
Single	$ 69-99.00	Check
Double	$ 69-99.00	AE/DC/MC/V

Four impeccably restored, turn-of-the-century Victorian homes and surrounding tree-shaded lawns form a one acre sanctuary in the downtown Hanford Historic District. The *Irwin Street Inn* offers a step back in time to a period of grace and gentility with its leaded glass windows, preserved wood detailing, period artifacts and close attention to historic accuracy -

California

all combined to recreate the late nineteenth century ambiance at its best. Thirty delightfully appointed rooms and suites, each with its own bath, offer Victorian charm with contemporary convenience. Each room is different - each with is own character. Rooms with lavish four-poster beds, antique armoires and period furniture are made even more comfortable with cable TV, radios and phones. In the morning, guests are treated to a continental breakfast featuring, among other offerings, the Inn's own *Morning Glory Muffins*. Our elegant restaurant occupies the lower floor of one of the four Victorian homes. Breakfast, lunch and dinner are served, depending upon the season, in high-style in the interior dining room area or outdoors on the gracious awning-covered veranda with its sweeping view of the grounds. Within easy strolling distance is the Hanford Historic District with elegant Court House Square, numerous restaurants and shops, all enthusiastically embracing a turn-of-the-century spirit. Guests may also enjoy the use of the pool on the grounds. **DISCOUNTS:** Corporate rates, *AARP, AAA* **AIRPORT:** Fresno Airport-35 mi **RESERVATIONS:** Credit card number for deposit to guarantee reservation. Friday, Saturday & Holiday rates slightly higher; Sunday night discounted 25%; rates do not include hotel taxes. **BROCHURE:** Yes **PERMITTED:** Children, pets, smoking **CONFERENCES:** Facilities for business meetings, banquets; spacious grounds for perfect weddings, receptions and private parties **LANGUAGES:** Limited Spanish, Portuguese [R07FPCA2-368]

Healdsburg Inn On The Plaza	Healdsburg CA
Genny Jenkins	110 Matheson 95448
707-433-6991	**Res Times** 9am-9pm

Rates:	**Pvt Bath** 9	**Payment Terms:**
Single	$ 85-160.00	Check
Double	$ 85-160.00	MC/V

A quiet place in the center of town where history and hospitality meet. This historic Wells Fargo Building of 1890 now accommodates our Bed and Breakfast. Enjoy browsing through our gift, quilt and antique shops on the main floor. A grand staircase in the art gallery takes you to the guest rooms, most with fireplaces and clawfooted tubs, each furnished in antiques and decorated in sunrise/sunset colors. All nine rooms include queen size beds, private bathrooms, fluffy towels and your own rubber duckie; central air and heat, telephones, TV's, VCR's and video library are available upon request. The solarium and roof garden provide a charming common area for guests to meet for breakfast or afternoon wine and popcorn. The full country breakfast includes a hot entree, fresh fruit, cereals, assorted breads and muffins, orange juice, teas and our special blend coffee; champagne brunch on weekends. Coffee, assorted teas and cookies available 24 hours. Convenient to wine tasting, restaurants,

California

antique, galleries, shopping, canoeing and hiking. **AIRPORT:** San Francisco-80 mi **DISCOUNTS:** Three nights and longer stays. **RESERVATIONS:** Credit card number for deposit to guarantee reservation, 3 day cancel policy for refund less $15 service fee **BROCHURE:** Yes **PERMITTED:** Children by arrangement, wine, smoking outdoors only, no pets **LANGUAGES:** English [Z08GPCA2-374]

**Rockwood Lodge			**Homewood CA**
Louis Reinkens/Constance Stevens		5295 W Lake Blvd 96141-0266	
800-LE TAHOE 916-525-5273			**Fax** 916-525-5949
Rates:	**Pvt Bath** 3	**Shared Bath** 2	**Payment Terms:**
Single	$ 135.00	$ 100.00	Cash
Double	$ 250.00	$ 125.00	

This Thirties-style Chalet beckons guests with a warm, friendly atmosphere of Lake Tahoe's magical west shore, just down the road from Fleur Du Lac, a lakeside villa where *Godfather Part II* was filmed. Originally built as a second home in the mid-thirties, your hosts completely renovated this "Old Tahoe-Style" home of stone, knotty pine and hand-hewn beams into the perfect mountain chalet for romantics. Guest suites are named for actual places around Lake Tahoe and offer a range of furnishings and decor from a feather bed with a puffy down comforter, Laura Ashley curtains and fabrics, Early American and European furnishings, and a private bath with brass fixtures, a pedestal wash basin and a welcomed 20th century convenience - a seven foot long Roman tub with double showers. Added amenities include a complement of body lotions and shampoos, cozy terry cloth bathrobes and bedtime chocolates discretely placed on the nightstand. A full complimentary breakfast in the dining room offers selections of homemade fruit crepes, Lou's special "Dutch Baby" - a breakfast souffle, all complemented by fresh-squeezed orange juice, yogurt and granola to begin your day. Conveniently located for skiers, its a short drive to Squaw Valley and Alpine Meadows and within easy walking distance to Homewood Ski Area. Apres-ski amenities are close by with one of Lake Tahoe's most celebrated European-style restaurants - *Swiss Lakewood* within walking distance. Staying at *Rockwood* means leaving your car parked because you're within walking distance of great dining, sights and activities. **RESERVATIONS:** Payment in full within ten days of booking **PERMITTED:** Drinking, (outdoor shoes not permitted in house because of white carpeting) **BROCHURE:** Yes **AIRPORT:** Reno Cannon-55 mi **DISCOUNTS:** Upgrades, when available [Z07GPCA2-380]

Fairwinds Farm B&B	**Inverness CA**
Joyce Goldfield	PO Box 581 04037

California

415-663-9454

Res Times 24 Hrs

Rates:	**Pvt Bath** 1	**Payment Terms:**
Single	$ 125.00*	Check
Double	$ 125.00*	

The ultimate secluded getaway! High atop Inverness Ridge, amidst towering bishop pines and bays, with direct access to 68,000 acres of Point Reyes National Seashore. One large (1000 sq ft) cottage, living room, central heat plus a large fireplace with wood, fully-equipped kitchen, full bath, private garden with pond and swing, deck-top hot tub with ocean view! Amenities include barnyard animals, library, TV, stereo, VCR (movies!) typewriter, guitar, binoculars, beach chairs and umbrella, robes and beach towels. Quaint, rustic and cozy. A very special hideaway, secluded and private, the only light visible from the farm is the lighthouse on Farallon Islands. There's a queen size bed and futon couch in the living room with a double bed in the loft bedroom and a crib is available. A generous country breakfast is provided with baked goodies and fresh fruit, gourmet coffee and tea and homemade jam. For evenings movies by the fire, special cookies, cheese cakes, popcorn and chocolate bars are provided. Ocean and bay beaches, meadows of wildflowers, forested mountain tops - to explore and photograph. Whale watching in winter, birdwatching year-round - you'll find wild deer, elk, fox, bobcat and raccoons as well. Horseback riding and biking available in the National Park outside your front door! **AIRPORT:** San Francisco & Oakland-1 hr **PACKAGES:** Stay 7 nights, pay for 6. **RESERVATIONS:** Deposit required, 30 day cancel policy for refund. Check-in 3pm, late arrival only with prior arrangements, add 10% county tax to room rates. *$25 for each additional person **BROCHURE:** Yes **PERMITTED:** Children, social drinking **LANGUAGES:** Sign language [R05FPCA2-12697]

National Hotel			**Jamestown CA**
Steve Willey			Main St 95237
209-984-3446			**Res Times** 8am-10pm

Rates:	**Pvt Bath** 5	**Shared Bath** 7	**Payment Terms:**
Single	$ 55-65.00	$ 45-55.00	Check
Double	$ 65-75.00	$ 55-65.00	MC/V

An 1859 restored and gateway setting to the Mother-Lode Country!! The Wild West lives again!! One of the oldest continuously operating hotels in California. Full breakfast included. **RESERVATIONS:** Deposit required to hold room, cancellation notice of 5 days for full refund. **BROCHURE:** Yes **PERMITTED:** Children 8-up, limited drinking & smoking. **CONFERENCES:** Yes, for groups to 15 persons including gourmet dining. [E02BCCA-6216]

California

Murphys Jenner Inn	**Jenner CA**
Sheldon & Richard Murphy	10400 Hwy One 95450-0069
800-732-2377 707-865-2377	**Res Times** 10am-8pm

Rates:	**Pvt Bath** 11	**Payment Terms:**
Single	$ 50-110.00	Check
Double	$ 70-150.00	MC/V

Fifteen miles of sandy beaches, hundreds of acres of state parks with hiking trails through magnificent redwoods, pines and cypress, an ocean that continuously washes away the earth's impurities . . . all of nature's gifts are abundant just seventy scenic miles north of the Golden Gate Bridge on Coastal Highway One. Spend time on the beach just sitting, walking or meditating! Pick fresh herbs and wild mushrooms, catch a steelhead or seabass for dinner, whale-watch in winter or canoe the Russian River! Choose one of ten guest rooms which are furnished in varying decor including some with river and ocean views, hot tub, open-fire woodstoves, antique and wicker furnishings, quilts, books, houseplants, personal loving touches and without TV or phones! Several beach-side vacation rental homes are also available. A restaurant on the grounds offer Continental Cuisine featuring local seafoods, meats, vegetarian dishes and fine wines from the local Russian River Valley wineries. **RESERVATIONS:** One night's deposit in advance, 7 day cancel policy less $10 service fee. Full payment at check-in. **BROCHURE:** Yes **PERMITTED:** Children, limited pets, smoking outdoors on decks only **CONFERENCES:** Yes, the Terra Nova Institute at Salmon Creek Beach, just 8 miles south of the Inn. **Weddings by the Sea** are directed by Mrs Sheldon Murphy [Z01EPCA-399]

Kern River Inn B&B	**Kernville CA**
Marti Andrews/Mike Meeham	119 Kern Rive Dr 93238
619-376-6750	**Res Times** 8am-10pm

Rates:	**Pvt Bath** 6	**Payment Terms:**
Single	$ 65-75.00	Check*
Double	$ 75-85.00	MC/V

The brand new *Kern River Inn Bed & Breakfast* is truly a home away from home for people who enjoy personal service and western hospitality. Located on the Kern River in the quaint western town of Kernville,CA in the southern Sierras within Sequoia National Forest. Only three driving hours north of Los Angeles. The Inn features six tastefully, individually decorated country bedrooms, all with private baths and river views. Some rooms include fireplaces, whirlpool tubs, sitting areas, queen and king size beds, and wheelchair access. Relax with new friends in our country traditional parlor or enjoy refreshments on the front porch while you

California

enjoy the view of the park and river. An expanded continental breakfast features homebaked giant cinnamon rolls, special cereals, fresh fruit, juices, coffee and teas. Year round activities include fishing, golf, white-water rafting, kayaking, mountain biking, hiking, Lake Isabella, water sports and downhill skiing at Shirley Meadows ski area. Restaurants, parks, museums and antique shops are within walking distance, and it's just a short drive to the high country and the beautiful giant redwoods. **DISCOUNTS:** Special group and others, inquire at res time. **AIRPORT:** Bakersfield-45 mi **PACKAGES:** *Honeymoon, Birthday, Anniversary, Special Occasion.* **RESERVATIONS:** One night's or 50% of length of stay (which ever is greater), late arrival by arrangement, 7 day cancel policy; two or more room require 14 day notice for refund; Arrival 3-6pm, checkout 11 am. **BROCHURE:** Yes **PERMITTED:** Drinking & children 12-up, smoking on porches only - outside **CONFERENCES:** Yes, small retreat for 10-12 persons [R10DPCA-14351]

**Carriage House	**Laguna Beach CA**
Dee & Thom Taylor	1322 Catalina St 92651
714-494-8945	

Rates:	**Pvt Bath** 6	**Payment Terms:**
Single	$ 95-150.00	Check
Double	$ 95-150.00	

One of *Laguna's Designated Historical Landmarks*, this New Orleans-style Inn is located in the heart of the Village and just a few houses away from the beautiful beaches of the Pacific Ocean! Each guest room is individually decorated from the Springtime freshness of the Lilac Time Suite to the tropical coolness of Green Palms with emerald greens and white touches in wicker! All guest rooms are suites with sitting rooms and most have a fully-equipped kitchen. A spectacular courtyard is surrounded by the guest rooms and is the focal point for relaxation among the tropical plants and the splashing fountains. You'll never know who you might meet here because a number of celebrities (Linda Lavin, Jane Withers & Lauren Hutton) have already discovered the charm of this wonderful Inn. Your hosts are committed to service and you'll start each morning with a Complimentary continental plus breakfast served outdoors in the courtyard beneath a carrotwood tree covered with moss while the fresh ocean breeze reminds you the ocean is just a few steps away. In their usual California-custom, Dee & Vern treat each guest, upon arrival, to a complimentary bottle of California wine, fresh fruit and flowers in their rooms. **AIRPORT:** LA & San Diego are 75 minutes away (Laguna is midway) **DISCOUNTS:** Yes, inquire at res time **RESERVATIONS:** One night's deposit at res time, 7 day cancel policy for refund, two night min on weekends **BROCHURE:** Yes **PERMITTED:** Children, limited drinking, limited smoking [Z07GPCA2-409]

California

Laguna Pacifica	**Laguna Beach CA**
*Robin Nahin	
800-383-3513 310-498-0552	**Res Times** 24 Hrs

Rates:	**Pvt Bath** 1	**Payment Terms:**
Single		Check
Double	$ 85.00	MC/V

We invite you to stay at our romantic and sunny Bed & Breakfast by the sea! Enjoy our personal hospitality while you bask in the sun and drink in the **unobstructed 180 degree ocean view**. This suite is in breathtaking Laguna Beach - 2 blocks from the shoreline. *Lover's Cove* is only 3-1/2 blocks away. This generous private-entry two-room suite with private bath, sundeck and elevator, is decorated in soft colors, antiques with a queen size 4-poster bed, including a fingertip library. The living room features a full sofa bed, cable TV/VCR, indoor dining and kitchenette. Fruit, candy and fresh flowers adorn your quarters. A spacious 20 by 20 foot sundeck offers a dining table with umbrella, lounge chairs and an array of native vegetation. Our registered nurse nutritionist creates a variety of full breakfasts with scrumptious homecooked dishes. She will cater to those with special dietary requests. We are located just 1 hour from Los Angeles and San Diego, and only 1/2 hour from *Disneyland*. Laguna's internationally renown art festivals are a must. **RESERVATIONS:** One night's deposit to guarantee reservations **PERMITTED:** Children under 6 mo/over 5 years, limited pets, limited drinking, smoking outdoors **BROCHURE:** Yes **CONFERENCES:** Small gatherings of less than 25 persons, including weddings **LANGUAGES:** Fluent French, English, Italian, German, Spanish, Serbo-Croatian **DISCOUNTS:** Yes, inquire at res time **AIRPORT:** Orange County-15-20 mins [R05FPCA1-16967]

Terrace Manor	**Los Angeles CA**
Sandy & Shirly Spillman	1353 Alvarado Terrace 90006
213-381-1478	

Rates:	**Pvt Bath** 5	**Payment Terms:**
Single	$ 70-100.00	Check
Double	$ 70-100.00	AE/MC/V

A *National Registered Landmark* built c1902, this residence is an excellent example of hardwood flooring, stained and leaded glass windows, and ornate hardwood carvings. Antique furnishings and host collectibles complete the excellent decor of all rooms. Full Complimentary breakfast included with room. Complimentary wine upon arrival. Close to Chinatown, Little Tokyo, Magic Castle and Dodger's stadium. **BROCHURE:** Yes **PERMITTED:** Limited children [E11ACCA-425]

California

Big Canyon Inn	Lower Lake CA
John & Gretchen Wiegand 707-928-5631	11750 Big Canyon Rd 95457

Rates:	**Pvt Bath** 1	**Payment Terms:**
Single	$ 55.00	Check
Double	$ 65.00	

A secluded and peaceful home on a hilly twelve acres of pines and oaks beneath Cobb Mountain provides guests an opportunity to relax with nature's beauty surrounding them. Enjoy the many outdoor recreational activities: hike the mountains and search for Lake Country diamonds, enjoy the wildflowers blooming each Spring or the changing colors in the Fall, go fishing, or enjoy the wine tasting at nearby wineries. You'll have a separate suite with a private entrance, kitchenette and bath. You'll enjoy the wood-burning stove during the cooler months. Private airport pick-ups arranged at Hoberg Airport. **RESERVATIONS:** One night's deposit to hold room; arrival by 6:30 pm unless other arrangements have been made **PERMITTED:** Children, drinking [C11ACCA-435]

Casa Larronde	Malibu CA
Jim & Charlou Larronde 213-456-9333	PO Box 86 90265-0086

Rates:	**Pvt Bath** 2	**Payment Terms:**
Single	$ 70.00	Check
Double	$ 85.00	

Walk among the stars in Malibu near surfer's beach with over 4,000 sq ft of luxury including full glass windows, fireplace, outdoor wood deck for sunbathing. World-traveled hosts also enjoy entertaining if you desire. Full complimentary breakfast included. With beach activities close at hand and star watching with movie stars for neighbors. [C11ACCA-437]

**Stallup House*	Malibu Hills CA
*Ed & Ann Stallup 800-383-3513 310-493-0552	**Res Times** 24 Hrs

Rate:	**Pvt Bath** 1	**Shared Bath** 2	**Payment Terms:**
Single	$ 65.00	$ 50.00	Check
Double	$ 65.00	$ 50.00	MC/V

Magnificent 180° whitewater view of the Malibu coastline and Santa Monica Bay. Filled with paintings and folk art, the home reflects the interests of the well-travelled teacher hosts. Large decks are on two sides

California

of the house with a small balcony off the master suite. This suite consists of a large bedroom with king size bed, sitting room/loft and bathroom. Downstairs are two rooms, one with twin beds; the other has a double bed. Continental breakfasts are served, consisting of fresh fruits, cereals, juice, coffee and tea, home-baked muffins and a variety of jams. While viewing the sunsets from the deck, complimentary wine is available. A three and a half mile drive up a winding road from the Pacific Coast highway makes an automobile essential. Santa Monica is a 25 min drive, downtown Los Angeles is 50 mins, LAX 50 mins, Getty Museum 20 mins, Universal Studio 50 mins, Pepperdine Univ 20 mins and Santa Barbara 1-3/4 hrs. **RESERVATIONS:** One night's deposit **BROCHURE:** No **PERMITTED:** Children, drinking **LANGUAGES:** Some Spanish [R05FPCA2-16895]

**Oak Meadows, too	**Mariposa CA**
Don & Francie Starchman	5263 Hwy 140N 95338
209-742-6161	**Res Times** 4pm-9pm

Rates:	**Pvt Bath** 6	**Payment Terms:**
Single	$ 59.00	Check
Double	$ 59-89.00	MC/V

Just a short drive to Yosemite National Park. *Oak Meadows, too* is located in the Historic Gold Rush town of Mariposa, at the intersection of Hwy 49 and Hwy 140N. *Oak Meadows, too* was built in 1985 with New England architecture and turn-of-the-century charm. A stone fireplace greets your arrival in the guest parlor, where a continental plus breakfast is served each morning. Take a walking tour of Mariposa, see the California State Mining & Mineral Museum or just relax in your comfortably furnished room. All rooms have private baths and are furnished with handmade quilts, brass headboards, and charming wallpapers. **RESERVATIONS:** First night's deposit, 3 day cancel policy for refund, add 9% tax **SEASONAL:** Closed Christmas **BROCHURE:** Yes **PERMITTED:** Limited children, drinking **LANGUAGES:** French, German [Z07GPCA2-2916]

**Grey Whale Inn	**Mendocino CA**
Colette & John Bailey	
800-382-7244 707-964-0640	**Res Times** 8am-8pm

Rates:	**Pvt Bath** 14	**Payment Terms:**
Single	$ 60-140.00	Check
Double	$ 80-160.00	AE/DIS/MC/V

Refer to the same listing name under Fort Bragg CA for a complete description. [M04FPCA2-16854]

California

**John Dougherty House	**Mendocino CA**
David & Marion Wells	571 Ukiah St 95460
707-937-5266	

Rates:	**Pvt Bath** 6	**Payment Terms:**
Single	$ 95-165.00	Check
Double	$ 95-165.00	MC/V

Stop a while .... and enjoy California as it was one hundred and twenty--five years ago. Built in 1867, the *Historic John Dougherty House* offers some of the best ocean and bay views in the historic village of Mendocino - while just steps away from great restaurants and shopping. The Main House is furnished with period country antiques reminiscent of the 1860's and provides a quiet peaceful nights sleep seldom experienced in today's urban lifestyles. All of the guest rooms include a private bath, queen size bed and are furnished with antiques and individually decorated, accented with dried flower wreaths and arrangements gathered from our garden. Most of the rooms feature color cable TV, a small refrigerator and a woodburning stove. Breakfast is served by a crackling fire in the historic New England-style keeping room where guests are surrounded by period country antiques, handstenciled walls and a view of Mendocino Bay and the Pacific Ocean. The expansive full complimentary breakfast includes homemade scones and breads, a large selection of locally grown fresh fruit - decorated with edible flowers from our English garden. In-addition, you'll sample natural honey, Almond Granola with yogurt, hot entree and a large selection of natural cereals. Breakfast is also a pleasant time to share your daily plans with the other guests and your hosts .... where you'll learn there's canoeing up the Big River, hiking the headlands, beaches and tidepools along the rugged coast. Mendocino, a National Historic Preservation Area, is near nine state parks where you can enjoy whale watching, green fern canyons, lush botanical gardens and majestic redwoods. The arts thrive with numerous craft shops and galleries offer items unique to the area. **DISCOUNTS:** Special winter rates **AIRPORT:** San Francisco-175 mi; Santa Rosa-90 mi. **PACKAGES:** Inquire at res time **RESERVATIONS:** One night's deposit within 5 days of making reservation; 7 day cancel policy for refund less $15 service fee. Two night min weekends **BROCHURE:** Yes **PERMITTED:** Drinking, limited children. [I07GPCA2-12703]

California

**Goose & Turrets	**Montara CA**
Raymond & Emily Hoche-Mong	835 George St 94037-0937
415-728-5451	**Res Times** 8am-10pm

Rates:	**Pvt Bath** 5	**Payment Terms:**
Single	$ 85-110.00	Check
Double	$ 85-110.00	AE/DISC/MC/V

At the *Goose & Turrets* you'll find geese on the pond .... hummingbirds in the fuschias .... Mozart on the tape deck .... bread baking in the oven .... a wood fire in the living room .... down comforters to cuddle under .... and surf and foghorns in the distance. *The Goose & Turrets* has helped folks unwind for a long time. In the early 1900's, San Francisco Bohemians rode the Ocean Shore Railroad to Montara Beach and Art Colony. During Prohibition, the adventurous indulged in the forbidden along the sparsely patrolled coast. The cannon flanking the front door date from our time as the Spanish American War Veterans Country Club. Today Montara is a peaceful seaside village of horse ranches and straw flower farms. This 1908 italian villa is a family-run bed and breakfast where you are pampered with tea and tasty things in the afternoon and a full four-course breakfast in the morning. Menus change daily. Only 20 minutes from San Francisco Airport, the *Goose & Turrets Bed and Breakfast* is also only 1/2 mile from a clean uncrowded Pacific beach. Nearby are restaurants, galleries, tidepools, golf, hiking, horseback riding, and remnants of the area's lurid past during Prohibition. Montara is a small village 25 miles south of San Francisco and 8 miles north of historic Half Moon Bay. It's a convenient headquarters for excursions to Silicon Valley or Berkeley to the east, Monterey Aquarium and Carmel to the south, and San Francisco, Muir Woods, and Sausalito to the north. Hosts Raymond and Emily Hoche-Mong are pilots and have traveled the world. Living in Nashville, Key West, Beirut and Cairo has acquainted them with the customs and cuisines of those places famous for food and hospitality. Their personal art and artifact collections enliven the guest and common rooms. **DISCOUNTS:** 15% Mon-Thursday, *AARP & ASU*; 10% any stay of five nights **AIRPORT:** San Francisco Intl-20 mins; Half Moon Bay-2 mi (pick-up for GA pilots & sailors at HMB & Pillar Point by prior arrangement) **RESERVATIONS:** Credit card guarantee or check for full amount; 72-hour cancellation policy **BROCHURE:** Yes **PERMITTED:** Drinking, children **CONFERENCES:** Yes, maximum 15 people for day events; reunions and meetings not requiring more than five bedrooms **LANGUAGES:** Nous parlons français, English [K08GPCA2-6205]

California

**Babbling Brook Inn	**Monterey CA**
Helen King	
800-866-1131 408-427-2437	**Res Times** 7am-11pm
	Fax 408-427-2457
Rates: **Pvt Bath** 12	**Payment Terms:**
Single $ 85-150.00	Check
Double $ 85-150.00	AE/DC/MC/V

Refer to the same listing name under Santa Cruz for a complete description. [M11BCCA-4604]

**Monterey Hotel - 1904	**Monterey CA**
Deborah Alexander	406 Alvarado St 93940
800-727-0960 408-375-3184	**Res Times** 24 Hrs
Rates: **Pvt Bath** 44	**Payment Terms:**
Single $ 95.00-up	Check
Double $ 95.00-up	AE/DC/MC/V

Established in 1904 and lovingly restored to its original elegance, The *Monterey Hotel* was reopened in 1987. Located in the center of downtown Monterey, only two blocks from Fisherman's Wharf, The Center and State Historic Park. It is surrounded by shops, restaurants and boutiques. All rooms are filled with custom period furnishings plus antique style beds with down comforters. The Master Suites offer jacuzzi-spa tubs, fireplaces and wet-bars. Mornings begin with a complimentary Continental breakfast buffet served in the lobby courtyard garden area. Freshly brewed coffee & teas, a variety of muffins, breads & pastries, cereals, seasonal fruits, plus the latest edition of the newspaper help start your day. Afternoon wine & cheese is provided around the cozy fireplace in the lobby. Meals available. **RESERVATIONS:** Deposit or credit card for one night's stay at res time, 72 hr cancel policy. **DISCOUNTS:** Group and corporate rates available. **BROCHURE:** Yes **PERMITTED:** Children; Non-smoking **CONFERENCES:** Yes, 900 sq ft total space. Two conference rooms are available for 5 to 50 people [Z11BPCA-6523]

**Mount Shasta Ranch B&B		**Mount Shasta CA**
Bill & Mary Larsen		1008 W A Barr Rd 96967
916-926-3870		**Fax** 916-926-6882
Rates: **Pvt Bath** 4	**Shared Bath** 5	**Payment Terms:**
Single $ 70.00	$ 55.00	Check
Double $ 80.00	$ 60.00	AE/MC/V

This Northern California, two-story ranch home offers affordable elegance

California

in a historical setting. Built in 1923 by HD "Curley" Brown as a thoroughbred horse ranch, the original guest accommodations include the main house and several cottages and bungalows. Today, guests still enjoy the unique atmosphere and mood of those early years. The magnificent home has four spacious guestrooms, a separate carriage house with five bedrooms and a two-bedroom cottage. Guestrooms are furnished with antiques, queen size beds, most offer mountain views and the rooms in the main house offer enormous baths. Amenities include drinks, snacks, piano, game room with ping pong and pool table, a large hot spring spa and beautiful sunsets enjoyed on the outdoor veranda. A full complimentary breakfast begins your day - awakening to the aroma of imported coffee. Mount Shasta provides more than a spectacular backdrop for the *Mount Shasta Ranch* - there's downhill and x-country skiing, fishing, sailing, swimming, three golf courses, fish hatchery, museums and an enthusiastic climb of 14, 162 feet to the top. **RESERVATIONS:** Credit card number or one night's deposit, check-in 3-9pm or other time with prior arrangement. Two night min holiday summer weekends and stays in the cottage **PERMITTED:** Children, drinking, limited smoking **BROCHURE:** Yes **CONFERENCES:** Limited **DISCOUNTS:** 7th night free **AIRPORT:** Redding-60 mi; Sacramento-200 mi [Z07GPCA2-6198]

Murphys Hotel			Murphys CA
Robert Walker			457 Main St 95247
209-728-3444			**Res Times** 24 hours
Rates:	**Pvt Bath** 20	**Shared Bath** 9	**Payment Terms:**
Single	$ 60.00-Up	$ 50.00-Up	Check
Double	$ 70.00-Up	$ 60.00-Up	AE/MC/V

Turn-of-the-century "Gold Country" Inn c1856 listed as *National Historic Landmark* with guests' names such as Mark Twain and Horatio Alger on their register yet today!! Completely restored and furnished with period antiques and plenty of atmosphere to relive the Gold Fever!! You can even try the Presidential Suite where Ulysses S Grant stayed!! Hearty country breakfast included if you like, with other meals available in the dining room on the premises. **RESERVATIONS:** Airport pick-ups available at added cost. **BROCHURE:** Yes **PERMITTED:** Children, pets, smoking, and drinking. [C11ACCA-478]

**Arbor Guest House*		Napa CA
Bruce & Rosemary Logan		1436 G St 94559
707-252-8144		**Res Times** 7am-10pm
Rates:	**Pvt Bath** 5	**Payment Terms:**
Single	$ 80-110.00	Check

©*Bed & Breakfast Guest Houses & Inns of America, Memphis TN*

California

Double $ 80-110.00   AE/MC/V

After an eventful day touring, shopping and exploring the Napa and/or Sonoma wine country, *Arbor Guest House* is an inviting setting in which to relax and unwind. Enjoy refreshments at a garden patio table or before the glowing embers of the fireplace and the peaceful hospitality will envelop you. Each of the five guest accommodations is uniquely designed with comfortable queen beds, charming period furnishings, and private baths with clawfoot tubs/showers and pedestal sinks. The lovingly restored 1906 home is centrally heated and cooled while the carriage house rooms are individually heated and cooled. Extra beds are available for two rooms for a party of four or those desiring separate beds. The Colonial transition home and carriage houses are attractively surrounded by a vine-covered arbor, a stately sequoia, rose bushes, fruit & walnut trees and flowering shrubs. The interior features the garden motif throughout the inn with the wallpaper, window coverings, and a medley of antique furniture in brass, iron, oak, mahogany, wicker and etched glass. Within the intimate surroundings of this lovely retreat, you are pampered by the cheerful and thoughtful innkeepers in a manner suitable to an expensive resort. Continental breakfast includes freshly-baked breads, two selections of scones, croissants, coffee cakes, banana bread or nut breads with fresh juice and choice of hot beverages. **RESERVATIONS:** One night's deposit at res time, 72-hr cancel policy for refund, check-in 3-6pm **BROCHURE:** Yes **CONFERENCES:** Yes [Z08GPCA2-479]

**Blue Violet Mansion	**Napa CA**
Bob & Kathy Morris	443 Brown St 94559
707-253-2583	**Fax** 707-257-8205
Rates: **Pvt Bath** 7	**Payment Terms:**
Single $ 115-195.00	Check
Double $ 115-195.00	AE/MC/V

The *Blue Violet Mansion* has been lovingly restored by your hosts over the past four years and offers guests a blend of country living and Victorian elegance in the historic district of Napa. This elegant 1886 Queen Anne home was built for Emanuel Manasse, an executive at the Sawyer Tannery who developed innovative leather tanning techniques which remain in the leather wainscotting adorning the main foyer. Awarded the *Napa County Landmark Award of Excellence* for historic preservation,

California

your innkeepers pride themselves on catering to the romantic at heart and their Inn was chosen by Bill Gleeson to be included in his book, *50 Most Romantic Places In Northern California*, referring to the *Blue Violet Mansion* as the *"... cabernet of Napa Valley Inns."* Guests may choose from rooms with names such as *Queen Victoria, His Majesty, Garden Bower, Rose Room* or *The French Boudoir*. All rooms are spacious, sunfilled, peaceful and include complete guest services, amenities, with fireplaces and jacuzzi spas in many rooms. Special amenities such as private candlelight champagne dinners served ensuite, massage packages including two tables and two massage professionals, gift baskets, wine and food trays, flowers, picnic baskets - or whatever would make your stay complete and perfect can be arranged ahead of arrival. Napa is situated at the top of San Francisco Bay and is the gateway to the Napa and Sonoma Valleys and the Carneros Wine Region. In addition to the wineries, there are hot springs (one of the world's three Old Faithful Geysers), a natural petrified forest, Lake Hennessey and Lake Berryessa and beautiful mountain ranges. When not sightseeing, guests relax in the Victorian parlors or outside in the garden gazebo, verandah or shaded deck. A full complimentary breakfast is included. This comfortable Victorian home awaits your arrival. **RESERVATIONS:** Deposit required to guarantee reservation, 10 day cancel policy with 10% cancellation fee (less than 10 day cancel notice, refund only if rebooked), two day minimum stay **PERMITTED:** Children, drinking **BROCHURE:** Yes **CONFERENCES:** Small groups **DISCOUNTS:** Yes, inquire at res time **AIRPORT:** San Francisco-65 mi; Oakland-50 mi **PACKAGES:** *Golf, Hot Air Balloon, Massage* [I05GPCA2-14335]

**Churchill Manor	**Napa CA**
Joanna Guidotti/Brian Jensen	485 Brown St 94559
707-253-7733	**Res Times** 9am-9pm

Rates:	**Pvt Bath** 10	**Payment Terms:**
Single	$ 82.00	Check
Double	$ 149.00	AE/MC/V

Built in 1889 for local banker Edward Churchill, *Churchill Manor* is reputed to be the largest historic home built in Napa Valley. The magnificent three-story Mansion has been placed on the *National Register of Historic Places*. *Churchill Manor* rests on an acre of beautifully landscaped grounds and is surrounded by a sweeping veranda supported by large white columns. Entering through the original lead glass doors, one discovers four grand parlours, each with an elegant fireplace, carved redwood ceiling, mouldings and columns, a gorgeous sunroom with an original marble-tiled floor, and one guestroom. On the upper floors are nine more guest bedrooms, each with a private bathroom, several with fireplaces, two with jacuzzi spas and each decorated with an individual

California

theme. The entire home is furnished with lovely antiques, oriental rugs, brass and crystal chandeliers and a grand piano in the music room. Guests at the Manor enjoy coffee and tea along with fresh-baked cookies every afternoon, evening varietal wines with cheese and crackers, a full gourmet breakfast including omelettes and french toast, complimentary tandem bicycles for viewing Old Town Napa and nearby wineries, and croquet on the expansive lawns. **AIRPORT:** San Francisco-1 hr **DISCOUNTS:** Airline employees (25% S-Thur) **PACKAGES:** *Wine & Gourmet Dining Train, Balloon* **RESERVATIONS:** Deposit required, 72 hr cancel policy for refund; call if arriving late, Saturday nights require a two-night booking. **BROCHURE:** Yes **PERMITTED:** Children 12-up, limited drinking, limited smoking **CONFERENCES:** Groups to 50 during day periods, evening groups only if reserving all 10 guest rooms **LANGUAGES:** Spanish [I01FPCA2-482]

**Coombs/Inn The Park B&B			**Napa CA**
			720 Seminary St 94559
707-257-0789			**Res Times** 9am-6pm
Rates:	**Pvt Bath** 1	**Shared Bath** 3	**Payment Terms:**
Single	$ 135.00	$ 95-125.00	Check
Double	$ 135.00	$ 95-125.00	MC/V

One of the oldest and most beautiful residences in Napa Valley is this two-story Victorian home built in 1852 and completely restored and elegantly furnished with beautiful European and American antiques. Located in the lovely town of Napa and across the street from a small neighborhood park, guests can enjoy strolling the peaceful and tranquil setting or relaxing in the parlor while enjoying complimentary refreshments in front of a cozy fire. Guest rooms are furnished in various themes and include down comforters and pillows and luxurious terry robes and bath sheets. Continental breakfast is included and offers special house-blend coffees, croissants, homemade muffins & nutbread, juices, and seasonal fruits. You can relax in the pool, jacuzzi, or use one of the comp bikes for a leisure trip around town. The charming hosts will help arrange hot air balloon rides, champagne gourmet picnics, glider rides, mud baths or if you need help in choosing from all the excellent dining spots, you just need to ask. Menus of local restaurants, winery and local events information are available. **RESERVATIONS:** One night's deposi, 48 hour cancel notice for full refund **BROCHURE:** Yes **PERMIT**

California

TED: Drinking [A09APCA-489]

**Elm House	**Napa CA**
David & Betsy McCracken	800 California Blvd 94559
800-788-4356 707-255-1831	**Res Times** 7:30am-10pm

Rates:	**Pvt Bath** 16	**Payment Terms:**
Single	$ 79-130.00	Check
Double	$ 79-130.00	AE/MC/V

The Elm House, Napa Valley's most gracious new Inn, invites you to your home away from home. We wish to share the charm of The Valley with you by providing courteous and knowledgeable service. Sheltered by three magnificent historic elms, *The Elm House* is located at the gateway to the world-famous Napa Valley wine region. Our comfortable living room with its elegant furnishings and large Italian marble fireplace provides an engaging setting for conversation, reading or relaxation. In the adjoining courtyard, a spa/fountain invites guests to enjoy its soothing waters. Each morning guests are served a complimentary expanded continental breakfast of coffee, tea, fresh fruit, juices and assorted pastries and muffins. Modern construction provides sixteen sound-insulated guest rooms decorated in pine and attractive fabrics. The guest rooms have queen-sized beds, private baths, separate dressing vanities, individual temperature controls, remote TV, radios, phones and stocked refrigerators. Several rooms offer Italian marble fireplaces. For that special celebration, reserve our largest room with high ceilings, fireplace and chandeliers. Our staff is experienced in anticipating your every need, including the need for privacy. We are able to assist with restaurant reservations, winery tours, balloon rides, wine train packages and golf at some of the wine country's most beautiful courses. About an hour's drive from San Francisco, *The Elm House* is an elegant and ideal departure point to Napa Valley's numerous wineries and to historic Napa. **AIRPORT:** 1-1/2 Hrs to San Francisco **DISCOUNTS:** Business, some midweeks, inquire when calling **RESERVATIONS:** One night's deposit to guarantee with 72 hr cancel policy for refund **BROCHURE:** Yes **PERMITTED:** Children, drinking, limited smoking **CONFERENCES:** Yes, conference room for groups to twenty persons **LANGUAGES:** English [I05FPCA2-7065]

California

**Napa Inn	**Napa CA**
Doug & Carol Morales	1137 Warren St 94559
707-257-1444	**Res Times** 9:30am-8pm

Rates:	**Pvt Bath** 6	**Payment Terms:**
Single	$ 110-160.00	Check
Double	$ 110-160.00	DIS/MC/V

The *Napa Inn* is a beautiful three-story Queen Anne Victorian built in 1899 located on a quite residential street in the old historical section of Napa. The Inn has been recently redecorated in keeping with the Victorian Era including primarily Victorian furnishings, phonographs, books, musical instruments, china, and much more! A perfect Victorian hideaway! Complimentary afternoon refreshments are served in a large parlor and a full breakfast is served each morning in the formal dining room. Guest rooms are located on the second floor, each with a private bath, fireplace, queen-size bed and a sitting area. The entire third floor is devoted to one large suite which includes a king-size bed, private bath and a private balcony. The town of Napa is in the south end of Napa Valley, home to over two hundred wineries. In addition, guests can experience hot air ballooning, glider plane rides, lakes, biking, hiking, horse back riding, excellent restaurants, Napa Valley Wine Train and many historical landmarks. **DISCOUNTS:** Midweek **AIRPORT:** 60-miles. **RESERVATIONS:** Credit card # for authorization. Special arrangements made for late check-in **BROCHURE:** Yes [Z03FPCA2-492]

*Grandmeres Inn	**Nevada City CA**
Doug & Geri Boka	449 Broad St 95959
916-265-4660	

Rates:	**Pvt Bath** 6	**Payment Terms:**
Single	$ 90.00-Up	Check
Double	$ 120.00-Up	MC/V

Traditional French Country architecture residence is nestled in perfect setting in center Nevada City. *National Register of Historic Places* listing, relax in comfort and experience the ambience of turn-of-the-century France. Perfect place for social or business affairs. Hosts prepare gourmet breakfast for guests daily and served in the country kitchen or outdoors in the garden/patio area. **BROCHURE:** Yes **PERMITTED:** Children, limited. **CONFERENCES:** Dinner with catering by arrangement with space for seating 12-15 at dining and conferences. [C11ACCA-502]

**Red Castle Inn, Historic B&B	**Nevada City CA**
Conley & Mary Louise Weaver	109 Prospect St 95959

California

916-265-5135   **Res Times** 9am-9pm

Rates:	**Pvt Bath** 6	**Shared Bath** 2	**Payment Terms:**
Single	$ 80-105.00	$ 65.00	Check
Double	$ 85-110.00	$ 70.00	MC/V

High on a forested hillside where breezes linger on wide verandas, strains of Mozart echo through lofty hallways, chandeliers sparkle, the aura of another time prevails. Overlooking the "Queen City" of the Gold Country since before the Civil War, this imposing 1867 Gothic Revival Inn has welcomed travelers since 1964. *Gourmet Magazine* writes **"The Red Castle Inn would top my list of places to stay. Nothing else quite compares with it."** Every guest room is memorable in the four-story mansion located within the historic district steps away from antique shops, fine dining, dancing, performing arts, museums, art galleries, carriage rides, tennis courts and picnic areas. The landmark "Icicle" draped brick Inn is surrounded by terraced gardens and furnished comfortably in antiques. White-water rafting, swimming, hiking, fishing in lakes & rivers, alpine and nordic skiing, golfing and gold panning are nearby. The bountiful buffet breakfast and sumptuous afternoon tea receives rave reviews from every guest. *Sunset Magazine* writes **"attention to detail in this charming hostelry keeps rooms booked well in advance."** 8% tax applicable to room rate. **RESERVATIONS:** One nite's deposit within 10 days of res or credit card plus 5% for deposit; two night min on Sat nights (4/1-12/31) with 7 day cancel policy, 21 days for holidays or multiple rooms for full refund **BROCHURE:** Yes **PERMITTED:** Drinking, limited children. **CONFERENCES:** Yes up to 10 for informal business or social meetings [Z11CPCA1-6833]

Dahl House   **Newport Beach CA
Ron & Anne Dahl   2025 E Ocean Blvd 92661
714-673-3479   **Res Times** 8am-10pm

Rates:	**Pvt Bath** 2	**Payment Terms:**
Single	$ 50-75.00	Check
Double	$ 50-75.00	

Situated near the tip of the Balboa Peninsula in Newport Beach, the *Dahl House* is forty miles south of LAX and ten miles from the Orange County Airport and is perfectly located for beach and bay activities along California's *"Gold Coast"*. This charming home creates a cozy, intimate atmosphere with stained-glass, used brick, natural wood, and a raised-hearth fireplace. The downstairs *Brass Bedroom* is filled with antiques and has a recently-renovated bathroom. The upstairs *Loft Bedroom* has access to a large sun deck and upper "Crows Nest" for spectacular ocean, beach and city views. Disneyland and other local theme parks are only

©*Bed & Breakfast Guest Houses & Inns of America, Memphis TN*

California

minutes away, as are first-class shopping malls at South Coast Plaza and Fashion Island. Daily ferry service runs from Balboa to Catalina Island. Beach chairs and bicycles are provided and complimentary beverages, hors d'oeuvres and a delicious full breakfast are served. With only two guest rooms, guests may be assured of complete privacy and full personal attention to their needs. Business people and tourists alike will enjoy this relaxing location in this nearly crime-free residential neighborhood. Every effort will be made so your stay in Southern California will be an enjoyable and memorable one. **RESERVATIONS:** 50% deposit of length of stay, 14 day cancel policy **PERMITTED:** Children 6-up, drinking **AIRPORT:** LAX-40 mi; Orange County-10 mi **PACKAGES:** Inquire at res time. [Z07GPCA2-193]

**Boat & Breakfast USA	**Oakland CA**
Rob Harris/Andrew Roettger	40 Jack London Square 94607
510-444-5858 415-291-8411	**Res Times** 10am-6pm

Rates:	**Pvt Bath** 22	**Payment Terms:**
Single	$ 95-250.00	Check
Double	$ 95-250.00	AE/MC/V

Spend the night on a yacht! We've arranged for a select few private yachts to be available dockside for overnight guests. ***Take your Choice*** ... luxury power and sailing yachts from 35' to 75' - *perfect for a **Special Evening**!* All of the yachts are comfortably furnished with a main salon, separate sleeping quarters, head and shower, a galley with refrigerator, coffee maker and other appliances. A continental breakfast is included. Each yacht has is own unique amenities and include TV and stereo sound systems. To further enhance your stay, we can arrange private charters on the Bay, catered dinners, massage, limo service and more. Accommodations in San Francisco and San Diego. **RESERVATIONS:** 50% deposit upon booking, discounts for three nights and longer. Best check-in 2-6pm. $25 added charge for more than two guests. **BROCHURE:** Yes **PERMITTED:** Children, drinking **CONFERENCES:** Yes **LANGUAGES:** English, Hebrew [R04DPCA-11617]

***Bear Valley Inn**	**Olema CA**
Jo Ann & Ron Nowell	88 Bear Valley Rd 94950
415-663-1777	

Rates:	**Pvt Bath** 3	**Payment Terms:**
Single	$ 70.00	Check
Double	$ 85.00	

1899 classic Victorian farmhouse still retains its character and is

California

furnished with period decor and family heirlooms. Each room is furnished with period pieces and include either queen or king-size beds. Point Reyes National Park and Seashore offers visitors a spectacular year round treat of nature's artistry. Wildlife everywhere, you can even spend time whale watching in March/April and November/January. Full country breakfast included. **BROCHURE:** Yes [C11ACCA-519]

Centrella B&B Inn			**Pacific Grove CA**
*Maurine Diaz			612 Central Ave 93950
800-233-3372 408-372-3372			**Res Times** 7am-11pm
Rates:	**Pvt Bath** 24	**Shared Bath** 2	**Payment Terms:**
Single	$ 125-185.00	$ 90.00	Check
Double	$ 125-185.00	$ 90.00	AE/MC/V

This 19th Century Victorian received the *Gold Key Award*, *an International Award for Design Excellence for poetically combining the old with the new*. You find large open parlor rooms, lofty corridors, arched beams surrounding the attic suites - all combined with touches of Laura Ashley decor of contrasting colors of banana yellow, canary blue and rose-colored interiors. Nostalgic touches include clawfoot tubs with brass fixtures in some rooms, bedside candles, large beveled-glass windows along the north side of the Inn's parlor with an evening fire dancing across the glass. Evening relaxation brings complimentary hors d'oeuvres, sherry, wine or tea. Beautiful gardens of camellia and gardenia beds aflame in brilliant color and brick walkways surround the main house and lead to the Inn's private cottage suites. Pacific Grove is home to the Monarch butterflies that flock in droves each November only to depart during February and March - a sight travelers should experience. Monterey Peninsula provides breath-taking views while California sea otters play in the kelp beds just off shore - except for the occasional cracking sound of an abalone shell being opened for lunch. There's Fisherman's Wharf, Cannery Row and historic abodes and shops to visit along the wharf. A full sumptuous breakfast of fresh California fruit and pastries, fresh ground coffee and perhaps a waffle or egg entree is prepared to perfection. **DISCOUNTS:** Off-season and weekdays. **PACKAGES:** *Romance*, includes champagne and dinner **RESERVATIONS:** One night's deposit required; 2 night min on weekends and special holidays **BROCHURE:** Yes **PERMITTED:** Limited children, drinking **AIRPORT:** Monterey-15 mins **CONFERENCES:** Small groups to ten persons for meetings; up to thirty five persons for weddings **LANGUAGES:** Spanish, Italian, Portuguese [Z08GPCA2-527]

**Gatehouse Inn*	**Pacific Grove CA**
Ken & Joyce Cherry	225 Central Ave 93950

©Bed & Breakfast Guest Houses & Inns of America, Memphis TN

California

800-753-1881   408-649-1881

Res Times 8am-10pm
Fax 408-375-2539

Rates: **Pvt Bath** 8   **Payment Terms:**
Single $ 95-145.00   Check
Double $ 95-145.00   AE/MC/V

A light and airy Victorian home of Senator Benjamin F Langford was constructed in 1884 as a vacation home for his family. Situated in the quaint town of Pacific Grove, it is within easy walking distance of John Steinbeck's Cannery Row, home of Monterey Bay Aquarium and Fisherman's Wharf. With stunning views of the beautiful bay, this lovely Victorian has been fully restored to capture the essence of warmth of a graceful bygone era. The eight unique guest rooms are furnished with Victorian and 20th Century antiques and touches of Art Deco. There are fireplaces, private baths with claw-foot tubs, Queen-size beds with down comforters - no guest comforts have been overlooked here! This residence greets you with the warmth and hospitality of the turn-of-the-century, complete with an expanded continental breakfast to be enjoyed before a roaring fire with the other guests or else in the privacy of your room. Tea, sherry and hors d'oeuvres are served in the afternoon. Local sights and activities abound with famous museums, three world-renowned golf courses at Pebble Beach, elegant dining in numerous restaurants and in January, the annual migration of the Grey Whale can be watched with stunning views from the breakfast table. **RESERVATIONS:** One night deposit, cancel notice of 7 days prior to reservation date, except on holidays or for multiple rooms, when 20 day cancel notice is required. $10 service fee for cancellations. **BROCHURE:** Yes **PERMITTED:** Drinking, limited children, limited smoking [R02CPCA-9948]

Gosby House Inn   **Pacific Grove CA
Suzanne Russo   643 Lighthouse Ave 93950
408-375-1287   **Res Times** 7am-11pm

Rates: **Pvt Bath** 20   **Shared Bath** 5   **Payment Terms:**
Single $ 85-130.00 $ 100-105.00   Check
Double $ 85-130.00 $ 100-105.00   AE/MC/V

This classic Victorian Inn was built in 1887 with additions over the following years to accommodate seasonal visitors to Pacific Grove. Listed on the *National Historic Register*, this Inn is *featured in Pacific Grove's Annual Victorian Home Tour* each spring. A two-story wooden structure, the unique rounded tower entrance porch and large bay windows provide a special character. The common rooms are furnished with period antiques, floral print wallpaper, comfortable English style seating with a wood-burning fireplace in the beautiful parlor. The guest rooms are

California

inspired by the comfort and luxury of fine European Country inns. There are soft-colored wallpapers and wall-to-wall carpeting, off-white heirloom spreads, ruffled curtains, lace pillows, quilts, fresh fruit, plenty of green plantings and antique beds and furniture. Twelve guest rooms include fireplaces with small kitchens available in some. An old-fashioned garden including a winding brick path is a peaceful retreat for enjoying your full complimentary breakfast or just relaxing or talking over a cup of coffee. Breakfast in bed is available upon request. Comp night turn-down service and morning papers are included. Picnic lunches are available at a nominal charge. Welcoming guests for over a century, The Gosby House is one of nature's magnificent meetings of land and sea-the Monterey Peninsula. Treat yourself to a visit soon. **AIRPORT:** Monterey-20 mins. **PACKAGES:** *Dining Package* includes one night's stay and dinner, shared or private bath $125.00, fireplace room $140.00. **RESERVATIONS:** Credit card to guarantee room, 48 hr cancel policy. Less than 48 hr cancel notice, refund only if room is re-rented. **BROCHURE:** Yes **PERMITTED:** Children, drinking and limited smoking. **CONFERENCES:** Yes, business and social meetings to 20, including dining [Z01EPCA-528]

Maison Bleue Inn	**Pacific Grove CA**
Jeanne E Coles	PO Box 51371 93950
408-373-2993 408-373-1358	

Rates:	**Pvt Bath** 1	**Shared Bath** 2	**Payment Terms:**
Single	$ 125.00	$ 100.00	Check
Double	$ 125.00	$ 110.00	AE/DC/MC/V

A lovely romantic Country French "Home away from Home" completely restored to reflect the grace and hospitality of a stay in the French countryside and the finest of its kind on the beautiful Monterey Peninsula. Each room is individually furnished with Country French antiques and has its own unique flavor including queen & king canopied beds. A lavish full breakfast is served in the "Morning Room" or in bed if you like and includes fresh fruits, continental beverages and a gourmet entree to start your day. You're just minutes from world-renowned diving locations (picture perfect picnic spots too), Steinbeck's Cannery Row, the fabulous Monterey Bay Aquarium, beaches, world famous golf courses, shore-side recreation trails, theaters, seafood restaurants and plenty of shopping.. all minutes away and within walking distance. This quaint Inn is listed on the *Heritage Society Register* and is shown on the *Victorian Home Tour* and *Christmas At The Inns* during the year. Located between Carmel and Monterey, you'll be able to enjoy the *Home of the Monarch Butterfly* year-round. **RESERVATIONS:** Full payment within 7 days, 7-day cancel policy (10 days on holidays & special events) for full refund, check in 2-6:00pm, check-out 11am, late cancel & no show charge one night's lodging plus 10% **BROCHURE:** Yes **PERMITTED:** Limited children,

California

limited smoking, limited drinking **CONFERENCES:** Yes, groups to 10 persons [A09APCA1-530]

**Martine Inn	**Pacific Grove CA**
Marion & Don Martine	255 Oceanview Blvd 93950
800-852-5588 408-373-3388	**Res Times** 8am-9:30pm
	Fax 408-373-3896
Rates: **Pvt Bath** 19	**Payment Terms:**
Single $ 115-225.00	Check
Double $ 115-225.00	MC/V

"One of America's top twelve B&Bs" Country Inn, Feb 1992, indicates what guests experience in this 12,000 sq ft gracious Mansion resting high atop the cliffs of Pacific Grove - overlooking the rocky coastline of Monterey Bay. Your hosts have prepared an experience not to be missed, beginning with guest rooms furnished with authentic museum quality antiques (including an incredible Mahogany suite from the Marlaren Estates that was exhibited in the 1893 Chicago Worlds Fair), private bath, a fresh rose, a silver Victorian bridal basket filled with fresh fruit and spectacular views of the waves crashing against the rocks and/or a wood-burning fireplace (wood included) in some rooms. Guests awaken in the morning to the newspaper placed outside of your door while treated to a full breakfast served on old Sheffield silver, Victorian-style china, crystal and lace. Guests may relax during the day by enjoying one of the many selections in the library, sunbathe in the landscaped-enclosed courtyard or watch whales, sea otters, sailboat races from our parlor or sitting rooms. Play pool in the gameroom, relax in the spa/hot tub or share Don's vintage MG collection. Evening brings hors d'oeuvres in the parlor while enjoying the 1923 Knabe Reproducing Baby Grand and camaraderie of new friends. Within four blocks you'll find the Monterey Bay Aquarium and Cannery Row. A seven mile recreational trail offers walking, jogging or biking along the scenic coastline while within a five minute drive, you'll reach 17 Mile Drive, Carmel and Pebble Beach. Day trips take you to Monterey Wine Country, Big Sur and Hearst Castle. Each eventful day can finish with a relaxing bath or soaking in the clawfoot tub - and a nighttime Godiva mint placed on your pillow. Special requests for wine or chilled champagne, gifts or flowers, homemade picnic lunches and reservations are graciously provided. **RESERVATIONS:** Deposit in full, in advance, 72 hr cancel policy; prior arrangements for late arrivals **PERMITTED:** Children, drinking, limited smoking

California

CONFERENCES: Spectacular, intimate and memorable meetings, conferences and weddings created to suit your need **BROCHURES:** Yes **LANGUAGES:** AT&T language line **AIRPORT:** Monterey-10 mi **PACKAGES:** Yes, inquire at res time [I11EPCA2-531]

Seven Gables Inn	**Pacific Grove CA**
Susan Flatley	555 Oceanview Blvd 93950
408-372-4341 408-375-6641	

Rates:	**Pvt Bath** 14	**Payment Terms:**
Single	$ 95-155.00	Check
Double	$ 95-155.00	

"Lavish and Opulent" can only describe the details of this *Victorian Gem* nestled at the ocean's edge, dressed in the finest exterior Victorian yellow and sparkling white trim! There are spectacular views of the ocean and coastal mountains from every guest room; guests are lulled to sleep by the romantic surf outside. Museum-quality antiques & furnishings gives everyone an opportunity to **live like a queen for one day!** Outside you'll find a gorgeous profusion of flowers year-round, while inside you'll be treated to complimentary English-style "high tea & delicious homemade treats and imported cakes". Just outside of your doorway, you'll find a world-renowned ocean drive (17 miles) to Pebble Beach & Carmel. **RESERVATIONS:** Full payment upon reservation; 7-day cancellation policy for refund **BROCHURE:** Yes **LANGUAGES:** Spanish, French, Arabic [E02BCCA-534]

**Casa Cody*	**Palm Springs CA**
Frank Tysen/Therese Hayes	175 S Cahuilla 92262
800-231-CODY 619-320-9346	

Rates:	**Pvt Bath** 17	**Payment Terms:**
Single	$ 65-160.00	Check
Double	$ 65-160.00	AE/MC/V

This romantic, historic hideaway was founded by Buffalo Bill's niece, Harriet Cody in the 1920s. Nestled against the spectacular San Jacinto Mountains in the heart of Palm Springs Village, the Inn was recently restored in a Santa Fe motif with Saltillo tile floors, Southwestern pine furnishings and handwoven Dhurri rugs. *Casa Cody* consists of three single-story buildings featuring seventeen rooms, studios and one & two bedroom suites with private patios, fireplaces and kitchens. There are two heated pools and a secluded, tree-shaded whirlpool spa. *Casa Cody* has been highlighted in numerous travel articles ranging from the *New York Times* to the *Alaska Airlines* magazine; most recently in *Southern*

California

California: **50 Romantic Getaways**. If you're seeking relaxation, you've picked the right place. *Casa Cody* is the right place - fondly reminiscent of the original Palm Springs. **RESERVATIONS:** Credit card number or deposit required, 72 hr cancellation notice for refund **SEASONAL:** Summer rates $45-105.00 **PERMITTED:** Well-behaved children, pets, drinking, smoking **BROCHURE:** Yes **LANGUAGES:** French, Dutch **CONFERENCES:** Yes, small weddings and groups **DISCOUNTS:** Weekdays, summer **AIRPORT:** Palm Springs-2 mi [Z07GPCA2-9924]

Villa Royale	Palm Springs CA
Chuck Murawski & Bob Lee	1620 Indian Trail 92264
800-245-2314 619-327-2134	**Res Times** 8am-11pm
	Fax 619-322-4151
Rates: **Pvt Bath** 33	**Payment Terms:**
Single $ 75-325.00	Check
Double $ 75-325.00	AE/MC/V

An International Country Inn on a 3-1/2 acre tropical setting in beautiful Palm Springs offers guests an experience they won't forget. All thirty-three rooms are individually decorated with treasures from around the world creating an "old world charm" and ambience. The resort is a series of interior courtyards frames with statuesque pillars, cascading bougainvillea and hovering shade trees with pots of flowers and asymmetrical gardens with a musical fountain courtyard where classical music can frequently be overheard. Guests can relax around the pool/patio area or visit the wonderful Palm Canyon shops and night life. There are bikes for guests to use along with picnic lunches for a day's outing. A continental breakfast is served in the pool side dining room. **RESERVATIONS:** One night deposit with 5-14 day cancel policy depending upon the season **BROCHURE:** Yes **PERMITTED:** Drinking, smoking **LANGUAGES:** Spanish [E07BCCA-537]

Victorian On Lytton	Palo Alto CA
Susan & Maxwell Hall	555 Lytton Ave 94301
415-322-8555	**Res Times** 7am-8:30pm
Rates: **Pvt Bath** 10	**Payment Terms:**
Single $ 98.00	Check
Double $ 98-up	AE/MC/V

This lovely Victorian home c1895 was the first Bed & Breakfast in Palo Alto and has been completely renovated in what *Architectural Digest* comments*"... understated elegance"*! Each suite has been tastefully decorated with the charm and quietness of yesteryear and offers sitting parlors, private bath, and canopy or poster king, queen and double beds.

California

Relax with complimentary wine or sherry upon your arrival or with other guests in the "front room". Or just refresh yourself in the charming English Garden area outside. Continental breakfast is even served in your room each morning too! Close to center Palo Alto with all fine restaurants, cafes, theaters, and shops within walking distance. Enjoy that special occasion or business trip here! **RESERVATIONS:** Deposit at time of res, with a 10% cancellation charge with 10 day minimum notice **BROCHURE:** Yes **PERMITTED:** Limited drinking [A07GPCA2-538]

**Carriage House	**Point Reyes Station CA**
Felicity Kirsch	325 Mesa Rd 94956
415-663-8627	**Res Times** 7am-10pm

Rates:	**Pvt Bath** 2	**Payment Terms:**
Single	$ *110.00	Check
Double	$ *120.00	

The *Carriage House Bed & Breakfast Inn* is in coastal Marin, adjacent to Point Reyes National Seashore and Tomales Bay State Park; one hour north of San Francisco and one hour south of the Wine Country. Built in the 1920's, it has recently been remodeled into two spacious suites that are furnished with lovely antiques and folk art. Each suite has a comfortable queen size bed, living room with fireplace, full bath and complete kitchen. Quiet, privacy and warm hospitality abide here and a warm breakfast is brought to your suite. Wonderful old trees, flowers, beautiful sunrises and sunsets along with views of the countryside, soothe your senses. From this serene setting you can hike to Tomales Bay or to local village restaurants, galleries and shops. There are more than 100 miles of riding, hiking and bicycling trails in the Seashore Park as well as an 18 hole golf course nearby. Whales migrate along the miles of beaches during the winter - while wildflowers bloom profusely in the spring. This comfortable Bed & Breakfast is ideal for a private retreat, a romantic getaway or a vacation with family and friends. It can accommodate 10 comfortably. Child care is available with prior notice. **DISCOUNTS:** Yes, mid-week from Sept thru April **RESERVATIONS:** 50% deposit. *Two suites are available and include BR, LR, kitchen and wet bar **BROCHURE:** Yes **PERMITTED:** Smoking outside [Z07GPCA2-14357]

Ferrandos Hideway	**Point Reyes Station CA**
Greg & Doris Ferrando	12010 Hwy 1 94956
415-663-1966	**Fax** 415-663-1825

Rates:	**Pvt Bath** 3	**Payment Terms**
Single	$ 105.00	Check
Double	$ 120.00	

©*Bed & Breakfast Guest Houses & Inns of America, Memphis TN*

California

Ferrando's Hideaway
A Bed & Breakfast

A lovely contemporary-style home built in 1972 by your hosts offers two guest rooms along with a separate Cottage offering complete privacy. Great attention to detail in building and decorating brings a warm and harmonious atmosphere throughout the main house. The guest rooms are comfortably equipped with private baths and king size beds for luxurious resting. Rooms have a separate entrance and patio for privacy. There is a cozy sitting room which is shared by all guests who care to gather and warm up around the wood stove each evening. The Cottage is separated from the main house by a hot tub and a spacious vegetable garden and includes a fully equipped kitchen where guests can prepare breakfast at their leisure. Your hosts have thoughtfully filled the fridge with eggs fresh from their chickens, homemade bread, muffins, fresh fruit, cheese or yogurt, jam, coffee, herb teas and juice. Guests staying in the Cottage retire in a king size bed located in the loft and can relax on the sunny deck outdoors offering beautiful views of the rolling hills of West Marin. A full bath, wood stove and stereo insure a relaxful stay. A plentiful continental breakfast is served in the sunny breakfast room for guests staying in the main house. Guests are assured of complete relaxation by enjoying the hot tub along with taking advantage of a certified massage therapist who is available by appointment. Close to Point Reyes National Seashore, there's plenty of outdoor activities such as hiking, biking, birding, horseback riding, whale watching and miles of beautiful sand beaches. Sights include Tide Pools at Agate Beach, Tule Elk at Pierce Point Ranch, enjoying oysters at the Johnson Oyster Company, Audubon Canyon Ranch featuring unique egret and herons, Rouge et Noir (French cheese factory) and various galleries in Point Reyes and Inverness. **AIRPORT:** San Francisco Intl. Two night min on weekends. **RESERVATIONS:** Deposit required prior to arrival, 7 day cancel policy for refund less $15 service charge per night canceled. Less than 7 days, refund less service fee only if re-booked. **BROCHURE:** Yes **PERMITTED:** Children **CONFERENCES:** Yes, for groups to six **LANGUAGES:** German [K07GPCA2-15684]

**Jasmine Cottage	**Point Reyes Station CA**
Karen Gray	11561 Coast Rt #1 94956
415-663-1166	**Res Times** 8am-9pm

Rates:	**Pvt Bath** 1	**Payment Terms:**
Single	$ 115.00	Check
Double	$ 115.00	

California

The secluded privacy of these country cottages is the ideal arrangement in a Bed & Breakfast: all amenities of a Bed & Breakfast with the seclusion of a vacation home. Set in its own charming garden behind the owner's schoolhouse home, *Jasmine Cottage* is a complete home-away-from-home with a fully equipped kitchen, woodstove, garden room, naturalist's library, oak desk, queen beds, two twin beds, a romantic alcove, and beautiful views of sunsets. Only one hour north of San Francisco, one hour to Wine Country and just 5 minutes from the magnificent Point Reyes National Seashore on the California Coast! Last year's guests included four business executives on a weekend retreat, a caterer who wrote a cookbook, honeymooners starting an annual tradition, and dozens of families, who made the cottage their base exploring the national park. A secluded hot tub is set in the garden for relaxation. A full breakfast is included. Weekly rate of $650.00 plus tax Can sleep 10 persons between both cottages. **AIRPORT:** San Francisco-40 mi **RESERVATIONS:** 50% deposit at reservation time, bal upon arrival, 7 day cancel policy for refund. Check-in after 4pm, check-out at noon, 10% room tax not included **BROCHURE:** Yes **PERMITTED:** Children, drinking, limited pets, limited smoking (on patio) (Inquire about pet restrictions) [Z06FPCA2-2917]

East Brother Light Station			Point Richmond CA
Ruthie Benton			117 Park Place 94801
415-233-2385			

Rates:	**Pvt Bath** 2	**Shared Bath** 2	**Payment Terms:**
Single	$ 225.00	$ 200.00	Check
Double	$ 275.00	$ 240.00	

This turn-of-the-century lighthouse is reached by boat and offers guests a spectacular setting for San Francisco's night lights. All amenities are here to make your stay memorable, including continental breakfast and full dinner, with complimentary wine upon arrival. **BROCHURE:** Yes **PERMITTED:** Limited smoking, social drinking. [C11ACCA-552]

**Pillar Point Inn*		Princeton by the Sea CA
Richard Anderton		380 Capistrano Rd 94018
415-728-7377		

Rates:	**Pvt Bath** 11	**Payment Terms:**
Single	$ 125-160.00	Check
Double	$ 125-160.00	AE/MC/V

While this waterfront Inn boasts contemporary construction, the service and amenities are traditional European! The only harborside Bed &

California

Breakfast Inn on the San Mateo coast, each guest room offers a panoramic view of the harbor and waterside. An exciting fishing village history provides the decorating themes for each guest room which are reminiscent of a New England fishing village but in sunny California. Each guest room includes a ceramic-tiled fireplace for romantic evenings, entertainment centers, fridge, cozy window seats for waterfront star gazing and luxurious European featherbeds fit for a king or queen! A full breakfast is included in the country-styled parlor or enjoy breakfast in bed - complete with homebaked breads, fresh-squeezed orange juice, eggs, bacon, pancakes while getting ready to begin exploring the local sights. Nearby guests will find Ano Nuevo (state reserve for elephant seals), picturesque flower markets full of spring year-round, wineries and just a short drive is all of San Francisco. **RESERVATIONS:** One night's deposit, 72 hr cancel policy **BROCHURE:** Yes **PERMITTED:** Children, drinking **CONFERENCES:** Yes [R07BCCA-6206]

**Palisades Paradise B&B		**Redding CA**
Gail Goetz		1200 Palisades Ave 96003
916-223-5305		**Res Times** 4:30-10:00pm
Rates:	**Shared Baht** 2	**Payment Terms:**
Single	$ 55-65.00	Check
Double	$ 60-70.00	AE/MC/V

You feel you are in *Paradise* when you watch the magnificent sunsets from a lovely contemporary home overlooking the Sacramento River. Enjoy a spectacular view of the city, Shasta Bally and the surrounding mountains while you'll sleep to the sound of a flowing river and awake to the music of singing birds. You are always made to feel "special" here. Travelers and business people alike seek out the comfort and relaxed atmosphere of Palisades Paradise, in a quiet residential neighborhood. After dinner at one of the many fine restaurants in the area, you may choose to sit by the fire in the large living room with a wide-screen TV, relax in the old-fashioned porch swing under the Oak Tree, or soak your cares away in the garden spa before retiring to the "Sunset Suite" or the "Cozy Retreat" for a restful night of sleep. A continental plus complimentary breakfast is included each morning (full on weekends). Redding is the center of a naturally beautiful area. Come and enjoy fishing, rafting, swimming and boating on Whiskeytown Lake, Shasta Lake and the Sacramento River. For those who love to hike, Lasen Natl Park Mount Shasta, Castle Crags, Lake Shasta Caverns, Trinity Alps and Burney Falls Start Park are with a short driving distance. **PERMITTED:** Limited children, drinking, smoking outdoors only **RESERVATIONS:** Deposit required within 5 days after reserving, 5 day cancel policy for refund **BROCHURE:** Yes **DISCOUNTS:** Yes, inquire at res time **PACKAGES:** *Wedding* **AIRPORT:** Redding Municipal-7 mi [Z07FPCA2-6201]

California

Amber House B&B	**Sacramento CA**
Mike & Jane Richardson	1315 22nd St 95816
800-755-6526 916-444-8085	**Fax** 916-447-1548

Rates:	**Pvt Bath** 9	**Payment Terms:**
Single	$ 85-155.0	Check
Double	$ 90-195.00	AE/DC/MC/V

The *Amber House* offers deluxe accommodations in two meticulously restored vintage structures. *The Poet's Refuge*, a 1905 Craftsman-style home touched with period elegance offers five guest rooms, all with private bath and one with a jacuzzi tub for two. *The Artist's Retreat* is a fully restored 1913 Mediterranean style home which offers four luxurious guest rooms with marble-tiled baths and large jacuzzi bathtubs for two. The Van Gogh room in this home features a spectacular solarium bathroom with a heart-shaped jacuzzi tub and waterfall. All rooms have cable TV, private phones (modem ready) and central air conditioning. A full gourmet breakfast is served in the guest room, the dining room or on the outside patio. Complimentary bikes (and a bike for two) are available for guests use. Whatever your mood, you'll find the warm hospitality and personal attention you deserve. The Inn is located just eight blocks east of the state capitol and near other historical sights, shops and restaurants. **AIRPORT:** Sacramento Metro-12 mi **RESERVATIONS:** One night deposit or credit card number to guarantee reservation **BROCHURE:** Yes **PERMITTED:** Drinking, limited children **CONFERENCES:** Yes, for groups to twenty persons [Z07GPCA2-566]

Cinnamon Bear B&B	**Saint Helena CA**
Genny Jenkins	1407 Kearney St 94574
707-963-4653	**Res Times** 9am-9pm

Rates:	**Pvt Bath** 4	**Payment Terms:**
Single	$ 85-145.00	Check
Double	$ 85-145.00	MC/V

This classic 1904 Arts & Crafts home was home for Walter Metzner Family. Metzner was the mayor of Saint Helena for twenty years. Genny Jenkins bought the house from the Metzner estate to raise her three children. After the youngest left for college, she began renting rooms to overnight guests visiting the wineries. The *Cinnamon Bear* name developed from her oldest son's affection for a stuffed bear named Oliver, who saw him through tough exams at Stanford University. Stuffed bears started filling the house and entertaining the guests with all sorts of "unbearable" pranks. The home is furnished in the 1920's style with antiques, hardwood floors and oriental carpets. The four guest rooms are furnished with queen size beds, private bath rooms, central air and heat.

California

A full breakfast is served each morning in the dining room or on the spacious front porch. Breakfast includes a hot entree, fresh fruit, cereals, assorted breads and muffins, orange juice, teas and coffee. Afternoons: join us for refreshments in the parlor or relax by the fireplace. Puzzles, games and books are available Convenient to wineries, restaurants, shopping, galleries and biking. **RESERVATIONS:** Credit card number for deposit to guarantee reservation, 3-day cancel policy less $10 service fee **PERMITTED:** No children, smoking outdoors only, no pets **BROCHURE:** Yes **DISCOUNTS:** Yes, for 3 nights and longer stay **AIRPORT:** San Francisco-80 mi [R05FPCA1-16875]

**Ink House B&B	**Saint Helena CA**
Jim Annis/Ernie Veniegas	1575 St Helena Way 94574
707-963-3890	**Res Times** 8-10pm

Rates: **Pvt Bath** 4   **Payment Terms:**
Single   Check
Double $ 90-110.00

Classic Italianate Victorian Farmhouse built by Theron H Ink in 1884 situated in the heart of the famous Napa Valley Wine Country. Guests may relax in the parlor or the observatory situated on top of the house offering a 360 degree view of the vineyards. The four bedrooms with private baths are complete with period antique furnishings including beds, dressers, and finished with beautiful handmade quilts and lace curtains. Twelve foot ceilings on the first floor bring back the nostalgic 1880's including the 1870 pump organ and other antiques throughout the residence that is listed on the *National Register of Historic Places*. A homemade complimentary breakfast includes special recipe muffins and nutbread with juices, coffee/tea, and seasonal fruits. Enjoy your stay while visiting the mud baths, wineries, or try ballooning and tennis. **RESERVATIONS:** Full amount required at time of reservation. **BROCHURE:** Yes **PERMITTED:** Drinking. [A05APCA-588]

**Villa Saint Helena	**Saint Helena CA**
Ralph Cotton	2727 Sulphur Springs Ave 94574
707-963-2514	

Rates: **Pvt Bath** 3   **Payment Terms:**
Single $ 145-225.00   Check
Double $ 145-225.00   MC/V

A magnificent Mediterranean-style villa nestled on 20 acres provides a commanding view of the picturesque village of St Helenas and introduces guests to a Grand Dame of the Napa Valley! Dating from the 1940s, this

California

noble country place was the intimate hideaway of Hollywood celebrities and political leaders while today it's used on programs like *Falcon Crest*. Designed by Robert M Carrere, a master of classic architecture, the Villa balances country comfort and elegance. The 12,000 square foot residence offers Mexican tile floors, muted earth-tone colors, thick red brick walls, rambling white verandas, courtyards, swimming pool, fireplaces,and private entrances. The interior features a treasure-trove of eclectic period furnishings including many antique-filled rooms that offer warmth and informality with understated elegance. The three-quarter mile winding private drive leading away from this secluded location brings guests into the heart of exciting Napa Valleys' activities and sights. A complimentary continental breakfast is included with your room. **RESERVATIONS:** Full payment for entire stay at reservation time. **BROCHURE:** Yes **PERMITTED:** Drinking, limited smoking [R10BCCA-594]

**Caroles B&B	**San Diego CA**
Carole Dugdale/Mike O'Brien	3227 Grim Ave 92104
619-280-5258	**Res Times** 7am-10pm

Rates:	Pvt Bath 1	Shared Bath 7	Payment Terms:
Single	$ 75.00	$ 55.00	Check
Double	$ 75.00	$ 55.00	

A friendly congenial home close to all major attractions. Only 1-1/2 miles to the downtown area and also to the San Diego Zoo, located in the world-famous Balboa Park. This home, built in 1904 by the Mayor of San Diego, is decorated with family antiques and hand-made quilts. Guests are invited to play the piano. There is a large pool, a spa and a rose garden. The patio areas are filled with huge lovely tropical plants selected by Danny. Complimentary wine and cheese are served. The continental breakfast includes generous portions of fresh fruit. Michael or Carole are always there to provide warm personal attention to your needs, helping to insure a pleasurable stay in their Inn. Guests are conveniently located just one block from the city bus line. Additional meals (lunch & dinner) are available with added cost. **DISCOUNTS:** Extended stays over 4 nights **AIRPORT:** San Diego Lindburg-14 mins **RESERVATIONS:** 50% advance deposit (can be by check), with bal due upon arrival in cash or travelers check **BROCHURE:** Yes **PERMITTED:** Limited children, drinking, smoking **LANGUAGES:** Spanish [R11EPCA2-604]

**Harbor Hill Guest House	**San Diego CA**
Dorothy Milbourn	2330 Albatross St 92101
619-233-0638	**Res Times** 24 hours

Rates:	Pvt Bath 5	Payment Terms:

©Bed & Breakfast Guest Houses & Inns of America, Memphis TN

California

Single	$ 65-85.00*		Tvlrs Check
Double	$ 65-85.00*		MC/V

Overlooking San Diego Harbor, this charming tri-level residence full of character, craftsmanship, and comfort is located in the famous "Bankers Hill" area. Each level has private entrance, and private kitchen or kitchenette. Choose from rooms, with outstanding harbor view, sundeck, or overlooking the garden area, complete with gazebo. You'll be close to all points of interest including downtown, Balboa Park, Zoo, Old Town, Seaport Village, Sea World, Coronado Ferry. Half hour trolley ride to Mexico border. Ideal area for walkers, joggers, hikers. House is most convenient and comfortable for special occasions such as family reunions and special functions for up to 18 persons. Complimentary continental breakfast included. *$10 extra adult, children under 12, free **DISCOUNTS:** Yes, 4 days or longer stay **AIRPORT:** Lindberg-10 mins **RESERVATIONS:** Deposit required, one week cancellation policy for refund. **BROCHURE:** Yes **PERMITTED:** Children, drinking **CONFERENCES:** Accommodate groups to 16 for social events [A04EPCA2-607]

Surf Manor & Cottages   **San Diego CA
                                                   3949 La Cresta Dr 92107
619-225-9765

Rates: **Pvt Bath** 2   **Payment Terms:**
Single $ 75.00-plus   Check
Double

The surf is up in San Diego and the salt spray from the Pacific Ocean lets you know you are right on the beach with picturesque views in centrally located Ocean Beach. Or you can choose one of the few remaining "original beach cottages" in the desirable South Mission Beach area. All offer three room suites, including kitchen and private bath and furnished with antiques and English country prints with modern amenities including TV. The cottages offer a private garden area to enjoy the ocean breeze in the evening. Close to all attractions, Mission Bay, Sea World, San Diego Zoo, Cabrillo Monument, Old Town, Balboa Park. Stroll to the Ocean Beach Fishing Pier or the nearby village. Refrigerators are provisioned with everything needed for you to create your own continental or full English breakfast. **RESERVATIONS:** Weekly, monthly vacation rentals July/August, B&B accommodations remainder of year. Two night minimum rental. [A11CPCA-611]

Amsterdam Hotel   **San Francisco CA
Kanti Gopal   749 Taylor St 94018
800-637-3444   415-673-3277   **Res Times** 24 Hrs

©Bed & Breakfast Guest Houses & Inns of America, Memphis TN

California

Rates:	Pvt Bath 28	Shared Bath 6	Fax 415-673-0453
			Payment Terms:
Single	$ 60-69.00	$ 45.00	Check
Double	$ 69-75.00	$ 50.00	MC/V

A little bit of Europe in America with a great location in San Francisco just two blocks from Nob Hill and just a short cable car ride to all the exciting sights of Chinatown, Fisherman's Wharf, art galleries, Sausalito, legitimate theatre and fine restaurants. Built originally in 1909, the *Amsterdam Hotel* reflects the charm of a small European hotel with quality accommodations, friendly service at very modest rates. The clean and spacious rooms include color TV, cable, AM/FM radio, phones and totally renovated in 1993. A continental breakfast is served daily from 8-10:30am is included with your room. **RESERVATIONS:** One night's deposit or credit card at res time **BROCHURE:** Yes **PERMITTED:** Children, drinking **LANGUAGES:** German [Z05FPCA2-614]

**Art Center B&B Suites	**San Francisco CA**
Helvi & George Wamsley	1902 Filbert St 94123
415-567-1526 415-921-9023	**Res Times** 8am-9pm

Rates:	Pvt Bath 5	Payment Terms:
		Check
Single		
Double	$ 85-115.00	AE/DC/MC/V

Leave your heart in San Francisco!! This lovely 1857 *Country Inn* is fully restored into 4 Queen Suites with unusual period decor recalling the 1800's, with fireplaces in each suite, canopy beds in some, all with modern amenities. Relax in the garden patio or the artists/hosts art gallery & workshop, if classes aren't in session or you can join the class. Close to everything, you can walk everywhere in Old San Francisco: Golden Gate Bridge, China Town, Fisherman's Wharf, Nobb Hill, Fort Mason, or see the Art Circuit with help from your hosts. Sign-up for the 3 day art class before arriving to improve your skills! Private kitchen provisioned for your continental breakfast plus, self-prepared and other meals too if you want. **RESERVATIONS:** One week advance, one night's deposit at res time, refundable if canceled 10 days prior to arrival. Arrive after 2pm, late arrival by arrangement. **BROCHURE:** Yes **PERMITTED:** Children, limited drinking **CONFERENCES:** Enclosed rear deck and artist studio for groups to 13 **LANGUAGES:** Finnish [A04FPCA2-617]

**Babbling Brook Inn	**San Francisco CA**
Helen King	
800-866-1131 408-427-2437	**Res Times** 7am-11pm
	Fax 408-427-2457

California

Rates:	**Pvt Bath** 12	**Payment Terms:**
Single	$ 85-150.00	Check
Double	$ 85-150.00	AE/DC/MC/V

Refer to the same listing name under Santa Cruz CA for a complete description. [M05FCCA2-4352]

**Chateau Tivoli			**San Francisco CA**
Rodney Karr/Willard Gersbach			1057 Steiner St 94115
800-227-1647 415-776-5462			**Res Times** 9am-10pm
			Fax 415-776-0505
Rates:	**Pvt Bath** 4	**Shared Bath** 4	**Payment Terms:**
Single	$ 100-200.00	$ 80-125.00	Check*
Double	$ 100-200.00	$ 80-125.00	AE/MC/V

A Landmark Mansion, 1892 located in the center of Historic Alamo Square - *the greatest of The Famous Painted Ladies of San Francisco's Victorian Period!* Over five years and $750,000 in restoration has returned this famous landmark to her former glory. Filled with museum-quality antiques from the estates of the Vanderbilts, Charles de Gaulle, J Paul Getty and Madame Sally Stanford - guests experience the lavish lifestyle of the countless celebrities who stayed here. Resplendent with hardwood floors, grand oak staircase, stately columns, double parlors and restored 23k gold leaf trim. Guest rooms feature canopy beds, marble baths, balconies, views, fireplaces, stained glass, towers and turrets! The movie *Earthquake* from the 1930s starring Clark Gable and Jeanette McDonald is based on Ernestine Kreling's life story who was a former owner and proprietress of San Francisco's world famous Tivoli Opera and the *Chateau Tivoli*. Guests are just eight blocks from the San Francisco Opera House and Civic Center; six blocks to the Japan Center; seven minute drive to upper Fillmore Street with its famous restaurants and shops; ten minutes to Golden Gate Park and less than twenty minutes to Fisherman's Wharf, downtown and Chinatown. *Suites available from $200-up. **DISCOUNTS:** Yes, inquire at res time **MEALS:** Complimentary breakfast included, Continental weekdays, Full weekends. Other meals can be arranged **RESERVATIONS:** One night's deposit; 7 day cancel policy for refund less 10% fee based on entire length of stay; 14 day cancel notice for holiday periods, less than 7 day notice, no refund, *Checks require pre-approval **BROCHURE:** Yes **PERMITTED:** Children, drinking **CONFERENCES:** The *perfect locale for all special*

California

occasions - weddings, receptions, social events and business meetings for groups to 100 persons, catering can be arranged **LANGUAGES:** Spanish, German [K06FPCA1-10936]

*Friendly B&B Inn	**San Francisco CA**
Roy & Dale Roberts	3128 Friendly Ave 94122
415-622-9876	**Res Times** 8am-10pm

Rates:	**Pvt Bath** 4	**Shared Bath** 2	**Payment Terms:**
Single	$ 125.00	$ 110.00	Check
Double	$ 145.00	$ 125.00	AE/MC/V

Gorgeous Victorian restored Gingerbread Inn with all the trimmings, open verandas with lacework everywhere, stained & beveled glass windows, wide-planked floors, original carved woodwork, marble fireplaces and complete with oriental carpets, and beautiful antique furnishings. Canopied king-sized beds, down comforters and pillows, and modern bath including marble jacuzzi bath for two, sauna and hot tub outdoors. Full gourmet breakfast served in bed on sterling or outdoors overlooking the flowering garden area & pool. **RESERVATIONS:** Minimum 2 nite stay, full room rate deposit within 5 days of reservations. **BROCHURE:** Yes **PERMITTED:** Smoking, drinking, children 13-up [G02BFCA-6571]

**Goose & Turrets	**San Francisco CA**
Raymond & Emily Hoche-Mong	835 George St 94037-0937
415-728-5451	**Res Times** 8am-10pm

Rates:	**Pvt Bath** 5	**Payment Terms:**
Single	$ 85-110.00	Check
Double	$ 85-110.00	AE/DIS/MC/V

Refer to the same listing name under Montara, California for a complete description. [M08GPCA2]

**Grove Inn	**San Francisco CA**
Klaus & Rosetta Zimmerman	890 Grove St 94117
800-829-0780 415-929-0780	**Res Times** 9am-10pm

Rates:	**Pvt Bath** 14	**Shared Bath** 4	**Payment Terms:**
Single	$ 65-75.00	$ 60.00	Check
Double	$ 65-75.00	$ 60.00	AE/JCB/MC/V

The *Grove Inn*, a Bed & Breakfast place in the true European tradition, is surprisingly affordable, charming and intimate. It is part of the Alamo

California

Square Historic District, noted for its picture-postcard row of Victorian houses. The *Grove Inn* is located six blocks from the Opera House, Davies Symphonie Hall and the War Memorial with the Museum of Modern Art and the Herbst Theatre, Place of the signing of the United Nations Charter. The Inn was built during the **Gold Rush Era** as a residence and became a boarding house after the San Francisco Earthquake. The present owners renovated and refurbished the *Grove Inn* in 1983 and opened it to the public the same year. The guest rooms are individually furnished in the Victorian style. Most of the rooms have large bay windows and include a shower or tub/shower. A complimentary continental breakfast is included in the room rate. Your hosts will gladly answer any questions and will help in the planning of daily itineraries to make your stay most enjoyable. Group and family rates are available. **RESERVATIONS:** Deposit at res time; 7-day cancel policy for refund. Room rates do not include 12% hotel tax. **BROCHURE:** Yes **PERMITTED:** Children **LANGUAGES:** Italian, German [Z07GPCA2-631]

**Haus Kleebauer	**San Francisco CA**
Don Kern/Howard Johnson	225 Clipper St 94114
415-821-3866	**Res Times** 24 Hrs

Rates:	**Suite** 1	**Payment Terms:**
Single	$ 85.00	Tvlr Ck
Double	$ 85.00	AE/JCB/MC/V

Haus Kleebauer is in a storybook-like Victorian home with all the charm of San Francisco. Built in 1892 by Frederick Kleebauer and his son, the house retains all of its original beauty. Stained and etched glass windows, elaborate exterior trim and manicured gardens transport you back to an earlier era of refined elegance and charm. *Haus Kleebauer* offers a three-room suite with private entrance and bath accommodating up to five people with one queen-size bed in the bedroom and a full size sofa bed in the parlor, a Pullman kitchen (refrigerator, microwave) TV, VCR and stereo. *Haus Kleebauer* is conveniently located in one of San Francisco's premier neighborhoods, Noe Valley. As one of the city's first suburbs, **"the Valley"** offers a splendid display of original Victorian architecture. Within walking distance, you will find many interesting shops, galleries, restaurants and coffee houses. Just minutes away by street car or bus, you will find all the major tourist attractions that have made San Francisco America's Favorite City. Brochure and discounted

California

airport transportation available upon request. A complimentary full breakfast includes fresh fruit with choice of yogurt, juices, cold cereals, hot beverages, homemade jams and fresh bread, Belgium Waffles with fresh fruit and cream or French Toast and garnish. **RESERVATIONS:** 50% deposit of total amount, $85 cancellation fee, late arrivals only with prior arrangement **PERMITTED:** Children, drinking, limited pets **BROCHURE:** Yes **DISCOUNTS:** Yes, extended stay over 10 days **AIRPORT:** San Francisco-12 mi; Oakland-14 mi; San Jose-40 mi. Discount coupon available for Super Shuttle at San Francisco Intl **PACKAGES:** *Tour Packages* with front door pick-up [K07GPCA2-15610]

---

*Marina Inn	**San Francisco CA**
Suzie Baum	3110 Octavia 94123
415-928-1000	**Res Times** 24 Hrs

Rates:	**Pvt Bath** 40	**Payment Terms:**
Single	$ 55-75.00	Check
Double	$ 77-75.00	AE/MC/V

This four-story Victorian hotel, c1922, was completely redone in 1987 in the style of an English Country Inn, complete with large bay windows, intricate detailing and fresh light colors. **An oasis in the midst of the city.** The gracious pink and white marble lobby with high ceilings and country furnishings greet each guest and offers the amenities of a large hotel such as an elevator and barber shop. The second level offers a cozy sitting room with country furnishings and hardwood floors. A complimentary breakfast is served here each morning and a decanter of sherry is served each evening. The guest rooms offer pine furnishings, two-poster beds, a soft comforter, fresh flowers reminiscent of an English Inn. Evening turn-down service and a chocolate on your pillow ends each day. The *Marina Inn* is conveniently located near Union Street, the Marina Green, the Golden Gate Bridge and a fifteen minute stroll to Ghiradelli Square. The *Marina Inn* is a charming Inn with a friendly staff that's ready to help you enjoy your stay in San Francisco while offering reasonably-priced accommodations. **A great find in San Francisco!** **RESERVATIONS:** One night's deposit or credit card to guarantee reservation with 24 hr cancel policy for refund; less than 24 hour cancel notice, refund only if room is rebooked **BROCHURE:** Yes **PERMITTED:** Children, limited drinking [R09BCCA-6209]

**The Mansions Hotel	**San Francisco CA**
Robert Pritikin	2220 Sacramento St 94115
415-929-9444	**Res Times** 8am-10pm

| **Rates:** | **Pvt Bath** 21 | **Payment Terms:** |

©*Bed & Breakfast Guest Houses & Inns of America, Memphis TN*

California

Single	$ 129-350.00	Check
Double	$ 129-350.00	MC/V

The Mansions Hotel is two historic mansions interconnected by an interior corridor. The rates include a sumptuous breakfast, flowers in your room, nightly magic concerts, a performing ghost a billiard/game room sculpture gardens, the magic parlor and so much more. *The Mansions* also houses one of San Francisco's most important restaurants. *The Mansions* is minutes away from all of San Francisco's famous attractions -- but really a million miles away. *"Lovely, marvelous hospitality"* says former guest, Barbara Streisand. *"You jump back a century, slow down a bit and breath an atmosphere of forgotten elegance"*, says the *Christian Monitor*. *"Elegance to the Nth degree"*, says the *San Francisco Examiner*. The public rooms and private guest rooms feature a five million dollar collection of sculpture, antiques and treasures of art. The historic document museum in one of the parlors displays handwritten letters and documents of Lincoln, Thomas Edison, Houdini, John Hancock and more. The private guest rooms and suites are richly appointed and all have private baths. Your guest room may have a fireplace, a grand piano, a jacuzzi bath spa or any number of surprise amenities. Should you engage the Presidential Suite you will be surrounded by a library of more than 2000 books. Recent overnight guests include Robin Williams, Eddie Fisher, Susanne Sommers, Joe Montana, the late Andre Sakharov and countless luminaries from the world of theatre, the arts and business. But the omnipresent motif is magic which includes live performance of world-class magic every evening before dinner and the haunting but rather marvelous presence of documented ghost *Claudia*. Two blocks from Filmore Street with its elegant boutiques and restaurants, *The Mansions* is in the middle of San Francisco's most prestigious neighborhood, Pacific Heights. **RESERVATIONS:** Credit card commitments, three day cancellation notice required **PERMITTED:** Children 10-up, limited smoking, drinking **BROCHURE:** Yes **CONFERENCES:** Full conference facilities available **LANGUAGES:** Spanish, French **DISCOUNTS:** Yes, inquire at res time **AIRPORT:** San Francisco Intl-20 min car trip **PACKAGES:** Tailored to your specific needs and interests [J07FPCA1-632

California

Petite Auberge	**San Francisco CA**
Rich Revaz	63 Bush St 94108
800-365-3004 415-928-6000	**Res Times** 24 hours

Rates:	**Pvt Bath** 26	**Payment Terms:**
Single	$ 105-155.00	Check
Double	$ 105-155.00	AE/MC/V

This turn-of-the-century small hotel has been transformed into a French Country Inn in the Bed & Breakfast tradition. Guests step through a beveled glass doorway and almost into France! The downstairs lobby includes a lounge and dining room which is a gathering place for guests throughout the day and includes an inviting fireplace, antique furnishings, fresh flowers and lovely French country art. Afternoon wine and hors d'oeuvres are served here. The dining area is a cheery room which overlooks a small garden setting which offers a full breakfast of homemade breads, fresh seasonal fruit, cereals, muffins and special dishes, all with plenty of freshly brewed coffee and tea. The guest rooms are beautifully decorated to reflect a quaint French country mood and include antique and reproduction furniture. Each day begins with a morning paper and ends with nightly turndown service and a fancy chocolate for a nightcap. Conveniently located near Union Square, Nob Hill and the famous San Francisco cable car. For a touch of southern France in the midst of the city, try the *Petite Auberge* for a pleasant change. **RESERVATIONS:** Credit card to guarantee room, 24 hr cancel policy. **BROCHURE:** Yes **PERMITTED:** Children, limited smoking limited drinking **CONFERENCES:** Yes, complete facility for groups to 25 including gourmet dining and full social or business formats [R09BCCA-646]

Washington Square Inn		**San Francisco CA**
*Brooks Bayly		1660 Stockton St 94133
800-388-0220 415-981-4220		**Res Times** 24 Hrs
		Fax 415-397-7242

Rates:	**Pvt Bath** 10	**Share Bath** 5	**Payment Terms:**
Single	$ 95-180.00	$ 85-95.00	Check
Double	$ 95-180.00	$ 85-95.00	AE/DC/MC/V

The *Washington Square Inn* offers the charm and hospitality of a Country Inn - one block from Telegraph Hill in the heart of San Francisco's North Beach area. It is a special hotel for those who care about quiet and comfort with liberal tastes of elegance. The Inn provides a complimentary breakfast of flaky croissants, muffins, fresh fruit and our famous "Graffeo" coffee served in bed or at the table by the hearth. Afternoon tea is also served for guests and their visitors. Tea includes an array of cakes and cookies, cucumber sandwiches, complimentary wine and hors d'oeuvres. Friday evenings the Inn provides an informal wine tasting, giving visitors

California

a chance to sample some of California's best. Each of our rooms has been decorated and individually furnished with English and French antiques by San Francisco designer Nan Rosenblatt. Nan has created a European-style Inn which sits inside the Italian district, North Beach. For the vacationing visitor, the *Washington Square Inn* is the essence of San Francisco. The *Washington Square Inn* is located midway between downtown San Francisco and Fisherman's Wharf. The Inn overlooks Washington Square Park, views Coit Tower and is a stroll to Chinatown. The location provides easy access to buses and cable car lines. For those on business, we offer every convenience plus a pleasant change from the ordinary. Nightly rates range from $85-180.00. Most rooms have a private bath, all have phones and beautiful fresh flowers. Our staff has time to concentrate on guests' individual needs and wants and guests will be spoiled with individual terry cloth robes, thick thirsty towels, down pillows & comforters, handmilled soaps, a morning Wall Street Journal, local paper and polished shoes at your door - all complimentary of course! **DISCOUNTS:** Yes, inquire at res time. **AIRPORT** San Francisco Intl-35 mins. **RESERVATIONS:** Credit card to guarantee or one night paid in advance, 24 Hr cancel policy for refund or forfeit first night's deposit **BROCHURE:** Yes **PERMITTED:** Children, drinking, the Inn is entirely a *Non-smoking establishment* **DISCOUNT**: 20% for seniors **PACKAGES**: *Washington Square Sensation, North Beach Holiday* and *Little Italy Getaway* begins with breakfast in bed, afternoon tea, hors d'oeuvres, a bottle of champagne, valet parking for two for $125 to $210.00 [U01FPCA1-657]

**White Swan Inn	**San Francisco CA**
Rich Revaz	845 Bush St 94108
800-999-9570 415-775-1755	**Res Times** 24 Hrs

Rates:	**Pvt Bath** 26	**Payment Terms:**
Single	$ 145-160.00	Check
Double	$ 145-160.00	AE/MC/V

Built in 1908, just after the Great San Francisco earthquake, guests are

California

ideally located in the heart of the city in this fully renovated four-story hotel in the English tradition. Reminiscent of a bit of London, guests experience formal English decor which includes an English garden setting, curved bay windows, warm woods and handsome antique furnishings. Fireplaces welcome guests in all of the guest rooms & common rooms, including the living room, furnished with rich colors and the library done in the style of an English gentleman's club. A full breakfast is served in the dining room, just off the tiny secluded English garden and includes warm homemade baked goods, cereals, fresh fruit & juices and a hot dish with a fine selection of coffee and tea. The English theme continues to each guest room where warm polished woods, softly colored English wallpapers and prints, comfortable beds, a separate sitting area, fresh flowers and fruit, wet bar and fridge, TV and bedside phones meet every guest's wish. Nightly turndown service and towel change with a morning newspaper are provided. The pleasant and knowledgeable staff will arrange reservations for dinner, theatre or whatever and will make sure your shoes are polished and laundry is sent out. Within walking distance is Nob Hill, Union Square, Chinatown and the cable car. The perfect setting for the traveler who wants the intimacy of an inn and the service of a larger hotel. A place where guests return again and again. **RESERVATIONS:** Credit card guarantee or one night's deposit at res time, 24 hr cancel policy **BROCHURE:** Yes **PERMITTED:** Children, limited smoking, limited drinking **CONFERENCES:** Yes, seated groups to 30 persons and larger areas for receptions; full-time staff member handles all activities [R09BCCA-658]

Apple Lane Inn   San Jose CA
Doug & Diana Groom
408-475-6868   Res Times 8am-8pm

Rates:	**Pvt Bath** 3	**Shared Bath** 2	**Payment Terms:**
Single	$ 70.00	$ 60.00	Check
Double	$ 125.00	$ 85.00	DC/MC/V

Refer to the same listing name under Aptos CA for a complete description. [M05FPCA2-13073]

**Country Rose Inn   San Jose CA
Rose Hernandez
408-842-0441   Res Times 6-8am/8-10pm

Rates:	**Pvt Bath** 5	**Payment Terms:**
Single	$ 79-169.00	Check
Double	$ 79-169.00	AE/MC/V

©*Bed & Breakfast Guest Houses & Inns of America, Memphis TN*

California

Refer to the same listing name under Gilroy CA for a complete description. [M06FPCA1-11279]

Hensley House	San Jose CA
Sharon Layne	456 N 3rd St 95112
408-298-3537	**Res Times** 7am-10pm
	Fax 408-298-4676
Rates: **Pvt Bath** 5	**Payment Terms:**
Single $ 75.00	Check
Double $ 125.00	AE/DC/MC/V

Step into Victorian comfort and elegance reminiscent of great inns but with an intimate setting of just five guest rooms. From the moment you step inside the Inn, you will find a world of tranquility providing warm caring service to satisfy all guests - from weekend getawayers to business executives needing phones, TV, VCR and fax services. Guests discover a lavish-style of decor represented by fine French and English crafted antiques, crystal chandeliers and ancient stained glass windows capturing sparkles of sunlight and unique guest rooms like the Judge's Chambers featuring the comfort of a feather bed, wet bar, fireplace, whirlpool for two, English antiques and hand painted gilded ceilings and walls. Each room is unique, but each includes a queen feather bed, down comforters, TV, phone and VCR. Mornings bring a full complimentary breakfast of fresh ground coffee, expresso and cappuccino, fresh juices, fruits, muffins, croissants and a delicious entree. Wine, tea, hors d'oeuvres are served afternoons with high tea served Thursdays & Saturdays - where guests can relax beside the wood-burning fireplace with a good book. Located within walking distance of all downtown offices, courts, convention center and major restaurants - with light rail transport available for easy access to airport, Santa Clara and Silicon Valley. Prestigious private athletic club (pool, full gym, racketball, spa, restaurant, bar) available to guest. Full concierge at your service. **DISCOUNTS:** Yes, inquire at res time **AIRPORT:** San Jose Intl-5 mi **RESERVATIONS:** One night's deposit, 4 day cancel policy for refund; comp San Jose Airport pick-ups with prior arrangements **BROCHURE:** Yes **PERMITTED:** Drinking, limited children; a non-smoking Inn. **CONFERENCES:** From relaxed meetings, retreats, banquets, Victorian weddings, private parties - catering, private luncheons, dinners - let us know your needs, we do it all, groups to 75 [R05FPCA2-9958]

Arroyo Village Inn	San Luis Obispo CA
Gina Glass	818 Vista Brisa 93405
805-489-5926	**Res Times** 9am-10pm
Rates: **Pvt Bath** 7	**Payment Terms:**

©*Bed & Breakfast Guest Houses & Inns of America, Memphis TN*

California

Single $ 95-195.00   Check
Double $ 95-195.00   AE/DISC/MC/V

This award-winning, country Victorian Inn provides a delightful blend of yesterday's charm and hospitality with today's comforts and conveniences. Featuring seven unique garden-theme suites decorated in Laura Ashley prints with antique furnishings and special touches of window seats, skylights and balconies. A full gourmet breakfast is served in the parlor and teas and cordials are served in the late afternoon. Dinner available with prior notice and at added cost. Located half-way between Los Angeles and San Francisco in the heart of California's beautiful Central Coast, you're near Hearst Castle, San Luis Obispo, Pismo Beach, mineral spas, beaches and horseback riding on the beach and wineries. **DISCOUNTS:** Midweek Special: First night at regular price, 2nd night free on suites $145.00-up, excluding holidays. Seniors 20% **AIRPORT:** San Luis Obispo-15 mi **RESERVATIONS:** Full payment prior to arrival, late arrivals with prior arrangements **BROCHURE:** Yes **PERMITTED:** Children, drinking, limited smoking **CONFERENCES:** Groups 15-20 persons **LANGUAGES:** Italian, Spanish [Z07GPCA2-182]

Grand Cottages   **San Pedro CA**
Brigitte Clayton   809 S Grand Ave 90731
213-548-1240

Rates: **Pvt Bath** 4   **Payment Terms:**
Single $ 100.00   Check
Double $ 115.00   AE/DC/MC/V

Four quaint California bungalow cottages - an intimate hideaway with a "touch of class" in the Wharf Town of San Piedro. Just minutes from the Pacific, these cottages offer casual sophistication and convenience in a unhurried quiet neighborhood setting. Uniquely furnished, each cottage offers a different decor which might include fireplaces, antique, queen-size beds, private patio and front porch, full kitchen & living room. The *Grand Getaway for Lovers offers a special treat including breakfast in bed*! The VCR includes a copy of *Swing Shift* starring Goldie Hawn & Kurt Russell which was filmed on location at the Cottages! A full breakfast included and served in the Fireplace Room or your Cottage! **RESERVATIONS:** First night's full deposit by credit card or check at res time. **BROCHURE:** Yes **PERMITTED:** Drinking **CONFERENCES:** Yes including dining for groups to 10 persons. **LANGUAGES:** German, French, Spanish, Farsi [E02BCCA-6248]

**Casa Soldavini*   **San Rafael CA
Linda Soldavini-Cassidy   531 C St 94901

California

415-454-3140   **Res Times** 8-10pm

Rates:	**Pvt Bath** 1	**Shared Bath** 2	**Payment Terms:**
Single	$ 65.00	$ 60.00	Check
Double	$ 80.00	$ 70.00	

Built in the 1930's by grandfather Joseph Soldavini - your hostess shares her lovely home built in a quaint Italian neighborhood. While grandpa was a winemaker by trade, his lush gardens were his pride and joy and still flourish today. Located in Historic Mission San Rafael, guests can take a bike ride or picnic at a nearby park or museum - or relax on the front porch swing. Three lovely guest rooms are private, comfortable and furnished with original antiques and family heirlooms. Guests can relax in the large sitting room with piano, TV, VCR or they can enjoy the outdoor patio with a large built-in BBQ and fresh fruit and vegetables from the back garden. A complimentary continental breakfast includes fresh brewed hot beverages, juices and plenty of homebaked goods with special treats to tuck you in at night. Guests are within easy walking distance of many fine restaurants and just a short drive to San Francisco, Redwoods, beaches and much more. Your hosts can even provide a private massage therapist upon request! Kitchen privileges; phone available. **RESERVATIONS:** One night's deposit required; late arrivals with prior arrangement, 5 day cancel notice for refund **BROCHURE:** Yes **PERMITTED:** Pets with prior arrangements [Z05FPCA2-8157]

**Casa Del Mar Inn	**Santa Barbara CA**
Mike & Becky Montgomery	18 Bath St 93101
800-433-3097 805-963-4418	**Res Times:** 7am-10pm
	Fax 805-966-4240

Rates:	**Pvt Bath** 20	**Payment Terms:**
Single	$ 59-189.00	Check
Double	$ 59-189.00	DC/DISC/MC/V

A charming Mediterranean-style Bed & Breakfast Inn with a special home-like atmosphere, just steps away from the beach, harbor and wharf that combines the intimacy of a Bed and Breakfast Inn and the privacy of a small hotel close to elegant restaurants and fine shops. A wide variety of room types are available ranging from bungalow-style family suites with kitchens and fireplaces to cozy queens surrounding a private courtyard with lush gardens, meandering pathways and relaxing spa. Business travelers will appreciate fax, in-room modem hook-ups and comfortable work areas. Non-smoking available and handicap accessible available; CATV, phones, handicap accessible, private bath in all rooms. Amenities include a very generous continental breakfast with fruit and cereals and an evening wine and cheese buffet. **DISCOUNTS:** Seniors, business, travel agents, weekly & monthly rates **AIRPORT:** Santa

California

Barbara-10 mi **RESERVATIONS:** One night credit card deposit, 48 hr cancel policy **SEASONAL:** Rates vary **BROCHURE:** Yes **PERMITTED:** Children, drinking, smoking, limited pets **LANGUAGES:** German [Z057GCA2-11028]

**Cheshire Cat Inn B&B	**Santa Barbara CA**
*Margaret Goeden	36 W Valerio 93101
805-569-1610	**Res Times** 10am-9pm

Rates:	**Pvt Bath** 14	**Payment Terms:**
Single	$ 79-249.00	Check
Double	$ 89-249.00	MC/V

Victorian elegance for the romantic at heart and travelers seeking a relaxed family environment while traveling. Two of Santa Barbara's oldest homes have been magically restored to their former elegance with modern conveniences. High ceilings and pagoda-like bay windows create extraordinary atmosphere of comfort and charming public rooms where guests find large sitting areas with private nooks and corners for friendly conversation and a wood-burning fireplace. The guest rooms are uniquely decorated with either a queen or king brass bed, enhanced by beautiful Laura Ashley wallpapers and fabrics. English antiques grace charming sitting areas with gorgeous views and some with added extras such as a fireplace, patio or spa. Guest amenities include fresh flowers, private phones, chocolates and liqueurs in each guest room and complimentary guest bikes for touring Santa Barbara in the traditional style. A full gourmet breakfast of fresh-ground European coffees, pastries, fresh fruits and assorted juices are included. Complimentary regional wines are served Saturday evening guests. An outdoor brick patio courtyard joining the two stately homes is perfect for relaxing in comfortable seating, spa or within a beautiful gazebo. The *Cheshire Cat* is conveniently located four blocks from theatres, restaurants and shops. **DISCOUNTS:** Travel agents weekday FAM trips, call for details **AIRPORT:** Los Angeles LAX-2 hrs; Santa Barbara-10 mi **RESERVATIONS:** One night's deposit within 7 days of booking, one week cancel policy for refund less $15 service fee. **BROCHURE:** Yes **PERMITTED:** Drinking, limited children and smoking **CONFERENCES:** Meeting room for groups to ten persons **LANGUAGES:** Limited Spanish, French [R11EPCA2-677]

**Harbour Carriage House	**Santa Barbara CA**
Kimberly Pegram	420 W Montecito St 93101
800-594-4633 805-962-8447	**Res Times** 8am-8pm

Rates:	**Pvt Bath** 9	**Payment Terms:**
Single	$ 76.50	Check

California

Double $ 175.00   MC/V

Built as a private home around the turn-of-the-century and just two blocks from the beach in Santa Barbara, today guests can relax in this tranquil setting and still be in the center of things-to-do! The main house and its carriage house offer different themes and amenities to make it one of the best romantic Inns around town. Guest rooms in the Main House are named for different flowers (Queen Anne's Lace, Wisteria, Sweet Alyssum) with airy pastel colors, enhanced with greenery and large windows, furnished with English and French antiques and wicker touches. Some rooms feature spa tubs for two, private balconies, garden or mountain views, fireplaces and king or queen beds. A full gourmet breakfast, served in the solarium of the main house, often includes freshly squeezed orange juice, walnut coffee cake, poached pears with yogurt fruit sauce, a cheese, shrimp and mushroom strata with specially brewed coffee and tea. Nearby sights include the botanical gardens, live performing theatre, harbour cruises. beaches with swimming and surfing, fine restaurants and antiquing shopping. If you want to see Santa Barbara this is your place. Your charming hostess gladly helps guests find the right places of interest. **RESERVATIONS:** One night's deposit within 7 days of booking with 72 hr cancel policy, refund only if rebooked when less then 72 hr notice. **BROCHURE:** Yes **PERMITTED:** Children, drinking, limited children [R12BPCA-680]

Old Yacht Club Inn   **Santa Barbara CA
S Hunt/L Caruso/N Donaldson   431 Corona Del Mar Dr 93103
800-676-1676 805-962-1277   **Res Times** 8am-9pm

Rates:	**Pvt Bath** 9	**Payment Terms:**
Single	$ 80-145.00	Check
Double	$ 85-150.00	AE/MC/V

Dating from the *Roaring '20s* as Santa Barbara's temporary Yacht Club when their club washed out to sea, this gracious location was fully restored in 1980 and furnished with period pieces, classic European and Early American antiques while oriental rugs cover the hardwood floors creating the warm and "homey" feeling of another era. There are large light-filled rooms, a massive fireplace, and large covered porches surrounded with colorful hanging baskets of flowers. Guest rooms are individually decorated with an "old-fashioned touch" and include details such as flowers and sherry decanters with some including cozy sitting areas and balconies. The *Hitchcock House* next door includes four private-entry rooms exquisitely furnished with antique treasures and family heirlooms. The full breakfast is a memorable experience with fresh-brewed coffee, orange juice, fruit, baked breads and omelettes. The five-course dinner is available only to guests on Saturday evening and is

California

selected from the gourmet palate of your hostess, "Chefess" Nancy! All year-round activities are nearby: golf, tennis, fishing, horseback riding and quaint seaside shopping. Comp bikes, beach chairs and towels, and golfing privileges at private country club. **DISCOUNTS:** Midweek during off-season **AIRPORT:** Los Angeles Intl-90 mi; Santa Barbara-12 mi. **RESERVATIONS:** Deposit within 7 days, 7-day cancellation policy for refund, two night min on weekends **BROCHURE:** Yes **PERMITTED:** Children, limited drinking **CONFERENCES:** Yes, if entire Inn is reserved, conferences in common areas **LANGUAGES:** Spanish [Z07GPCA2-685]

Parsonage	**Santa Barbara CA**
Holli Harmon	1600 Olive St 93101
800-775-0352 805-962-9336	

Rates:	**Pvt Bath** 6	**Payment Terms:**
Single	$ 105-185.00	Check
Double	$ 105-185.00	AE/MC/V

Built in 1892 as a parsonage for the Trinity Episcopal Church, *The Parsonage*, one of Santa Barbara's most notable Queen Anne Victorians, has operated as a unique and memorable Bed & Breakfast Inn for over a decade. Lovingly restored to recapture the openness and grandeur of its distinctive light and cheerful rooms, *The Parsonage* has maintained the touches of rare bird'seye redwood throughout this historic structure. Unwind in the spacious living room by the fireplace as you make your dinner plans in one of the numerous local gourmet restaurants. Period furnishings and exquisite antique Oriental rugs create an unique and elegant atmosphere throughout the house and in each individually decorated room. Whichever room you choose, you will find the appointments peacefully pleasing, a comfortable king or queen bed and spotless facilities. Nestled between downtown Santa Barbara and the foothills in the quiet residential Upper East neighborhood, the grandiose home offers unparalled views of the city, Harbor and Channel Islands, in its premium rooms. The Inn is within walking distance of the mission and just a few short blocks from theatre going, dining and shopping in Historic Santa Barbara. Guests begin each morning with a relaxful generous full complimentary breakfast on the sundeck or in the formal dining room by the cozy fireplace. **AIRPORT:** Santa Barbara-10 mi; Los Angeles Intl-90 mi **DISCOUNTS:** Yes, inquire at res time **RESERVATIONS:** First night's deposit or credit card number to guarantee, bal upon arrival. Add 10% hotel room tax **BROCHURE:** Yes **PERMITTED:** Limited children, drinking [R04FPCA2-687]

**Simpson House Inn*	**Santa Barbara CA**
G Wilson/Glyn & Linda Davies	121 E Arrellaga 93101

California

800-676-1280 805-963-7067

Rates:	Pvt Bath 14
Single	$ 105-245.00
Double	$ 105-245.00

Res Times 8am-9pm
Fax 805-564-4811
Payment Terms:
Check
AE/DC/DISC/MC/V

A beautiful Eastlake-style Victorian home c1874 secluded in an acre of English gardens yet just a five minute walk to Santa Barbaras' restaurants, theatres, museums and shops. Lovingly restored by the host/owners, you can relax in the spacious sitting room with its fireplace and book-lined walls or in the gardens. Cottages, suites and rooms are elegantly appointed with oriental carpets, antiques, goose down beds and fresh flowers. Some feature private patios, woodburning fireplaces, jacuzzi tubs, VCRs and wet bars. Enjoy your full breakfast of fresh California juices and fruits, the finest of coffees and teas, homemade muffins and warm entrees on the veranda overlooking the spectacular gardens! Complimentary afternoon refreshments and local wine are served with hors d'oeuvres in a variety of gracious settings. Comp bikes for your use too! **AAA ♦♦♦♦, ABBA 4 Crown Rated, Grand Hotels Award -Best Bed & Breakfast, Southern California**, by travel writers and editors throughout the state, featured in numerous publications, including the cover and feature story in *Country Inns Magazine*, Feb, 1994. **DISCOUNTS:** 20% M-Thur, based upon availability **AIRPORT:** LA Intl-90 mi; Santa Barbara Airport-15 mi **DISCOUNTS:** Yes, inquire at res time **RESERVATIONS:** Deposit at res time, 7 day cancel policy for refund, late arrival with prior arrangements **BROCHURE:** Yes **PERMITTED:** Children, drinking, limited smoking **CONFERENCES:** Yes, groups to 25 person **PACKAGES:** Inquire at res time **LANGUAGES:** Spanish [Z08GP-CA2-689]

**Upham Hotel & Cottages	**Santa Barbara CA**
Jan Martin Winn	1404 De La Vina St 93101
800-727-0876 805-962-0058	**Res Times** 24 hours

Rates:	Pvt Bath 49
Single	$ 105.00-up
Double	$ 105.00-up

Payment Terms:
Check
AE/DC/MC/V

Established in 1871, making it **the oldest continuously operating hostelry in southern California**, this beautifully restored Victorian is situated on an acre of gardens in downtown Santa Barbara. Walk to museums, galleries, historical attractions, shops and restaurants. Accommodations are located in the Main House & Cottages. All rooms are individually decorated with period furnishings, antiques and beds with cozy comforters. Most cottages have fireplaces and most have private porches or patios. The Master Suite beckons with Jacuzzi-spa,

California

fireplace, wet-bar and private yard including a relaxing hammock! Complimentary Continental breakfast is served in the lobby & garden veranda. Freshly brewed coffee & tea, juices, a variety of muffins, breads & pastries, cereals, seasonal fruits plus the latest edition of the newspaper help start your day. Wine & cheese is provided around the lobby fireplace in late afternoon. Enjoy Louie's restaurant serving excellent California Cuisine for lunch and dinner. Special group and corporate rates are available. For that romantic weekend or mid-week retreat, the *Upham* is the answer! **DISCOUNTS:** Yes, inquire at res time **AIRPORT:** Santa Barbara Municipal; LA Intl-2 hrs **RESERVATIONS:** Deposit or credit card for first night's stay to guarantee res, 72 hr cancel policy. Check-in 3:00pm, check-out 12:00pm **BROCHURE:** Yes **PERMITTED:** Children, drinking **CONFERENCES:** Yes, 1875 sq ft **LANGUAGES:** Spanish [Z07GPCA2-692]

Madison Street Inn			Santa Clara CA
Ralph & Teresa Wigginton			1390 Madison St 95050
408-249-5541			**Res Times** 7am-10pm
Rates:	**Pvt Bath** 4	**Shared Bath** 2	**Payment Terms:**
Single	$ 75-85.00	$ 60.00	Check
Double	$ 75-85.00	$ 60.00	AE/DC/MC/V

An ideal location for all visitors to the Bay Area, travelers are assured of a restful night's stay after trips to nearby San Francisco and the Napa Valley, south to the Carmel-Monterey area or business trips to Bay Area firms. The *Madison Street Inn* is the culmination of an award winning restoration offering a gracious perspective of a different era. An ideal place for work or relaxation, there are five individually decorated rooms, all with phones, a sunny breakfast room overlooking flower filled gardens; a parlor decorated with authentic Victorian wall papers and museum-quality furnishings; and by special request, laundry, dry cleaning and fax services. The half-acre of landscaped gardens, highlighted with an arbor of fuschia-colored Bougainvillea, makes a perfect setting for spring and summer weddings or parties. The grounds around the pool and spa can easily accommodate 20-75 guests. The *Madison Inn* offers superb dining - whether its breakfast, luncheons, dinners or catered parties. The day begins with a complimentary full breakfast of juices, fresh fruit, baked muffins & breads and entrees of Eggs Benedict or Belgian Waffles. Dinners, by prior arrangement only,

California

brings Ralph's delicious entrees, such as Poached Salmon with Basil and Olive Butter or Individual Beef Wellington - all prepared with fresh herbs grown outside the kitchen door. Nearby sights include Winchester Mystery House, Great American Park, Rosicruician and Triton Museums. **DISCOUNTS:** Yes, inquire at res time. **AIRPORT:** San Jose-10 mins **RESERVATIONS:** One night's deposit with 4-day cancellation policy for full refund **BROCHURE:** Yes **PERMITTED:** Children **CONFERENCES:** Groups of 10-15 persons **LANGUAGES:** French [K03EPCA-695]

**Babbling Brook Inn	**Santa Cruz CA**
Helen King	1025 Laurel St 95060
800-866-1131 408-427-2437	**Res Times** 7am-11pm
	Fax 408-427-2457
Rates: **Pvt Bath** 12	**Payment Terms:**
Single $ 85-150.00	Check
Double $ 85-150.00	AE/DC/MC/V

Cascading waterfall, historic waterwheel and meandering brooks grace an acre of terraced gardens, fruit trees and redwoods surrounding this secluded Inn built in 1909 on the foundation of an 1870 tannery, a 1790 flour mill and the site of a 2,000 year-old Indian fishing village. Choose from 12 rooms in Country French decor located in four buildings beside the brook. All have private bath, telephone, TV, and most have cozy fireplaces, private decks and an outside entrance. Four rooms offer deep-soaking jet bathtubs. The Inn has off-street parking. Included in your stay is a full country breakfast featuring memorable egg casseroles served buffet-style in the large living room parlor between 8 and 10 am, so guests may arrive at their leisure. Afternoon tea and Mrs King's famous cookies, followed by evening wine and cheese served during the social hour with the other guests complimentary. The unusual Country Inn location is within walking distance of ocean beaches, wharf, boardwalk, shopping, tennis and historic homes. Three golf courses, two hundred restaurants and seven wineries are within 20 minutes! The narrow gauge railroad trip over old logging trails, elephant seals at Ano Nuevo Reserve, whale-watching, the annual winter haven of Monarch butterflies, deep-sea fishing, evening sails and antiquing are some of the "seeing/doing" ideas for this city on the North end of Monterey Bay. The weather is comparatively mild in winter and cool in the summer. ***AAA Approved, Mobil*** ★★★ ***Rated*** **RESERVATIONS:** 50% deposit for confirmed reservations, check-in 3-10:30pm **PERMITTED:** Drinking, children

California

and pets with restrictions **BROCHURE:** Yes **LANGUAGES:** Spanish, French, AT&T Language Service available **CONFERENCES:** Yes, groups to 8 to 12 persons **AIRPORT:** San Francisco Intl-90 min **PACKAGES:** *Getaway Special* 2 nights, 3 days for $175.00 includes champagne, discounts at local restaurants [I05FPCA1-696]

**Blue Spruce Inn	**Santa Cruz CA**
Pat & Tom O'Brien	
408-464-1137	**Res Times** 7am-10pm

Rates:	**Pvt Bath** 5	**Payment Terms:**
Single	$ 80-125.00	Check
Double	$ 80-125.00	AE/MC/V

Refer to the same listing name under Soquel, California for a complete description. [M07GPCA2]

*Channel Road Inn	**Santa Monica CA**
Susan Zolla	219 W Channel Rd 90402
310-459-1920	**Res Times** 7:30am-10pm
	Fax 310-454-9920

Rates:	**Pvt Bath** 14	**Payment Terms:**
Single	$ *95-200.00	Check
Double	$ *95-200.00	MC/V

Sitting on the back deck overlooking the sea and flowering hillside, it is difficult to believe one is in the hectic city of Los Angeles! But the *Channel Road Inn*, a 1910 colonial revival has been lovingly restored and graciously furnished to become one of the few Bed & Breakfasts in Los Angeles. In-addition to the fine antique furnishings in each of the 14 guest rooms, every guest will also find fresh fruit or flowers, embroidered linens, down pillows, cozy comforters or antique quilts, extra firm mattresses and thick bath robes. After a healthful breakfast of homebaked berry muffins, bread pudding and a variety of fresh California fruits, guests may bicycle (comp bikes available) along the beach bike path, or walk along the hillside nature trails. The John Paul Getty Museum is five minutes up the coast; the Santa Monica Pier, just one mile south. Horseback riding and tennis nearby. A seafood restaurant, Italian cafe and a fun Tex-Mex restaurant are within a block. Other fine

California

restaurants, museums, and shops are located in nearby Santa Monica or in the Pacific Palisades. The Inn is only twenty minutes from the airport or downtown LA. But with the gracious staff and the restful atmosphere of the Inn, many guests never wander far from the front porch. **AIRPORT:** 20 mins from LA Intl. **RESERVATIONS:** One night's deposit required at res time with 72 hr cancel policy for refund. Wheelchair accessible. *Corporate & weekly discounts available. **BROCHURE:** Yes **PERMITTED:** Children, drinking. **CONFERENCES:** Excellent facilities for social or business meetings/conferences. **LANGUAGES:** Spanish, French [I04FPCA2-8421]

**Melitta Station Inn	**Santa Rosa CA**
V Amstadter/D Crandon	5850 Melitta Rd 95409
707-538-7712	**Res Times** 8am-9pm

Rates:	**Pvt Bath** 4	**Shared Bath** 2	**Payment Terms:**
Single	$ 85.00	$ 75.00	Check
Double	$ 90.00	$ 80.00	MC/V

The *Melitta Station* is a turn-of-the-century railroad station which has been caringly and lovingly turned into a rustic American Country Bed & Breakfast Inn and family home with six guest rooms, a large sitting area which is warmed by a wood-burning stove, and a balcony that overlooks the surrounding pepperwood trees. Located in the middle of the Valley of the Moon, guests have their choice of activities, including biking, horseback riding, hiking or sailing in the several parks, located within minutes of the Inn. Guests may wish to visit some of the many wineries in the area or this historic towns of Sonoma and Calistoga, where they can enjoy mud baths, massages, hot air ballooning and glider rides. A full breakfast is included along with complimentary wine & cheese service in the early evening. Many fine restaurants are within a short drive for your dining experiences. **RESERVATIONS:** One night's deposit within 7 days of booking, 7 day cancellation policy for refund; check-in after 3pm, check-out 11am **BROCHURE:** Yes **PERMITTED:** Limited children [Z07GPCA2-2927]

**Pygmalion House B&B	**Santa Rosa CA**
Lola Wright	331 Orange St 95407
707-526-3407	**Res Times** 24 Hrs

Rates:	**Pvt Bath** 5	**Payment Terms:**
Single	$ 45-65.00	Check
Double	$ 50-70.00	MC/V

One of Santa Rosa's historical landmarks, this Grand Lady survived the

California

great earthquake and fire of 1906 and has been transformed into a fine example of Victorian Queen Anne architecture. Ideally located in a secluded residential street in Santa Rosa's "Old Town", it is within walking distance of Railroad Square, popular for its specialty shops and fine restaurants. The interior is an eclectic combination of unique colorful rooms each with a vintage claw foot tub and/or shower, central a/c & heat. Each morning a bountiful (full) breakfast is served in the country kitchen including fresh squeezed orange juice! Throughout the day guests are treated to complimentary soft drinks, bottled spring water and in the evening, there's coffee, snacks and tea while socializing around the fireplace in the double parlor or relaxing in their room. Your hostess is anxious to help guests with the many activities, including: Napa Valley & Sonoma County wineries, hot air ballooning, golfing, bike trails, the Northern California Coast, Muir Woods, Sausalito and much more **RESERVATIONS:** One night's deposit with 7 day cancel policy less $10 service fee, late cancel or no-show forfeits deposit **BROCHURE:** Yes **PERMITTED:** Children with special arrangements, smoking outside [Z04DPCA2-711]

**Sunrise B&B Inn	**Santa Rosa CA**
Bob & Denyse Linde	1500 Olivet Rd 95401
707-542-5781	**Res Times** 7am-9pm

Rates:	**Pvt Bath** 1	**Shared Bath** 2	**Payment Terms:**
Single	$ 85.00	$ 65.00	Check
Double	$ 95.00	$ 75.00	

Sunrise Bed & Breakfast is a contemporary home located 6 miles west of Santa Rosa in the Russian River Valley of Sonoma County's wine country where guests can unwind or enjoy the country. Your hosts are experienced hot air balloonists and guests can ride over Wine Country with them each morning. Located on a 2-1/2 acre vineyard, the *Sunrise Bed & Breakfast* offers its own labeled wine for guests to try. Guest rooms are large & airy and furnished with antiques, oak furniture, queen-size brass beds, oriental rugs and a new large suite has its own large private bath. A full Scottish complimentary breakfast includes fresh eggs, Canadian bacon, sausage, fresh ground coffee, fruit and preserves frequently served by your kilted host. Nearby sights include fifty-seven award winning wineries including Korbel and Deloach, Armstrong Redwood and Fort Ross State Parks, the Russian River and Lake Sonoma offer water sports and the Pacific Ocean is within 30 mins. Festivals occur year-round which include the annual Caledonia Club Highland Games & Bagpipe competition on Labor Day weekend *(the largest clan gathering in the world)* with all the sights of San Francisco just 60 miles to the South. **RESERVATIONS:** First night's full deposit, 72 hr cancel policy for full refund, check-in 4 pm and later **SEASONAL:** Close Holidays **BROCHURE:**

California

Yes **PERMITTED:** Drinking, limited children [R07BCCA-6290]

**Storybook Inn	**Skyforest CA**
Kathleen & John Wooley	Lake Arrowhead 92385
800-554-9208 909-336-1483	**Res Times** 8am-9pm

Rates:	**Pvt Bath** 10	**Payment Terms:**
Single	$ 98.00	Check
Double	$ 200.00	AE/DIS/MC/V

An excitingly different experience is offered in this Classical Hideaway offering romance and magical experiences in all ten different theme guest rooms. Snuggled atop San Bernardino Mountains, enjoy the spectacular 100 mile view of the snow capped mountains and the Pacific Ocean or relax in the glassed-in solarium & porches that bring in all the abundant wildlife. Furnishings include antiques and contemporary pieces throughout the guest and common rooms with fresh flowers sprinkled everywhere. This peaceful and serene setting includes a gorgeous stone fireplace and a three-story main lobby, hot tub, hors d'oeuvres, complimentary wine, outdoor activities at Lake Arrowhead, breath-taking nature trails for hiking, old-fashioned picnics with prepared lunches, and wonderful skiing in winter. A picturesque cabin "Call of the Wild" is available and offers privacy and a hunting lodge setting with open beam ceilings, stone fireplace and John's hunting and fishing trophies. A full gourmet breakfast is included daily along with the morning paper. Lunch and Dinner available. **DISCOUNTS:** 20-25% Mid-week, Seminars and other special events **AIRPORT:** Ontario CA-40 mins **PACKAGES:** *Swiss Alps Getaway, Honeymoon, Ski Trips, Weddings* which includes a romantic wedding gazebo and reception facilities **RESERVATIONS:** One night deposit, 7 day cancel policy, late arrival notice **BROCHURE:** Yes **PERMITTED:** Children, drinking, smoking outdoors on patio **CONFERENCES:** Meeting and dining location for seclusion and privacy for social or business up to 20 persons **LANGUAGES:** French, Italian, Spanish [I05FPCA1-722]

**Victorian Garden Inn	**Sonoma CA**
Ms Donna Lewis	316 E Napa St 95476
800-543-5339 707-996-5339	**Res Times** 8am-5pm

©*Bed & Breakfast Guest Houses & Inns of America, Memphis TN*

California

Rates:	Pvt Bath 3	Shared Bath 1	Payment Terms:
Single			Check
Double	$ 99-139.99	$ 79.00	AE/DC/MC/V

1870 Greek Revival residence and Woodcutter's Cottage are nestled within this wooded setting and lush garden area including private patio, and romantic atmosphere. Choose from three rooms/suites all with individual decor from a Merrimekko-styled blue and white room with wicker accents at the top of the "old water tower" to the Garden Room, with a queen size iron framed bed, classic Laura Ashley Rose wallcoverings & fabrics, wicker furnishings and garden-side with its own babbling brook. The Woodcutter's Cottage offers guests a Hunter Green and redwood decor, complete with clawfoot tub/shower, queen size brass bed, your own fireplace and sitting area. Gourmet breakfast included with lunch and snack breaks available with added cost. **RESERVATIONS:** First and last nights' deposit required in advance, 14 day cancel notice for refund less $10 service fee **DISCOUNTS:** Yes, inquire at res time **AIRPORT:** San Francisco-65 mi **BROCHURE:** Yes **PERMITTED:** Limited children, limited smoking **CONFERENCES:** Flexible for mid-week social or business style meetings, to 10 persons [Z03FPCA2-736]

Columbia City Hotel   **Sonora CA

Tom Bender
209-532-1479

Res Times 8am-10pm
Fax 209-532-7027

Rates:	Pvt Bath* 10	Payment Terms:
Single	$ 65-85.00	Check
Double	$ 65-85.00	AE/MC/V

Refer to the same listing name under Columbia, CA for a complete description. [M07GPCA2]

Blue Spruce Inn   **Soquel CA

Pat & Tom O'Brien
408-464-1137

2815 S Main St 95073
Res Times 7am-10pm

Rates:	Pvt Bath 5	Payment Terms:
Single	$ 80-125.00	Check
Double	$ 80-125.00	AE/MC/V

At the *Blue Spruce Inn*, guests enjoy the flavor of yesterday blended with the luxury of today in a friendly 1875 Victorian farm house. Each room derives its own mood from the handmade quilt on the queen-size bed which complements the representative work of a local artist displayed in the room. Accommodations offer gas fireplaces, some spa tubs or full

©Bed & Breakfast Guest Houses & Inns of America, Memphis TN

California

body showers, private entrances and deck areas. The window seat parlor is a place to read, play a game or watch the flowers grow. Just down the street, guests can enjoy fine dining, browse through antique shops or visit premier wineries. The day begins in the parlor or out in the garden with a bounteous complimentary breakfast of just-squeezed juice, fresh fruits, and baked breads, perhaps hearty blueberry pancakes or a baked ham stratta accompanied by steaming cups of coffee or tea. Beyond the neighborhood lies the entire Monterey Bay - the redwood groves in the mountains to the north; the blue Pacific shore to the south. Three State Parks in the area have extensive hiking, bicycle and horse trails, historic displays and beautiful beaches. When guests retire, pillows will be fluffed, robes laid out and a nightcap waiting to assure a perfect ending to a wonderful day. **DISCOUNT:** 10% Nov through Feb **AIRPORT:** 30 mi to San Jose. **RESERVATIONS:** One night's deposit with 48 hr cancel policy for refund less $10 service fee. Check-in 3-6pm, check-out 11am **BROCHURE:** Yes **PERMITTED:** Limited children, drinking & smoking **LANGUAGES:** Spanish [I07GPCA2-13226]

**Fogleson House "Valley View"	**Studio City CA**
*Robin Nabin	
800-383-3513 310-498-0552	**Res Times** 24 Hrs

Rates:	**Pvt Bath** 1	**Payment Terms:**
Single	$ 50.00	Check
Double	$ 60.00	

Located in the beautiful hills overlooking the San Fernando Valley, this home is a good base for exploring the Los Angeles area. It's close to freeways, the media district, shops and restaurants. Universal Studios is within walking distance. Guest accommodations consist of a comfortable, quiet room with double bed and single bed, TV and private bath. The bedroom is on the second floor, completely private from the rest of the house. There is a second bedroom upstairs which could accommodate a third person (child) and/or a crib for a baby. Breakfast is served in a sunny breakfast room or outdoors, weather permitting. Breakfast consists of fruit, juice, cereal, muffins and sometimes homemade pancakes or waffles and brewed coffee and tea. **DISCOUNTS:** Weekly stays - 7th day free **AIRPORT:** LAX-17 mi; Burbank-6 mi **RESERVATIONS:** One night's deposit, late arrival only with prior arrangements **PERMITTED:** Children **LANGUAGES:** German [R05FPCA2-16894]

California

Mayfield House		Tahoe City CA
Bruce & Cynthia Knauss		236 Grove St 96145
916-583-1001		**Res Times** 9am-5pm
Rates:	**Shared Bath** 5	**Payment Terms:**
Single	$ 85-115.00	Check
Double	$ 85-115.00	MC/V

Built in 1932 by Norman Mayfield, Lake Tahoe's pioneer builder, it represents one of the finest examples of the architecture unique to the area. Completely refurbished in 1979, guests relax in comfortably furnished rooms, including down comforters & pillows, his & her robes, brass & copper accents, striking Queen Anne and oak furnishings, lots of books and fresh flowers in each room and a quiet nook perfect for the full breakfast that's available for "in-bed" diners! A large living room with a stone fireplace is often a common meeting area for the guests and charming hostess who states *"there are no strangers at the Mayfield House, only friends who have not yet met"!* A perfect year-round location, there's x-country skiing and golf just across the street and within thirty minutes there are seventeen downhill and twelve Nordic ski areas. In summer guests are just a half-block from Lake Tahoe and Commons beach along with shops and restaurants with gambling right at the state line. The full breakfast is exquisite for variety and especially the homebaked favorites of apple strudel, sweet-potato muffins and Finnish pancakes with strawberry topping and sour cream. **RESERVATIONS:** 50% of full amount as deposit, 2 week cancel policy for refund, less $10.00 service fee. **BROCHURE:** Yes **PERMITTED:** Drinking [Z07GPCA2-761]

Touch Of Mexico B&B		Toluca Lake CA
*Robin Nabin		
800-383-3513 310-498-0552		**Res Times** 24 Hrs
Rates:	**Pvt Bath** 2	**Payment Terms:**
Single	$ 75.00	Check
Double	$ 75.00	

Toluca Lake is a very small, special enclave within blocks of five major studios where resident celebrities include Bob Hope, Roy Disney, Henry Winkler, Patrick Wayne, Dudley Moore, Jonathan Winters and many more. *Touch of Mexico* was designed after a Tusacny Hills monastery however the interior resembles a Mexican hacienda with Satillo tiled floors, arches and ceramic tiles from Mexico. The guest rooms have private full baths, king size bed, TV and an exterior door leading to the deck with a pool and spa. Children are welcomed with plenty of baby furniture and toys all ready. A continental breakfast includes fresh juice,

California

fruit, rolls, croissants or muffins and cereals. There are many ethnic restaurants and fun boutiques in this quaint little village setting to visit during your stay. **AIRPORT:** Burbank-10 mins; LAX-45 mins **RESERVATIONS:** One night's deposit to guarantee reservation **PERMITTED:** Children, drinking **LANGUAGES:** Spanish [R05FPCA2-16896]

Whites House	Torrance CA
Russell & Margaret White	17122 Farsmith Ave 90504
213-324-6164	

Rates:	**Pvt Bath** 2	**Payment Terms:**
Single	$ 40.00	Check
Double	$ 45.00	

Quiet suburban locale for this charming contemporary home with sunbathing deck, patio, fireplaces, and convenient to all sights within 30 mins to Disneyland, Marineland and Knott's Berry Farm. You'll feel right at home with these hospitable hosts. Continental breakfast included. **RESERVATIONS:** Airport & bus station pick-ups available at nominal charge. **PERMITTED:** Children, pets with advance notice, smoking & social drinking. [E11ACCA-771]

**Vichy Hot Springs Resort*	Ukiah CA
Gilbert & Marjorie Ashoff	2605 Vichy Springs Rd 95482
707-462-9515	**Res Times** 7:30am-10pm

Rates:	**Pvt Bath** 14	**Payment Terms:**
Single	$ 85.00	Check
Double	$ 125-160.00	All Major

Vichy Hot Springs Resort, a two hour drive north on Hwy 101 from San Francisco, is **one of California's oldest continuously operating hot springs resorts.** Opened in 1854 the original buildings have been completely renovated and individually decorated. Bed & Breakfast is offered for our guests in 12 rooms and two self-contained cottages. A few feet from your room await the 14 natural tubs built in 1860 and used by the rich and famous in California's history including Jack and Charmaigne London, Mark Twain, Teddy Roosevelt and his daughter Alice, Ulysses Grant and pugilists Jim Corbett and John L Sullivan. *Vichy* features naturally sparkling 90 degree mineral baths, a communal hot tub and olympic size pool that will gently caress your cares and stress away. The baths are backdropped by a five million year old travertine/onyx grotto, formed from the Spring. *Vichy* has 700 acres for your hiking, jogging, picnicking and mountain bicycling pleasure. *Vichy* offers Swedish massage, reflexology and herbal facials. A quiet healing

California

environment is what a stay at a mineral springs resort should be. *Vichy's* idyllic setting amidst native oak, madrone, manzanita, bay, fir, pine and buckeye will leave you refreshed, renewed and invigorated. An expanded complimentary breakfast is included in your room rate. **AIRPORT:** Santa Rosa-60 mi **PACKAGES:** One week stay, 7th nite free. Massage therapy available on-site. **RESERVATIONS:** Deposit at res time, 4 day cancel policy for refund; late arrivals accommodated. **BROCHURE:** Yes **PERMITTED:** Children, drinking, smoking (outside only) Bathing suits required in mineral baths and pools. **CONFERENCES:** Yes with space from 400 to 4400 sq ft. **LANGUAGES:** Spanish [Z07GPCA2-10038]

**Clocktower Inn	Ventura CA
Dale Sedgemeyer	181 E Santa Clara St 93001
800-727-1027 805-652-0141	**Res Times** 24-hr
Rates: **Pvt Bath** 50	**Payment Terms:**
Single $ 85.00-Up	Check
Double $ 95.00-Up	AE/DISC/DC/MC/V

In 1985, interior designer Tom Brooks was commissioned to create an Inn from the existing structure of 1940 California/Spanish firehouse and clocktower! Southwestern style fiber wall hangings, original art, beamed ceilings, handsome wood furnishings and a large fireplace have transformed the firehouse into the easy grace and simplicity of the *Clocktower Inn*. Located in the heart of historic downtown Ventura, it is surrounded by a park and adjacent to the Mission and Historical downtown Ventura, it is surrounded by a park and adjacent to the Mission and Historical Museum. The State Beach, restaurants, antique shops, boutiques and County Fairgrounds are all within easy walking distance. The two-story guest wings are accessed by elevator and Spanish tiled stairs. Most rooms have private balconies or patios and several include fireplaces. Mornings begin in the glass-covered Atrium with a Complimentary continental breakfast buffet. Freshly-brewed coffee and teas, juices, a variety of muffins, breads and pastries, cereal, seasonal fruits plus the latest edition of the newspaper help start your day . In late afternoon enjoy complimentary wine and cheese around the lobby fireplace. Three conference rooms are available for groups from 5 to 100 in comfortable Santa Fe style. Special corporate & group rates available. **RESERVATIONS:** Deposit for first night's stay to guarantee res, 72-hr cancel policy **BROCHURE:** Yes **PERMITTED:** Children, no smoking **CONFERENCES:** Yes, 1900 sq ft **LANGUAGES:** Spanish [Z11BPCA-785]

*La Mer	Ventura CA
Gisela & Michael Baida	411 Poli St 93001
805-643-3600	

California

Rates:	Pvt Bath 5	Payment Terms:
Single	$ 80.00	Check
Double	$ 110.00	AE/MC/V

Authentic c1890 Victorian with hillside locale offering splendid ocean views and a historic landmark now. Just three blocks from the beach. The restored guest rooms are decorated with family touches and handicrafts or lounge in the pleasant yard and gardens. Sumptuous Bavarian breakfast is included with fresh fruits, Black Forest ham, homemade sweet rolls or other fresh pastries. **RESERVATIONS:** Two night stay on weekends **BROCHURE:** Yes **PERMITTED:** Children 14-up **LANGUAGES:** German, Spanish [E11ACCA-787]

**Coleens California Casa			**Whittier CA**
Coleen Davis			PO Box 9302 90608
310-699-8427			Res Times 7am-7pm

Rates:	Pvt Bath 3	Shared Bath 1	Payment Terms:
Single	$ 60.00	$ 55.00	Check
Double	$ 65.00	$ 60.00	

Come to the top of the hill and find your own quiet paradise. This home is located less than five minutes from #605 Freeway and is near #5 and #60 highways, yet seems to be in a rural area. The quiet peacefulness is enhanced by the luxuriant patio where you may enjoy the sunshine along with a full breakfast prepared by your *home economist hostess.* Other meals available with prior arrangement and nominal fee. She will direct you to the nearby Disneyland, Knott's Berry Farm and other Los Angeles attractions. Accommodations include: (a) large king size bed with electric adjustment and extra large PB, with private entrance and (b) two extra long twin bed with PB, (c) double bed with private entrance and SD and (d) extra long twin bed with PB. After your sightseeing, enjoy wine and cheese as the sun sets and the lights of the city flicker from below. The view from the deck is enchanting. You may dine here with previous arrangements. Well-behaved children over 12 are welcome. This home is near tennis, is excellent for jogging and is five minutes to Whittier College. Excellent hiking is found in the canyon nearby. *Home is thirty minutes east of LA in a quiet, uncongested and historic Quaker Town.* **RESERVATIONS:** Payment by check in advance to guarantee reservation **BROCHURE:** Yes **PERMITTED:** Children, drinking, smoking outdoors only **AIRPORT:** LAX, Ontario, Long Beach **CONFERENCE:** Yes, large patio and deck with chairs and seating **LANGUAGES:** Spanish [Z08GPCA2-2929]

California

Oak Meadows, too	Yosemite CA

Don & Francie Starchman
209-742-6161   **Res Times** 4pm-9pm

Rates: **Pvt Bath** 6   **Payment Terms:**
Single $ 59.00   Check
Double $ 58-89.00   MC/V

Refer to the same listing name under Mariposa CA for a complete description. [M11BCCA-9461]

Burgundy House	Yountville CA

Denna Roque   6711 Washington St 94599
707-944-0899   **Res Times** 7am-9pm

Rates: **Pvt Bath** 5   **Payment Terms:**
Single $ 105.00   Check
Double $ 120.00

Originally a brandy distillery, this c1870 structure is solidly built with 22" thick walls of local fieldstone and river-rock well combined in harmonious manner to bring comfort and warmth to guests. You are in a choice location of the famous Napa Valley, ideally located for exploring the magnificent wine growing region. Terraced mountains with Reisling and Chardonnay grapes are close by and closer yet, you'll find shade and privacy in our sheltered garden where roses bloom profusely. The rustic character of the residence is complimented by antique country furniture, comfortable beds, and colorful quilts. Fresh flowers and a decanter of local wine greet all guests. Full breakfast is included buffet-style and includes cereals, juice, coffee, tea, pastries and muffins, fresh fruits as-well-as egg dishes or casseroles enjoyed indoors or in the outdoor garden area for the perfect beginning of your day. Local activities include: wine tasting, bicycling, ballooning and plenty of sight-seeing. **RESERVATIONS:** First night's deposit to hold reservation, 2 night min on weekends, 5-day cancellation notice for refund less a $15.00 handling charge, check-in 2:00pm **BROCHURE:** Yes **PERMITTED:** Drinking **LANGUAGES:** German [A07GPCA2-801]

Oleander House	Yountville CA

John & Louise Packard   7433 St Helena Way 94599
800-788-3057 707-944-8315

Rates: **Pvt Bath** 5   **Payment Terms:**
Single $ 115-150.00   Check
Double $ 115-150.00   MC/V

©*Bed & Breakfast Guest Houses & Inns of America, Memphis TN*

California

Country French two-story home featured in the *New York Times*, combines the best of old world design with modern amenities and is located at the entrance to the spectacular and unique Napa Valley, midway between the champagne cellars of Domaine Chandon and the Robert Mondavi Winery! Guests enjoy the spacious high-ceiling rooms with private balconies offering beautiful valley views, full private baths with gleaming solid brass fixtures and pedestal sinks, cozy wood-burning fireplaces, comfortable queen-size beds, antiques and Laura Ashley wallcoverings and fabrics. Fresh-brewed coffee beckons guests to the large dining room furnished with antiques and fine art each morning to enjoy a full complimentary breakfast. Daily activities could include soaring over the valley in hot air balloons, gliders or helicopters; luxuriating in the mineral spas with mudbaths and massages, golf, tennis, horse back riding, cycling; delightful shopping and fine dining at the numerous excellent restaurants. Upon your return, you can relax on the patio and sample a complimentary soft drink or brandy, while the sun set dances over the distant mountain tops . . . enjoying the delightful fragrance of star jasmine blending into the cool evening breeze. **AIRPORT:** San Francisco or Oakland-70 mi **RESERVATIONS:** One night's deposit by credit card required, 7 day cancel policy, two night min on weekends & holidays. **BROCHURE:** Yes **PERMITTED:** Drinking **CONFERENCES:** Small meetings for 10-12 persons **LANGUAGES:** Some Japanese [Z05FPCA2-804]

California

Ahwahnee
OL-NIP GOLD TOWN
209-683-2155

Alameda
*GARRATT MANSION
415-521-4779

*WEBSTER HOUSE
415-523-9697

Albion
ALBION RIVER INN
707-937-1919

**FENSALDEN INN
707-937-4042

WOOL LOFT
707-937-0377

Alleghany
*KENTON MINE
LODGE
916-287-3212

Alpine
CEDAR CREEK INN
619-445-9605

Alturas
DORRIS HOUSE B&B
916-233-3786

Amador City
*CULBERTH HOUSE
209-267-0440

IMPERIAL HOTEL
800-242-5594

*MINE HOUSE INN
209-267-5900

Anaheim
ANAHEIM B&B
714-533-1884

**ANAHEIM
COUNTRY INN
800-755-7801

Anderson
PLANTATION HOUSE
800-950-2827

Angels Camp
COOPER HOUSE B&B
209-736-2145

UTICA MANSION INN
209-736-4209

Angelus Oaks
WHISPERING PINES
909-794-2962

Angwin
BIG YELLOW
SUNFLOWER B&B
707-965-3885

*FOREST MANOR
707-965-3538

Aptos
APPLE LANE INN
408-475-6868

**BAYVIEW HOTEL
B&B
408-688-8654

*MANGELS HOUSE
408-688-7982

Aquanga
CHIHUAHUA VALLEY
INN

Arcata
LADY ANNE
VICTORIAN INN
707-822-2797

PLOUGH AND THE
STARS
707-822-8236

Arnold
LODGE AT MANUEL
MILL B&B
209-795-2622

Arroyo Grande
**ARROYO VILLAGE
INN
805-489-5926

GUEST HOUSE
805-481-9304

*ROSE VICTORIAN
INN
805-481-5566

Aspen
LAZY 7 GUEST
RANCH

Auburn
*DRY CREEK INN
916-878-0885

*LINCOLN HOUSE
916-885-8880

POWERS MANSION
916-885-1166

VICTORIAN HILL
HOUSE
916-885-5879

Avalon
*GARDEN HOUSE
310-510-0356

GLENMORE PLAZA
HOTEL
800-4-CATALA

California

*GULL HOUSE
310-510-2547

HOTEL ST LAUREN
310-510-2299

HOTEL VILLA
PORTOFINO
310-510-0555

ISLAND INN

MAVILLA INN
310-510-1651

OLD TURNER INN
310-510-2236

SEACREST INN
310-510-0196

ZANE GREY PUEBLO
HOTEL
310-510-0966

Avila Beach
SAN LUIS BAY INN
805-595-2333

Bakersfield
*HELEN K B&B
805-325-5451

Ballard
BALLARD INN
805-688-7770

Bass Lake
DUCEYS ON THE
LAKE
805-528-3098

Baywood Park
**BAYWOOD B&B INN
805-528-8888

Ben Lomond

*CHATEAU DES
FLEURS
408-336-8943

*FAIRVIEW MANOR
408-336-3355

Benicia
*CAPT DILLINGHAMS
800-544-2278

CAPT WALSH HOME
707-747-5653

*UNION HOTEL
707-746-0100

Berkeley
B&B ACCOMMODA-
TION IN BERKELEY
510-548-7556

FLOWER GARDEN
B&B
510-644-9530

FRENCH HOTEL
510-548-9930

GRAMMA'S INN
510-549-2145

HILLEGASS HOUSE
510-548-5517

VICTORIAN HOTEL
510-540-0700

Big Bear
*EAGLES NEST
909-866-6465

Big Bear City
**GOLD MOUNTAIN
MANOR
909-585-6997

Big Bear Lake
CATHYS COUNTRY
COTTAGE
800-544-7454

KNICKERBOCKER
MANSION
909-866-8221

MOONRIDGE MANOR
909-585-0457

WAINWRIGHT INN
909-585-6914

Big Bend
ROYAL GORGES
RAINBOW LODGE
916-426-3661

Big Sur
DEETJENS BIG SUR
INN
408-667-2377

LUCIA LODGE
408-667-2391

POST RANCH INN
800-527-2200

VENTANA INN

Bishop
CHALFANT HOUSE
619-872-1790

*MATLICK HOUSE
619-873-3133

Blairsden
ELWELL LAKES
LODGE
916-836-2347

GRAEAGLE LODGE
916-836-2511

©Bed & Breakfast Guest Houses & Inns of America, Memphis TN

California

Blue Jay
*EAGLES LANDING
909-336-2642

Bodega
*SCHOOL HOUSE INN
707-876-3257

*TAYLORS ESTERO
VISTA INN
707-876-3300

Bodega Bay
BAY HILL MANSION
707-875-3577

BODEGA HARBOR
INN
707-875-3594

SEA HORSE GUEST
RANCH
707-875-2721

Bolinas
BLUE HERON INN
415-868-1102

BOLINAS VILLA
415-868-1650

GARDEN PUMP
HOUSE
415-868-0243

RITAS B&B
415-868-0113

STAR ROUTE INN
415-868-2502

THOMAS WHITE
HOUSE INN
415-868-0279

WHARF ROAD B&B
415-868-1430

Bonita
*BURLEY RANCH
619-479-9838

Booneville
ANDERSON CREEK
707-895-3091

*BEAR WALLOW
RESORT
707-895-3335

*TOLL HOUSE INN
707-895-3630

Boonville
BOONVILLE HOTEL
707-895-2210

COLFAXS GUEST
HOUSE
707-895-3241

FURTADOS
HIDEAWAY
707-895-3630

Brentwood
DIABLO VISTA B&B
415-634-2396

Bridgeport
BRIDGEPORT HOTEL
619-932-7380

**CAIN HOUSE
800-433-CAIN

Burbank
BELAIR
818-848-9227

Burlingame
BURLINGAME B&B
415-344-5815

SISTER MOON INN

Calistoga
*BRANNAN
COTTAGE INN
707-942-4200

CALISTOA COUNTRY
LODGE
707-942-5555

CALISTOGA INN
800-845-3632

CALISTOGA
WAYSIDE INN
707-942-0645

*CHRISTOPHERS
INN
707-942-5755

*CULVERS,
A COUNTRY INN
707-942-4535

*FOOTHILL HOUSE
707-942-6933

GOLDEN HAVEN
HOT SPRINGS
707-942-6793

HIDEAWAY
COTTAGES
707-942-4108

HILLCREST B&B
707-942-6334

LA CHAUMIERE
707-942-5139

LARKMEAD
COUNTRY INN
707-942-5360

LE SPA FRANCAIS
707-942-4636

©Bed & Breakfast Guest Houses & Inns of America, Memphis TN   141

California

MEADOWLARK
COUNTRY HOUSE
707-942-5651

MOUNT VIEW HOTEL
707-942-6877

MOUNTAIN HOME
RANCH
707-942-6616

OLD TOLL ROAD INN

PINE STREET INN
707-942-6829

*QUAIL MOUNTAIN
B&B
707-942-0316

REBECCA'S SHADOW
OF CALISTOGA
707-942-9463

*SCARLETTS
COUNTRY
707-942-6669

*SILVER ROSE INN
707-942-9581

**THE ELMS B&B
INN
800-235-4316

**THE PINK
MANSION
800-238-7465

*TRAILSIDE INN
707-942-4106

WASHINGTON ST
LODGING
707-942-6968

*WINE WAY INN

707-942-0680

**WISHING WELL INN
707-942-5534

ZINFANDEL HOUSE
707-942-0733

Cambria
*BEACH HOUSE
800-549-6789

BLUE WHALE INN
805-927-4647

CAMBRIA LANDING
805-927-1619

CAMBRIA PINES BY
THE SEAS
805-927-4200

HOMESTAY

*OLALLIEBERRY INN
805-927-3222

*PATRICK, J HOUSE
805-927-3812

*PICKFORD HOUSE
805-927-8619

Camino
SEVEN MILE HOUSE
916-644-7740

Capistrano Beach
CAPISTRANO
EDGEWATER INN
714-240-0150

COUNTRY BAY INN
714-496-6656

Capitola
INN AT DEPOT HILL

408-462-3376

Capitola Valley
SUMMER HOUSE
408-475-8474

Cardiff By the Sea
CARDIFF BY THE SEA

WHALE HOUSE
619-942-1503

Carlsbad
PELICAN COVE INN
619-434-5995

Carmel
CANDLE LIGHT INN
408-624-6451

*CARRIAGE HOUSE
INN
800-433-4732

COACHMANS INN
800-336-6421

*COBBLESTONE INN
800-833-8836

COLONIAL TERRACE
INN
408-624-2741

CYPRESS INN
408-624-3871

DOLPHIN INN
408-624-5356

FOREST LODGE
408-624-7023

GROSNEVOR'S
GARDEN
408-624-3190

California

HAPPY LANDING INN
408-624-7917

HIGHLANDS INN
408-624-3801

HOFSAS HOUSE
800-421-0000

HOLIDAY HOUSE
408-624-6267

HOMESTEAD
408-624-4119

HOUSE OF ENGLAND
408-624-3004

LINCOLN GREEN INN
800-262-1262

MARTIN HOUSE B&B
408-624-2232

MISSION RANCH
800-538-8821

*MONTE VERDE INN
800-328-7707

NORMANDY INN

SAN ANTONIO
HOUSE
408-624-4334

SANDPIPER INN AT THE BEACH
800-633-6433 (CA)
408-624-6433

SEA VIEW INN
408-624-8778

*STONEHOUSE INN
800-544-9183

STONEPINE ESTATE
RESORT
408-659-2245

SUNDIAL LODGE
408-624-8578

SUNSET HOUSE
408-624-4884

SVENDSGAARDS INN
408-624-1511

TALLY HO INN
408-624-2232

TICKLE PINK INN
408-624-1244

VAGABONDS HOUSE
800-262-1262

WAYFARER INN

WAYSIDE INN
408-624-5336

Carmel Calley
LOS LAURELES
LODGE
408-659-2233

Carmel Valley
ROBLES del RIO LODGE
800-883-0843

VALLEY LODGE
408-659-2261

Carmel-by-the Sea
*GREEN LANTERN
INN
408-624-4392

PINE INN
800-228-3851

SAN CARLOS LODGE
800-831-3008

Carpinteria
*D&B SCHROEDER
RANCH
805-684-1579

Castro Valley
LORES HAUS
415-781-1553

Catalina Island
*INN ON MT ADA
310-510-2030

SAND CASTLE B&B
310-510-0682

Catheys Valley
CHIBCHAS INN
209-966-2940

Cazadero
CAZANOMA LODGE
707-632-5225

TEN AKER WOOD
707-632-5328

TIMBERHILL RANCH
707-847-3258

Chatsworth
OAKRIDGE MANOR
818-998-7547

Chester
BIDWELL HOUSE
916-258-3338

BULLARD HOUSE
916-342-5912

Chico
MUSIC EXPRESS INN
916-345-8376

©Bed & Breakfast Guest Houses & Inns of America, Memphis TN   143

California

O'FLAHERTY HOUSE
916-893-5494

PALMS OF CHICO
916-343-6868

Chula Vista
BROOKSIDE FARM
619-421-8698

Clearlake
*MUKTIP MANOR
707-994-9571

Cloverdale
ABRAMS HOUSE INN
707-894-2412

VINTAGE TOWERS
707-894-4535

YE OLDE SHELFORD HOUSE
800-833-6479

Colfax
BEAR RIVER MTN FARM
916-878-8314

Coloma
*COLOMA COUNTRY INN
916-622-1225

VINEYARD HOUSE
916-622-2217

Columbia
COLUMBIA CITY HOTEL
209-532-1479

Colusa
*O ROURKE MANSION
916-458-5625

Coronado
CORONADO VILLAGE
619-435-9318

VICTORIAN HOUSE 1894-DANCE STUDIO
619-435-2200

Coto De Caza
STRATTONS INN ON THE CREEK
714-858-0503

Coulterville
JEFFREY HOTEL
209-878-3417

SHERLOCK HOLMES
800-354-5679

Crescent City
PEBBLE BEACH B&B
707-464-9086

Crescent Mills
CRESCENT HOTEL
916-284-9905

Crest Park
BRACKEN FERN MANOR
909-337-2055

Crowley Lake
RAINBOW TARMS
619-935-4556

Dana Point
BLUE LANTERN INN
800-234-1425

Davenport
NEW DAVENPORT B&B
408-425-1818

Davis

UNIVERSITY INN
916-756-UNIV

Death Valley
FURNACE CREEK RESORT
619-786-2345

Del Mar
BLUE DOOR
619-755-3819

*GULLS NEST
619-259-4863

*ROCK HAUS
619-481-3764

Desert Hot Springs
TRAVELERS REPOSE
619-329-9584

Dinsmore
DINSMORE LODGE
707-574-6466

Dinuba
AGUS RANCH
310-591-6617

Dorrington
DORRINGTON
209-795-5800

Dorris
HOSPITALITY INN
916-397-2097

Downieville
SIERRA SHANGRI LA
916-289-3455

Dulzura
*BROOKSIDE FARM
619-468-3043

Dunsmuir

California

DUNSMUIR INN
916-235-4534

El Cerrito
DOLPHIN B&B
510-527-9622

Elk
ELK COVE INN
707-877-3321

GREEN DOLPHIN INN
707-877-3342

GREENWOOD PIER INN
707-877-9997

GRIFFIN HOUSE
707-877-3422

HARBOR HOUSE
707-877-3203

SANDPIPER HOUSE INN
707-877-3587

Elkcreek
STONY CREEK RETREAT
800-643-7183

Encinitas
INNCLINE B&B
619-944-0318

Escondido
*HALBIGS HACIENDA
619-745-1296

Eureka
A WEAVERS INN
707-443-8119

CAMELLIA COTTAGE
707-445-1089

CARTER HOTEL
415-444-8062

*CARTER HOUSE
707-445-1390

DALY INN
800-321-9656

*EAGLE HOUSE INN
707-442-2334

AN ELEGANT VICTORIAN MANSION
707-444-3144

HEUERS VICTORIAN INN
707-445-7334

HOLLANDER HOUSE
707-443-2419

*HOTEL CARTER**
707-444-8062

IRIS INN
707-445-0307

*OLD TOWN B&B INN
800-331-5098

SHANNON HOUSE
707-443-8130

Fallbrook
LA ESTANCIA INN
619-723-2888

Fawnskin
INN AT FAWNSKIN
909-866-3200

Ferndale
*FERNDALE INN
707-786-4307

FREITAS HOUSE INN
707-786-4000

GINGERBREAD MANSION
800-952-4136

SHAW HOUSE INN
707-786-9958

Fish Camp
KAREN'S YOSEMITE INN
800-346-1443

NARROW GAUGE INN
209-683-7720

Folsom
FOLSOM HOTEL

PLUM TREE INN
916-351-1541

Fort Bidwell
*FORT BIDWELL HOTEL
916-279-6199

Fort Bragg
AVALON HOUSE
707-964-5555

BLUE ROSE INN
707-964-3477

CLEONE LODGE
707-964-2788

COLONIAL INN
707-964-9979

*COUNTRY INN
707-964-3737

GLASS BEACH B&B

©*Bed & Breakfast Guest Houses & Inns of America, Memphis TN*   145

California

707-964-6774

GREY WHALE INN
800-382-7244

JUG HANDLE INN
707-964-1415

NOYO RIVER LODGE
800-628-1126

OCEANVIEW LODGE
707-964-1951

ORCA INN
707-964-5585

PINE BEACH INN
707-964-5603

PUDDING CREEK INN
800-227-9529

RIVERVIEW HOUSE
707-964-5236

ROUNDHEDGE INN
707-964-9605

Freestone
GREEN APPLE INN
707-874-2526

Fremont
*LORD BRADLEY'S INN
415-490-0520

MARGOT'S CONTINENTAL LODGE
415-657-8862

Fresno
VICTORIAN
209-233-1988

Garberville
BENBOW INN
707-923-2124

RANCH HOUSE
707-923-3441

Garden Grove
HIDDEN VALLEY B&B
714-636-8312

Gasquet
PATRICK CREEK LODGE
Idw-Idwld Op

Georgetown
*HIST AMERICAN RIVER
800-245-6566

Geyserville
CAMPBELL RANCH INN
707-857-3476

*ISIS OASIS LODGE
707-857-3524

Gilroy
COUNTRY ROSE INN
408-842-0441

Glen Ellen
*GAIGE HOUSE
707-935-0237

*GLENELLY INN
707-966-6720

JACK LONDON LODGE
707-938-8501

JVB VINEYARD
707-966-4533

STONE TREE RANCH
707-996-8173

TANGLEWOOD HOUSE
707-996-5021

TOP O'THE WORLD LODGE
707-938-4671

Glendale
SHROFF B&B HOME
818-507-0774

Glenhaven
KRISTALBERG B&B
707-274-8009

Goleta
CIRCLE BAR B RANCH
805-968-1113

Grass Valley
*ANNIE HORANS
916-272-2418

*DOMIKES INN
916-273-9010

GOLDEN ORE HOUSE B&B
916-272-6870

*HOLBROOKE & PURCELL HOUSE
916-273-1353

*MURPHYS INN
916-273-6873

*SWAN LEVINE HOUSE
916-272-1873

Green Valley Lake

146 ©Bed & Breakfast Guest Houses & Inns of America, Memphis TN

California

SERENITY SUMMIT
909-867-4109

Gridley
MC CRACKEN'S INN
916-846-2108

Groveland
GROVELAND HOTEL
800-273-3314

HOTEL CHARLOTTE
209-962-6455

Gualala
GUALALA HOTEL
707-884-3441

NORTH COAST COUNTRY INN
800-959-4537

OLD MILANO HOTEL
707-884-3256

SAINT ORRES
707-884-3303

WHALE WATCH BY THE SEA
800-942-5342

Guerneville
CAMELOT RESORT
707-869-2538

*CREEKSIDE INN
800-776-6586

*ESTATE
707-869-9093

FERN GROVE INN
800-347-9083

*RIDENHOUR RANCH HOUSE
707-887-1033

RIVER LANE RESORT
707-869-2323

*SANTA NELLA HOUSE
707-869-9488

WILLOWS
707-869-3279

Half Moon Bay
CYPRESS INN
800-83-BEACH

HALF MOON BAY B&B

LITTLE CREEK MANSION
415-747-0810

*MILL ROSE
800-829-1794

OLD THYME INN
415-726-1616

SAN BENITO HOUSE
415-726-3425

ZABALLA HOUSE B&B
800-77B NB4U

Hanford
IRWIN STREET INN
209-583-8791

Healdsburg
*BELLE DE JOUR INN
707-431-9777

*CAMELLIA INN
800-727-8182

FRAMPTON HOUSE
707-433-5084

GEORGE ALEXANDER HOUSE
707-433-1358

*GRAPE LEAF INN
707-433-8140

*HAYDON HOUSE
707-433-5228

HEALDSBURG INN ON PLAZA
707-433-6991

L'AUBERGE DU SAN SOUCI
707-431-1110

LYTTON SPRINGS INN
707-431-1109

*MADRONA MANOR
800-258-4003

*RAFORD HOUSE
707-887-9573

Helena
MEADOWOOD RESORT
707-963-4602

Helmet
GRACIOUS ENGLISH MANOR
909-625-0555

Hollywood
CHATEAU MARMONT
213-656-1010

Homewood
ROCKWOOD

California

LODGE
800-LE TAHOE

Hope Valley
SORENSENS RESORT
800-423-9949

Hopland
HOPLAND HOUSE
707-744-1404

Idyllwild
SILVER PINES LODGE
909-659-4335

STRAWBERRY CREEK INN
909-659-3202

WILKUM INN B&B
909-659-4087

Independence
WINNEDUMAH COUNTRY INN

Inverness
ALDER HOUSE B&B
415-669-7218

*ARK
415-663-9338

*BLACKTHORNE INN
415-663-8621

DANCING COYOTE BEACH
415-669-7200

FAIRWINDS FARM B&B
415-663-9454

GRAY WHALE UPSTAIRS
415-669-1330

INVERNESS VALLEY INN
415-669-7250

MACLEAN HOUSE
415-669-7392

MANKAS INVERNESS LODGE
415-669-1034

MOORINGS
415-669-1464

ROSEMARY COTTAGE
415-663-9338

SANDY COVE INN
415-669-1233

*TEN INVERNESS WAY
415-669-1648

TREE HOUSE
415-663-8720

Ione
*HEIRLOOM
209-274-4468

Isleton
DELTA DAZE INN
916-777-7777

Jackson
ANN MARIES COUNTRY INN
800-729-4287

BROADWAY HOTEL
209-223-3503

COURT STREET INN
209-223-0416

*GATE HOUSE INN
209-223-3500

*WEDGEWOOD INN
800-933-4393

WINDROSE INN
209-223-3650

Jamestown
JAMESTOWN HOTEL
209-984-3902

*NATIONAL HOTEL
209-984-3446

PALM HOTEL
209-984-3429

ROYAL HOTEL
209-984-5271

SHEETS N'EGGS B&B
209-984-0915

Jamul
LIONS HEAD INN
619-463-4271

Jenner
**MURPHYS JENNER INN
800-732-2377

SALT POINT LODGE
707-847-3234

SEA COAST HIDEAWAYS
707-847-3278

STILLWATER COVE RANCH
707-847-3277

TIMBER COVE INN

California

Julian
BUTTERFIELD B&B
619-765-2179

CAROLE'S PLACE
619-765-0251

FAIR OAKS B&B
619-765-0704

*JULIAN GOLD RUSH HOTEL
619-765-0201

JULIAN LODGE
619-765-1420

JULIAN WHITE HOUSE
619-765-1764

MOUNTAINSIDE
619-765-1295

PINE HILLS LODGE
619-765-1100

PINECROFT MANOR
619-765-1611

SHADOW MOUNTAIN LODGE
619-765-0323

VILLA IDALEEN
619-765-1252

Kelsey
MOUNTAINSIDE B&B
916-626-0983

Kernville
**KERN RIVER INN B&B
619-376-6750

Kingsburg

KINGSBURG SWEDISH INN
209-897-1022

Klamath
REQUA INN
707-482-8205

Knights Ferry
*KNIGHTS FERRY HOTEL
209-881-3271

Kyburz
STRAWBERRY LODGE
916-659-7200

La Jolla
*B&B INN AT LA JOLLA
619-456-2066

IRISH COTTAGE
619-454-6075

PROSPECT PARK INN
800-433-1609

SCRIPPS INN
619-454-3391

La Porte
LOST SIERRA INN
916-675-2525

Lafayette
DONNER COUNTRY INN
916-547-5574

Laguna Beach
**CARRIAGE HOUSE
714-494-8945

*CASA LAGUNA INN
800-233-0449

*EILERS INN
714-494-3004

HOTEL CALIFORNIA
714-497-1457

HOTEL FIRENZE
714-497-2446

INN AT LAGUNA BEACH
714-494-7535

**LAGUNA PACIFICA
800-383-3513

SPRAY CLIFF
714-499-4022

Lake Arrowhead
BLUEBELLE HOUSE
909-336-3292

CARRIAGE HOUSE B&B
909-336-1400

CHATEAU DUE LAC
909-337-6488

LAKEVIEW LODGE
909-337-6633

*SADDLEBACK INN
909-336-3571

Lake Elsinore
DEBORAHS B&B

Lakeport
FORBESTOWN INN
707-263-7858

Leggett
BELL GLEN RESORT
707-925-6425

©Bed & Breakfast Guest Houses & Inns of America, Memphis TN

California

Lemon Cove
LEMON COVE B&B
209-597-2555

Little River
FOOLS RUSH INN
707-937-5339

GLENDEVEN
707-937-0083

HERITAGE HOUSE
707-937-5885

LITTLE RIVER INN

Lodi
*WINE & ROSES
COUNTRY INN
209-334-6988

Long Beach
APPLETON PLACE
B&B 310-432-2312

CRANES NEST
310-435-4084

LORD MAYOR'S INN
310-436-0324

SEASHORE MANOR

Los Alamos
UNION HOTEL
805-344-2744

Los Angeles
CALIFORNIA HOME
HOSPITALITY
213-390-1526

CENTURY CITY INN

*CHANNEL ROAD INN
310-459-1920

*EASTLAKE
VICTORIAN
213-250-1620

HERB GARDEN B&B
213-465-0827

LAGUNA PACIFICA
800-383-3513

SALISBURY HOUSE
800-373-1778

SOLVANG CASTLE
INN
805-688-9338

***TERRACE MANOR**
213-381-1478

WEST ADAMS B&B
213-737-5041

Los Banos
MERCY HOT SPRINGS

Los Gatos
COURTSIDE
408-395-7111

LA HACIENDA INN
408-354-9230

Los Olivos
COUNTRY COTTAGE
805-688-1395

LOS OLIVOS GRAND
HOTEL
800-446-2455

RED ROOSTER
RANCH
805-688-8050

ZACA LAKE
805-688-4891

Los Osos
BAYVIEW HOUSE
805-528-3098

GERALDAS B&B
805-528-3973

Lotus
GOLDEN LOTUS
916-621-4562

Lower Lake
*BIG CANYON INN
707-928-5631

SWISS CHALET
707-994-7313

Loyalton
*CLOVER VALLEY
MILL HOUSE
916-993-4819

Malibu
*CASA LARRONDE
310-456-9333

MALIBU COUNTRY
CLUB
310-457-9622

Malibu Hills
**STALLUP HOUSE
800-383-3513

Mammoth Lakes
JAGERHOF LODGE
619-934-6162

*SNOW GOOSE INN
800-874-7368

TAMARACK LODGE
619-934-2442

Mariposa
BOULDER CREEK

California

B&B
209-742-7729

CHALET ON THE
MOUNT
209-966-5115

DICK & SHIRLS B&B
209-966-2514

DUBORDS RESTFUL
NEST
209-742-7127

FITCH HAVEN
209-966-4738

*GRANNYS GARDEN
209-377-8342

*MEADOW CREEK
RANCH & B&B
800-955-8843

**OAK MEADOWS,
too**
209-742-6161

*PELENNOR B&B AT
BOOTJACK
209-966-2832

SCHLAGETER HOUSE
209-966-2471

VISTA GRANDE B&B
209-742-6206

WINSOR FARMS B&B
209-966-5592

Mc Cloud
FRANCOIS' GREY
SQUIRREL INN
916-964-3105

JOANIES B&B

916-964-3160

MCCLOUD GUEST
HOUSE
916-964-3160

STONEY BROOK INN
916-369-6118

Mendocino
1021 MAIN ST GUEST
HOUSE
707-937-5150

AGATE COVE INN
800-527-3111

AMES LODGE
707-937-0811

BIG RANCH INN
707-937-5322

BIG RIVER LODGE
707-937-5615

BLACKBERRY INN
707-937-5281

BLUE HERON INN
707-937-4323

BREWERY GULCH
INN
707-937-4752

CYPRESS HOUSE
707-937-1456

GREY WHALE INN
800-382-7244

HEADLANDS INN
707-937-4431

HILL HOUSE
707-937-0554

**JOHN
DOUGHERTY HOUSE**
707-937-5266

JOSHUA GRINDLE
INN
707-937-4143

KELLYS ATTIC
707-937-5588

*MACCALLUM
HOUSE
707-937-0289

MAMA MOON
GARDENS
707-937-4234

MENDOCINO BAY
TRADING CO
707-937-5266

*MENDOCINO FARM
HOUSE
707-937-0241

MENDOCINO HOTEL
707-937-0511

*MENDOCINO
VILLAGE INN
707-937-0246

OSPREY HILL
707-937-4493

RACHEL'S INN
707-937-0088

SEA GULL INN
707-937-5204

SEA ROCK
707-937-5517

SEARS HOUSE INN

©*Bed & Breakfast Guest Houses & Inns of America, Memphis TN*   151

California

707-937-4076

SS SEAFOAM LODGE
707-937-1827

*STANFORD INN BY
THE SEA
800-331-8884

STEVENSWOOD
LODGE
800-421-2810

WHITEGATE INN
707-937-4892

Middletown
BROOKHILL INN
707-928-5029

*HARBIN HOT
SPRINGS
707-987-2477

NETHERCOTT INN
707-987-3362

Midpines
HAPPY MEDIUM
209-742-6366

HOMESTEAD GUEST
RANCH
209-966-2820

SIERRA B&B
209-966-5478

Mill Creek
ST BERNARD LODGE

Mill Valley
MOUNTAIN HOME
415-381-9000

SYCAMORE HOUSE
415-383-0612

Mokelumne Hill
HOTEL LEGER
209-286-1401

Montara
FARALLONE HOTEL
415-728-7817

**GOOSE &
TURRETS
415-728-5451

MONTARA B&B
415-728-3946

Monte Rio
HIGHLAND DELL INN
800-767-1759

*HUCKLEBERRY
SPRINGS
707-865-2683

RIO VILLA BEACH
RESORT
707-865-1143

VILLAGE INN
707-865-2304

Montecito
SAN YSIDRO RANCH
805-969-5046

Monterey
**BABBLING BROOK
INN
800-866-1131

CARTER ART
GALLERIES B&B
408-655-0177

*DEL MONTE BEACH
INN
800-727-4410

JABBERWOCK
408-372-4777

*MARTINE INN
800-852-5588

MERRITT HOUSE
408-646-9686

**MONTEREY
HOTEL (1904)
800-727-0960

OLD MONTEREY INN
408-375-8284

SPINDRIFT INN
408-646-8900

VICTORIAN INN
800-225-2902

Monterio
HOUSE OF 1000
FLOWERS
707-632-5511

Morgana
HALLMANS
415-376-4318

Moss Beach
SEAL COVE INN
415-728-7325

Mount Shasta
CAROLYN'S INN
TOWN
916-926-6078

**MT SHASTA
RANCH B&B
916-926-3870

*WARD'S BIGFOOT
RANCH
916-926-5170

California

Muir Beach
PELICAN INN
415-383-6000

Murphys
*DUNBAR HOUSE
B&B 1880
209-728-2897

MURPHYS HOTEL
209-728-3444

Napa
**ARBOR GUEST
HOUSE**
707-252-8144

*BEAZLEY HOUSE
707-257-1649

**BLUE VIOLET
MANSION**
707-257-8205

BOWEN MANOR

BROOKSIDE
VINEYARD
707-944-1661

CANDLELIGHT INN
707-257-3717

CEDAR GABLES INN
707-224-7969

CHATEAU
707-253-9300

**CHURCHILL
MANOR**
707-253-7733

CLARION INN
707-253-7433

COOMBS/INN THE

PARK B&B
707-257-0789

COUNTRY GARDEN
INN
707-255-1197

CROSS ROADS INN
707-944-0646

CRYSTAL ROSE
VICTORIAN INN
707-944-8185

ELM HOUSE
800-788-4356

*GALLERY OSGOOD
B&B INN
707-224-0100

*GOODMAN HOUSE
707-257-1166

*HENNESSEY HOUSE
707-226-3774

LA BELLE EPOQUE
707-257-2161

LA RESIDENCIA INN
707-253-0337

NAPA INN
707-257-1444

OAK KNOLL INN
707-255-2200

OAKVILLE RANCH
707-944-8612

*OLD WORLD INN
707-257-0112

ROCKHAVEN
707-944-2041

STAHLECKER
HOUSE
707-257-1588

*SYBRON HOUSE
707-944-2785

TALLL TIMBER
CHALETS
707-252-7810

VILLAGE INN
707-257-2089

YESTERHOUSE INN
707-257-0550

Napa Valley
*RANCHO CAYMUS
INN
707-963-1777

National City
DICKINSON/BOAL
MANSION
619-477-5363

Nevada City
DOWNEY HOUSE
800-258-2815

FLUMES END
916-265-9665

*GRANDMERES INN
916-265-4660

KENDALL HOUSE
916-265-0405

NATIONAL HOTEL
916-263-4551

PALLY PLACE
916-265-5427

*PARSONAGE

©Bed & Breakfast Guest Houses & Inns of America, Memphis TN

California

916-265-9478

*PIETY HILL INN
916-265-2245

**RED CASTLE INN,
HIST B&B
916-265-5135

Newcastle
VICTORIAN MANOR
916-663-3009

Newport Beach
**DAHL HOUSE
714-673-3479

DORYMANS INN
714-675-7300

*LITTLE INN ON THE
BAY
800-538-4466

*PORTIOFINO
HOTEL
714-673-7030

Nice
FEATHER BED
RAILROAD COMPANY
707-274-4434

Nipomo
LINANES
805-929-5444

Nipton
HOTEL NIPTON
619-856-2335

Norden
NORDEN HOUSE
916-426-3326

North Fork
YE OLDE SOUTH
FORK INN
209-877-7025

North Hollywood
LA MAIDA HOUSE
818-769-3857

Northridge
*HIDEAWAY HOUSE
818-349-5421

Oakhurst
CHATEAU DE
SUREAU
209-683-6860

Oakland
BEDSIDE MANOR
510-452-4550

**BOAT &
BREAKFAST USA
510-444-5858

ROCKRIDGE B&B
510-655-1223

WASHINGTON INN
510-452-1776

Occidental
HEART'S DESIRE INN
707-874-1311

Ojai
OJAI B&B
800-422-OJAI

OJAI MANOR HOTEL
805-646-0961

SALUBRIUM
805-649-4577

THEODORE
WOOLSEY HOUSE
805-646-9779

WHEELER HOT
SPRINGS

Olema
*BEAR VALLEY INN
415-663-1777

*OLEMA INN
415-663-9559

*POINT REYES
SEASHORE LODGE
415-663-9000

ROUNDSTONE FARM
415-663-1020

Olympic Valley
CHRISTY HILL INN
916-583-8551

DOLPHINS HOME
916-581-0501

Ontario
RED LION INN
909-983-0909

Orange
COUNTRY COMFORT
714-532-2802

Orinda
HEIDI HAUS
503-388-0850

Orland
INN AT SHALLOW
CREEK FARM
916-865-4093

STEARMAN HOUSE

Orosi
*VALLEY VIEW
CITRUS RANCH
209-528-2275

California

Oroville
JEANS RIVERSIDE
B&B
916-533-1413

SILVER HAVEN
HIDEAWAY
916-534-3344

Pacific Grove
**CENTRELLA B&B
INN**
800-233-3372

DOWN UNDER INN
408-373-2993

GATEHOUSE INN
800-753-1881

GOSBY HOUSE INN
408-375-1287

*GREEN GABLES INN
800-722-1774

LIGHTHOUSE LODGE
408-655-2111

**MAISON BLEUE
INN**
408-373-2993

MARTINE INN
800-852-5588

*OLD ST ANGELA INN
800-873-6523

PACIFIC GARDENS
INN
408-646-9414

*ROSEROX COUNTRY
INN
408-373-ROSE

*SEVEN GABLES INN
408-372-4341

Palm Springs
CASA CODY
800-231-CODY

GARBO INN
619-325-6737

HACIENDA LAS
PALMAS
619-325-6374

*INGLESIDE INN
619-325-0046

LE PETIT CHATEAU
619-325-2686

*PEPPER TREE INN
619-325-9124

RAFFLES PALM
SPRINGS
619-320-3949

SAKURA, JAPANESE
B&B INN
619-327-0705

SUNBEAM INN

*VILLA ROYALE
800-245-2314

Palo Alto
COWPER INN
415-327-4475

HOTEL CALIFORNIA
415-322-7666

*VICTORIAN ON
LYTTON
415-322-8555

Pasadena
DONNYMAC IRISH
INN
818-440-0066

Paso Robles
ALMOND VIEW INN
805-238-4220

ROSELEITH B&B
805-238-5848

Petaluma
7TH STREET INN
707-769-0480

CAVANAGH INN B&B
707-765-4657

Philo
PHILO POTTERY INN
707-895-3069

Piercy
HARTSOOK INN
707-247-3305

Pismo Beach
*PISMO LANDMARK
805-773-5566

Placerville
CHICHESTER
HOUSE
800-831-4008

FLEMING JONES
HOMESTEAD
916-626-5840

HIST COMBELLACK
BLAIR HOUSE
916-622-3764

JAMES BLAIR
HOUSE
916-626-6136

©Bed & Breakfast Guest Houses & Inns of America, Memphis TN

California

*RIVER ROCK INN
916-622-7640

RUPLEY HOUSE INN
916-626-0630

Pleasanton
PLUM TREE INN
415-426-9588

Plymouth
INDIAN CREEK
800-24-CREEK

SHENANDOAH INN
209-245-4491

Point Arena
COAST GUARD HOUSE
707-882-2442

POINT ARENA LIGHTHOUSE
707-882-2777

WAGNERS WINDHAVEN
707-884-4617

Point Reyes
BURGERS BEDS
415-663-1410

DRAKES COTTAGE
415-663-9373

HOLLY TREE INN
415-663-1554

INVERNESS PARK PLACE
415-663-9515

NEON ROSE
415-663-9143

*THIRTY NINE CYPRESS WAY
415-663-1709

TRADEWINDS
415-663-9326

Point Reyes Station
**CARRIAGE HOUSE
415-663-8627

COUNTRY HOUSE
415-663-1627

EUREKA HOUSE

FERRANDOS HIDEWAY
415-663-1966

GALLERY COTTAGE

HORSESHOE FARM COTTAGE
415-663-9401

*JASMINE COTTAGE
415-663-1166

KNOB HILL
415-663-1784

LONDON HOUSE
415-388-2487

MARSH COTTAGE
415-669-7168

WINDSONG COTTAGE
415-663-9695

Point Richmond
*EAST BROTHER LIGHT STATION
415-233-2385

Pope Valley
JAMES CREEK RANCH

Portola
UPPER FEATHER B&B
916-832-0107

Posey
ROADS END
805-536-8668

Princeton by the Sea
**PILLAR POINT INN
415-728-7377

Qunicy
*FEATHER BED
916-283-0102

Ranch Palos Verdes
BY THE SEA
310-377-2113

Rancho Cucamonga
*CHRISTMAS HOUSE B&B INN
909-980-6450

Rancho Santa Fe
THE INN

Red Bluff
BUTTONS & BOWS
916-527-6405

CARLSBAD GUEST RANCH
OP-OP #2

*FAULKNER HOUSE
916-529-0520

JARVIS MANSION
916-527-6901

California

JETER VICTORIAN INN
916-527-7574

Redding
CABRAL HOUSE ON CHESTNUT
916-244-3766

PALISADES PARADISE B&B
916-223-5305

REDDINGS B&B
916-223-2494

TIFFANY HOUSE B&B
916-244-3225

Redlands
GEORGIANNA MANOR
909-793-0423

MOREY MANSION B&B
909-793-7970

Redondo Beach
SEA BREEZE B&B
310-316-5123

Redwood City
VIRGINIA CITY RAIL COMPANY
415-369-5405

Redwood Valley
OLSON FARMHOUSE
707-485-7523

Reedley
HOTEL BURGESS
209-638-6315

REEDLEY COUNTRY INN
209-638-6333

Ridgecrest
*JERRYS B&B
916-446-3138

Riverside
NELLE LETHERS
714-683-3267

Running Springs
SPRING OAKS B&B
909-867-9636

Rutherford
AUBERGE DU SOLEIL
707-963-1211

Sacramento
AMBER HOUSE B&B
800-755-6526

*AUNT ABIGAILS B&B
800-848-1568

*BRIGGS HOUSE
916-441-3214

*DRIVER MANSION INN
916-455-5243

*HARTLEY HOUSE
916-447-STAY

RIVER ROSE, A COUNTRY INN
916-443-4248

RIVERBOAT DELTA KING
916-444-KING

STERLING HOTEL
800-365-7660

Saint Helena
*AMBROSE BIERCE HOUSE
707-963-3003

AUBERGE B RISEBOIS
707-963-4658

BALE MILL INN
707-963-4545

*BARTELS RANCH
800-932-4002

BELL CREEK B&B
707-963-2383

*BYLUND HOUSE B&B
707-963-9073

*CHESTLESON HOUSE
707-963-2238

CINNAMON BEAR B&B
707-963-4653

CREEKSIDE INN
707-963-7244

CREEKWOOD
707-963-8590

DEER RUN INN
800-843-3408

ELSIES CONN VALLEY INN
707-963-4614

ERIKAS HILLSIDE
707-963-2887

FARMHOUSE

California

707-963-3431

HARVEST INN
800-950-8466

HOTEL ST HELENA
707-963-4388

INK HOUSE B&B
707-963-3890

JUDY RANCH HOUSE
707-963-3081

*OLIVER HOUSE B&B

707-963-4089

PRAGER WINERY
B&B
707-963-3713

SHADY OAKS
COUNTRY INN
707-963-1190

*SPANISH VILLA
707-963-7483

TOLLERS GUEST
COTTAGE

TRUBODY RANCH
B&B
707-255-5907

VILLA ST HELENA
707-963-2514

*WHITE RANCH
707-693-4635

*WINE COUNTRY INN
800-473-3463

San Andreas
BLACK BART INN

COURTYARD B&B
209-754-1518

ROBINS NEST
209-754-1076

THORN MANSION
209-754-1027

San Clemente
CASA DE FLORES
B&B
619-498-1344

CASA TROPICANA
619-492-1234

JEANS RETREAT
619-492-1216

San Diego
ABIGAIL
619-583-4738

CAROLES B&B
619-280-5258

CASTAWAY INN
619-298-5432

COTTAGE
619-299-1564

**HARBOR HILL
GUEST HOUSE**
619-233-0638

HILL HOUSE B&B
619-239-4738

HORTON GRAND
800-999-1886

INN BY THE PARK
619-232-1253

*KEATING HOUSE

INN
619-239-8585

MONETS GARDEN
619-464-8296

QUINCE STEET
TROLLEY
619-422-7009

SHEPARDS
619-582-3972

SKYVIEW II
619-584-1548

**SURF MANOR
& COTTAGES**
619-225-9765

VERAS COZY COR-
NER
619-296-1938

San Francisco
1818 CALIFORNIA
415-885-1818

ABIGAIL HOTEL
800-243-6510

ADELAIDE INN
415-441-2261

*ALAMO SQUARE
INN
800-345-9888

ALBION HOUSE
415-621-0896

ALEXANDER INN

**AMSTERDAM
HOTEL**
800-637-3444

California

ANDREWS HOTEL
415-563-6877

ANSONIA B&B
415-672-2670

ARCHBISHOPS
MANSION
800-543-5820

**ART CENTER B&B
SUITES**
415-567-1526

AURORA MANOR
415-564-2400

B&B INN
415-921-9784

B&B NEAR THE PARK
415-753-3574

**BABBLING BROOK
INN**
800-866-1131

BOCKS B&B
415-664-6842

CAROUSEL B&B

CASA ARGUELLO
415-752-9482

CHATEAU TIVOLI
800-227-1647

CLEMENTINAS BAY
BRICK
415-431-8334

COMMODORE INTL
415-885-2464

DOLORES PARK INN
415-621-0482

*ED & MONICA
WIDBURG

*EDWARD II INN
800-GREATINN

FAY MANSION INN
415-921-1816

FORDS B&B
602-776-1564

FOUR SISTERS INN
415-775-6698

*FRIENDLY B&B INN
415-622-9876

GARDEN STUDIO
415-753-3574

*GOLDEN
GATE HOTEL
800-835-1118

**GOOSE &
TURRETS**
415-728-5451

GROVE INN
800-829-0780

HAUS KLEEBAUER
415-821-3866

*HYDE PARK SUITES
415-771-0200

*INN -
SAN FRANCISCO
800-359-0913

INN AT THE OPERA
415-753-3574

INN AT UNION
SQUARE

800-288-4346

*INN ON CASTRO
415-861-0321

JACKSON COURT
415-929-7670

KENSINGTON
PARKLE
PETIT MANOIR
415-864-7232

MAJESTIC
415-441-1100

MARINA INN
415-928-1000

MILLEFIORI INN
415-433-9111

MOFFATT HOUSE
415-661-6210

*MONTE CRISTO
415-931-1875

*NO NAME
VICTORIAN B&B
415-931-3083

NOB HILL
LAMBOURNE
415-433-2287

NOLAN HOUSE
800-736-6526

OBRERO HOTEL
415-989-3960

PACIFIC BAY INN
800-445-2631

PACIFIC HEIGHTS
INN

©Bed & Breakfast Guest Houses & Inns of America, Memphis TN   159

California

415-776-3310

PENSIONE
SAN FRANCISCO
415-864-1271

PETITE AUBERGE
800-365-3004

QUEEN ANN INN
800-227-3970

*RED VICTORIAN
B&B INN
800-GO BANDB

REDWOOD INN
800-221-6621

SAN REMO HOTEL
415-776-8688

SHERMAN HOUSE
415-563-3600

SPENCER HOUSE
415-626-9207

*SPRECKELS
MANSION
415-861-3008

ST FRANCIS YACHT
CLUB
415-931-3083

*STANYAN
PARK HOTEL
415-751-1000

**THE MANSIONS
HOTEL**
415-929-9444

UN PLAZA HOTEL
UNION STREET INN
415-346-0424

VICTORIAN INN ON
THE PARK
800-435-1967

**WASHINGTON
SQUARE INN**
800-388-0220

WHITE SWAN INN
800-999-9570

WILLOWS B&B INN
415-431-4770

San Gregorio
*RANCHO SAN
GREGORIO
415-747-0722

San Jose
APPLE LANE INN
408-475-6868

*BRIAR ROSE
408-279-5999

**COUNTRY ROSE
INN**
408-842-0441

HENSLEY HOUSE
408-298-3537

MRS K'S RETREAT
408-371-0539

O NEIL'S
408-996-1231

San Juan Bautista
B&B SAN JUAN
408-623-4101

**COUNTRY ROSE
INN**
408-842-0441

*San Juan
Capistrano*
HOTEL CALIFORNIA
714-496-9444

San Leandro
BEST HOUSE B&B
415-351-0911

San Luis Obispo
ADOBE INN
805-549-0321

**ARROYO VILLAGE
INN**
805-489-5926

GARDEN STREET
INN
805-545-9802

*HERITAGE INN
805-544-7440

MADONA INN
805-543-3000

San Miguel
DARKEN DOWNS
EQUESRE INN
805-467-3589

RANCH B&B
805-463-2320

VICTORIAN MANOR
805-467-3306

San Paula
FERN OAKS INN
805-525-7747

San Pedro
GRAND COTTAGES
213-548-1240

San Rafael

160 ©*Bed & Breakfast Guest Houses & Inns of America, Memphis TN*

California

**CASA SOLDAVINI
415-454-3140

OLE RAFAEL B&B
415-453-0414

PANAMA HOTEL
800-899-3993

San Ramon
GOLD QUARTZ INN
209-267-0747

San Ysidro
TRINGHAMS B&B

Santa Ana
OLD OAK TABLE
714-639-7798

Santa Barbara
ARLINGTON INN
805-965-6532

*BATH STREET INN
800-788-BATH

*BAYBERRY INN
805-682-3199

*BLUE QUAIL INN
800-549-1622

BRINKERHOFF B&B INN
805-963-7844

**CASA DEL MAR INN
800-433-3097

**CHESHIRE CAT INN B&B
805-569-1610

COTTTAGE
805-682-4997

*GLENBOROUGH INN
805-996-0589

**HARBOUR CARRIAGE HOUSE
800-594-4633

LONGS SEAVIEW B&B
805-687-2947

OCEAN VIEW GUEST HOUSE
805-966-6659

OLD MISSION HOUSE
805-569-1914

**OLD YACHT CLUB INN
800-676-1676

*OLIVE HOUSE
800-786-6422

*PARSONAGE
800-775-0352

**SIMPSON HOUSE INN
800-676-1280

*TIFFANY INN
805-963-2283

**UPHAM HOTEL GARDEN COTTAGES
800-727-0876

VALLIS VIEW
805-969-1272

*VILLA D'ITALIA
805-687-6933

*VILLA ROSE INN
805-966-0851

Santa Clara
**MADISON STREET INN
408-249-5541

Santa Cruz
*ADELLA VILLA
408-321-5195

APPLE LANE INN
408-475-6868

**BABBLING BROOK INN
800-866-1131

BANGERTS
408-476-1906

**BLUE SPRUCE INN
408-464-1137

CHATEAU VICTORIAN
408-458-9458

*CLIFF CREST INN
408-427-2609

*DARLING HOUSE
408-458-1958

HERON HOUSE
408-429-8963

PLEASURE POINT INN
408-475-4657

SEA & SAND INN
408-427-3400

VICTORIAN HOUSE
800-421-6662

Santa Maria
SANTA MARIA INN

California

805-928-7777

Santa Monica
*CHANNEL ROAD INN
310-459-1920

SOVERIGN AT SANTA MONICA
800-331-0163

Santa Paula
GLEN TAVERN INN
805-525-6658

LEMON TREE INN
805-525-7747

Santa Rosa
BELVEDERE INN
707-575-1857

COOPERS GROVE RANCH
707-526-3135

GABLES
707-585-7777

*GEE-GEE'S B&B HOME
707-833-6667

*HILLTOP HOUSE
707-944-0880

MELITTA STATION INN
707-538-7712

PYGMALION HOUSE B&B
707-526-3407

SUNRISE B&B INN
707-542-5781

*VINTERS INN
800-421-2584

Saratoga
EDEN VALLEY PLACE
408-867-1785

INN AT SARATOGA
408-867-5020

Sausalito
ALTA MIRA HOTEL
415-332-1309

BUTTERFLY TREE
415-383-8447

CASA MADRONA HOTEL
800-288-0502

SAUSALITO HOTEL
415-332-4155

Scotia
SCOTIA INN
707-764-5683

Sea Ranch
SEA RANCH LODGE
707-785-2371

Seal Beach
*SEAL BEACH INN & GARDENS
310-493-2416

VILLA PACIFICA
213-594-0397

Sebastopol
O'HAGANS GUEST HOUSE
707-823-4771

Shelter Cove
SHELTER COVE B&B

707-986-7161

Sherman Oaks
SCOTT VALLEY INN
916-467-3229

Sierra City
BUSCH HERINGLAKE COUNTRY INN

HIGH COUNTRY INN
916-862-1530

Sierraville
CONSCIOUSNESS VILLAGE
916-994-8984

Skyforest
STORYBOOK INN
800-554-9208

Soda Springs
SERENE LAKES LODGE
916-426-9001

Solvang
CHIMNEY SWEEP INN
800-824-6444

DANISH COUNTRY INN
805-688-2018

EL RANCHITO
805-688-9517

KRONBORG INN
805-688-2383

SOLVANG INN
805-688-3248

SUNFLOWER HOUSE
805-688-4492

California

Somerset
FITZPATRICK WINERY
& LODGE
209-245-3248

Somis
RANCH DE SOMIS
805-987-8455

Sonoma
CHALET B&B
707-938-3129

**COLUMBIA CITY HOTEL
209-532-1479

COUNTRY COTTAGE
707-938-2479

EL DORADO INN
707-996-3030

*HIDDEN OAK
707-996-9863

KATE MURPHY COTTAGE
707-996-4359

MAGLIULO'S
PENSIONE
707-996-1031

SONOMA HOTEL
707-996-2996

*THISTLE DEW INN
707-938-2909

*TROJAN HORSE INN
800-899-1925

**VICTORIAN GARDEN INN
800-543-5339

VINEYARD INN
707-938-2350

Sonora
*BARETTA GARDENS
209-532-6039

GUNN HOUSE
209-532-3421

LA CASA INGLESA
209-532-5822

LAVENDER HILL INN
209-532-9024

*LLAMAHALL GUEST RANCH
209-532-7264

*LULU BELLES
209-533-3455

*RYAN HOUSE B&B
800-831-4897

SERENITY - A B&B
800-426-1441

SONORA INN
209-532-7468

VIA SERENA RANCH
209-532-5307

Soquel
**BLUE SPRUCE INN
408-464-1137

Soulsbyville
WILLOW SPRINGS
COUNTY INN
209-533-2030

South Lake Tahoe
*CHRISTIANA INN
916-544-7337

South San Francisco
OYSTER POINT
MARINA INN
415-737-7633

Stinson Beach
CASA DEL MAR
415-868-2124

SHORELINE HOUSE
415-868-1062

Stockton
OLD VICTORIAN INN
209-462-1613

Studio City
FIGS COTTAGE
818-769-2662

**FOGELSON HOUSE "VALLEY VIEW"
800-383-3513

Summerland
INN ON SUMMER HILL
800-999-8999

*SUMMERLAND INN
800-999-8999

Sunset Beach
SUNSET B&B INN
310-592-1666

Susanville
ROSEBERRY HOUSE
916-257-5675

Sutter Creek
*FOXES IN SUTTER CREEK
209-267-5882

GOLD QUARTZ INN

©Bed & Breakfast Guest Houses & Inns of America, Memphis TN

California

800-752-8738

HANFORD HOUSE
209-267-0747

NANCY & BOBS
9 EUREKA ST INN
209-267-0342

SUTTER CREEK INN
209-267-5606

Tahoe City
CHANEY HOUSE
916-525-7333

COTTAGE INN
916-581-4073

LAKESIDE HOUSE
916-588-8796

MAYFIELD HOUSE
916-583-1001

RIVER RANCH
916-583-4264

TAHOE VINTAGE INN

Tahoma
ALPENHAUS
COUNTRY INN
916-525-5000

Temecula
*LOMA VISTA B&B
909-676-7047

Templeton
COUNTRY HOUSE
INN
805-434-1598

Thomasville
QUAIL COUNTRY
B&B

912-226-7218

Three Rivers
CORT COTTAGE
209-561-4671

REDWOOD MANOR
209-561-4145

Toluca Lake
TOUCH OF MEXICO B&B
800-383-3513

Tomales
TOMALES COUNTRY INN
707-847-9992

US HOTEL
707-878-2742

Torrance
NOONE GUEST HOUSE
310-328-1837

*WHITES HOUSE
213-324-6164

WILD GOOSE
310-325-3578

Trinidad
LOST WHALE
707-677-3425

TRINIDAD B&B
707-677-0840

Trinity Center
CARRVILLE INN
916-266-3511

Truckee
ALTA HOTEL
916-587-6668

BRADLEY HOUSE

HILLTOP LODGE
916-587-2545

MOUNTAIN VIEW INN
916-587-5388

TRUCKEE HOTEL
B&B
916-587-4444

Tuolumne
OAK HILL RANCH
209-928-4717

Twain Harte
*TWAIN HARTES B&B
209-586-3311

Twentynine Palms
CIRCLE C
619-367-7615

TOWER HOMESTEAD
619-367-7936

Ukiah
*OAK KNOLL B&B
707-468-5646

SANFORD HOUSE
707-462-1653

VICHY HOT SPRINGS RESORT
707-462-9515

Upper Lake
NARROWS LODGE
707-275-2718

Valley Ford
INN AT VALLEY FORD
707-876-3182

California

VALLEY FORD HOTEL
707-876-3600

Venice
VENICE BEACH HOUSE
310-823-1966

Ventura
BAKER INN
805-652-0143

*BELLA MAGGIORE
800-523-8479

**CLOCKTOWER INN
800-727-1027

*LA MER
805-643-3600

ROSEHOLM
805-649-4014

Visalia
SPALDING HOUSE
209-739-7877

Volcano
ST GEORGE HOTEL
209-296-4458

VOLCANO INN
209-296-4959

Walnut Creek
*GASTHAUS ZUM BAREN
415-934-8119

MANSION AT LAKEWOOD
800-477-7898

Warner Springs
WARNER SPRINGS RANCH
619-782-4219

West Covina
HENDRICK INN
818-919-2125

Westport
BOWENS PELICAN INN
707-964-5588

DEHAVEN VALLEY FARM 707-961-1660

HOWARD CREEK RANCH
707-964-6725

Whittier
BENELL INN

*COLEENS CALIFORNIA CASA
310-699-1527

Williams
WILBUR HOT SPRINGS
916-473-2306

Willits
DOLL HOUSE
707-459-4055

Windsor
*COUNTRY MEADOW INN
707-431-1276

Yosemite
**OAK MEADOWS, too
209-742-6161

TELAROS WAWONA
209-375-6582

Yosemite Natl Park
WALDSCHLOSS
209-372-4958

Yountville
BORDEAUX HOUSE
707-944-2855

**BURGUNDY HOUSE
707-944-0899

MAGNOLIA HOTEL
707-944-2056

NAPA VALLEY RAILWAY INN
707-944-2000

**OLEANDER HOUSE
800-788-3057

VINTAGE INN
707-944-1112

WEBBER PLACE
707-944-8384

Yreka
3RD STREET INN
916-842-7058

MCFADDENS INN
916-842-7712

Yuba City
*HARKEY HOUSE B&B
916-674-1942

MOORE HOUSE
916-674-8559

Colorado

Cottonwood Inn			**Alamosa CO**

J & George Mordecai-Sellman
800-955-BNBE 719-589-3882

123 San Juan 81101
Res Times 8am-9pm

Rates:	**Pvt Bath** 3	**Shared Bath** 2	**Payment Terms:**
Single	$ 56.00	$ 46-48.00	Check
Double	$ 60.00	$ 50-52.00	MC/V

A lovely turn-of-the-century home where hospitality is a way of life with your charming hosts. This elegant and very affordable lodging is in the heart of the San Luis Valley offering beautiful scenic nature trails for hiking, biking and picnicking. Each guest room is uniquely decorated with comfortable antique furnishings and art work from area artists. Your hosts will be glad to help plan your visit to local sights of: Wolf Creek, Monarch, Taos, Rio Costilla & Cuchara ski areas, Cumbres and Toltec Railroad, The Great Sand Dunes, Monte Vista & Alamosa National Wildlife Refuge and the Creede Repertory Theatre. A hearty family-styled full breakfast is included in the rate and is served in the comfortable dining room. **RESERVATIONS:** One night's deposit at res time or credit card, 7 day cancel policy less $10 fee **BROCHURE:** Yes **PERMITTED:** Limited children, drinking **CONFERENCES:** Yes, small groups to 9 persons. **LANGUAGES:** Spanish [E08BCCO-6079]

Snow Queen Victorian Inn			**Aspen CO**

Norma Dolle/Larry Leduingham
303-925-8455

124 E Cooper Ave 81611
Fax 303-925-8455

Rates:	**Pvt Bath** 5	**Shared Bath** 2	**Payment Terms:**
Single	$ 50-85.00	$ 45-75.00	Check
Double	$ 50-85.00	$ 45-75.00	MC/V

Within easy walking distance to the center of town and local activities, the *Snow Queen Lodge* is just minutes away from the Gondola and shuttle busses to the surrounding ski areas too. The *Snow Queen Lodge* is a romantic and charming Victorian home built in 1886 with modern amenities and Victorian furnishings. This family-operated lodge specializes in a friendly and congenial atmosphere with western hospitality. There are a variety of rooms all named after famous silver mines with most offering private baths and two units include kitchen facilities. Reasonable year round rates vary between off-season (summer, spring,

Colorado

fall) and four winter rate schedules. Off-season rates listed in heading; Seasonal rates are: Low 11/24-12/18, Holiday 12/19-1/2, Mid 1/2-2/6 and High 2/6-3/27. The woodburning fireplace in the lounge is a favorite gathering place for relaxing, watching TV or visiting with others. Smoking is allowed in rooms. A lovely outdoor hot tub is available for guests to relax in while enjoying the beautiful view of Aspen Mountain. A continental breakfast is included in your room rate and there are afternoon parties/get-togethers from tine to time. Studio loft apartments next door are available. **DISCOUNTS:** More than one week **PACKAGES:** Yes, inquire at res time **RESERVATIONS:** 50% deposit within 7 days, bal 30 days before arrival/45 days-holidays. Cancel policy; refund if 30/45 days before arrival less $20 per person; less than 30/45 days, only if rebooked **SEASONAL:** Rates vary **BROCHURE:** Yes **PERMITTED:** Children, drinking, smoking **AIRPORT:** Aspen Airport-3 mi **LANGUAGES:** Some German, Spanish **PACKAGES: Ski** [K07GPCO2-2939]

The SNOW QUEEN BED & BREAKFAST

124 East Cooper Avenue
Aspen, Colorado 81611
(303) 925-8455

On Golden Pond B&B	Avada CO
Katy Kula	7831 Eldridge 80005
303-424-2296	**Rws Times** 8am-9pm
Rates: **Pvt Bath** 5	**Payment Terms:**
Single $ 60-100.00	Check
Double $ 60-100.00	

"European hospitality and relaxing country comfort" is assured in this custom-built two story home located on ten acres with dramatic views of the mountains, prairies and downtown Denver from the wrap around verandahs - and in a secluded Rocky Mountain foothill setting just fifteen miles west of Denver. Choose from five uniquely decorated guest rooms including Italian Provincial with king bed and large jacuzzi, African motif including a hanging bed, fireplace and large jacuzzi; a romantic Victorian room and an Oriental furnished setting with brass bed where you'll awaken to the beauty of the natural pond and native birds. Each room has a large sliding glass door framing the gorgeous views and which opens onto your private deck. The great room offers a crackling fire, TV, VCR, games and books in a very comfortable setting. Your German hostess provides an extensive breakfast served on the deck or indoors and a late afternoon "kaffeklatsch" with fresh-brewed coffee and pastries. A gazebo on a natural fishing pond on the grounds provides

Colorado

exciting wildlife viewing while the soaking in the hot tub or swimming laps in the pool will keep you fit. Nearby foothills offer excellent hiking, biking, country roads and horseback riding trails. Of course, all of Denvers' activities and sights are just minutes away. Your host Kathy is a German native who enjoys an active lifestyle and looks forward to sharing her home with you. **RESERVATIONS:** 50% deposit required, 7 day cancel notice for refund less $15 service fee **BROCHURE:** Yes **LANGUAGES:** German **PERMITTED:** Smoking outdoors [R03GPCO2-13241]

**Boulder Victoria Historic B&B	**Boulder CO**
Jacki or Kirsten	1305 Pine St 80302
303-938-1300	

Rates:	**Pvt Bath** 7	**Payment Terms:**
Single	$ 88.00	Check
Double	$ 153.00	AE/MC/V

The *Boulder Historic Bed & Breakfast* is a showcase of classic elegance in the heart of downtown Boulder. Just two blocks from the famous Pearl Street Pedestrian Mall, this distinctive inn is within easy walking distance to shops, restaurants and nightspots, as well as year-round mountain activities and the University of Colorado campus. Originally built in the 1870's, The *Boulder Victoria* has recently been renovated to reflect its original Victorian grandeur. Guests experience the charm and personal service of a bed and breakfast, and the amenities and modern conveniences of a fine hotel. The seven beautifully appointed guest rooms, each with a private bath and telephone, are furnished with period antiques, queen size brass beds and down comforters. Many rooms also feature steam showers and/or private balconies or patios. A European-style continental breakfast buffet is served on the flagstone terrace or in the bay-windowed dining room. The elegant parlour provides and inviting atmosphere for afternoon tea and cookies, and a glass of port wine in the evening. Above the north wing of the inn, a spacious canopied patio is an ideal setting for catered receptions and meetings. **DISCOUNTS:** Corporate **AIRPORT:** Stapelton, Denver-35 mi **RESERVATIONS:** Credit card number to guarantee reservation, 7 day cancel policy for refund. **BROCHURE:** Yes **PERMITTED:** Drinking **CONFERENCES:** Meeting space in parlour and canopied patio **LANGUAGES:** Spanish, German [R09EPCO2-14847]

**Allaire Timbers Inn	**Breckenridge CO**
Jack & Kathy Gumph	9511 Hwy #9/S Main St 80424
800-624-4904 303-453-7530	**Res Times** 10am-8pm

Colorado

Rates: **Pvt Bath** 10   **Payment Terms:**
Single $ 115-230.00   Check
Double $ 115-230.00   AE/DC/MC/V

The *Allaire Timbers Inn* is the intimate way to experience Breckenridge. Nestled in the trees at the south end of historic Main Street, this new log and stone Bed & Breakfast was **designed and built in 1991 with every comfort of its guests in mind.** Eight lodge rooms are named for historic Colorado mountain passes and each is uniquely decorated according to its name history. Each has a private bath and deck. Two elegant suites, the Summit and Breckenridge, boast a private fireplace and hot tub, as well as a private bath and deck. Join friends by a crackling fire in the log & beam Great Room. Relax in the Sunroom, or read in the Loft, all designed for you to share quiet times together. After a full day of activities, unwind in the large rejuvenating spa located on the main deck which offers spectacular views of the Ten Mile Range. The *Allaire Timbers* is located in the heart of Summit County, home of four major ski resorts and four championship golf courses. The *Allaire Timbers Inn* is wheelchair accessible, Gourmet breakfasts, afternoon treats and personalized hospitality makes The *Allaire Timbers* the perfect getaway in Colorado. Check with innkeeper for cancel policy for less than 30 days. Check-in 3-7pm, late arrivals only with prior arrangements, check-out 11am **AIRPORT:** Denver Intl-100 mi **RESERVATIONS:** 50% deposit within 10 day of booking, balance due 30 days prior to arrival; reservations within 30 days of arrival, bal due at res time; 30 day cancel policy for full refund **BROCHURE:** Yes **PERMITTED:** Children 13-up, drinking, maximum 2 persons per guest room **CONFERENCES:** Yes, perfect setting for small retreats and groups to 20 persons [Z07GPCO2-15317]

Cotten House   **Breckenridge CO
Peter & Georgette Contos   102 S French St   80424
303-453-5509

Rates: **Pvt Bath** 1   **Shared Bath** 2   **Payment Terms:**
Single $ 60.00 $ 50-55.00   Check
Double $ 60.00 $ 50-55.00   Yes*

In the heart of beautiful Breckenridge is this exciting 1886 Victorian home which is listed on the *National Historic Register* that has been fully restored in the theme of the mining era of the **Gold Rush of the 1860's**. The guest rooms are furnished in individual themes with the name of *Colorado Room* with a four-poster queen bed and down bedding; *Victorian Room*, with turn-of-the-century furnishings, hardwood floors in a romantic setting; *Room With A View* overlooks the ski slopes and town and offers a relaxing Southwest American decor. The private and shared baths include antique clawfoot tubs. The common room has a beautiful

Colorado

view of the Breckenridge ski area and includes TV, VCR, books, games and a comfortable atmosphere. Phone service, ski and bike storage are available along with on-site parking and laundry facilities. A 7 day, full menu complimentary breakfast and afternoon refreshments are offered. Conveniently located, winter skiing is available right at your door-step, via a free shuttle bus; nightlife, restaurants, shopping and many other activities are within walking distance, including summer festivals which shouldn't be missed. Members of *Innkeepers of Colorado, American B&B Assoc* and ***AAA Approved***. **RESERVATIONS:** Non-refundable deposit by check within 5 days of reservation, arrival from 4-6 pm, unless prior arrangements have been made. *Credit card accepted only for deposit guarantee. Winter rates: $70-90.00 **PERMITTED:** Children, limited drinking **SEASONAL:** Rates vary **BROCHURE:** Yes **LANGUAGES:** French, Greek **AIRPORT:** Denver Stapleton - 1-1/2 to 2 Hrs **PACKAGES: *Honeymoon, Anniversary, Roses & Champagne, Gift Certificates*** [Z07GPCO2-16379]

Cottonwood Hot Springs Inn	Buena Vista CO
Kathy Manning/Dian Key	aka Cottonwood Pass Rd 81211
800-241-4119 719-395-6434	**Res Times** 9am-10pm

Rates:	**Pvt Bath** 15	**Payment Terms:**
Single	$ 32-42.00*	Check
Double	$ 37-47.00*	DC/MC/V

Travelers are invited to our relaxing Country Inn, nestled high in the Rocky Mountains surrounded by the National Forest and a pleasant bubbling brook, just 5.5 mi west of the picturesque town of Buena Vista. There are three creekside cabins with kitchens, 12 guest rooms, a bunkhouse, tipi and campsites. This retreat revolves around the pure natural hot mineral spring, spas, sauna and exercise room. This area was historically noted for its healing waters and as a power spot by the Ute Indians & others. Your hosts advocate the tradition of self-responsibility for healing, living in balance with nature and one another and the healing of Mother Earth. A variety of private sessions are available for massage therapy, energy balancing, rebirthing, past life regressions and group discussions. The friendly and caring staff insure your stay will be a special experience whether you are here to play, relax, learn, share, grow, heal or celebrate life. Ideal for small group retreats, healthful vacations, meetings, workshops and seminars. Unlimited recreational activities in the area include; rafting, hiking, skiing, rock hounding, horse back riding, sightseeing, bicycling, fishing, exploring and golf. A family-style restaurant offers delicious nutritional meals in a spacious dining room with a cozy fireside conversation area. All meals are available at added cost; an American Plan for $25.00 per person, daily **AIRPORT:** Denver Stapleton-2.5 hrs **DISCOUNTS:** 10 or more in a group;

Colorado

10% for 3 nights, 25% for 7 nights **RESERVATIONS:** 25% deposit, rooms not held after 8pm unless notified of late arrival. *Winter rates $32-37.00. **BROCHURE:** Yes **PERMITTED:** Limited pets, children, smoking, drinking **CONFERENCES:** Can accommodate up to 200 persons in single or divided rooms for smaller groups [R10DPCO-13243]

**Cheyenne Cañon B&B Inn	**Colorado Springs CO**
John & Barbara Starr	2030 W Cheyenne Blvd
719-633-0625	**Fax** 719-633-8826

Rates:	**Pvt Bath** 7	**Payment Terms:**
Single	$ 65-105.00	Check
Double	$ 75-115.00	

Opened in January, 1994, this exceptionally spacious 1920's Mission-style mansion of over 13,000 square feet is situated at the mouth of two canyons in one of Colorado's most spectacular locations. Features of the Inn include the Great Room (with its seven foot tall windows overlooking the mountains and canyons) and seven unique, private bath guestrooms, each decorated for a different region of the world. The Hacienda has a king carved Santa Fe style bed, private sitting room with canyon views, bath with 6-foot jacuzzi tub plus a hand painted sink from Mexico. The Lodge (Colorado theme) has a king Aspen canopy bed and offers awesome views of Cheyenne Mountain. The king size bed in the Tea House (Oriental) yields to some of the most beautiful sunrises anywhere. Rounding out the tour are the Villa (Italy), Chalet (Switzerland), Cabana (Caribbean) and the Hut (Africa). Numerous hiking and mountain biking trails start at the doorstep. The Inn is minutes from the famous 5-star Broadmoor Hotel and all Pikes Peak area attractions. There is also a private Hot Tub Room available for use by reservation (no additional charge). A full breakfast features quiches, specialty fruit dishes and more is served each morning. **RESERVATIONS:** One night or 50% of length of stay, which ever is greater **PERMITTED:** Limited children, drinking **BROCHURE::** Yes **AIRPORT:** Denver-65 mi; Colorado Springs-7 mi **CONFERENCES:** Yes, groups to thirty five **LANGUAGES:** French [R08GPCO2-18993]

**Holden House-1902 B&B Inn	**Colorado Springs CO**
Sallie & Welling Clark	1102 W Pikes Peak Ave 80904
719-471-3980	**Res Times** 9am-9pm

Rates:	**Pvt Bath** 6	**Payment Terms:**
Single	$ 70-105.00	Check
Double	$ 70-105.00	AE/CB/DC/DISC/MC/V

Colorado

Built by Isabel Holden, the widow of a wealthy Colorado Springs businessman, this 1902 storybook Victorian and 1906 carriage house are centrally located near historic "Old Colorado City", in a residential area. The Inn was lovingly restored by the Clarks in 1985 and is furnished with antiques, family treasures and heirloom quilts. Named for Colorado mining towns, the six individually decorated guest rooms are furnished with queen beds, period furnishings and down pillows. The inn also boasts four romantic suites with "tubs for two", fireplaces, mountain views and more! Gourmet breakfasts - served in the formal dining room, might include blueberry-corn muffins, Sallie's famous Eggs Fiesta, fresh fruit, gourmet coffee, tea and juice. Complimentary refreshments, 24-hour coffee and tea, homemade cookies and turn-down service are just a few of the Holden House's special touches. Sallie & Welling will be happy to help in planning your itinerary. Colorado Springs is nestled at the base of 14,100 ft Pikes Peak and offers a variety of activities from scenic beauty to cultural attractions. Spend a few days, a week or more. You'll find plenty to keep you busy. **AAA & Mobil Approved**. Friendly cats Mingtoy and Muffin in residence. **Aspiring Innkeeper Seminars and Gift Certificates**. **PACKAGES: Romance**, stay 2 or more nights in the Aspen or Independence Suites and have breakfast in bed for $10 additional to room rate **AIRPORT:** Colorado Springs-10 mi; Denver Stapleton-70 mi **RESERVATIONS:** One night or 50% deposit (which ever is more) 8 day cancel policy $15 service fee, 30 day cancel notice for special events, minimum stay holidays/weekends/High Season, handicap accessible rooms available **BROCHURE:** Yes **PERMITTED:** Drinking, No Smoking [Z07GPCO2-6081]

**Room At The Inn B&B	**Colorado Springs CO**
Jan, Chick & Kelly McCormick	618 N Nevada Ave 80903
719-442-1896	**Res Times** 10am-8pm

Rates:	**Pvt Bath** 7	**Payment Terms:**
Single	$ 75-110.00	Check
Double	$ 80-115.00	AE/DISC/MC/V

The recently opened and restored *Room At The Inn* features the romance, charm and hospitality of the Victoria Era, while pampering guests with in-room whirlpool tubs for two, fireplaces, fresh cut flowers and evening turn-down service. Guests are enticed to relax on the wrap around porch or in our outdoor hot tub while enjoying spectacular views of the mountains by day and the illuminated Gothic spires of an adjacent historic church at night. A short stroll takes you to the many unique restaurants, coffee houses and shops of a vibrant downtown or through the beautiful campus of Colorado College and neighboring parks, The Fine Arts Center, United States Olympic Training Center and the Numismatic Museum are all within close proximity. The Inn is a classic

Colorado

Queen Anne Victorian with a three-story turret and seven styles of fish scale siding. The guest rooms feature queen size beds, period antiques, oriental rugs, private baths, original wall paintings and a/c. One guest room is wheel chair accessible. The smell of fresh ground coffee and homemade muffins invites you to a delicious full breakfast served in the dining room or on the porch. Bananas Foster French Toast or Raspberry Cheese Blintz accompanied by fresh-squeezed orange juice and seasonal fresh fruit are just samples of the breakfast fare. Afternoon refreshments greet guests upon their arrival. The Inn is a perfect haven to retreat to after a busy day at work or a day of enjoying the numerous attractions of the Pikes Peak region. **RESERVATIONS:** One night or 50% of length of stay (which ever is greater) deposit required within 7 days of booking, 14 day cancel policy for refund **PERMITTED:** Limited children **BROCHURE:** Yes **DISCOUNTS:** Off-season, extended stays **CONFERENCES:** Yes, groups to fourteen **AIRPORT:** Colorado Springs Municipal-8 mi [I08GPCO2-18835]

**Castle Marne	**Denver CO**
Jim & Diane Peiker	1572 Race St 80206
800-92 MARNE 303-331-0621	

Rates:	**Pvt Bath** 9	**Payment Terms:**
Single	$ 65-145.00	Check
Double	$ 75-145.00	AE/DC/MC/V

Come, fall under the spell of one of Denver's Grandest Historic Mansions. Built in 1889, *Castle Marne* is considered by many to be the finest example of "America's most eclectic architect", William Lang. Your stay at Castle Marne combines old world elegance and Victorian charm with modern convenience and comfort. Each room is a unique experience in pampered luxury. Carefully chosen furnishings combine period antiques, family heirlooms and exacting reproductions to create a mood of long ago elegance. Whether your stay is for business, vacation or a honeymoon, it will be unforgettable in one of our luxury suites. Two rooms have jetted whirlpool tubs, three rooms have the original clawfooted tubs with shower rings and all have showers and pedestal sinks. Gourmet full breakfast of fresh fruits, homebaked breads, muffins and hot entree is included; afternoon tea is served daily. Castle Marne is located in the heart of one of Denver's most historic neighborhoods, minutes from the finest cultural, shopping, dining and sightseeing attractions. **RESERVATIONS:** One

Colorado

night's deposit within 7 days of booking, cancel policy of $25 service fee if canceled less than 5 days prior to arrival date, no refund if less than 48 hr cancel notice **BROCHURE:** Yes **PERMITTED:** Drinking **CONFERENCES:** Yes [Z11CPC0-8371]

**Cheyenne Cañon B&B Inn	**Denver CO**
John & Barbara Starr	
719-633-0625	**Fax** 719-633-8826

Rates:	**Pvt Bath** 7	**Payment Terms:**
Single	$ 65-105.00	Check
Double	$ 75-115.00	

Refer to the same listing name under Colorado Springs, Colorado for a complete description. [M08GPCO2]

**Haus Berlin B&B	**Denver CO**
Christiana & Dennis Brown	1651 Emerson St 80218
303-837-9527	**Res Times** 7am-10pm
	Fax 303-837-9527

Rates:	**Pvt Bath** 4	**Payment Terms:**
Single	$ 80-120.00	Check
Double	$ 80-120.00	AE/MC/V

Haus Berlin, a recently renovated Victorian townhouse, has three guest rooms and one suite offering private bath, shower, inroom phones and special touches such as king or queen size beds dressed in luxurious, all-cotton linens and down comforters. Located on a quiet tree-lined street where the architecture reflects the charm of the turn-of-the-century, business and leisure travelers appreciate the closeness of Denver's central business district. all rooms reflect urban elegance while providing the warmth and feeling of European tradition. The main floor offers a library/sitting room, a morning parlor with fresco walls, iron and wicker furnishings befit a definite Mediterranean feeling while the breakfast room offers a cozy Country French theme. The furnishings are eclectic as are the original paintings and pieces of art. This is truly a different Bed and Breakfast! A continental plus breakfast includes hot beverages, juices, jam, cereals and fresh baked goods or guests may choose traditional German bread, cold cuts and cheese. Come and discover us and Denver - at the foothills of the Rocky Mountains! Cable TV, fax and complimentary beverages are available **RESERVATIONS:** One night deposit, 7 day cancel policy **BROCHURE:** Yes **PERMITTED:** Limited children, drinking **AIRPORT:** "New" Denver Intl-30 min **LANGUAGES:** German [R04GPCO2]

Colorado

Queen Anne B&B Inn — Denver CO

Tom King
800-432-4667   303-296-6666

2147 Tremont Place 80205
Res Times 7am-11pm
Fax 303-296-2151

Rates:	Pvt Bath 14	Suites	Payment Terms:
Single	$ 75-125.00	$ 135-155.00	Check
Double	$ 75-125.00	$ 135-155.00	AE/DISC/MC/V

Facing quiet Benedict Fountain park in the Clement Historic District of Downtown Denver are the Inn's two side-by-side *National Register* Victorians (1879/1886). They are within easy walking distance of the Capitol, US Mint, 16th Street Mall, Convention Center, most offices, Larimer Square, museums and many fine restaurants. Because of the Inn's downtown location, and the Inn's quiet friendly atmosphere, businessmen and women are half of the Inns' guests. There are fourteen guest rooms including four gallery suites dedicated to famous artists: Audubon, Calder, Remington and Rockwell. Fresh flowers, chamber music, period antiques, direct dial phones and private baths are in all rooms. Six guest rooms offer special deep tubs and one room features a fireplace. The Inn is air conditioned for your year round comfort. There is plenty of free parking and a no-tipping policy is in effect. Complimentary full breakfast (ensuite if you wish) and evening beverages are included. Your knowledgeable innkeepers will suggest seeing-doing-shopping in and around Denver, arrange dinner reservations at nearby restaurants, tours and sport activities (perhaps see a working gold mine or take a horsedrawn carriage ride to dinner downtown?), or advise you about other B&Bs in Colorado. The Inn's twenty-nine awards include: **Best Ten B&B In The USA, Twelve Most Romantic B&Bs In The Nation, Best Of Denver, Seven Most Romantic Destinations in Colorado.** RESERVATIONS: Full payment within two weeks of booking reservation, 50% if more than 4 mos in advance, with bal due 30 days prior to arrival; cancel policy: 3 day cancel notice for full refund except holidays (two weeks notice) or groups of 3 rooms or more (30 day notice) Diners Card Accepted **PERMITTED:** Children **BROCHURE:** Yes **DISCOUNTS:** *AAA*, Corporate, Groups **PACKAGES:** *Mid-Week* (11/1-5/31), *Three Day Holiday Weekends* **AIRPORT:** Denver Intl **LANGUAGES:** Spanish **CONFERENCES:** Groups to 15 indoors, to 75 outdoors [K03GPCO2-840]

Room At The Inn B&B — Denver CO

Jan, Chick & Kelly McCormick

618 N Nevada Ave

Colorado

719-442-1896

Res Times 10am-8pm

Rates:	**Pvt Bath** 7	**Payment Terms:**
Single	$ 75-110.00	Check
Double	$ 80-115.00	AE/DISC/MC/V

Refer to the same listing name under Colorado Springs, Colorado for a complete description. [M08GPCO2]

---

*Victoria Oaks Inn			**Denver CO**
Clyde Stephens			1575 Race St 80206
303-355-1818			

Rate:	**Pvt Bath** 1	**Shared Bath** 8	**Payment Terms:**
Single	$ 69.00	$ 39.00	Check
Double	$ 79.00	$ 59.00	AE/DC/MC/V

An elegant 1896 Mansion, restored to its former glory provides warmth and hospitality as a home travelers love to come home to. It retains the original oak woodwork, tile fireplaces, dramatic hanging staircase and ornate brass chandelier. The nine guest rooms are furnished with stylish, restored antiques from the turn-of-the-century, with leaded glass windows creating a play ground of colors while providing a panoramic view of the city. The individual character of *Victoria Oaks Inn* is designed for your personal comfort in your home away from home. As a small inn, we offer personalized services not often available in larger hotels. Our concierge is on-hand to accommodate your needs, provide assistance and information. An inspiring continental breakfast of fresh squeezed orange juice, blended coffee and teas, and a choice of fresh pastries, croissants, bagels and fresh fruits. Evenings bring complimentary wine. Whether business or leisure, guests are conveniently located to Denver's business, financial, shopping and tourist attractions such as the Historic Capitol Hill District, the *Unsinkable Molly Brown House*, Botanic Gardens and within walking distance is Denver's City Park and 72 acre zoo, Museum of Natural History, Laserium and Imax Theater. **RESERVATIONS:** One nights deposit required, 48 hr cancel policy for refund **PERMITTED:** Drinking, smoking **BROCHURE:** Yes **CONFERENCES:** From meetings to dining - the *Victoria Oaks Inn* provides full service designed to meet your particular needs **AIRPORT:** Stapleton-7 mi [R12EPCO2-842]

**Leland House B&B Suites		**Durango CO**
The Komick Family		712 E Second Ave 81301
303-385-1920		**Res Times** 7am-7pm

Rates:	**Suites** 5	**Studio** 4	**Payment Terms:**

Colorado

Single	$ 112.50	$ 76.50	Check
Double	$ 135.00	$ 85.00	MC/V

The *Leland House Bed & Breakfast Suites* offer distinctive overnight lodging in historic downtown Durango. The property is a lovingly restored historic Inn built in 1927, steps away from Durango's Main Avenue and a variety of charming shops and excellent restaurants. There are six one bedroom suites with private bath, fully equipped kitchens, full or queen size beds, queen size sofa sleepers and living rooms, and our studios with a combined bedroom/living area, partially equipped kitchenette, private bath and either queen or full size beds. There's cable TV, daily maid service, private on-site parking and cribs for small children. Guests awake to freshly baked breads and muffins served with the complimentary full breakfast each morning. Complimentary refreshments are offered at an afternoon social hour. Sights include Durango-Silverton train. Mesa Verde National Park, PRCA Rodeo with excellent skiing at Purgatory, hiking, biking and rafting, kayaking and fishing the Animas River. Full concierge services include information, reservation service, guided tours, train tickets and picnic arrangements. **RESERVATIONS:** One night deposit to guarantee reservation, 7 day cancel policy for refund **PERMITTED:** Children, drinking **BROCHURE:** Yes **DISCOUNTS:** Yes, inquire at res time **SEASONAL:** Rates vary **AIRPORT:** La Plata-16 mi **PACKAGES:** Yes, inquire at res time [Z07GPCO2-17793]

Penny's Place			Durango CO
Penny O'Keefe		1041 County Rd 307 81301	
303-247-8928		**Res Times** 8am-4pm	
Rates:	**Pvt Bath** 1	**Shared Bath** 2	**Payment Terms:**
Single	$ 60-70.00	$ 40-50.00	Check
Double	$ 65-75.00	$ 44-55.00	MC/V

Penny's Place is eleven picturesque, paved miles from downtown Durango, located on 26 acres in quiet, rolling countryside overlooking the spectacular La Plata Mountains. There are deer and meadowlarks visiting most days. There is a gabled ceiling room with a king-size bed that has a private entrance, deck, bath, kitchenette and washer & dryer. The room has a marvelous view of the mountains from the deck. A spiral staircase joins this room to the common room with a hot tub, satellite TV and woodburning stove. Also available is another gabled-ceiling room with a queen-size brass bed that shares a bath with a room with a four-poster double bed. A full breakfast is served including homemade bread, jams and syrup. Dietary restrictions upon request and flexible breakfast time. A visit of several days is recommended to see the wonderful sites of the Durango area, including Narrow Gauge Train, Mesa Verde, hiking, horseback riding, fishing and skiing at Purgatory Ski Area. **AIRPORT:**

Colorado

LaPlata Field, Durango-5 mi **RESERVATIONS:** One night's deposit, 7 day cancel policy for refund, check-in 4-6pm, other by prior arrangement, two night minimum stay required during summer **BROCHURE:** Yes **PERMITTED:** Drinking, limited children [R11DPCO-12489]

**River House B&B	**Durango CO**
Crystal Carroll/K&L Enggren	495 Animas View Dr 81301
800-254-4775 303-247-4775	

Rates:	**Pvt Bath** 7	**Payment Terms:**
Single	$ 50-70.00	Check
Double	$ 65-85.00	DC/MC/V

The elegant simplicity of southwest living is enjoyed by guests at *River House Bed & Breakfast*, one of Durango's largest and finest homes. Just on the north edge of Durango you'll enjoy vacation living at its best, on the river with views of the Animas Valley and in a true European B&B manner but with American style. Each guest room is uniquely furnished and named after some of the enchanting rivers of the San Juan Mountains such as the Rio Grande River Room or the Gunnison River Room which has a king size bed, a large library and a clawfoot tub for soaking while enjoying your favorite passages. Each day begins with a full complimentary breakfast in the early morning sun-filled Atrium with its astonishing proportions. Common rooms include an exercise room. living room with fireplace, wet bar, game room and large screen cable TV, snooker table and an outdoor therapeutic hot tub dubbed *"Rainbow Hot Springs"*, after one our favorite spots in the Rockies. Additional meals are available, including special diets and healthy gourmet-style, at added cost and with prior arrangements. We invite you to experience our lifestyle and hospitality in the Colorado tradition. **RESERVATIONS:** One night's deposit, 14 day cancel policy for refund, otherwise, refund only if room is rebooked **PERMITTED:** Children, limited drinking **BROCHURE:** Yes **CONFERENCES:** Yes, weddings, receptions, meetings for 16 to 100 persons **DISCOUNTS:** Yes, inquire at res time **AIRPORT:** Durango-20 mi **PACKAGES:** Yes, inquire at res time [Z07GPCO2-849]

---

*Scrubby Oaks B&B	**Durango CO**
Mary Ann Craig	1901 Florida Rd 81302
303-247-2176	**Res Times** 8am-5pm

Rates:	**Shared Bath** 3	**Payment Terms:**
Single	$ 40.00	Check
Double	$ 50.00	

Lovely two story home nestled upon ten acres of country overlooking

Colorado

Animals Valley and enclosed by mountain peaks. Enjoy the outdoors among the trees & gardens surrounding the patio while enjoying breakfast where strawberry waffles are a specialty of the hostess. Relax around the warm fireplace in the kitchen in winter and the year-round sauna. **BROCHURE:** Yes **PERMITTED:** Children and social drinking. [E11ACCO-2944]

**Vagabond Inn B&B			**Durango CO**
Ace & Mary Lou Hall			2180 Main Ave 81301
303-259-5901			**Res Times** 24 Hrs
Rates:	**Pvt Bath** 8		**Payment Terms:**
Single	$ 36-125.00		Check
Double	$ 36-125.00		AE/DC/MC/V

Enjoy the down-home comfort of the *Vagabond Inn*. This unique and charming bed & breakfast has 8 rooms, each different from the other. The Bridal Suite has a hand-carved four-poster bed and a heart-shaped hot tub in the room. All rooms have color TV, very comfortable beds, and some have waterbeds and/or fireplaces. Guests receive a continental breakfast and a complimentary glass of wine each day of their stay. Message and wake-up service, reasonable rates and an outdoor hot tub are some of the other amenities that await you at the *Vagabond Inn*. Visit us and see the splendor of southwest Colorado in any season. Ride the Durango & Silverton Narrow Gauge Train. See the ancient Anazasi Indian Ruins. Ski Purgatory. Sample food from over seventy restaurants, and experience Durango while you stay at our *"turn-of-the-century roadhouse"*. Durango has plenty of nightlife and old-fashioned fun if you've got the notion. It's a perfect match for some of the best skiing Colorado has to offer. We accept most major credit cards. Sorry no pets permitted. Call or write for more information. We're looking forward to your stay with us! **AIRPORT:** La Plata County Airport 17 mi **DISCOUNTS:** Yes **RESERVATIONS:** One night's deposit at res time, 24 hr cancel policy for full refund, except Holiday seasons when 2 wk notice required **BROCHURE:** Yes **PERMITTED:** Children, smoking, drinking **CONFERENCES:** Yes [Z11DPCO-8460]

**Blue Lake Ranch			**Durango (Hesperus) CO**
David Alford			16919 Hwy 140 81326
303-385-4537			**Res Times** 8am-8pm
Rates:	**Pvt Bath** 2	**Shared Bath** 2	**Payment Terms:**
Single	$ 95-125.00	$ 70.00	Check
Double	$ 95-125.00	$ 70.00	

©*Bed & Breakfast Guest Houses & Inns of America, Memphis TN*

Colorado

Homesteaded in the early 1900s by Swedish immigrants, *Blue Lake Ranch* has evolved from a simple homestead to a luxurious, European-style Estate. The main house with antique and flower-filled rooms, is surrounded by gardens that supply Blue Lake Ranch's various businesses with lavender for jelly, heirloom seeds and everlasting flowers. From every room there is a view of the magnificent mountains that form a backdrop to the lake and the grazing herds of sheep. There is absolute privacy and quiet without another house in sight. At the cabin, overlooking a lake, window boxes of geraniums cascade to the outside deck. Furnished in Southwestern-style, there are three rooms equally comfortable for a couple or a group. Dramatic shifts of clouds pass over the lake; deer graze below in open meadows; and star-gazing is unparalled. A full European-style buffet breakfast and afternoon tea are included in the room rate. *Blue Lake Ranch* is 20 minutes from Durango and close to Mesa Verde with hiking in the San Juan Mountains. **RESERVATIONS:** 50% deposit of total stay within 7 days of booking, bal due 30 days prior to arrival, 30 day cancel policy for full refund; less than 30 days total amount forfeited unless re-rented for the same time. **BROCHURE:** Yes **PERMITTED:** Children, drinking **LANGUAGES:** French [Z11DPCO-847]

**Mad Creek B&B			**Empire CO**
Heather & Mike Lopez			PO Box 404 80438
303-569-2003			

Rates:	**Pvt Bath** 1	**Shared Bath** 2	**Payment Terms:**
Single	$ 59.00	$ 39.00	Check
Double	$ 69.00	$ 49.00	MC/V

1881 Victorian Cottage with old mountain charm! Antiques, family heirlooms, original artwork and unique artifacts of the past adorn the house. The common area includes a snowshoe style loveseat in a bay window. Relax in front of the rock fireplace while watching a movie, pursue the library filled with local lore, or plan your next adventure with our guides and maps. Your rooms are furnished with antiques, down comforters, knotty pine floors and other pleasantries. Complimentary x-country skis, snowshoes and mountain bikes are available for guests, including the outdoor hot tub. A full complimentary breakfast is included. On the continental divide at over 8600 foot altitude, Empire's picturesque star-shaped mountain valley is conveniently located within minutes of some of the best Colorado has to offer. Located just 42 miles west of Denver, Empire and its surrounding Historic Communities are living visions of a colorful mining past. Six major ski areas and wonderful back-country trails are 15-45 minutes away. Summer fun includes rafting, hiking, mountain biking, horseback rides, fishing and train rides. Scenic drives, Mine Tours, unique shopping and gourmet dining all year-round. Come - join us! **RESERVATIONS:** Credit card number for one night's deposit, 7

Colorado

day cancel policy for refund **BROCHURE:** Yes **PERMITTED:** Children 10-up, No smoking or pets **LANGUAGES:** Some Spanish **AIRPORT:** Denver Stapleton-45 mins **PACKAGES:** *Downhill Mountain Bike Tours, Raft Trips* [R03GPCO2-16667]

**Eagle Cliff House	**Estes Park CO**
Nancy & Mike Conrin	PO Box 4312 80517
303-586-5425	

Rates:	**Cottages** 3	**Payment Terms:**
Single	$ 65-95.00	Check
Double	$ 65-95.00	

Eagle Cliff House is a warm and friendly Bed and Breakfast nestled in ponderosa pines at the base of Eagle Cliff Mountain in Estes Park. We invite you to relax in the comfort of soft colors native to Southwestern decor combined with the beautiful woods used in American antiques. We invite you to enjoy the enticing aromas of a hearty country breakfast served in our bright and sunny breakfast nook. Tender homemade breads and rolls and fresh fruit greet you each morning. With our abundant full breakfast and an *every-ready cookie jar of delicacies* - you'll be ready for a full day of activities. The guest rooms and a separate cottage are variously furnished in turn-of-the-century country antiques, American Southwest decor and a Victorian theme. The Victorian Cottage is a private, romantic retreat featuring a queen size bed, fully stocked kitchenette and a sunny deck for enjoying the natural setting. Within walking distance of Rocky Mountain National Park, your hosts are expert backpacking and hiking enthusiasts and are happy to share their knowledge of the local areas. Summers offer a full complement of golf, hiking, tennis, swimming and horseback riding while winters feature excellent x-country skiing, snowshoeing - with spectacular views year-round. The quaint village of Estes Park offers an abundance of Western history, unique shops and restaurants. Your hosts can help with special touches such as flowers, champagne, fruit, cheese, balloons -just let them know. **RESERVATIONS:** Credit card number accepted only for one night deposit (or cash, check), two week cancel policy for refund less $10 service fee. Two night stay weekends requested **PERMITTED:** Children, drinking **BROCHURE:** Yes **LANGUAGES:** Some Spanish **AIRPORT:** Denver Stapleton-2 hrs [Z07GPCO2-16785]

**Hardy House	**Georgetown CO**
Carla & Mike Wagner	605 Brownell 80444
303-569-3388	**Res Times** 8am-9pm

Rates:	**Pvt Bath** 4	**Payment Terms:**

©*Bed & Breakfast Guest Houses & Inns of America, Memphis TN*

Colorado

Single	$ 63-67.00	Check
Double	$ 73-77.00	MC/V*

Quaint ten room red Victorian home which began life in 1877 invites guests to a special experience relaxing by the pot-belly stove or resting beneath feather comforters, in this charming home. Period furnishings throughout, guests can choose one of the four rooms/suites: *Victoria Suite, Ruby Room* or *Under the Eaves*. All with period decor, private baths, fireplaces and an outdoor hot tub. A gourmet candlelight breakfast is included in summer and winter. You're just ten minutes from the "best skiing" in Colorado. Plenty of hiking at 14,000 ft altitude including picnics along mountain streams or in the meadowlands. Flowers and carriage rides by request, complimentary bikes for guests to use. **RESERVATIONS:** Full payment is required 7-10 days after booking, 7 day cancel policy for refund, 30 day cancel notice for special events, holiday or ski groups *MC/V accepted only to hold, payment by cash or check is required **BROCHURE:** Yes **PERMITTED:** Children limited, drinking **AIRPORT:** Denver Intl-45 min **PACKAGES:** *Anniversary, Honeymoon* [Z08GPCO2-862]

**Dove Inn			**Golden CO**
Sue & Guy Beals			711 14th St 80401-1906
303-278-2209			**Res Times** 8am-8pm
			Fax 303-278-4029
Rates:	**Pvt Bath** 4	**Shared Bath** 2	**Payment Terms:**
Single	$ 44.00	$ 44.00	Check
Double	$ 66.00	$ 51.00	AE/DC/MC/V

Charming 1878-1886 Country Victorian residence on beautifully landscaped grounds and mature plantings is nestled in the foothills of West Denver, offering some of the best scenery Colorado has to offer. This residence offers all the Victorian features with dormers, angled ceilings, large bay windows, and other points of interest. Each guest room offers a unique decor. A spacious second floor room is furnished with a writing table and a spectacular view overlooking Golden and the foothills. An exciting room includes an antique 7-foot bathtub. All rooms include phone, TV, a/c with beds and cribs available. A full or continental breakfast is included. Nearby attractions included: Coors Brewery tour, Colorado School of Mines, Colorado RR Museum, Golden Gate Canyon State Park, Rocky Mountain National Park with plenty of skiing within an easy drive. Denver is just a twenty minute drive. **DISCOUNTS:** 10% stays 7 days or longer **AIRPORT:** Denver Stapleton Intl-20 mi **SEASONAL:** Closed Christmas **RESERVATIONS:** Deposit or credit card number to hold room; notify if arriving after 9 pm, 48 hr cancel policy. Airport shuttle is available. *Shower facility. **BROCHURE:** Yes **PERMITTED:** Limited children, limited drinking, limited smoking [Z03FPCO2-867]

Colorado

**Mary Lawrence Inn	**Gunnison CO**
Jan Goin	601 N Taylor 81230
303-641-3343	

Rates:	**Pvt Bath** 5	**Payment Terms:**
Single	$ 63-79.00	Check
Double	$ 69-85.00	MC/V

Built in 1885 and named for its long-time owner, *The Mary Lawrence Inn* was restored as a B&B in 1988. Rooms are furnished with Victorian antiques, hand-stenciled walls, home-made quilts, colorful art work, desks, fans and radios. A complimentary breakfast is imaginative and creative and served around an expandable table and differs each day. Menus take into account whether children are among the guests, and there's always a choice of juices and a wide range of hot beverages. Guests will find a sitting room filled with books, games and maps of the area. There's a fenced yard with deck, play house and picnic area for the children. Summer offers nearby lakes for fishing and boating while x-country skiing begins right outside of your door and downhill skiing at Crested Butte is jus 30 mins away. **AIRPORT:** Gunnison-2 mi **PACKAGES:** *Ski Packages* start at $46/person including B&B and lift ticket. **RESERVATIONS:** Credit card number to guarantee one night's deposit, late arrival only with prior arrangements. Airport pick-up available with prior arrangements. **BROCHURE:** Yes **PERMITTED:** Children, drinking [Z07GPCO2-9028]

**Apple Blossom Inn			**Leadville CO**
Maggie Senn			120 W Fourth St 80461
800-982-9279 719-486-2141			**Res Times** 8am-8pm

Rates:	**Pvt Bath** 3	**Shared Bath** 5	**Payment Terms:**
Single	$ 65.00	$ 49.00	Check
Double	$ 69.00	$ 54.00	MC/V

You are invited to enjoy an authentic slice of Colorado's rich past in this lovingly restored and tastefully decorated home. Built in 1879 by a prominent Leadville banker and business man whose holdings included interests in various lucrative mines such as The Little Pittsburgh and Little Johnny. His wife Estelle, earned the reputation of a gracious hostess because of the numerous parties and events they hosted. This lovely home retains many of their Victorian touches such as the beautiful crystal and brass lights, fireplaces adorned with Florentine tile, beveled mirrors, stained glass windows and maple and mahogany inlaid floors. The six guest rooms are uniquely furnished ranging from warm and cozy to large and sunny. Guests are welcomed into both of the charming living rooms, to enjoy the piano or the many board games or to choose a book

Colorado

from among the many selections on our shelves. A full complimentary breakfast is included and can be served in the dining room or your guest room. Packed lunches and delicious home-cooked dinners are available with prior arrangements. Complimentary hot and cold beverages are always available along with a full cookie jar of homemade goodies! Your hostess is ready to help plan your stay from finding the best fishing spot to locating baby sitters - just let her know. **AIRPORT:** Denver-110 mi **DISCOUNTS:** 10% for seniors (over 64) & corporate **PACKAGES:** *Ski Packages* from $49/ person including lift ticket; *Summer Package* from $39/person with museum passes **RESERVATIONS:** One night or 50% due within 7 days after reservation, 14 day cancel policy for refund, less than 14 days, refund only if rebooked, late arrival and check out only with prior arrangements **BROCHURE:** Yes **PERMITTED:** Children, drinking, limited pets, limited smoking **CONFERENCES:** Ideal for groups with sleeping facilities for 13-22 persons. [R05FPCO2-16407]

Grays Avenue Hotel			**Manitou Springs CO**
Tom & Lee Gray			711 Manitou Ave 80829
719-685-1277			

Rates:	**Pvt Bath** 6	**Shared Bath** 4	**Payment Terms:**
Single			Check
Double	$ 70.00	$ 50.00	

Queen Anne shingle Victorian which was built c1880's and in the center of the historic district and is the oldest continuously used hotel in Colorado. Guest rooms are furnished with antiques and spacious. You're close to all Colorado's major attractions here; Pike's Peak, Cog RR, Seven Falls, Air Force Academy, and Mt Manitou incline. Full country breakfast included. **PERMITTED:** Children 9-up **CONFERENCES:** Yes, social and business groups to 15 persons [C11ACCO-880]

Inn At Chalk Cliffs			**Nathrop CO**
Phyllis Terry			16557 County Rd #162 81236
719-395-6068			**Res Times** 7am-Noon

Rates:	**Pvt Bath** 2	**Shared Bath** 2	**Payment Terms:**
Single	$ 50.00	$ 50.00	Check
Double	$ 60.00	$ 60.00	MC/V

The *Inn at Chalk Cliffs* is nestled beneath breathtaking Mount Princeton (14,197 ft) and looks out onto Mt Antero (14,269 ft). It is located near the geographic center of Colorado and within 20 miles of the Continental Divide between the towns of Salida and Buena Vista. This is the ideal getaway for people who enjoy the outdoors, photography and geothermal

Colorado

mineral hot springs. Spectacular sunrises greet guests from our patios each morning while birds sing and wildlife makes regular appearances. The *Inn at Chalk Cliffs* is located in the Heart of the Rockies and enjoys 300 days (average) of sunshine making our locale the ideal spot for vacations year-round. Hike, bike, fish, golf, hunt (in season), snowmobile, raft the Arkansas River, ski the local slopes or visit a historic mining town - all within minutes of our cozy retreat. At night, view the setting sun going behind the Rockies and warm up to a snug fire in the crisp mountain summer night air. We have three spacious rooms and one smaller one for our guests sleeping comfort. A hearty full breakfast including many specialties awaits guests in the mornings. Let us make your vacation a memorable one. Experiences - *join us for a vacation you won't forget.* **AIRPORT:** Colorado Springs-115 mi; Denver-130 mi **DISCOUNTS:** Yes, inquire at res time **RESERVATIONS:** Full deposit required, 50% for extended stays. **BROCHURE:** Yes **PERMITTED:** Children 6+, limited smoking, limited drinking [Z04FPCO2-15172]

**Main Street House	**Ouray CO**
Dave Vince	Box 87 81427
303-325-4317	

Rates:	**Pvt Bath** 3	**Payment Terms:**
Single	$ 30-40.00	Check
Double	$ 45.55.00	

The *Main Street House* is a superbly renovated turn-of-the-century residence now consisting of three suites, each with a distinct identity, which blends modern conveniences with Victorian Charm! The Hayden Mountain Suite occupies the entire second floor. A spacious living room is joined by a large bedroom furnished with an antique dresser, walk-in closet king-size bed. The Oak Creek Suite located on the ground floor features a studio design with a small greenhouse. Its sleeping section contains a queen-size bed and the living area is furnished with a futon sofa that converts to a double bed. A large private deck off the greenhouse offers an excellent view of Oak Creek Canyon. The Cascade Suite, also on the ground level, contains a queen-size bed and a futon sofa that converts to a double . The Hayden Mtn & Oak Creek Suites have modern & fully equipped kitchens. All suites offer spectacular views of the San Juan Mtns, private entries, exterior decks, Victorian woodwork and private tiled baths. Guests have exclusive use of a landscaped courtyard & play area. Located on Main Street in the heart of Ouray's National Historic District, you're within easy walking distance of Ouray's famous Box Canon Park, Cascade Falls and the Ouray Hot Springs Pool. Continental breakfast included **RESERVATIONS:** One night's deposit at res time **BROCHURE:** Yes **PERMITTED:** Children, pets, smoking, drinking [RO6ACCO-5902]

Colorado

Saint Elmo Hotel	**Ouray CO**
The Lingenfelters	426 Main St 81427
303-325-4951	**Res Times** 8am-10pm
	Fax 303-325-0348
Rates: **Pvt Bath** 9	**Payment Terms:**
Single $ 84.00	*Check
Double $ 84.00	AE/DISC/MC/V

The *Saint Elmo Hotel* was built in 1898 as a miner's hotel in the booming mining era of the day, in the San Juan Mountains of southwestern Colorado. Today the *Saint Elmo* is a beautifully restored nine room, Victorian Bed and Breakfast Inn with antiques (many thought to be original pieces) in the guest rooms and common areas. A breakfast buffet of juice, homemade muffins and breads, cold cereal and a special entree of the day, awaits overnight guests each morning in the sunny breakfast room with its magnificent view of the surrounding mountains. The very popular Bon Ton Restaurant is located in the hotel, serving dinner nightly and a Sunday champagne brunch. Ouray sits in one of the most picturesque mountain settings that one will ever see, and has been known as *"The Switzerland of America"* for over a hundred years. **AIRPORT:** Denver Stapleton-325 mi **PACKAGES:** Two night special including dinner **RESERVATIONS:** Credit card number for deposit required to guarantee reservation. *Local checks accepted only **BROCHURE:** Yes **PERMITTED:** Children, drinking [Z07GPCO2-889]

*Orchard House	**Palisade CO**
William & Stephanie Schmid	3573 E 1/2 Rd 81526
303-464-0529	**Res Times** Anytime
Rates: **Pvt Bath** 2	**Payment Terms:**
Single $ 60.00	Check
Double	MC/V

Enjoy the spectacular views of Mount Garfield, Lincoln and Grand Mesa from this 4000 sq ft charming home set on its own peach orchard. Offers guests a large king-size room along with twin beds downstairs in this separate guest house complete with its own private entrance and full kitchen. A full country breakfast is included where you can sample your host's talents for preparing Eggs Benedict, French toast, omelets with all the extras. Dinners are also available at added cost. Plenty of things to see and do here and your knowledgeable hosts are most anxious to help you with any plans. **RESERVATIONS:** Pre-payment with reservation, 72-hr cancellation policy for refund **BROCHURE:** Yes **PERMITTED:** Children, pets, smoking, drinking [E02BCCO-6069]

Colorado

**Castillo de Caballeros		Salida CO
Cheri Rost		PO Box 89 81201
719-539-2002		**Res Times** 5-9pm

Rates:	**Shared Bath** 4	**Payment Terms:**
Single	$ 37-45.00	Certified Check
Double	$ 37-45.00	

Quaint nine-room red Victorian home which began life in 1877 invites guests to a special experience relaxing by the pot-belly stove or resting beneath feather comforters, in this charming home. Period furnishings throughout, guests can choose one of the three rooms/suites: Victoria Suite. Ruby Room or Under the Eaves. All with period decor and king beds in some rooms, private or *designated baths and an anniversary/birthday candlelight & champagne dinner service available upon request!! A savory Continental plus breakfast in the Summer and a Full breakfast in Winter is included. You're just ten minutes from the "best skiing" in Colorado at Loveland Basin! Plenty of hiking at 14,000 ft altitude including picnics along mountain streams or in the meadowlands. Any trout you catch will be graciously prepared by the hostess for your meal. Flowers & carriage rides by request. **RESERVATIONS:** $15.00 non-refundable deposit required at res time. Responsible for full room cost if canceled with 14 days of reservation date. **BROCHURE:** Yes **PERMITTED:** Children 10-up [R05APCO-862]

**Alpine Inn B&B			Telluride CO
Denise & John Weaver			PO Box 2398
800-707-3344 303-728-6282			**Res Times** 10am-9pm

Rates:	**Pvt Bath** 6	**Shared Bath** 2	**Payment Terms:**
Single	$ 65-220.00	$ 50-130.00	Check
Double	$ 65-220.00	$ 50-130.00	MC/V

We invite you to experience the *"magic of Telluride"* in one of it's original landmark hotels - now restored to a charming Bed & Breakfast. Each of the eight guest rooms transport you back to a Victorian Era filled with handmade quilts, armoires, soft colors and a touch of elegance. King, queen and single bed accommodations with private baths create a comfortable atmosphere suited for a variety of guestneeds. Our honeymoon suite has kitchen facilities, whirlpool tub

©*Bed & Breakfast Guest Houses & Inns of America*

Colorado

and a private terrace looking out to Ingram Falls and the ski mountain. Each morning enjoy a full breakfast served in our sunroom or on the veranda. After a day of activity, relax in the hot tub while soaking-up the **"best hot tub views in town".** During the summer, Telluride hosts a variety of festivals which include Bluegrass, Wine, Film and Jazz as well as a few other eclectic treats like the Mushroom and Talking Gourds festivals. All are within walking distance of the Inn. During winter, Telluride is a skier's paradise. Within two blocks of the Inn, the ski lifts take you to the **most beautiful place you will ever ski.** Over 1000 acres of skiing terrain will excite skiers of all levels. Lift lines are virtually non-existent. Your hosts invite you to experience **views that will take your breath away** and a town that retains very much of its historical ambiance. Both Telluride and the *Alpine Inn* have strong environmental objectives and hope you will share in our commitment. **RESERVATIONS:** One night's deposit (50% winter and festival periods), within 7 days of booking, balance due upon arrival, bal required 45 days prior to arrival during winter and festival periods **BROCHURE:** Yes **PERMITTED:** Children 11-up, drinking **DISCOUNTS:** Yes, inquire at res time **AIRPORT:** Telluride, Montrose, Grand Junction **PACKAGES:** *Skiing* [I08GPCO2-15743]

Pennington's Mountain Inn	Telluride CO
Judy & Michale MacLean	PO Box 2428 81435
800-543-1437 303-728-5337	**Res Times** 24 Hrs

Rates:	**Pvt Bath** 12	**Payment Terms:**
Single	$ 95-155.00*	Check
Double	$ 95-155.00*	AE/DC/MC/V

A B&B Resort that's more like everyone's dream home surrounded by the unrivaled scenic beauty of the Rocky Mountains while nestled along side the 12th fairway on Telluride's Championship 18 hole course. The Inn is reminiscent of a picture-perfect postcard and features warm & comfortable French country decor, spacious rooms with queen & king beds all with panoramic views of Colorado's most beautiful mountains. Each guest room includes a private refrigerator stocked with refreshments and snacks - all included in the room rate. There's more too; a full breakfast with specialties of blueberry pancakes, eggs Benedict, fresh ground coffee & tea served in your room or dining room - a complimentary Happy Hour (4-6 daily) with wine, brandy, champagne, hot tea & hors d'oeuvres. A library, indoor jacuzzi & steam room, game room, ski lockers, laundry facilities, kitchen for preparing snacks and mountain bikes for your use. Outdoors is world class alpine skiing, x-country Nordic trails, snowmobiling, ice skating, sleigh rides and in spring & summer there's golf, tennis, hiking, fishing, white-water rafting and plenty of sightseeing in Telluride. Courtesy airport pick-up and free ski shuttle. **RESERVATIONS:** First

Colorado

night's deposit 21 days from res date incl 8.29% tax; 30 day cancel policy for refund, bal due on arrival. *Rates higher during seasonal peaks. **BROCHURE:** Yes **PERMITTED:** Children, drinking, limited smoking **CONFERENCES:** Yes for groups to 25 persons including special room rates **PACKAGES:** Yes, inquire at res time [R07BCCO-8458]

**San Sophia	**Telluride CO**
Dianne & Gary Eschman	330 W Pacific Ave 81435
800-537-4781 303-728-3001	**Res Times** 8am-9pm

Rates:	**Pvt Bath** 16	**Payment Terms:**
Single	$ 95-195.00	Check
Double	$ 95-195.00	AE/MC/V

Elegant and new luxurious sixteen room Inn with spectacular views of the surrounding 13,000 foot mountains. Located one block from the Telluride downtown Historic District. Also one block from the Oak Street ski lift and 1/2 block from the San Miguel River. Breakfast on the east facing dining deck or inside an exclusive dining area. West facing deck offers afternoon sunning while enjoying complimentary wine & cheese. The *San Sophia* has been featured in many travel articles and is considered by the *American Bed & Breakfast Association* as the "***Top Inn in Colorado***", *Innside America*, June 1989 proclaims "*... one of the most deluxe and romantic inns in America*". Amenities include full gourmet buffet breakfast, afternoon apres ski, luxuriously appointed rooms all with brass beds, "bathtubs for two", original art work and cable TV. Guests can enjoy spectacular views in the observatory, a gazebo with jacuzzi, ski lockers, ski boot dryers, garden and underground parking. ***True Western Hospitality*** and knowledgeable hosts make for an unforgettable stay! **RESERVATIONS:** 50% deposit per night of stay within 10 days, less than 30 days prior to arrival, entire amount due at res time, 30 day cancel policy less $20 service fee. Less than 30 days notice, only if rebooked **SEASONAL:** Rates vary **BROCHURE:** Yes **PERMITTED:** Children 10-up, drinking, smoking outdoors only, no pets. **CONFERENCES:** Excellent for groups to 25 including A/V: 6x8 ft projection screen, large screen TV, VCR, slide projectors **LANGUAGES:** English **AIRPORT:** Telluride-5 mi **DISCOUNT:** Travel agents and Skiamericard. [I07GPCO2-8459]

Colorado

Two Bars Seven Ranch	**Virginia Dale CO**
Polly Schaffer	PO Box 398 80548
303-742-6072	**Res Times** 9am-9pm

Rates: **Pvt Bath** 7   **Payment Terms:**
Single $ 59.00   Check
Double $ 69.00

A 7,000 acre cattle & horse ranch setting places you right in the Great Outdoors!! Hearty ranch breakfast served daily to start you on your daily outdoor adventure. **BROCHURE:** Yes **PERMITTED:** Children, pets, smoking, social drinking [C11ACCO-919]

Colorado

Alamosa
*COTTONWOOD INN
800-955-BNBE

Allenspark
ALLENSPARK LODGE
303-747-2552

LAZY H RANCH
303-747-2532

WILD BASIN LODGE
303-747-2454

Arriba
TARADO MANSION
303-768-3468

Arvada
KB KANOPY
800-432-4435

ON GOLDEN POND
303-424-2296

TREE HOUSE
303-431-8352

Aspen
ALPINA HAUS
800-24-ASPEN

ASPEN MANOR
303-925-3001

ASPEN SKI LODGE
303-925-3434

BRASS BED INN
303-925-3622

CHRISTIANA LODGE
303-925-3014

CHRISTMAS INN
303-925-3822

CRESTHAUS LODGE
800-925-7081

FIRESIDE INN
303-772-7678

HEARTHSTONE HOUSE
303-925-7632

HEATHERBED LODGE
303-925-7077

HOTEL LENDAO
800-321-3457

INNSBRUCK INN
303-925-2980

INVERNESS B&B
303-925-8500

LITTLE RED SKI HAUS
303-925-3333

MOUNTAIN HOUSE
303-920-2550

POMEGRANATE INN
303-525-4012

*SARDY HOUSE
800-321-3457

**SNOW QUEEN VICTORIAN INN
303-925-8455

ST MORITZ LODGE
303-925-3220

TIPPLE INN
800-321-7025

ULLR LODGE
303-925-7696

Ault
EASTRIDGE FARMS
303-834-2617

Avada
ON GOLDEN POND
303-424-2296

Bailey
GLEN-ISLE ON THE PLATTE

Basalt
ALTAMIRA RANCH INN
303-927-3309

SHENANDOAH INN
303-927-4991

Bayfield
DEER VALLEY RESORTS
303-884-2600

Beaver Creek
INN AT BEAVER CREEK
303-845-7800

POSTE MONTANE LODGE
303-845-7500

Berthoud
PARRISH COUNTRY SQUIRE
303-772-7678

Black Hawk
GILPIN HOTEL
303-582-5012

Boulder
BLUEBIRD LODGE

©Bed & Breakfast Guest Houses & Inns of America, Memphis TN   191

Colorado

303-443-6475

**BOULDER VICTORIA HISTORIC B&B
303-938-1300

*BRIAR ROSE B&B
303-442-3007

HOTEL BOULDERADO

MAGPIE INN
303-449-6528

PEARL STREET INN
800-232-5949

ROOM WITH A VIEW

SALINA HOUSE
303-442-1494

SANDY POINT INN
303-530-2939

Breckenridge
**ALLAIRE TIMBERS INN
800-624-4904

BROWN HOTEL
303-453-0084

**COTTEN HOUSE
303-453-5509

DAYTONS NORDIC INN
303-453-6617

*FIRESIDE INN
303-453-6456

SWISS INN
303-453-6489

WILLIAMS HOUSE B&B
303-453-2973

Buena Vista
ADOBE INN
303-395-6340

BLUE SKY INN
303-395-8865

BLUEBIRD RIDGE B&B
719-395-2336

*COTTONWOOD HOT SPRINGS INN
800-241-4119

TROUT CITY INN
719-495-0348

Carbondale
AMBIANCE INN
303-963-3597

ASPEN VALLEY B&B
303-963-2628

BIGGERSTAFF HOUSE
303-963-3605

CRYSTAL RIVER INN
303-963-3902

HARMONY HOUSE
303-963-3369

Cascade
EASTHOLME
719-684-9901

SUE'S GUEST HOUSE
719-684-2111

Cedaridge

CEDARS EDGE
303-856-6836

MELINDA MEADOWS
303-856-6384

Clark
HOME RANCH
303-879-1780

Colorado Springs
1894 VICTORIAN
719-630-3322

BLACK FOREST B&B
719-495-4208

**CHEYENNE CAÑON B&B INN
719-633-0625

*GRIFFINS HOSPITALITY HOUSE
719-599-3035

*HEARTHSTONE INN
719-473-4413

**HOLDEN HOUSE-1902 B&B INN
719-471-3980

PAINTED LADY B&B
719-473-3165

**ROOM AT THE INN
719-442-1896

Creede
CREEDE HOTEL
719-658-2608

Crested Butte
ALPINE LACE B&B
303-349-9857

Colorado

BRUMDER HEARTH
303-349-6253

CLAIM JUMPER
303-349-6471

CRESTED BEAUTY
303-349-1201

CRISTIANA GUEST
HAUS B&B
303-349-5326

FOREST QUEEN
HOTEL
303-349-5336

GOTHIC INN
303-349-7215

NORDIC INN
303-349-5542

PURPLE MOUNTAIN
LODGE
303-349-5888

TUDOR ROSE B&B
303-349-6253

Cripple Creek
IMPERIAL HOTEL
303-689-2713

Delores
MOUNTAIN VIEW
B&B
800-228-4592

RIO GRANDE
SOUTHERN HOTEL

Delta
DELTA-ESCALANTE
RANCH
303-874-4121

Denver
CAMBRIDGE CLUB
303-831-1252

CASTLE MARNE
800-92 MARNE

**CHEYENNE CAÑON
B&B INN**
719-633-0625

HAUS BERLIN B&B
303-837-9527

MERRITT HOUSE
B&B
303-861-5230

MOUNTAIN MANSION
303-486-0655

OXFORD
303-228-5838

QUEEN ANNE INN
800-432-INNS

ROOM AT THE INN
719-442-1896

*VICTORIA OAKS
INN
303-355-1818

Dillon
ANNABELLES B&B
303-468-8667

BLUE VALLEY GUEST
HOUSE
800-530-3866

PTARMIGAN MTN
B&B
303-468-5289

Divide

SILVERWOOD B&B
AT DIVIDE
719-687-6784

Dolores
LITTLE SOUTHFORK
RANCH B&B
303-882-4259

SIMON DRAW GUEST
HOUSE
303-565-8721

Durango
COUNTRY SUNSHINE
800-383-2853

ELK MEADOWS INN
303-247-4559

GENERAL PALMER
HOTEL
800-523-3358

*JARVIS SUITE
HOTEL
800-824-1024

**LELAND HOUSE
B&B SUITES**
303-385-1920

LOGWOOD B&B
800-369-4082

PENNYS PLACE
303-247-8928

**RIVER HOUSE
B&B**
800-544-0009

*SCRUBBY OAKS
B&B
303-247-2176

STRATER HOTEL

Colorado

800-247-4431

TALL TIMBER
303-259-4813

**VAGABOND INN
303-259-5901

VICTORIAN INN
303-247-2223

Durango(Hesperus)
**BLUE LAKE RANCH
303-385-4537

Duray
HISTORIC WESTERN B&B
303-325-4645

Eaton
VICTORIAN VERANDA
303-454-3890

Edwards
LODGE AT CORDILLERA
800-548-2721

Eldora
GOLDMINER HOTEL
800-422-4629

Empire
**MAD CREEK B&B
303-569-2003

PECK HOUSE
303-569-9870

Estes Park
ANNIVERSARY INN
303-586-6200

ASPEN LODGE & GUEST RANCH
303-586-8133

BALDPATE INN
303-586-6151

BLACK DOG INN
303-586-0374

COTTENWOOD HOUSE
303-586-5104

EAGLE CLIFF HOUSE
303-586-5425

EMERALD MANOR
303-586-8050

INN AT ROCK'N RIVER
800-448-4611

*RIVERSONG A B&B
303-586-4666

SAPPHIRE ROSE INN
303-586-6607

*STANLEY HOTEL
800-ROCKIES

TERRACES
303-586-9411

*WANEKS LODGE AT ESTES
303-586-5851

WIND RIVER RANCH
303-586-4212

Fort Collins
*ELIZABETH STREET GUEST HOUSE
303-493-BEDS

EMERALD MANOR
303-223-1396

HELMSHIRE INN
303-493-4683

SHINING MOUNTAINS INN
303-586-5886

Frisco
FRISCO LODGE
800-279-6000

GLENA ST MOUNTAININN
303-668-3224

LARK B&B
303-668-5237

MAR DEIS MOUNTAIN RETREAT
303-668-5337

TWLIGHT INN
303-668-5008

WOODS INN INTL LTD
303-668-3389

Garnby
DROWSY WATER RANCH
303-725-3456

Georgetown
*HARDY HOUSE
303-569-3388

Glen Haven
INN OF GLEN HAVEN
303-586-3897

Glenwood Springs
ADDUCCIS INN
303-945-9341

HIDEOUT

Colorado

303-945-5621
HOTEL COLORADO

HOTEL DENVER
303-945-6565

KAISER HOUSE B&B
303-945-8827

TALBOTT HOUSE
303-945-1039

Gold Hill
GOLD HILL INN
303-443-6461

Golden
**DOVE INN
303-278-2209

JAMESON INN
303-278-2209

Granby
SHADOW MOUNTAIN
RANCH
303-887-9524

Grand Junction
CIDER HOUSE B&B
303-242-9087

GATEHOUSE
303-242-6105

JUNCTION COUNTRY
INN
303-241-2817

Grand Lake
WINDING RIVER
RESORT
303-627-3215

Grant
TUMBLING RIVER
RANCH
303-838-5981

Green Mountain Falls
COLUMBINE LODGE
719-684-9062

OUTLOOK LODGE
719-684-2303

Gunnison
**MARY LAWRENCE INN
303-641-3343

WAUNITA HOT
SPRINGS RANCH
303-641-1266

Gypsum
7-W GUEST RANCH
303-524-9328

SWEETWATER
CREEK RANCH
303-524-9301

Hot Sulphur Springs
RIVERSIDE HOTEL
303-725-9996

Hotchkiss
MIDWAY INN
303-527-3422

YE OLDE OASIS
303-872-3794

Idaho Springs
ST MARYS GLACIER

Ignacio
KELSALLS UTE
CREEK RANCH
303-563-4464

Keystone
KEYSTONE RESORT
VILLAGE
303-468-5251

*SKI TIP LODGE
303-468-4202

La Veta
1899 INN
719-742-3576

Lake City
ADOBE B&B
303-944-2642

CINNAMON INN
303-944-2641

CRYSTAL LODGE
303-944-2201

MONCRIEF
MOUNTAIN RANCH
303-944-2796

MOSS ROSE B&B
303-366-4069

OLD CARSON INN
303-944-2511

Leadville
**APPLE BLOSSOM INN
800-982-9279

DELAWARE HOTEL
800-748-2004

LEADVILLE
COUNTRY INN
800-748-2354

WOOD HAVEN
MANOR B&B
800-748-2570

©*Bed & Breakfast Guest Houses & Inns of America, Memphis TN*   195

Colorado

Limon
MIDWEST COUNTRY INN
719-775-2373

Littleton
HUCKLEBERRY INN

Loveland
SYLVAN DALE RANCH

*THE LOVELANDER
800-866-0621

Lyons
PEACEFUL VALLEY LODGE

ROCK N' RIVER B&B
800-448-4611

Manitou Springs
BILLYS COTTAGE
719-685-1828

*GRAYS AVENUE HOTEL
719-685-1277

ON A LEDGE
800-530-8253

PEACEFUL PLACE B&B
719-685-1248

RED CRAGS B&B
719-685-1920

RED STONE CASTLE
719-685-5070

SUNNYMEDE B&B
719-685-4619

TWO SISTERS INN
719-685-9684

Marble
INN AT RASPBERRY RIDGE
303-963-3025

Meeker
SNOW GOOSE B&B
303-878-4532

Meredith
DIAMOND J GUEST RANCH
303-927-3222

FRYINGPAN RIVER RANCH
303-927-3570

Minturin
*EAGLE RIVER INN
800-344-1750

Monte Vista
*MONTE VILLA INN

Montrose
FIFTH STREET B&B
303-249-4702

Morrison
*CLIFF HOUSE LODGE
303-697-9732

Mosca
DUNES COUNTRY INN
719-378-2356

Nathrop
INN AT CHALK CLIFFS
719-395-6068

Northrup
CENTERVILLE INN
303-539-4786

DEER VALLEY RANCH
303-395-2353

Norwood
BACK NARROWS INN
303-327-4417

Ohio City
GOLD CREEK INN

Olathe
UNCOMPAHGRE CABIN
303-323-6789

Ouray
DAMN YANKEE B&B
800-845-7512

HOUSE OF YESTERDAY
303-325-4277

KUNZ HOUSE
303-325-4220

****MAIN STREET HOUSE**
303-325-4317

MANOR B&B
303-325-4574

OURAY 1898 HOUSE
303-838-4167

****ST ELMO HOTEL**
303-325-4951

WEISBADEN SPA & LODGE
303-325-4347

WESTERN HOTEL
303-325-4645

Colorado

Pagosa Springs
DAVIDSONS COUNTRY INN
303-264-5863

ECHO MANOR
303-264-5646

ROYAL PINE INN
800-955-0274

Palisade
*ORCHARD HOUSE
303-464-0529

Paonia
ET'S B&B
303-527-3300

Parshall
ASPEN CANYON RANCH
303-725-3518

BAR LAZY J GUEST RANCH
303-725-3437

Pine
MEADOW CREEK B&B
303-838-4167

Pueblo
ABRIENDO INN
719-544-2703

Red Cliff
PILGRIMS INN
303-827-5333

Redstone
AVALANCHE RANCH
303-963-2846

*CLEVEHOLD MANOR
800-643-4887

HISTORIC REDSTONE INN
303-963-2526

Ridgeway
MACTIERNANS SAN JUAN RANCH
303-626-5360

Rifle
COULTER LAKE GUEST RANCH
303-625-1473

Salida
**CASTILLO DE CABALLEROS
719-539-2002

PONDEROSA LODGE

POOR FARM COUNTRY INN
800-373-4995

VICTORIAN MANOR
719-539-4112

Shawnee
NORTH FORK RANCH
303-838-9873

Silver Plume
BREWERY INN
303-571-1151

Silverthorne
ALPEN HUTTE LODGE
303-468-6336

Silverton
ALMA HOUSE
303-387-5336

ALPINE HOUSE
303-387-5628

CHRISTOPHER HOUSE
303-387-5857

*FOOLS GOLD INN
303-387-5879

GRAND IMPERIAL HOTEL
303-387-5527

SMEDLEYS B&B
303-387-5423

*TELLER GUEST HOUSE
800-342-4338

WINGATE HOUSE B&B
303-387-5423

WYMAN HOTEL
303-387-5372

Snowmass
MOUNTAIN CHALET
800-843-1579

Steamboat Springs
BEAR POLE RANCH
303-879-0576

CRAWFORD HOUSE
303-879-1859

HABOR HOTEL
303-543-8888

INN AT STEAMBOAT
303-879-2600

SCANDINAVIAN LODGE
800-233-8102

*SKI VALLEY LODGE

Colorado

303-879-7749

STEAMBOAT SPRINGS
303-879-5724

VISTA VERDE GUEST RANCH
800-526 RIDE

Steamboat Village
SCANDINAVIAN LODGE
303-879-0517

Sterling
CREST HOUSE
303-522-3753

Telluride
**ALPINE INN B&B
303-728-6282

BEAR CREEK B&B
800-338-7064

CIMARRON LODGE
303-728-3803

*DAHL HAUS
303-728-4158

JOHNSTONE INN
800-628-4750

NEW SHERIDAN HOTEL
303-728-4351

OAK STREET INN
303-728-3383

*PENNINGTON'S MOUNTAIN INN
800-543-1437

**SAN SOPHIA

800-537-4781

SKYLINE GUEST RANCH
303-728-3757

VICTORIAN INN
303-728-3684

Twin Lakes
INN OF THE BLACK WOLF

TWIN LAKES NORDIC LODGE
303-486-0440

Vail
BLACK BEAR INN
303-478-1304

GASTHOF GRAMSHAMMER
303-476-5626

MOUNTAIN WEAVERY
303-476-5539

SITZMARK LODGE
303-476-5001

Vallecito Lake
WIT'S END
303-884-4113

Victor
PORTLAND HOUSE
800-669-2102

Virginia Dale
*TWO BARS SEVEN RANCH
303-742-6072

Winter Park
ALPEN ROSE B&B
303-726-5039

BEAU WEST B&B
800-473-5145

ENGLEMANN PINES
800-992-9512

GASTHAUS EICHIER HOTEL
303-726-5133

GELMARK B&B
800-424-2158

MILLERS INN

OUTPOST INN
303-726-5346

SOMETHING SPECIAL: A B&B
303-726-5360

TEMPLES ANGLEMARK
303-726-5354

WOODSPUR LODGE

Woodland Park
HACKMAN HOUSE
719-687-9851

LOFTHOUSE
719-687-9187

PIKES PEAK PARADISE
800-728-8282

WOODLAND HILLS LODGE
719-621-8386

Yellow Jacket
WILSONS PINTO BEAN FARM
303-562-4476

Hawaii

Doris Epp-Reichert | **Aiea Oahu HI
*Doris Epp
800-999-6026 808-487-1228

99-442 Kekoa Place 96701
Res Times 24 Hrs
Fax 808-261-1228

Rates: **Pvt Bath** 1
Single
Double $ 500.00 Week

Payment Terms:
Check

In the mountains above Pearl Harbor, this great setting for a family or friends traveling together. A private unit in a residential home with a large yard, tropical fruit trees. A private entrance leads to two bedrooms, bath, living room and a complete kitchen with stove, refrigerator, dishwasher, appliance, dishes and etc. The refrigerator is provisioned with morning breakfast. Owners don't smoke and don't have children or pets. Just five minutes to large shopping centers, entertainment and just a twenty minute drive to Waikiki and other beach areas. Beautiful hiking trails in nearby reserve. A great escape from the crowded tourist areas. **BROCHURE:** Yes **PERMITTED:** Children, smoking, drinking **LANGUAGES:** English, German, Spanish [R05FPHI2-16887]

Papaya Paradise B&B | **Kailua Oahau HI
Bob & Jeanette Martz
808-261-0316

395 Auwinala Rd 96734
Res Times 6am-9pm

Rates: **Pvt Bath** 2
Single $ 60.00
Double $ 60.00

Payment :
Tvlrs Checks

Papaya Paradise is located in Kailua on the windward side of Oahu approximately 20 miles from the Honolulu Airport and Waikiki. It's private, quiet, tropical and removed from the hectic activity of Waikiki but still only 20 mins away for those who want an evening's entertainment. All major attractions on the island can be reached within 90 mins from *Payaya Paradise* . . Kailua Beach, a beautiful uncrowded four miles of white sandy beach, offering all of the water sports is just a short walk . . . there are two bedrooms each with 2 beds, ceiling fans, a/c, cable color TV and private bath and private entrances. A full breakfast which includes fresh Papaya (when available from our own grove) is served on the lanai overlooking a 20 by 40 pool and jacuzzi which is surrounded by tropical plants, trees and Hawaiian flowers. Mount Olomana is in the

Hawaii

background. A 17 cu ft refrigerator is available for our guests use, along with beach towels, mats, hats, chairs and coolers. Bob is a full-time host who enjoys cooking, baking and sharing his hawaiian experience with his guests. **RESERVATIONS:** 20% deposit at time of reservation, add 9% tax **BROCHURE:** Yes **PERMITTED:** Drinking, smoking; limited children. [R11CPHI-11834]

**Kailua Plantation House	**Kona HI**
Rose Singarella	75-5948 Alii Dr 96740
808-329-3727	**Res Times** 24 Hrs

Rates:	**Pvt Bath** 5	**Payment Terms:**
Single	$ 120-175.00	Check
Double	$ 120-175.00	AE/MC/V

A tropical paradise awaits you at the *Kailua Plantation House* in Kona on the Big Island of Hawaii. This newly constructed Inn is perched on a promontory of black lava rocks with an unobstructed view of the Pacific Ocean. Each guest room in this oceanfront inn boasts a private bath as well as a private lanai. Awaken to the aroma of freshly ground and brewed Kona coffee and a continental breakfast featuring fresh tropical fruits, breads and muffins. Enjoy a leisurely breakfast in the living area - elegantly designed with high ceilings, exposed dropped beams, crown moldings and fan lights - or outside by the dipping pool and jacuzzi. Watch migrating whales while you sunbathe on the lanai in soft ocean breezes. Savor a glass of wine as the sun gently slips into the water. Within walking distance are tennis facilities, fine restaurants and shops. The *Kailua Plantation House* retains its secluded beauty. For the traveler who seeks the niceties of an oceanfront resort yet desires the coziness and charm of a bed and breakfast, the Kailua Plantation House offers the best of both worlds. **DISCOUNTS:** 10% to Hawaiian residents **AIRPORT:** Keahole Airport-10 mi **RESERVATIONS:** 50% deposit of full length of stay **BROCHURE:** Yes **PERMITTED:** Children 12-up, drinking, limited smoking (outside) **LANGUAGES:** French [R10DPHI-14586]

**Ahinahina Farm B&B	**Maui HI**
Mike & Annette Endres	Kula 96790
800-241-MAUI 808-878-6096	**Res Times** 24 Hrs

Rates:	**Pvt Bath** 3	**Payment Terms:**
Single	$ 75-90.00	Check
Double	$ 75-90.00	

Let us show you Maui the way it really is; hundred mile views of ocean and mountains, rainbows and flowers, gentle breezes, peace and quiet.

Hawaii

Both our studio cottage and the two bedroom cottage are separate from the main dwelling, affording maximum privacy for guests. Each accommodation has a large covered deck with outdoor table and chairs for relaxation. The studio cottage has a queen bed, efficiency kitchen, color TV, sofa and chair for reading and a table for two for a gracious double accommodation. The two bedroom cottage offers a full kitchen, including dishwasher, clothes washer, drier, two full bedrooms (queen in one, twin beds in the other) color TV with VCR, full dining and living room. Both accommodations have beautiful views of Mount Haleakala, the central valley of Maui and the ocean to the North and South of the island. We offer only the highest quality of accommodation and hospitality and to the discriminating visitor we say *"E komo mai"* - *(Welcome to our home).* **AIRPORT:** Kahului Maui HI-20 mins. **RESERVATIONS:** 50% deposit required with bal due upon arrival. Payment by check only in advance of arrival, 14 day cancel policy less one night's lodging fee, 3 day min in 2 bedroom cottage **BROCHURE:** Yes **PERMITTED:** Drinking and children 12-up [Z03FPHI2-13862]

**Oceanfront, Doris Epp	**Kailua Oahu HI**
*Doris Epp 800-999-6026 808-263-4848	19 Kai Nani Place 96734 **Res Times** 24 Hrs **Fax** 808-261-6573
Rates: **Pvt Bath** 2 Single $ 75.00 Double $ 75.00*	**Payment Terms:** Check

Beachfront, quiet executive residence, an area of million dollar properties, perfectly private, miles of white sand beaches, away from the maddening crowds and *Hawaii Too!* That's not all - guests to this island paradise have a separate wing with a private entrance, two-room suite with private bath, king-size bed, color cable TV, phone with the second room offering a double and single bed, a full kitchen area that includes a fridge, micro-wave, bar-type sink, elect appliances for preparing anything at home. A patio outside of the glass sliding doors offers additional privacy. Within a five minute walk are grocery stores, bus lines and restaurants. Honolulu is just 15 mins driving, Waikiki and the airport are just 30 mins driving. There's horseback riding, tennis, golf and windsurfing close-by. The refrigerator is provisioned for your comp breakfast each morning. **RESERVATIONS:** 50% deposit at res time, plus 9% room tax. *$85 a night for 3 or more guests. Rooms are rented to one private party at a time. Weekly rates are $475 and monthly $1500.00 **BROCHURE:** Yes **PERMITTED:** Children, smoking, drinking **LANGUAGES:** German, Spanish, English [Z05FPHI2-8181]

Hawaii

Kilauea Lodge	**Volcano Village HI**
The Jeytes	PO Box 116 96785
808-967-7366	
	Fax 808-967-7367
Rates: **Pvt Bath** 12	**Payment Terms:**
Single $ 80-125.00	Check
Double $ 85-125.00	MC/V

KILAUEA LODGE

Nestled in the pine trees atop Kilauea Mountain, *Kilauea Lodge* presents the perfect lodging for the visitor to Hawaii Volcanoes National Park. Located in Volcano Village, a mile from the park entrance, *Kilauea Lodge* is a charming YMCA lodge converted to a Country Inn in 1988 by the owners/hosts, Lorna and Albert Jeyte. Twelve rooms with private baths are decorated in the style of old Hawaii and country New England. Six of the rooms are furnished with fireplaces and the other six have central heating. Due to the 3700 foot elevation, nights and mornings can be quite cool. A hearty breakfast is included with the room. The lodge dining room, open nightly for dining alongside the famous *Fireplace of Friendship* features continental cuisine with a touch of local flavor. **"A superb restaurant only a stone's throw from your pillow"** said *Conde Nast*, November 1990. The cuisine reflects the style of Chef Albert who hails from northern Germany and his wife Lorna, born and raised in Hawaii. *Volcano Village* is located 26 miles from Hilo Airport and 100 miles from Kona Airport. Old Hilo Town is a charming plantation community being restored to reflect its former history. Volcanoes National Park features museums, trails, craters to explore, an active volcano and the splendors of Madame Pele herself. Volcano Golf Course is three miles from the lodge and sightseeing helicopter service is located nearby. **RESERVATIONS:** One night deposit by cash or money order; 3 day cancel notice for refund, 2 night min on holidays. **BROCHURE:** Yes **PERMITTED:** Children, drinking and limited smoking **LANGUAGES:** German, English [O05FPHI2-8182]

Hawaii

Aiea Oahu
DORIS EPP-REICHERT
800-999-6026

Anahola, Kauai
MAHINA KAI
808-822-9451

Captain Cook
ADRIENNE B&B
800-328-9726

SOUTH POINT B&B
808-929-7466

Haibu, Maui
HAIKULEANA B&B
INN PLANTATION
808-575-2890

Hana
HANA PLANTATION
800-657-7723

Hana, Maui
KAIA RANCH & CO
808-248-7725

Hanalei
HAENA HIDEAWAY
808-826-9522

Holualoa
HOLUALOA INN
808-324-1121

Honaunau
DRAGONFLY RANCH
800-487-2159

Honolulu
HALE O KAHALA
808-732-5889

JOHN GUILD INN
800-634-5115

Kailua
SHEFFIELD HOUSE
808-262-0721

WILD ORCHID B&B
808-262-5015

Kailua Oahau
PAPAYA PARADISE
808-261-0316

Kamuela
WALMEA GARDENS COTTAGE
808-885-4550

Kaneohe, Oahu
EMMA'S ROOMS
808-239-7248

Kauai
HALE AHA HOSPITALITY HOUSE
800-826-6733

KAY BARKERS B&B
808-822-3073

POIPU PLANTATION
808-742-6757

VICTORIA PLACE
808-332-9300

Kohala Coast
BUNGALOWS OF MAUNA LANI BAY
800-367-2323

Kola, Kaui
POIPU PLANTATION
808-742-7038

Koloa
KONA OCEAN INN
800-552-0095

Kona
KAILUA PLANTATION HOUSE
808-329-3727

Kukuihaele
HAMAKUA HIDEAWAY
808-775-7425

Lahaina
PLANTATION INN
800-433-6815

Maui
AHINAHINA FARM
800-241-MAUI

BLOOM COTTAGE
808-878-1425

CHAUNCE & BETTYS
808-572-2347

Na'Alehu
NUTT HOUSE
808-929-9940

Napli, Maui
COCONUT INN
800-367-8006

Oahu
OCEANFRONT, DORIS EPP
800-999-6026

Pahoa, Kalapana
KALANI HONUA
808-965-7828

Volcano Village
KILAUEA LODGE
808-967-7366

©Bed & Breakfast Guest Houses & Inns of America, Memphis TN

Idaho

*Jessens B&B — Ashton ID

Nieca C Jessen
208-652-3356
Hwy 20 83420

Rates:	**Pvt Bath** 2	**Shared Bath** 2	**Payment Terms:**
Single	$ 40.00	$ 35.00	Check
Double	$ 45.00	$ 40.00	AE

Close to Yellowstone National Park, Jackson Hole, Wyoming, this contemporary & comfortable home offers guests a chance for relaxing and enjoying the pleasant hosts. Continental breakfast included. **PERMITTED:** Children. [C11ACID-1204]

*Pension Hermine — Blackfoot ID

Hermine Balbi
208-684-3857
937 W 200 South 83221
Res Times 8am-8pm

Rates:	**Pvt Bath** 2
Single	$ 35.00
Double	$ 45.00

Your hostess (French, German, Latin teacher at Blackfoot High School) shares her modern ranch home located on 28 acres of countryside pleasure. Guest will find horses, cows, sheep, one goat and dogs and cats in this relaxing, natural setting. The clean air, beautiful landscape and relative solitude offers guests a peaceful setting for visiting Idaho. A full breakfast is included and lunch and dinner are available upon request. Nearby Blackfoot (10,000 pop) is in the lower extension of the Teton Mountains and is an agricultural town (potatoes, wheat, cattle) without industry. There an indoor pool, two movie theaters, good restaurants and a picturesque lake with picnic areas. Sightseeing includes Yellowstone National Park, Teton National Park, Salt Lake City, Jackson Hole Wyoming, Sun Valley and Craters of the Moon, Lava Hot Springs, Ice Caves with year-round events which include rodeos, horse races, chariot races, Wild West Days. Guests can enjoy swimming, skiing, water-skiing, canoeing and rafting, horseback riding, fishing, hiking and hand gliding **RESERVATIONS:** Deposit requested to hold reservation **BROCHURE:** Yes **PERMITTED:** Children, pets, drinking, smoking **LANGUAGES:** German, French [E08BCID-1205]

Idaho

Idaho Heritage Inn	**Boise ID**
Tom & Phyllis Lupher	109 W Idaho 83702
208-342-8066	**Res Times** 9am-9pm

Rates:	**Pvt Bath** 4	**Shared Bath** 1	**Payment Terms:**
Single	$ 60-85.00	$ 55-60.00	Check
Double	$ 60-85.00	$ 55-60.00	AE/MC/V

Built for Henry Falk in 1904, this fine residence served as the home for many of Idaho's famous personalities including Governor Clark and Senator Frank Church until the present owners began their restoration efforts in 1987. Listed on the *National Register of Historic Places*, all of the rooms are comfortably and charmingly complete with private baths, period furnishings and crisp linens. All of the charm of yesteryear remains with diamond-pane french doors, oak flooring, oriental carpeting and beautiful woodwork throughout. Located in Boise's historic Warm Springs District, guests enjoy the geothermal hot baths year-round. Boise State U is less than a mile away. A continental breakfast includes fresh-squeezed orange juice, choice of beverages, fresh fruit in season, oven-warmed breads & muffins, homemade jams & preserves, all delivered to your room each morning. Airport pick-up service in the Inn's classic car is available with prior notice along with sightseeing tours, ski outings and comp bikes for touring. **RESERVATIONS:** One night's deposit within one week of booking to guarantee room, 48 Hr cancel policy **BROCHURE:** Yes **PERMITTED:** Children, drinking **CONFERENCES:** Yes, groups to 70 persons [E04CCID-10149]

Sleeping Place Of The Wheels	**Coeur D'Alene ID**
Donna & Wallace Bedord	PO Box 5723 83814
208-765-3435	

Rates:	**Shared Bath** 3	**Payment Terms:**
Single	$ 38.00	Check
Double	$ 48.00	

Pleasant residence that invites children and adults to stop and visit. Wagon wheels line the entrance to this location along with flower gardens & tall pine trees. Guests pick fresh fruit from trees in summer. The home decor includes handmade quilts. **BROCHURE:** Yes **PERMITTED:** Children, pets [C11ACID-1212]

Idaho City Hotel	**Idaho City ID**
Don and Pat Campbell	215 Montgomery St 83631
208-392-4290	

Idaho

Rates:	**Pvt Bath** 5	**Payment Terms:**
Single	$ 38-50.00	Check
Double	$ 45-55.00	AE/MC/V

A true Western hotel from the 1930's located near hot springs and includes a backyard creek that splashes past the guests' rooms, and furnished with authentic antiques in a town that's listed as a *National Historic Site*. Just 45 minutes from Boise, you'll enjoy the freshness and natural setting here. Full country breakfast included. **RESERVATIONS:** Deposit required at res time **BROCHURE:** Yes **PERMITTED:** Children, pets, smoking, drinking [C11ACID-1221]

---

*Angel Of The Lake **Sandpoint ID**
410 Railroad Ave   83864
208-263-0816

Rates:	**Pvt Bath** 3	**Shared Bath** 6	**Payment Terms:**
Single	$ 52.00	$ 44.00	Check
Double	$ 66.00	$ 52.00	AE/MC/V

Right next to the lakeshore is this centrally located inn offering guests convenience and great hospitality. Year-round outdoor sporting activities available including hiking, swimming and all water sports, skiing. Full complimentary breakfast starts off your day. **BROCHURE:** Yes **PERMITTED:** Children [C11ACID-1232]

---

*Pine Street Inn **Wallace ID**
Jean McCorkle   177 King St   83873
208-752-4391

Rates:	**Pvt Bath** 2	**Shared Bath** 4	**Payment Terms:**
Single	$ 48.00	$ 43.00	Check
Double	$ 55.00	$ 48.00	MC/V

Quaint Country Inn snuggled in a hillside pine setting overlooking a historic silver mining town with Placer Creek running through the backyard. Plenty of outdoor activities including mining for your own silver. Continental breakfast included. **BROCHURE:** Yes **PERMITTED:** Children, smoking, drinking [C05ACID-1238]

Idaho

Ashton
JESSENS B&B
208-652-3356

Blackfoot
PENSION HERMINE
208-684-3857

Boise
IDAHO HERITAGE INN
208-342-8066

IDANHA

MACKAY BAR RANCH

NENDELS INN
208-344-7971

SUNRISE
208-345-5260

VICTORIAS WHITE HOUSE
208-362-0507

Caldwell
MANNING HOUSE B&B
208-459-7899

Cascade
WAPITI MEADOW RANCH
208-382-4336

Coeur D'Alene
BLACKWELL HOUSE
208-664-0656

CRICKET ON THE HEARTH B&B
208-664-6926

GABLES
208-664-5121

GREENBRIAR B&B INN
208-667-9660

INN THE FIRST PLACE
208-667-3346

KATIES WILD ROSE
208-756-9474

MCFARLAND B&B
208-667-1232

SLEEPING PLACE OF THE WHEELS
208-765-3435

Grangerville
TULIP HOUSE
208-983-1034

Hagerman
CARY HOUSE
208-837-4848

Haley
COMFORT INN
208-788-2477

Harrison
MARYANNES ON O'GARA BAY
208-689-3630

PEGS B&B PLACE
208-689-3525

Horseshoe Bend
RIVERSIDE B&B
208-793-2408

Idaho City
IDAHO CITY HOTEL
208-392-4290

Idaho Falls

LITTLETREE INN
208-523-5993

Indian Valley
INDIAN VALLEY INN
208-256-4423

Irwin
MCBRIDES B&B
208-483-4221

Kamiah
WHITEWATER RANCH
208-935-2568

Kellogg
MONTGOMERY INN
800-SNOW FUN

Ketchum
ASPEN INN

BUSTERBACK RANCH
208-774-2217

HEIDELBERG INN
208-726-5361

IDAHO COUNTRY INN
208-726-1019

LIFT HAVEN INN
208-726-5601

PINNCALE CLUB
800-521-2515

POWDERHORN LODGE
208-726-3107

RIVER STREET INN
208-726-3611

©*Bed & Breakfast Guest Houses & Inns of America, Memphis TN*

Idaho

Kooskia
THREE RIVERS RESORT
208-926-4430

Laclede
RIVER BIRCH FARM
208-263-3705

Lava Hot Springs
LAVA HOT SPRINGS
208-776-5830

RIVERSIDE INN
800-733-5504

ROYAL HOTEL B&B
208-776-5216

Lenore
HARPERS BEND RIVER INN
208-486-6666

Lewiston
CARRIAGE HOUSE B&B
208-746-4506

DAHMEN GUEST HOUSE
208-799-9020

Lowman
HAVEN LODGE

Mc Call
HOTEL MCCALL MTN INN
208-634-8105

NORTHWEST PASSAGE B&B
208-634-5349

Meridian
HOME PLACE

208-888-3857

Moscow
BEAUS BUTTE
208-882-4061

THE COTTAGE
208-882-0778

TWIN PEAKS INN
208-882-3898

VAN BUREN HOUSE
208-882-8531

Naples
DEEP CREEK INN
208-267-2373

Norman
GRANDVIEW LODGE

Northfork
CUMMINGS LAKE LODGE
208-865-2424

INDIAN CREEK RANCH
208-394-2126

Plummer
OWL CHALET
208-686-1597

Pocatello
HOLMES RETREAT
208-232-5518

MOUNTAIN RETREAT B&B
208-234-7114

Riggins
THE LODGE B&B
208-628-3863

Saint Maries
KNOLL HUS
208-245-4137

Salmon
HERITAGE INN
208-756-3174

Sandpoint
*ANGEL OF THE LAKE
208-263-0816

Shoup
SMITH HOUSE B&B
208-394-2121

Stanley
IDAHO ROCKY MTN RANCH
208-774-3544

REDFISH LAKE LODGE
208-774-3536

SAWTOOTH HOTEL
208-774-9947

Wallace
JAMESON B&B
208-556-1554

*PINE STREET INN
208-752-4391

Weiser
GALLOWAY MANSION
208-549-2659

Yellow Pine
ALPINE VILLAGE

YELLOW PINE LODGE
208-382-4336

Montana

Bad Rock Country B&B	**Bigfork MT**

Jon & Sue Alper
800-422-3666 406-892-2829

Rates:	**Pvt Bath** 3	**Payment Terms:**
Single	$ 75-85.00	Check
Double	$ 85-95.00	AE/DC/MC/V

Refer to the same listing name under Columbia Falls MT for a complete description. [M07FPMT2-17787]

Odauchain Country Inn	**Bigfork MT**

Mrs Margot Doohan
406-837-6851

675 Ferndale Dr 59911

Rates:	**Pvt Bath** 2	**Shared Bath** 2	**Payment Terms:**
Single	$ 75.00	$ 65.00	Check
Double	$ 85.00	$ 75.00	MC

Genuine log cabin, furnished with frontier antiques and art works, set on five acres of wilderness. Picture perfect locale for enjoying glorious views, wildlife, nature trails, and waterfowl. Full country breakfast included. **BROCHURE:** Yes **PERMITTED:** Children limited [C11ACMT-2203]

Sacajawea Inn	**Bozeman MT**

Jane & Smith Rodel
800-821-7326 406-285-6515

Res Times 24 Hrs

Rates:	**Pvt Bath** 33	**Payment Terms:**
Single	$ 45.00	Check
Double	$ 55-85.00	AE/DC/MC/V

Refer to the same listing name under Three Forks MT for a complete description. [M10EPMT2-16116]

Torch & Toes B&B	**Bozeman MT**

Ron & Judy Hess
406-586-7285

309 S Third Ave 59715
Res Times 8am-10pm

©Bed & Breakfast Guest Houses & Inns of America, Memphis TN

Montana

Rates:	Pvt Bath	4	Payment Terms:
Single	$ 55.00		Check
Double	$ 65-70.00		MC/V

Set back from the street, this Colonial Revival house is centrally located in one of Bozeman's historic districts. Lace curtains, leaded glass windows and period pieces remind one that this is a house with a past. While trying to decide what to call their bed & breakfast enterprise, Ron and Judy happened upon an old photo of the first pieces of the Statue of Liberty to arrive in the United States: the torch and her foot. Taken by the whimsy, they dubbed their home the *Torch and Toes*, hanging the framed photo in the entry-way as much to amuse guests as to explain the off-beat name. Ron is a professor of architecture and Judy is a weaver. Their home is furnished in a charming blend of nostalgic antiques, humorous collectibles and fine furnishings. A full complimentary breakfast includes a special egg dish, fresh fruit and muffins or coffee cake. There are three guest rooms on the second floor all with private baths. In-addition, there is a converted carriage house that can sleep up to six persons complete with a private bath and kitchenette. Nearby attractions include blue-ribbon trout streams, hiking, skiing, the Museum of the Rockies and Yellowstone National Park. **DISCOUNTS:** Yes, inquire at res time **AIRPORT:** Gallatin Field-8 mi **RESERVATIONS:** One night's deposit or credit card number to guarantee reservation **BROCHURE:** Yes **PERMITTED:** Children **CONFERENCES:** Yes, for groups to 10 persons **LANGUAGES:** French [R05FPMT2-9033]

Bad Rock Country B&B	Columbia Falls MT
Jon & Sue Alper	480 Bad Rock Dr 59912
800-422-3666 406-892-2829	

Rates:	Pvt Bath	3	Payment Terms:
Single	$ 75-85.00		Check
Double	$ 85-95.00		AE/DC/MC/V

An elegant Country Home on thirty acres, fifteen miles from the entrance to Glacier Park. Look out on magnificent, 7200 foot high Columbia Mountain, just two miles away, and the majestic peaks of Glacier Park. Located in a beautiful valley that reaches to those mountains, surrounded by open fields and groves of tall pine trees. Central to all of Flathead Valley's fabulous activities: hiking, fishing, golf, white-water rafting, horseback riding, x-country and downhill skiing, snowmobiling, all available with expert guides and equipment. Three guest rooms, queen beds, private baths, phones; three living rooms; secluded hot tub with time reserved exclusively for each guest; Old West antiques. Full breakfast, hearty Montana-style, featuring items such as Montana Potato Pie, huckleberry muffins and buffalo steaks. **ABBA Three Crown rating**

Montana

for excellence in attractiveness, warmth, furnishings, cleanliness and innkeeper hospitality, **AAA Approved**. **AIRPORT:** Kalispell Intl-10 mi **PACKAGES:** Custom designed to meet your interests upon request. **RESERVATIONS:** One night's deposit to guarantee reservation **BROCHURE:** Yes **PERMITTED:** Children 10-up, drinking [R07FPMT2-16782]

**Huckleberry Hannah's B&B	**Eureka MT**
Jack & Deanna Doying	3100 Sophie Lake Rd 59917
406-889-3381	**Res Times** Evenings

Rates: **Pvt Bath** 5   **Payment Terms:**
Single $ 40.00   Check
Double $ 65.00   DC/MC/V

All wrapped-up in over 5,000 square feet of old-fashioned, country-sweet charm, *Huckleberry Hannah's Montana Bed and Breakfast* is the answer to vacationing in Northwestern Montana. Sitting on fifty wooded acres, and bordering a fabulous trout-filled lake with gorgeous views of the Rockies, this bed and breakfast depicts a quieter time in our history ... a time when the true pleasures of life represented a walk in the woods or a moonlight swim. Or maybe just a little morning relaxation in a porch swing, sipping a fresh cup of coffee, and watching a colorful sunrise. A complimentary continental breakfast is included with your stay. Deanna Hansen-Doying is a retired tourism marketing specialists. Her hobby is collecting and developing wonderful recipes, cooking, baking and taking the research for this book off her waistline. She now lives on a lake near Eureka Montana with four horses, three cats, two dogs and one husband (not necessarily in that order), where she is currently writing the next book in the *Huckleberry Hannah Series*, and operating *Huckleberry Hannah's Montana Bed and Breakfast*. **RESERVATIONS:** 50% on long term stays, walk-ins welcomed as vacancies are available, lake cottage available **PERMITTED:** Children 13-up, limited pets, smoking outdoors only **BROCHURE:** Yes **DISCOUNTS:** 10% Senior citizens **AIRPORT:** Kalispell Intl-60 mi; County Private airport-4 mi [R07FPMT1-17204]

**Bad Rock Country B&B	**Kalispell MT**
Jon & Sue Alper	
800-422-3666 406-892-2829	

Rates: **Pvt Bath** 3   **Payment Terms:**
Single $ 75-85.00   Check
Double $ 85-95.00   AE/DC/MC/V

Refer to the same listing name under Columbia Falls MT for a complete description. [M07FPMT2-17785]

©*Bed & Breakfast Guest Houses & Inns of America, Memphis TN*

Montana

**Huckleberry Hannah's B&B	**Kalispell MT**
Jack & Deanna Doying	
406-889-3381	**Res Times** Evenings

Rates:	**Pvt Bath** 5	**Payment Terms:**
Single	$ 40.00	Check
Double	$ 65.00	DC/MC/V

Refer to the same listing name under Eureka MT for a complete description. [M07FPMT2-17790]

**Sacajawea Inn	**Three Forks MT**
Jane & Smith Rodel	PO Box 648 59752
800-821-7326 406-285-6515	**Res Times** 24 Hrs

Rates:	**Pvt Bath** 30	**Payment Terms:**
Single	$ 49.00	Check
Double	$ 49-99.00	AE/DC/MC/V

Since William Howard Taft was president, people have enjoyed the gracious hospitality of the *Sacajawea Inn* a *National Landmark* which is listed on the *National Historic Register*. The Inn, named after Sacajawea, a guide of the Lewis & Clark Expedition, was built in 1910 and today the original lofty wood beams and polished hardwood floors form the main lobby. The ambience is casual elegance - from the rocking chairs and large veranda to comfortable nostalgic guest rooms all with private baths. A perfect location from which to explore the Gallatin Valley, including the Lewis & Clark Caverns, Madison Buffalo Jump state Monument, Three Forks Museum and the Museum of the Rockies - the area is renowned for Blue Ribbon trout fishing on the Jefferson, Madison and Gallatin Rivers. In-addition, there's excellent hunting for deer, elk, geese, ducks and pheasants. Yellowstone National Park is just a two hour drive from the front door. Excellent skiing, biking, hiking are nearby and a public golf course is within walking distance of the Inn. Dinner is served nightly with breakfast and lunch served during the summer. **AAA** ♦♦♦ **Rated DISCOUNTS:** *AAA, AARP* **AIRPORT:** Bozeman-25 mins. **PACKAGES:** *Hunting & Fly Fishing* **RESERVATIONS:** Deposit or credit card to guarantee reservations; 24 hr cancel policy **BROCHURE:** Yes **PERMITTED:** Children, drinking, limited pets **CONFERENCES:** Yes, meetings room for groups to seventy **LANGUAGES:** Some Spanish [R10EPMT2-14208]

---

*Foxwood Inn	**White Sulphur Springs MT**
Shane & Shelly Dempsey	1 Sportsman Lane 59656
406-547-3918	

Montana

Rates:	**Shared Bath** 16	**Payment Terms:**
Single	$ 35.00	Check
Double	$ 40-50.00	MC/V

A renovated 1890's "poor farm" featuring sixteen individually decorated guest rooms. The Inn is located in the middle of the mountains in west central Montana. Guests can enjoy guided fishing tours, floating trips, horseback riding, downhill and x-country skiing. Guided tours can be arranged for historical and photographic outings. Enjoy great outdoors and western hospitality. Located midway between Yellowstone and Glacier Park areas, customized vacation packages and trips can be arranged. **RESERVATIONS:** 50% deposit at res time, late arrivals must notify 5 days in advance to obtain refund **BROCHURE:** Yes **PERMITTED:** Children, pets, drinking, limited smoking **CONFERENCES:** Yes for groups to 30 persons [E06BCMT-2225]

Bad Rock Country B&B — **Whitefish MT**
Jon & Sue Alper
800-422-3666   406-892-2829

Rates:	**Pvt Bath** 3	**Payment Terms:**
Single	$ 75-85.00	Check
Double	$ 85-95.00	AE/DC/MC/V

Refer to the same listing name under Columbia Falls MT for a complete description. [M07FPMT2-17786]

---

*Duck Inn — **Whitefish MT**
Ken & Phyllis Adler   1305 Columbia Ave   59937
406-862-DUCK

Rates:	**Pvt Bath** 10	**Payment Terms:**
Single		Check
Double	$ 59.00	MC/V

Relaxing views of Big Mountain and Whitefish River make this ideal spot for both indoor and outdoor activities. Guest rooms include iron or brass beds, cozy fireplace, deep soak tubs, and a balcony. Outdoors you have fishing, hunting, canoeing, nature trails, swimming, and boating. Close to Glacier National Park. Jacuzzi available too. Continental breakfast included. **BROCHURE:** Yes **PERMITTED:** Children, smoking & drinking. [E11ACMT-2223]

Montana

**Huckleberry Hannah's B&B	**Whitefish MT**

Jack & Denna Doying
406-889-3381

Res Times Evenings

Rates: **Pvt Bath** 5
Single $ 40.00
Double $ 65.00

Payment Terms:
Check
DC/MC/V

Refer to the same listing name under Eureka MT for a complete description. [M07FPMT2-17791]

Montana

Big Sky
LONE MOUNTAIN RANCH
406-995-4644

Big Timber
LAZY K BAR RANCH
406-537-4404

THE GRAND
406-932-4459

Bigfork
AVERILLS FLATHEAD RANCH

BAD ROCK COUNTRY B&B
800-422-3666

BIGFORK INN

BURGGRAFTS COUNTRYLANE B&B
406-837-4608

ODAUCHAIN COUNTRY INN
406-837-6851

SCHWARTZ FAMILY
406-837-5463

Bozeman
CROSSCUT RANCH

LEHRKIND MANSION
406-586-1214

SACAJAWEA INN
800-821-7326

SILVER FOREST INN
406-586-1882

TORCH & TOES B&B

406-586-7285

VOSS INN B&B
406-587-0982

Butte
COPPER KING MANSION
406-782-7580

Columbia Falls
BAD ROCK COUNTRY B&B
800-422-3666

*MOUNTAIN TIMBERS LODGE
406-387-5830

Essex
IZAAK WALTON INN
406-888-5700

Eureka
GRAVE CREEK B&B
406-882-4658

HUCKLEBERRY HANNAH'S B&B
406-889-3381

Gallatin Gateway
GALLATIN GATEWAY
800-626-4886

Great Falls
CHALET B&B INN
406-452-9001

MURPHY'S B&B
406-452-3598

PARK GARDEN B&B
406-727-8127

SOVEKAMMER INN
406-453-6620

THREE PHEASANT INN
406-453-0519

Helena
SANDERS-HELENAS B&B
406-442-3309

Hilger
VAN HAUR RANCH

Kalispell
BAD ROCK COUNTRY B&B
800-422-3666

HUCKLEBERRY HANNAH'S B&B
406-889-3381

Missoula
GOLDSMITH B&B
406-721-6732

Nevada City
NEVADA CITY HOTEL
406-843-5377

Pary
CHICO HOT SPRINGS
800-HOT-WADA

Polsom
*BORCHERS OF FINLEY POINT

Polson
HAMMONDS B&B
406-887-2766

Pompys Pillar
BYXBE RANCH

Red Lodge
PITCHER GUEST HOUSE

©*Bed & Breakfast Guest Houses & Inns of America, Memphis TN*

Montana

406-446-2859

*WILLOWS INN
406-446-3913

Ronan
TIMBERS
406-676-2089

Saint Igantius
MISSION MOUNTAINS

406-745-4331

Sheridan
*KING'S REST

Stevensville
COUNTRY CABOOSE
406-777-3145

Sula
CAMP CREEK INN
B&B
406-821-3508

Three Forks
**SACAJAWEA INN
800-821-7326

Townsend
HIDDEN HOLLOW
HIDEAWAY
406-266-2322

Troy
BULL LAKE GUEST
RANCH
406-295-4228

Turah
COLONIAL HOUSE,
A B&B
406-258-6989

Victor
WILDLIFE

OUTFITTER GUEST
RANCH

Virginia City
FAIRWEATHER INN

West Yellowstone
SPORTSMAN'S HIGH
800-272-4227

*White Sulphur
Springs*
*FOXWOOD INN
406-547-3918

Whitefish
**BAD ROCK
COUNTRY B&B
800-422-3666

DANCING WATERS

*DUCK INN
406-862-DUCK

GARDEN WALL B&B
406-862-3440

**HUCKLEBERRY
HANNAH'S B&B
406-889-3381

Wise River
SUNDANCE LODGE
MONTANA

Nevada

Deer Run Ranch B&B	Carson City NV
David & Muffy Vhay	5440 Eastlake Blvd 89704
702-882-3643	**Res Times** 8am-8pm

Rates: Pvt Bath 2 **Payment Terms:**
Single $ 75-85.00 Check
Double $ 75-85.00 MC/V

Relax and unwind on 200 of the most beautiful acres in Western Nevada. Our working alfalfa ranch is located just eight miles north of Carson City, and 22 miles south of Reno, Nevada. Watch the deer in the fields, enjoy the smell of western sage and listen for the cry of the coyotes at night. Our unique architect-designed-and-built western ranch house, shaded by tall cottonwood trees, over-looks our pond, Washoe Valley and the Sierra Nevada Mountains to the West. Two comfortable guest rooms (queen size beds) have private baths, window seats, spectacular views and lots of privacy. Both guest rooms share the sitting room with wood-burning wood stove, dining area, guest refrigerator, TV/VCR and other amenities. The owner's pottery studio and woodshop are on the premises. Full ranch breakfasts include house specialties and fresh fruits and vegetables from our garden. Recreation at the ranch includes swimming in our above ground pool, horseshoes, hiking, biking, ice skating on the pond in winter. (We supply the skates and hot chocolate!) We are conveniently close to golf, skiing, casinos and showrooms and many excellent restaurants. **DISCOUNTS:** Specials **AIRPORT:** Reno-22 mi **RESERVATIONS:** 50% deposit required at res time, 7 day cancel policy for full refund, max stay one week (a county restriction) **SEASONAL:** Closed holidays **BROCHURE:** Yes **PERMITTED:** Children (10-up), drinking, smoking outdoors [R09EPNV2-15663]

Winters Creek Ranch	Carson City NV
Mike & Pat Stockwell	1201 Hwy 395 N 89701
702-849-1020	

Rates: Pvt Bath 2 **Payment Terms:**
Single Check
Double $ 85.00 MC/V

Historic horse ranch c1865 on 50 acres of ponderosa pines with theme guest rooms of Oliver's Nook, Nevada Room, or Colonial Room. Spectacu-

Nevada

lar views of Sierra Nevadas, hot tub, and complimentary wine and hors d'oeuvres in evening. Virginia City, Lake Tahoe, Carson City & Reno nearby. **BROCHURE:** Yes **PERMITTED:** Children, drinking, limited pets. Full Western breakfast served outdoors, weather permitting [E11ACNV-2-240]

Old Pioneer Garden			Imlay NV
Mitzi & Lew Jones			Star Rt 89418
702-538-7585			
Rates:	**Pvt Bath** 4	**Shared Bath** 12	**Payment Terms:**
Single	$ 45.00	$ 35.00	Check
Double	$ 50.00	$ 40.00	

c1861 frontier ranch set in a Nevada mining town along canyon walls, perfect for solitude and experiencing the western outdoors. Picturesque setting with babbling brook, deer, rabbits and other fauna & flora. Fourteen acres for fishing, swimming in creeks, water sports. Family style meals prepared from the home garden!! **BROCHURE:** Yes **PERMITTED:** Children, pets, drinking [E11ACNV-2245]

Hotel Lamoille		Lamoille NV
Ron & Pam Druck		PO Box 1208 89828
702-753-6363		**Res Times** 9am-11pm
Rates:	**Pvt Bath** 3	**Payment Terms:**
Single	$ 65.00-Up	Check
Double	$ 65.00-Up	MC/V

Located just 20 miles from Elko, the tiny town of Lamoille, a picturesque agricultural community offers a quiet peaceful setting for those who like out-of-the-way places. Visitors find stunning mountain scenery in the lush glacier-carved Lamoille Canyon. High alpine lakes provide exceptional fishing opportunities along with numerous hiking trails, streams and ponds. Snowmobiling, x-country skiing and helicopter skiing are available, inquire at time of reservation. Home of the Annual Cowboy Poetry in late January. National Basque Festival every 4th of July. An 18 hole golf course is within 20 minutes. Gambling in large casinos. Our restaurant, the Pine Lodge, offers excellent night-time dining and a saloon for those who enjoy spirits and fun times. The guest rooms are comfortable with queen size beds and one room offers a king size bed and hot tub. A full breakfast is included in your room rate and dinner is available. **DISCOUNTS:** Yes, inquire at res time **AIRPORT:** Elko Regional-20 mi **RESERVATIONS:** Full deposit in advance, 5 day cancel policy for full refund less $5 handling fee; 50% refund if less than 5 days

Nevada

notice **BROCHURE:** Yes **PERMITTED:** Drinking, smoking, limited children, limited pets **CONFERENCES:** Yes for small groups [Z04FPNV2-15061]

Deer Run Ranch B&B		**Reno NV**
David & Muffy Vhay		
702-882-3643		**Res Times** 8am-8pm
Rates:	**Pvt Bath** 2	**Payment Terms:**
Single	$ 75-85.00	Check
Double	$ 75-85.00	MC/V

Refer to the same listing name under Washoe Valley NV for a complete description. [M09EPNV2-16108]

*Edith Palmers Country Inn			**Virginia City NV**
Erlene & Norm Brown			South B St 89440
702-847-0707			**Res Times** 8am-6pm
Rates:	**Pvt Bath** 1	**Shared Bath** 4	**Payment Terms:**
Single	$ 75.00	$ 70.00	Check
Double	$ 80.00	$ 80.00	MC/V

The 1862 country home of Nevada's first wine merchant in Victorian design, and today offering a gourmet restaurant in the former stone wine cellar. Walking distance from historic sights of Virginia City and close to Lake Tahoe and Reno. Country full breakfast of freshly ground coffee, eggs, and homemade breads and pastries. Meals available on premises. **PERMITTED:** Social drinking. [E11ACNV-2997]

Nevada

Carson City
DEER RUN RANCH
702-882-3643

ELLIOT CHARTZ
HOUSE
702-882-5323

SAVAGE MANSION
702-847-0574

***WINTERS CREEK
RANCH**
702-849-1020

East Ely
STEPTOE VALLEY
INN
702-289-8687

Gardnerville
REID MANSION
702-782-7644

Genoa
GENOA HOUSE INN
702-782-7075

ORCHARD HOUSE
702-782-2640

WALLEYS HOT
SPRINGS
702-782-8255

Goldfield
SUNDOG B&B
702-485-3438

Imlay
***OLD PIONEER
GARDEN**
702-538-7585

Incline Village
HAUS BAVARIA
800-GO TAHOE

Lamoille
BREITENSTEIN
HOUSE
702-753-6351

HOTEL LAMOILLE
702-753-6363

Lamorlle
PINE LODGE
702-753-6363

Paradise Valley
STONE HOUSE C
OUNTRY INN
702-578-3530

Reno
**DEER RUN RANCH
B&B**
702-882-3643

LACE & LINEN
702-826-3547

Silver City
HARDWICKE HOUSE
702-847-0215

Smith
WINDYBRUSH
RANCH
702-465-2481

Sparks
BLUE FOUNTAIN B&B
702-359-0359

Tahoe City
*COTTAGE INN AT
LAKE TAHOE
916-581-4073

Tonopah
MIZAPAH HOTEL

Truckee

RICHARDSON
HOUSE
916-587-7585

Virginia City
CHOLLAR MANSION
702-847-9777

***EDITH PALMERS
COUNTRY INN**
702-847-0707

GOLD HILL HOTEL
702-847-0111

HOUSE ON THE HILL
702-847-0193

Winnemucca
STAUFFER HOUSE
702-623-2350

Yerington
ARBOR HOUSE
702-463-2991

ROBRIC RANCH
702-463-3515

New Mexico

Casita Chamisa B&B	Albuquerque NM
Kit & Arnold Sargeant	850 Cahmisal Rd NW 87107
505-897-4644	

Rates:	Pvt Bath 2	Shared Bath 1	Payment Terms:
Single	$ 75.00	$ 70.00	Check
Double			MC/V

A lovely country guest house and main adobe home with indoor pool, just 15 minutes to downtown Albuquerque with an archaeologist host who delights in showing guests around local excavations. Close to ski area plus all homemade breads and cakes for breakfast. Bikes, hot tub, and hearty Southwestern breakfast are included. **BROCHURE:** Yes **PERMITTED:** Children, smoking, drinking, limited pets [E11ACNM-3957]

**Hacienda Vargas B&B*	Albuquerque NM
Paul & Jule DeVargas	
505-867-9115	Res Times 8:30am-6pm
	Fax 505-867-1902

Rates:	Pvt Bath 4	Payment Terms:
Single	$ 69-89.00	Check
Double	$ 69-109.00	MC/V

Refer to the same listing name under Santa Fe NM for a complete description. [M07GPNM2]

**Inn At Paradise*	Albuquerque NM
Lefty, Billie, Coroie	10035 Country Club 87114
505-898-6161	Res Times 24 Hrs

Rates:	Pvt Bath 15	Payment Terms:
Single	$ 50.00	Check
Double	$ 60-110.00	MC/V

Located on the first tee of the lush Paradise Hills Golf Club, you can experience golf course living at its finest. Whether you are spending an executive retreat with your company, having a competitive tournament with family and friends, or taking a romantic holiday with that special someone, the Inn is a great getaway. Each of our newly remodeled rooms

New Mexico

features original art work on consignment from local artists and craftsmen, so bring your eye for style. We also have suites available with fireplaces and kitchens. Start your morning with fresh juice, coffee and fresh pastries. Relax and enjoy the sunrise or head out for an early round of golf. Bring your family and friends and plan your next fiesta at the Full Moon Saloon. While in Albuquerque, ride the world's longest tram up the Sandia Mountains, just twenty minutes from the Paradise Hills Golf Resort, shop in Old Town, ski Santa Fe or Taos, or visit the historic Indian pueblos. Ask us about arranging a hot air balloon ride while here in the ballooning capital of the west. You'll find a complete pro shop, restaurant and lounge, Caring Hands massage, award-winning Rede to Cater and Sun Country Amateur Golf Assoc **RESERVATIONS:** Credit card deposit required to guarantee, contact property for cancellation policy **BROCHURE:** Yes **DISCOUNTS:** Corporate, groups **LANGUAGES:** German, some French **CONFERENCES:** Yes **AIRPORT:** Albuquerque- 20 mi **PACKAGES:** *Skiing, Golf* [R04GPNM2-18202]

Sierra Mesa Lodge		Alto NM
Harry & Lila Goodman		Ft Stanton Rd 88312
505-336-4515		**Res Times** 8am-10pm
Rates:	**Pvt Bath** 5	**Payment Terms:**
Single	$ 65.00	Check
Double	$ 75.00	MC/V

Nestled into a two-and-a-half acre hillside overlooking the magnificent Captain Mountains. Bountiful woods and meadows surround this elegant inn designed for relaxation and privacy. Enjoy thoughtful service, quiet charm and the warm hospitality of New Mexico's friendliest Inn. We offer five charming guest rooms with private baths, each individually decorated (Victorian, French Country, Oriental, Country Western and Queen Anne). Comforters and goose down pillows, graceful period furniture, brass and four poster beds, rockers and chaise lounges - tasteful elegance blended with modern comforts. Start your day with a generous gourmet breakfast of waffles, quiches or omelettes, fruits and freshly baked breads. Join us in the late afternoon for coffee, tea and pastries and in the evening for wine, cheese and conversation, or relax in the Inn's indoor hot tub spa! The Inn, located near Ruidoso is close to restaurants, shops, "Ski Apache" ski basin, Ruidoso Down racetrack, Lincoln National Forest and day trips to Carlsbad Caverns, White Sands, National Monument and the historical town of Lincoln - home of Billy-the-Kid. **RESERVATIONS:** One night's deposit within 7 days of booking or credit card to hold room with 7-day cancellation policy for full refund. **BROCHURE:** Yes **PERMITTED:** Children 15-up, drinking [R02BCNM-6321]

New Mexico

**Jones House Inn	**Chama NM**
Sara Jayne Cole	Terrace & Third 87520
505-756-2908	

Rates:	**Pvt Bath** 4	**Shared Bath** 2	**Payment Terms:**
Single	$ 65.00	$ 50.00	Check
Double	$ 85.00	$ 60.00	AE/MC/V

Enjoy the friendly, comfortable atmosphere of this lovely historic home. Across from the Cumbres-Toltec Scenic Railroad, this Inn is a Rail Fans Dream Come True! Our library is full of railroad books and train videos. We offer a train package that includes meals and the train ticket. Within walking distance to the Sargent Wildlife Preserve and the Chama River. **AIRPORT:** Albuquerque Intl-3 hr drive **RESERVATIONS:** Deposit or credit card number for one night's stay, 7 day cancel policy for refund **BROCHURE:** Yes **PERMITTED:** Limited children, drinking **PACKAGE:** *Train With Meals* [R05FPNM2-11109]

*Lodge At Cloudcroft	**Cloudcroft NM**
Mike Coy	Corona Place 88317
800-842-4216 505-682-2566	**Res Times** 24 Hrs

Rates:	**Pvt Bath** 59	**Payment Terms:**
Single		Check
Double	$ 55-155.00 EP*	AE/DIS/MC/V

Perched atop New Mexico's Southern Rockies at 9000 feet, guests are treated to fiery sunsets and starbright nights in a unique natural setting and wilderness offering wild bears and grazing elk among the verdant pine, blue spruce and golden aspen. Constructed in 1899 as a haven to escape the heat and relax, *The Lodge* has been meticulously restored inside and out; dressed with rich wood moldings, turn-of-the-century furnishings, antique fixtures, mounted game and lazy paddle fans. Each guest room has been restored and individually decorated including cozy high beds filled with down quilts for cool evenings. Dining is excellent with New Mexico's most award-wining chef blending continental cuisine and exquisite sunsets for a marvelous evening. There are ghost towns, horse racing, state parks, observatories, trout fishing, over 500 prehistoric cave drawings, Billy the Kid's stomping grounds and much more. Don't miss this historic mountain railroad resort. **RESERVATIONS:** Credit card to guarantee, 7 day cancel policy for refund less $10 service fee; one night's lodging if cancel notice is less than 72 hrs. **PACKAGES:** *Ski, Golf* **BROCHURE:** Yes **PERMITTED:** Children, smoking, drinking **CONFERENCES:** Yes with five meeting rooms offering complete A/V, excellent corporate retreat **LANGUAGES:** Spanish [R10BCNM-3962]

©Bed & Breakfast Guest Houses & Inns of America, Memphis TN

New Mexico

**Sandhill Crane B&B	**Corrales NM**
Carol Hogan/Philip Thorpe	389 Camino Hermosa 87048
800-375-2445 505-898-2445	**Res Times** 3pm-7pm
	Fax 505-898-2445
Rates: **Pvt Bath** 3	**Payment Terms:**
Single $ 75-85.00	Check
Double $ 85-95.00	MC/V

The *Sandhill Crane* is an extensively renovated rambling adobe hacienda situated on two and a half beautifully landscaped acres. Wisteria draped walls surrounding peaceful patios contribute to the feeling of privacy and solitude. Large common areas feature awesome views of nearby mountains. In warm weather guests can enjoy one of Phil's homestyle breakfasts on the patio while being entertained with a dazzling display of hummingbirds or an occasional feisty Roadrunner. The effect of living in an adobe combines the richness of history and the diversity of the New Mexican culture. Owners Carol Hogan and Phil Thorpe planned every detail of the remodeling. Carol traveled the state to find unusual furniture and decorative art including a variety of carved birds which have been added to her extensive collection of duck decoys. American Indian wall hangings and rugs complement her selection of Southwestern bedding and linens. A fine contemporary art collection includes works by local artists and adds to the over all feeling of intimacy and comfort. Three individually decorated guest rooms offer guests a choice in accommodations, including a two room suite with a kitchenette and a queen pull-out for added space. It's only a short walk to the small village of Corrales where not much has changed since it was settled in the 1700's. Amenities include a hot tub, cable TV, nearby horseback riding and therapeutic massages. When asked why people choose their B&B, the couple refers to comments left by guests while staying at the *Sandhill Crane B&B*, *"warm, unique, creative, restful."* **RESERVATIONS:** One night's deposit, 50% if longer, 14 day cancel policy for refund **PERMITTED:** Limited children, smoking outdoors **BROCHURE:** Yes **DISCOUNTS:** Extended stays and some midweeks **CONFERENCES:** Groups of 6-8 **AIRPORT:** Albuquerque-25 min **PACKAGES:** Yes, inquire [R07GPNM2-18764]

*Casa del Rio	**Espanola NM**
Eileen & Mel Vigil	PO Box 92 87532
800-333-2267 505-753-2035	
Rates: **Pvt Bath** 1	**Payment Terms:**
Single $ 70.00	Check
Double $ 70.00	MC/V

Casa Del Rio, a totally modern Bed and Breakfast, reflects the peace,

New Mexico

beauty and charm of New Mexico without compromising high standards for service and authenticity. This private guesthouse is appointed with local handmade crafts, rugs, bed coverings and furniture. A traditionally designed viga and latilla ceiling reflects the soft light of a kiva fireplace. The guest beds can be arranged as one king or two twin beds. A modern bath finished in handmade Mexican tile completes this comfortable, yet traditional New Mexico accommodation. A patio and window brings magnificent views of wild life which include eagles and whooping cranes. Occasionally guests are treated to the vocalizations of the local coyotes enjoying the crisp night air. Your hosts invite guests to enjoy their ranch on which they breed Arabian horses and fine wool sheep. A full breakfast, including special dietary needs, is included with your room and is served in the main house each morning. Nearby sights/activities include: Ghost Ranch Living Museum, Rio Grande Gorge, skiing, bicycling, hiking and fishing. Located equi-distance from Santa Fe or Taos, both towns offer guests an interesting day trip. **RESERVATIONS:** 50% deposit of total amount at res time, 14 day cancel policy less 10% service fee **BROCHURE:** Yes **PERMITTED:** Limited drinking, limited smoking **LANGUAGES:** Spanish [R09BCNM-3968]

Llewellyn House	**Las Cruces NM**
Linda & Jerry Lundeen 505-526-3327	618 S Alameda 88005

Rates:	**Pvt Bath** 14	**Payment Terms:**
Single	$ 55-70.00	Check
Double	$ 65-85.00	MC/V

Fourteen room adobe home furnished in western decor with large living/dining room and art gallery. Perfect spot for business or social meetings, including dining. Continental breakfast included. **BROCHURE:** Yes **PERMITTED:** Children 12-up, limited smoking, drinking **LANGUAGES:** Spanish [E11ACNM-3971]

Carriage House B&B Antiques			**Las Vegas NM**
Kera Anderson 505-454-1784			925 6th Street 87701

Rates:	**Pvt Bath** 3	**Shared Bath** 5	**Payment Terms:**
Single	$ 54.00	$ 39.00	Check
Double	$ 59.00	$ 44.00	

Listed on *National Register of Historic Places* is this fully restored three-story Victorian residence & Carriage House, complete with antiques and family heirlooms, some of which are for sale!! Balconies off some

©*Bed & Breakfast Guest Houses & Inns of America, Memphis TN*

New Mexico

bedrooms offer exciting views overlooking a beautiful neighborhood of Victorian residences. Full Western breakfast included. **BROCHURE:** Yes **PERMITTED:** Limited smoking and children. [E11ACNM-3972]

**Sierra Mesa Lodge	**Ruidoso NM**

Harry & Lila Goodman
505-336-4515

Res Times 8am-10pm

Rates:	**Pvt Bath** 5	**Payment Terms:**
Single	$ 65.00	Check
Double	$ 75.00	MC/V

Refer to the sane listing name under Alto NM for a complete description. [M02BCNM-6587]

**Adobe Abode	**Santa Fe NM**

Pat Harbour, Innkeeper
505-983-3133

202 Chapelle 87501
Res Times 8am-9pm
Fax 505-983-3133

Rates:	**Pvt Bath** 5	**Payment Terms:**
Single	$ 90-150.00	Check
Double	$ 95-150.00	DC/MC/V

As the spectacular landscape of New Mexico welcomes you like an old friend, so will this inviting and intimate European-styled Bed & Breakfast, just 3 blocks from the Plaza and a minute's walk to the best restaurants, museums and shopping. In an important Santa Fe historic district, this 84-year-old adobe home maintains its old world feeling despite extensive renovation to add every modern convenience. Decorated with sophistication and flair, there's authentic Southwest charm in vigas, native New Mexican furniture and Indian art, rugs and unusual artifacts. There are two delightful guest rooms in the main house, both with private baths featuring oversized art-tiled showers and sharing a large living room with fireplace. Also in the main house is a new two-room Provence Suite, queen size bed, full size living room and large bath. Three rooms with private bath in a Courtyard Compound, private entrances off a flower filled patio and all are pure Santa Fe Style. All six rooms offer the amenities of a fine country inn, including terrycloth robes, bath accessories, designer linens, private phones, writing desks and private color cable TV's. Full gourmet breakfast offers fresh-squeezed juice, fresh fruit, an assortment of homemade muffins and changing daily entrees. **AIRPORT:** Albuquerque-60 mi **RESERVATIONS:** One night deposit on all reservations, 10 day cancel policy for refund less 10% service fee, 4-6pm check-in **BROCHURE:** Yes **PERMITTED:** Children 11 yrs-up, drinking, limited smoking **CONFERENCES:** Yes, for groups to 12 persons if entire

Inn is booked; includes a large living room and patio **LANGUAGES:** Some Spanish, French [Z07GPNM2-11107]

**Alexanders Inn			**Santa Fe NM**
Carolyn Lee			529 E Palace 87501
505-986-1431			**Res Times** 7:30am-10pm
Rates:	**Pvt Bath** 5	**Shared Bath** 1	**Payment Terms:**
Single	$ 85-150.00	$ 75.00	Check
Double	$ 85-150.00	$ 75.00	MC/V

*Featuring the **best of American Country Charm** - Alexanders is located in a lovely residential neighborhood on the town's historic east side. Built in 1903, the Inn has been newly renovated to offer modern comfort and convenience along with the romance and charm of earlier, simpler times. The Inn is lovingly decorated with stenciling, plants, antiques and collectibles creating a warm, relaxing and nurturing ambiance. Each delightfully different guest room is spacious, sun-filled and charming and furnished with your personal comfort in mind, including luxurious down comforters and fluffy bathrobes. A complimentary continental breakfast is served ensuite or on the veranda overlooking a grassy lawn lined with fragrant lilacs and shade trees and includes homemade breads or muffins, homemade granola, yogurt, freshly ground coffee and tea. Homemade cookies and chips and salsa are served in the warm homey kitchen each afternoon. Your hosts are pleased to help you with sightseeing plans while here, including the town's numerous art galleries, Indian pueblo history, hiking and skiing, rafting places, musical and theatrical events and the various shopping areas. Complimentary bikes are available for guests along with guest privileges at the El Gancho Health Club. A world of warmth and hospitality awaits travelers at Alexander's Inn in Santa Fe.* **DISCOUNTS:** 10% for weekly stays **AIRPORT:** Albuquerque Intl-1 hr **RESERVATIONS:** One night's deposit (50% if longer than 2 nights) within 7 days of booking; 7 day cancel policy for refund less $10 service fee, two night min on weekends **BROCHURE:** Yes **PERMITTED:** Children 6-up, quiet dogs, drinking **LANGUAGES:** French [R07FPNM2-11108]

**Canyon Road Casitas		**Santa Fe NM**
Trisha Ambrose		652 Canyon Rd 87501
800-279-0755 505-988-5888		**Res Times** *10am-5pm
Rates:	**Pvt Bath** 2	**Payment Terms:**
Single	$ 85-145.00	Check
Double	$ 95-145.00	AE/DC/MC/V

New Mexico

Located on Santa Fe's famous Canyon Road within walking distance to distinctive art galleries, numerous museums, unique shops and historic landmarks. Luxury accommodations are featured in this 100-year-old Historic Territorial adobe. The large suite offers southwestern designer furnishings including a separate dining room, kiva fireplace, queen & double beds, separate rooms, original art work and private bath with shower and tub. Both guest rooms have kitchenettes, down quilts & pillows, feather beds, queen & double beds, separate entrances, with completely quiet, private patio full of local flowers. Truly a four-season retreat. Knowledgeable hostess will make dinner reservations and will help with local sightseeing in the most picturesque 100-square-miles of America, offering mountains, valleys, deserts, and plenty of dramatic contrasts. A continental breakfast is included. A complimentary bottle of wine greets all guests upon their arrival. **RESERVATIONS:** One night's fee or 50% of stay with 10-day cancellation policy for refund, *24-hr answering machine, $15 per extra person **BROCHURE:** Yes **PERMITTED:** Children, drinking, smoking outdoors, local kennel available for pet boarding **LANGUAGES:** Spanish [Z11DPNM-6586]

**Dos Casas Viejas	**Santa Fe NM**
Jois & Irving Belfield	610 Agua Fria St 87501
505-983-1636	**Res Times** 8am-8pm

Rates:	**Pvt Bath** 5	**Payment Terms:**
Single	$ 145-195.00	Check
Double	$ 145-195.00	MC/V

A special Inn . . . in a special city. Within the heart of picturesque Santa Fe is a small special Inn, *Dos Casas Viejas* (Two Old Houses). The two historical buildings have recently been restored to their 1860's architecture representing the three cultures of Santa Fe; Anglo, Indian and Hispanic. A spacious brick patio surrounded by six foot high adobe walls leads to each guest room (all with private entrance), French doors open into rooms containing original vigas, Mexican tiled floors and wood-burning kiva fireplaces. The rooms are furnished with authentic Southwest antiques and original art; all rooms have phones, TV and private baths. Cozy down comforters and pillows, fresh linens and canopy beds (in some rooms) insure a comfortable night's rest. The main building houses the lobby/library and dining area where guests can relax on an overstuffed sofa next to the fire with a novel - or outdoors on sunny days, next to the 40' lap pool with a cascading fountain. A complimentary continental European breakfast is available indoors or out. Centrally located, *Dos Casa Viejas* enables you to discover Santa Fe's renowned galleries, shops, museums and the finest restaurants in the Southwest. We believe the place you stay should be as wonderful as the city you visit. We hope you find *Dos Casas* meets this standard. **AIRPORT:** Albuquerq-

New Mexico

ue-65 mi **RESERVATIONS:** One night tariff due within 7 days of booking; arrival time 3-6pm, late arrival only by special arrangement, 14 day cancel policy for refund **BROCHURE:** Yes **PERMITTED:** Drinking, limited children [Z07GPNM2-15805]

**Grant Corner Inn			**Santa Fe NM**
Louise Stewart & Pat Walter			122 Grant Ave 87501
505-983-6678			**Res Times** 8am-8pm
Rates:	**Pvt Bath** 10	**Shared Bath** 2	**Payment Terms:**
Single	$ 70.00	$ 80.00	Check
Double	$ 140.00	$ 95.00	MC/V

A charming country setting complete with a white picket fence and gazebo is offered in this large residence c1900's of a former wealthy New Mexican ranching family. Completely restored and furnished by Pat, a designer-builder and Louise, an interior designer, with antique furnishings that provide a warm and charming atmosphere. You'll find each guest room uniquely furnished with brass and four-poster beds, armories, works of art, and treasures from around the world. Continuing the *European tradition of Bed & Breakfast*, Pat creates culinary delights for a full morning meal before either a crackling fire in the dining room or on the veranda in summer. The varied menu includes treats such as banana waffles, eggs Florentine, New Mexican souffle and accompanied by freshly ground European coffee, fresh squeezed orange juice, fresh fruit and homemade rolls and jellies. Complimentary wine is offered guests in the evening and you're just two blocks' strolling distance from Santa Fe's historic plaza. Other gourmet meals available at added cost & prior arrangements. **RESERVATIONS:** One night's full rate minimum or 1/2 full length of stay within 10 days of reservation, refund if canceled 10 day prior to res date less 15% service charge **BROCHURE:** Yes **PERMITTED:** Limited children, limited drinking **CONFERENCES:** Yes, groups to 20 persons **LANGUAGES:** Spanish [A07GPNM2-3988]

**Hacienda Vargas B&B		**Santa Fe NM**
Paul & Jule Vargas		PO Box 307 87001
505-867-9115		**Res Times** 8:30-6pm
		Fax 505-867-1902
Rates:	**Pvt Bath** 4	**Payment Terms:**
Single	$ 69-89.00	Check
Double	$ 69-109.00	MC/V

This historic stagecoach stop and Indian trading post *Adobe Hacienda* dates back to the 1700's, and has been completely restored and elegantly decorated with antiques. A charming courtyard is home to a two hundred

New Mexico

year old tree and a historic chapel. The four beautiful guest rooms offer fireplaces, private baths and private entrances. One room includes a two-person jacuzzi tub while a hot tub and barbecue are available for guests to use. Situated on two acres by the Rio Grande and thirty minutes south of Santa Fe and north of Albuquerque on the historic El Camino Real, guests enjoy the majestic views of the New Mexico Mesas and Sandia Mountain, golf, fishing, snow skiing and horseback riding nearby. A full country breakfast, prepared by a New Mexican chef, gets everyone started for a full day of activities. **AAA Rated**, Member NM B&B Assoc **RESERVATIONS:** One nights deposit or 50% of length of stay, which ever is greater **PERMITTED:** Children 13-up, drinking, smoking outside only **SEASONAL:** Rates vary **BROCHURE:** Yes **LANGUAGES:** Spanish, German **DISCOUNTS:** 10% Seniors **AIRPORT:** Albuquerque-20 mi **PACKAGES:** *Romance*, includes champagne and breakfast in room [R07GPNM2-19206]

Inn Of The Animal Tracks   Santa Fe NM
Daun Martin   707 Paseo de Peralta 87501
505-988-1546

Rates: **Pvt Bath** 4   **Payment Terms:**
Single $ 95-105.00   Check
Double $ 95-105.00

Your charming hostess relocated to Santa Fe from San Diego to begin this special Inn offering a harmonious, peaceful, fun-loving environment for travelers. Guest rooms are named after different animal (and their spirit) offering unique decor. Choose from the "Soaring Eagle", an airy room with six large windows, a fireplace that invites lofty, contemplative thoughts to the "Gentle Deer" which offers pale pastels, oatmeal and cream colors with a queen-size platform bed, hardwood floors and viga. Other rooms are the "Playful Otter" and the "Loyal Wolf". With names such as these, guests may put aside all that robs them of their joy of life. Full homemade breakfasts are offered in the "Sign of The Buffalo" room with special recipe yeast breads, fresh juices, fruits and innovative egg entrees. Summer breakfast is outdoors on the patio area, picnic baskets available. **BROCHURE:** Yes [E09BCNM-8947]

Preston House   Santa Fe NM
Singe Bergaman   106 Faithway St 87501
505-982-3465

Rates: **Pvt Bath** 4   **Shared Bath** 2   **Payment Terms:**
Single $ 65.00-Up $ 55.00-Up   Check
Double $ 75-105.00 $ 65.00-Up   MC/V

New Mexico

Listed on the *National Register of Historic Places*, this fine example of Queen Anne includes fine antique furnishings and decor, family heirlooms, plenty of quilts and handicrafts. Continental plus breakfast included. Complimentary wine/sherry. **BROCHURE:** Yes **PERMITTED:** Limited children, limited smoking [E11ACNM-3994]

**El Rincon B&B	Taos NM
Nina Meyers	114 Kit Carson 87571
505-758-4874	**Res Times** 24 Hrs

Rates:	**Pvt Bath** 12	**Payment Terms:**
Single	$ 49-129.00	Check
Double	$ 49-129.00	AE/MC/V

Described in Frank Waters classic book of the Southwest, *The Man Who Killed Deer*, once the home of La Dona Luz Lucero De Martinez, the sister-in-law of the famous (or infamous) Padre Martinez; the former world-renown restaurant *La Donna Luz* - guests are truly living in Taos History. Located in the heart of historic Taos, you're across the street from Kit Carson's home - just 1/2 block from Old Town Plaza and within walking distance of museums, art galleries and shops. Each room is unique with its own surprises; a large collection of fine art, both contemporary and from the early days is distributed throughout the large adobe. All rooms have private baths, most have a small refrigerator, TV, VCR and stereo. During warm months, breakfast is served in a colorful outdoor patio or before a warming fire in an ancient fireplace during the cooler periods. Your hostess, Nina Meyers (an artist in her own right), is the daughter of Ralph Meyers, a well-known Indian trader, writer and craftsman of early Taos. Fifty feet away is the oldest trading post in Taos (also named El Rincón) which is still operated by Rowene Martinez, Ralph's widow. Your host, Paul "Paco" Castillo, is Nina's son and shares his family's rich background and knowledge of New Mexico. **RESERVATIONS:** One night's deposit or credit card number, 7 day cancel policy for refund less $7.50 service fee **PERMITTED:** Children, pets, smoking, drinking **BROCHURE:** Yes **LANGUAGES:** Spanish, English **AIRPORT:** Albuquerque-130 mi [Z07GPNM2-13961]

**Hacienda del Sol	Taos NM
Marcine & John Landon	PO Box 177 87571
505-758-0287	**Res Times** 7am-9pm

Rates:	**Pvt Bath** 9	**Payment Terms:**
Single	$ 55-95.00	Check
Double	$ 65-120.00	

New Mexico

Selected by *USA Weekend*, as *"one of America's 10 Most Romantic Inns."* Once part of Art Patroness Mabel Dodge Luhan's estate, *Hacienda del Sol* is a 180 year old adobe adjoining the 95,000 acre Taos Pueblo Indian Lands. With 1.2 acres of tree-shaded grounds, the nine room Inn offers country ambiance just 1-1/2 miles north of the Taos Plaza. With viga ceilings, arched pueblo-styled doorways, and large, quiet rooms, the Inn takes visitors back to the days when famous author Frank Waters wrote *People of the Valley* in what is now one of the B&B's larger guest rooms. Handcrafted Southwest furnishings, original works of art (many for sale), fireplaces and down comforters add to the warm feeling of this special place. One room features its own huge jacuzzi tub with a large skylight above and another has its own steam room. Outdoors, just steps from the Reservation, and with an unobstructed view of Taos Mountain is a large Hot-Tub and deck. Complimentary snacks are served in the evening. Breakfast includes home-baked specialties, hot entrees, fresh fruit and a secret blend of coffee. **RESERVATIONS:** 50% deposit or one night's rate (whichever is greater); 10-day cancel policy for refund, less $15; deposit forfeited if less than 10 days **BROCHURE:** Yes **PERMITTED:** Children, drinking, smoking permitted outdoors only **CONFERENCES:** Yes, if entire facility is booked [Z07GPNM2-4004]

Mabel Dodge B&B   Taos NM

                                                  240 Morada Lane 87571
800-84-MABEL 505-758-9465

                                                  Fax 505-751-0431
Rates: **Pvt Bath** 5   **Shared Bath** 4   **Payment Terms:**
Single $ 65.00 $ 55.00   Check
Double $ 75.00 $ 65.00

Historic home of Mabel Dodge Luhan offers historical setting for guests today. Stay where DH Lawrence, Georgia O'Keefe and other famous guests collected their thoughts in this pleasant setting. Full breakfast included. **BROCHURE:** Yes **PERMITTED:** Children, smoking, limited drinking. [E11ACNM-4007]

Mountain Light B&B   Taos NM
Gail Russell   PO Box 241 87571
505-776-8474

Rates: **Pvt Bath** 2   **Shared Bath** 1   **Payment Terms:**
Single $ 45.00 $ 40.00   Check
Double $ 55.00 $ 45.00

Enjoy gorgeous views from this adobe-style residence of a well-known photographer who will introduce you to all that's here and help with

New Mexico

camera tips if you need. Full breakfast is included. **RESERVATIONS:** Deposit required at res time **BROCHURE:** Yes **PERMITTED:** Children, limited smoking **LANGUAGES:** Photography & the West! [E11ACNM-4009]

Plum Tree AYH-Hostel & B&B			Taos NM
		Box A-1 Hwy 68 Pilar 87531	
800-678-PLUM 505-758-4696		**Res Times** 8am-10pm	
Rates:	**Pvt Bath** 3	**Shared Bath** 3	**Payment Terms:**
Single	$ 32-47.50	$ 17.50*	Check
Double	$ 55.00	$ 30.00*	AE/MC/V

A place in the country. Pilar is a centuries-old village along the banks of the Rio Grande, located between the cultural centers of Taos and Santa Fe. The country setting is ideal for viewing nature or getting involved in many outback activities and adventures! The *Plum Tree* is a friendly place, offering good food and comfortable lodging at low costs. A common kitchen is available for all guests. A continental breakfast is included and is served in our art gallery. Take a raft trip down the Rio Grande and hike the Sangre de Christos. We offer fine art workshops in the summer; painting, photography, drawing and paper making. Family get-togethers and groups are welcomed. **RESERVATIONS:** One night's deposit or 50% of total at res time; 48 hr cancel policy - 30 days if holiday stays **BROCHURE:** Yes **PERMITTED:** Children, limited pets, limited smoking, limited drinking [E11BCNM-4011]

New Mexico

Albuquerque
ADOBE & ROSES
505-898-0654

CASAS DE SUENOS
505-247-4560

*CASITA CHAMISA
505-897-4644

CORNER HOUSE
505-295-5000

**HACIENDA
VARGAS B&B
505-867-9115

**INN AT PARADISE
505-898-6161

LIGHTENING FIELD
505-898-5602

SARABANDE B&B
505-345-4923

WE MAUGER INN
505-242-8755

Alto
LA JUNTA

*SIERRA MESA
LODGE
505-336-4515

Aztec
AZTEC RESIDENCE
HOTEL

Carlsbad
LA CASA MUNECA
B&B
505-887-1891

Cedar Crest
ELAINES B&B
505-281-2467

NORMA GREMORE
505-281-3092

Chama
**JONES HOUSE INN
505-756-2908

OSO RANCH &
LODGE
Chimayo
CASA ESCONDIDA
800-643-7201

HACIENDA RANCHO
DE CHIMAYO
505-351-2222

LA POSADA DE
CHIMAYO
505-351-4605

Cimarron
CASA DEL GAVILAN
800-445-5251

ST JAMES HOTEL
505-376-2664

Cloudcroft
ALL SEASONS B&B
505-682-2380

*LODGE AT
CLOUDCROFT
800-842-4216

Coolidge
STAUDER'S NAVAJO
LODGE

Corrales
ALBUQUERQUE
YOURS TRULY
505-898-7027

CORRALES INN B&B
505-897-4422

**SANDHILL CRANE
800-375-2445

Costilla
COSTILLA B&B
505-586-1683

Deming
SPANISH STIRRUP
GUEST HOUSE
505-546-3165

Dixon
LA CASITA
GUESTHOUSE
505-579-4297

Eagles Nest
LAGUNA VISTA
LODGE
505-377-6522

El Prado
BLUE STAR
RETREAT
505-758-4634

SALSA DEL SALTO
505-776-2422

Elephant Butte
ELEPHANT BUTTE
INN

Espanola
*CASA DEL RIO
800-333-2267

LA PUEBLA HOUSE
505-753-3981

Galisteo
GALISTEO INN
505-982-1506

New Mexico

Glenwood
LA CASITA

LOS OLMOS GUEST
RANCH
505-539-2311

Kingston
BLACK RANGE
LODGE
505-895-5652

Las Cruces
ELMS
505-524-1513

*LLEWELLYN HOUSE
505-526-3327

Las Vegas
*CARRIAGE HOUSE
B&B ANTIQUES
505-454-1784

PLAZA HOTEL
505-425-3591

Lincoln
CASA DE PARTON
505-653-4676

Los Alamos
CASA DEL REY
505-672-9401

LOS ALAMOS B&B
505-662-6041

ORANGE STREET
B&B
505-662-2651

WILSON HOUSE B&B
505-662-7490

Los Ojos
*CASA DE MARTINEZ

Mescalero
INN OF THE
MOUNTAIN GODS

Mesilla
MESON DE MESILLA
505-525-9212

Ojo Caliente
INN AT OJO
505-583-2428

Portales
HARPERS
505-356-3773

Ranchos De Taos
DON PASCUAL
MARTINEZ B&B
505-758-7364

RANCHOS RITZ B&B
505-758-2640

TWO PIPE B&B
505-758-4770

Raton
RED VIOLET INN
505-445-9778

Ruidoso
SHADOW MOUNTAIN
LODGE
505-257-4886

**SIERRA MESA
LODGE
505-336-4515

San Juan Pueblo
CHINGUAGUE
COMPOUND
505-852-2194

Sandia Peak
PINE CONE INN

505-281-1384

Santa Fe
**ADOBE ABODE
505-983-3133

ADOBE GUEST
HOUSE
505-983-9481

**ALEXANDERS INN
505-986-1431

ARIUS COMPOUND
800-735-8453

**CANYON ROAD
CASITAS
800-279-0755

CANYON ROAD
COMPOUND
505-982-8859

CASA DE LA CUMA
505-983-1717

DANCING GROUND
OF THE SUN
800-645-5673

**DOS CASAS
VIEJAS
505-983-1636

DUNSHEES
505-982-0988

EL PARADERO
505-988-1177

**GRANT CORNER
INN
505-983-6678

**HACIENDA
VARGES B&B

©Bed & Breakfast Guest Houses & Inns of America, Memphis TN

New Mexico

505-867-9115

*INN OF THE
ANIMAL TRACKS
505-988-1546

INN OF THE
VICTORIAN BIRD
505-455-3375

*INN ON THE
ALAMEDA
505-984-2121

LA POSADA
DE SANTA FE
505-621-7231

POLLYS GUEST
HOUSE
505-983-9781

*PRESTON HOUSE
505-982-3465

*PUEBLO BONITO
505-984-8001

RANCHO
ENCANTADO
800-722-9339

SUNSET HOUSE
505-983-3523

TERRITORIAL INN
505-989-7737

WATER STREET INN
505-984-1193

Silver City
BEAR MOUNTAIN
GUEST RANCH
505-538-2538

CARTER HOUSE

505-388-5485

Socorro
EATON HOUSE
505-835-1067

Taos
AMERICAN ARTISTS
GALLERY HOUSE
505-758-4446

AMIZETTE INN
505-776-2451

BLUE DOOR B&B
505-758-8360

BROOKS STREET INN
505-758-1489

CASA BENAVIDES
505-758-1772

CASA DE LAS
CHIMENEAS
505-758-4777

CASA DE MILAGROS
505-758-8001

CASA EURPOA
505-758-9798

EL MONTE LODGE

**EL RINCON B&B
505-758-4874

**HACIENDA DEL
SOL
505-758-0287

HISTORIC TAOS INN
800-TAOS INN

HOTEL LA FONDA DE
TAOS

505-758-2211

LA POSADA DE TAOS
505-758-8164

LAUGHING HORSE
INN
505-758-8350

*MABEL DODGE
B&B
800-84-MABEL

*MOUNTAIN LIGHT
B&B
505-776-8474

*PLUM TREE
AYH-HOSTEL & B&B
800-678-PLUM

RUBY SLIPPER
505-758-0613

SAN GERONIMO
LODGE
800-828-TAOS

SILVERTREE INN
505-758-3071

STAGEBRUSH INN
505-758-2254

STEWART HOUSE
B&B
505-776-2913

Taos Ski Valley
HOTEL EDELWEISS
505-776-2301

Truchas
RANCHO ARRIBA
B&B
505-689-2374

Oregon

Chanticleer Inn	Ashland OR

Jim & Nancy Beaver
503-482-1919
120 Gresham St 97520

Rates: **Pvt Bath** 7   **Payment Terms:**
Single $ 75.00   Check
Double $ 85-100.00

Charm and warmth in this country residence offering antique furnishings, patio garden, and fluffy comforters for all guests. Close to ski lifts, including discounts. Full breakfast included. **BROCHURE:** Yes **PERMITTED:** Children and drinking. [E11ACOR-4272]

Cowslips Belle	Ashland OR

Jon & Carmen Reinhardt
503-488-2901
159 N Main St 97520

Rates: **Pvt Bath** 4   **Payment Terms:**
Single $ 57-87.00   Check
Double $ 62-92.00   MC/V

This darling Craftsman home of 1913 remains essentially as then with the original woodwork and bevel glass throughout the residence. Vintage furnishings include canopy, brass & iron beds, stained glass windows, antique quilts and tiffany-style lamps and beautiful garden views from each guest room in the main house. Your hosts have tended to everything for your comfort including fresh flowers to brighten each room! A scrumptious full breakfast includes roasted Italian coffee and espresso. Guests are within three blocks of walking to shops, restaurants, Lithia Park and the Shakespearean Theatres. **RESERVATIONS:** One night's deposit within 7 days of booking, 14 day cancel policy, check-in 3pm, check-out 11am **BROCHURE:** Yes **PERMITTED:** Drinking, smoking outdoors only [E10BCOR-4277]

Hersey House B&B	Ashland OR

Gail Orell
503-482-4563
451 N Main St 97520
Res Times 8am-8pm

Rates: **Pvt Bath** 4   **Payment Terms:**

Oregon

Single	$ 65.00	Check
Double	$ 65.00	MC/V

c1900's saltbox Victorian that has been restored and furnished with period decor and family heirlooms, nestled among lovely garden areas. Furnished with antiques, queen beds and plenty of love and charm to satisfy even the most discriminating guest. **RESERVATIONS:** Deposit required at res time with refund if canceled **SEASONAL:** 4/1-10/15 **BROCHURE:** Yes **PERMITTED:** Children 13-up. [E11ACOR-4279]

Iris Inn	Ashland OR
Vicki Lamb	59 Mazanita St 97520
503-488-2286	**Res Times** 8am-9pm

Rates:	**Pvt Bath** 5	**Payment Terms:**
Single	$ 81.00	Check
Double	$ 95.00	MC/V

The *Iris Inn* is situated in a quiet neighborhood with views of the Valley and the Mountains surrounding this Rogue Valley setting. Guests often spend time relaxing on the deck overlooking the Rose Garden, when not at the award-winning Oregon Shakespeare Festival, Historic Jacksonville, The Britt Music Festival, Crater Lake and local wineries. The peaceful ambiance of this 1905 Victorian Inn is enhanced with antique furnishings and custom amenities making it a great place not only when traveling but for those special occasions, birthdays and anniversaries. Each guest room reflects the innkeeper's thoughtfulness in making your stay enjoyable with special touches of hospitality - such as the guest robes. Elegant and creative breakfast starts your day - specialties such as Peaches 'n Cream French Toast, Crepes, Apple Pancakes and fresh baked buttermilk Scones bring guests back again and again.   Following breakfast, nearby activities might include fishing, rafting, downhill and cross country skiing - all nearby, or a full day of wonderful sightseeing. **RESERVATIONS:** Deposit or credit card number required within 7 days of booking with 10 day cancel policy for refund less $10 service fee **PERMITTED:** Limited children, limited drinking, smoking outdoors **BROCHURE:** Yes **LANGUAGES:** Spanish, French, Greek, English **AIRPORT:** Medford-12 mi [Z07GPOR2-4281]

Neil Creek House	Ashland OR
Gayle Netro	341 Mowetza Dr 97520
503-482-6443	

Rates:	**Pvt Bath** 2	**Payment Terms:**
Single	$ 95.00	Check

Oregon

Double $ 115.00

Five acre compound offering European style rustic setting with pond, antique furnishings, and fluffy comforters on queen-size beds. Full gourmet breakfast, pool, bikes, sitting room, and comp wine. **BROCHURE:** Yes **PERMITTED:** Limited smoking **LANGUAGES:** French, German [E11ACOR-4285]

**Franklin Street Station B&B	**Astoria OR**
Renee Caldwell	1140 Franklin St 97103
800-448-1098 503-325-4314	**Res Times** 24 Hrs

Rates:	**Pvt Bath** 6	**Payment Terms:**
Single	$ 58-110.00	Check
Double	$ 63-115.00	MC/V

Featured in the Los Angeles Times Travel Section and excellent ratings in many B&B guide books, this Victorian home is decorated beautifully and reflects the early years of Astoria with its ornate craftsmanship, built by Shipbuilder Ferdinand Fisher. We are the closest of all Bed & Breakfasts in Astoria, to the downtown area. Within walking distance to museums and restaurants. Our accommodations include six rooms, three of which have views of the Columbia River and three are two-room suites, with all rooms offering private baths. Try our Captain's Quarters which features a beautiful view of the Columbia River and downtown, queen size bed, fireplace, TV, VCR, stereo plus a luxurious bath with clawfoot tub, brass shower and fixtures. Very private! Our full complimentary breakfast is served either at 8:30 or 9:30 and includes our specialty of Belgium Waffles, sausage, fresh fruit, juice and coffee. We will make your stay a memorable one and know you'll return again. **AIRPORT:** Portland Intl-90 mi **DISCOUNTS:** Lower winter rates **BROCHURE:** Yes **PERMITTED:** Children, drinking [R05FPOR2-16874]

**Grandview B&B	**Astoria OR**
Charleen Maxwell	1574 Grand 97103
800-488-3250 503-325-5555	**Res Times** 9am-9pm

Rates:	**Pvt Bath** 6	**Payment Terms:**
Single	$ 39-87.00	Check
Double	$ 39-92.00	DC/MC/V

Wonderful Columbia River view in a light, cheerful 3-story Victorian, located on Historical Homes Walking Tour. Rooms/suites have queen beds, country decor, hardwood floors, books, and fluffy comforters. Walk to superb Maritime Museum, Columbia Lightship, Heritage Museum and

Oregon

100-year-old churches. Ships from many nations dock here, and some allow tours. Golf, clam-digging, beachcombing, surfing, boating, and tennis are close-by. Hike to "Astoria Column" or stroll on the college campus; boat watch or bird watch. Two hours from Portland on the Northwest tip of Oregon. Continental-plus breakfast includes tea-coffee, hot cocoa, cider, milk, fruit and juices and two or more kinds of fresh muffins. *Reservations for large groups or for exclusive uses of the home or Inn need to be arranged well in advance, 30 day cancellation policy notice in writing for deposit refund for conferences. **RESERVATIONS:** Full amount due at time of res or credit card guarantee to hold room, 24-hr cancel policy for full refund; add 6% room tax; check-in by 6 pm. *Large groups see description. Travel agents commissions payable except July and August bookings **BROCHURE:** Yes **PERMITTED:** Children, 10-up, no smoking, no drinking **CONFERENCES:** Limited to fifteen persons for accommodations [Z07GPOR2-6337]

**Yankee Tinker B&B	**Beaverton OR**
Jan & Ralph Wadleigh	5480 SW 183rd Ave 97007
800-TINKER 2 503-649-0932	**Res Times** 9am-5pm

Rates:	**Pvt Bath** 1	**Shared Bath** 2	**Payment Terms:**
Single	$ 65.00	$ 50-55.00	Check
Double	$ 75.00	$ 60.00	AE/DC/MC/V

"A handcrafted New England experience in the heart of Washington County". Located 10 miles west of Portland in a peaceful residential neighborhood. From here, visit wineries, farmers' markets, historical sights as well as the dramatic Columbia River Gorge and grand Oregon beaches. Three distinctive guest rooms with comfortable beds are graced by handmade quilts, antiques, family heirlooms and includes a/c. Guest sitting room features a fireplace & TV; private yard has spacious deck and gardens. Memorable breakfasts, served alfresco weather permitting, are designed to accommodate special dietary needs and your schedule. The mouth watering choices might include blueberry pancakes or muffins, peaches'n cream french toast or herbed omelettes. The traditional Yankee offering of pie for breakfast is available for the hearty eater. Benefit from "all the extras" that make your business or leisure travel successful. The *Yankee Tinker's* warmth and hospitality will convince you to linger an extra day or two as well as planning your return visit. **RESERVATIONS:** One night deposit/credit card number with 72 hr cancel policy for refund **BROCHURE:** Yes **DISCOUNTS:** Yes, for extended stays **PERMITTED:** Drinking, limited children [Z07GPOR2-8918]

***Mirror Pond House**	**Bend OR**
Beryl Kellum	1054 NW Harmon Blvd 97701

Oregon

503-389-1680

Rates:	**Pvt Bath** 2	**Payment Terms:**
Single	$ 70.00	Check
Double	$ 80.00	

Relax and reflect while staying at this charming Cape Cod on the water and next to a wildlife refuge for enjoying nature at its best. Year-round retreat with interesting host that will give directions to all sights, including excellent snow skiing in winter. Full breakfast included.
RESERVATIONS: Deposit is necessary to hold room **BROCHURE:** Yes
PERMITTED: Children 12-up, smoking, drinking [E11ACOR-4301]

Wheelers B&B			**Coburg OR**
Joe & Isabel Wheeler			404 E McKinzy 97401
503-344-1366			

Rates:	**Pvt Bath** 2	**Shared Bath** 2	**Payment Terms:**
Single	$ 40.00	$ 35.00	Check
Double	$ 50.00	$ 40.00	

Completely private setting close to the famous *Coburg Inn* with its ghosts. Quiet country atmosphere in the National Historic Town just north of Eugene Oregon. Full breakfast included. **BROCHURE:** Yes **PERMITTED:** Children, limited smoking [E11ACOR-4308]

Campbell House, A City Inn		**Eugene OR**
Myra Plant		252 Pearl St 97401
800-264-2519 503-343-1119		**Res Times** 8am-11pm
		Fax 503-343-2258

Rates:	**Pvt Bath** 14	**Payment Terms:**
Single	$ 70-220.00	AE/MC/V
Double	$ 75-225.00	

"Classic elegance, exquisite decor and impeccable service" ... Old world elegance and charm, nestled on the East side of Skinner's Butte, over looking the city of Eugene, in the National Historic District. The *Campbell House, A City Inn*, built in 1892 and fully restored as an elegant fourteen room Inn. You will sense the hospitality as you stroll up the curved walk, surrounded by acres of lawn, flowers and a hillside of natural landscaping. You feel at-once welcome the moment you enter through the French doors into the charming and elegant lobby with marble floor, open staircase and gracious innkeeper. Just beyond the lobby is the parlor, dining room and library, each with majestic views of the city, offering several sitting areas with wing back chairs and an

Oregon

extensive selection of fine leather bound books and videos (mysteries and classics). Each of the beautiful fourteen guest rooms have private bath, TV with VCR, telephone and all the amenities' one would find in a small European hotel. Selected rooms feature: gas fireplaces, four-poster bed and jetted or claw footed bath tub. Ideally located just three blocks away from downtown, the performing arts Hult Center, the Fifth Street public market with several unique shops, fine restaurants and charming antique stores. Leisure adventures include: hiking, rock climbing, bicycling (two blocks away is the river with miles of bike paths), golfing, jogging, and we also make arrangements for fishing or white-water rafting trips down one of the most scenic rivers in the nation. **RESERVATIONS:** Deposit required to guarantee room and house retreat and package events **PERMITTED:** Children, limited drinking, smoking in outside courtyard **BROCHURE:** Yes **DISCOUNTS:** Corporate midweek (Sun-Thur) **AIRPORT:** Eugene-15 mi **CONFERENCES:** Three separate meeting rooms for groups **PACKAGES:** *Business Retreats, Weddings, Theater, Romance Getaway* [I08GPOR2-20014]

**Kjaers House In The Woods	**Eugene OR**
Eunice & George Kjaer	814 Lorane Hwy 97405
503-343-3234	**Res Times** 8am-8pm

Rates:	**Pvt Bath** 1	**Shared Bath** 1	**Payment Terms:**
Single	$ 40.00	$ 40.00	Check
Double	$ 65.00	$ 55.00	

Urban convenience and suburban tranquility describe this 1910 Craftsman-Style home in a park-like setting with covered porches and swing from which to enjoy the deer, birds and wildflowers. Even though a shopping center is just six blocks away - deer and raccoon are almost daily visitors. Your hosts gladly share their interest and knowledge of wildflowers with their guests along with giving wildflower seeds and plants to guests to start in their home gardens. This lovely home is located within walking distance to hiking, biking, jogging trails and parks. Many museums, art galleries, theaters, the U of Oregon and fine restaurants are within four miles. The *House In The Woods* has been in operation since 1984 and is furnished with antiques, Oriental carpets and an unusual square rosewood grand piano as well as a wonderful music and record library which guests enjoy browsing through to hear their favorite songs. A full complimentary breakfast is planned for the guest's convenience and

Oregon

includes specialties of the house featuring local cheeses, nuts and fruits. Inspected by the *Eugene Area B&B Assoc, Oregon B&B Guild & members of PAII* **AIRPORT:** Mahlon Sweet Airport-15 mi **DISCOUNTS:** Travel agents, seniors, extended stays-7th night free **RESERVATIONS:** One night's deposit, 72 hr cancel policy for full refund. Check-in 4-6pm, other by prior arrangement, check-out by 11am, add 9.5% room tax to above rates **BROCHURE:** Yes **PERMITTED:** Limited drinking, children over 12 **CONFERENCES:** Meeting room available for up to 15 persons **LANGUAGES:** German [Z07GPOR2-4323]

Lorane Valley B&B	Eugene OR
Esther & George Ralph 503-686-0241	86621 Lorane Hwy 97405

Rates:	**Pvt Bath** 1	**Payment Terms:**
Single	$ 55.00	Check
Double	$ 69.00	MC/V

Four and one-half miles from the hustle and bustle of downtown Eugene is a haven of tranquility. The *Lorane Valley Bed & Breakfast* is a beautiful, new two level cedar home set on twenty-two acres of wooded hillside overlooking the picturesque Lorane Valley and presided over by a small herd of Angus cattle. Guests can enjoy the luxurious combination of rich antique furnishings and the convenience of a thoroughly modern home. Catering to one party at a time, secluded accommodations include a bedroom with a king-size bed, window seat and plant window. The private bath contains a shower, tub and Jacuzzi. Additional amenities are a full English breakfast, fresh-cut flowers, a split of French champagne and a wide assortment of reading materials. Come and relax in the sedate beauty of the Oregon countryside. The *Lorane Valley Bed & Breakfast* is an excellent choice for families or individuals who want to retreat to country comforts. **RESERVATIONS:** Deposit required by credit card number **BROCHURE:** Yes **PERMITTED:** Limited children [R09BCOR--6356]

**Pine Meadow Inn*	Grants Pass OR
Maloy & Nancy Murdock 503-471-6277	**Res Times** 8am-9pm **Fax** 503-471-6277

Rates:	**Pvt Bath** 3	**Payment Terms:**
Single	$ 95-110.00	Check
Double	$ 95-110.00	

© *Bed & Breakfast Guest Houses & Inns of America, Memphis TN*

Oregon

Refer to the same listing name under Merlin, Oregon for a complete description. **RESERVATIONS:** One night's deposit per room required within 7 days of booking, 7 day cancel policy for full refund **PERMITTED:** Children 8-up, drinking **BROCHURE:** Yes **AIRPORT:** Medford-40 min [M09GPOR2]

**Riverbanks Inn	**Grants Pass OR**
Myrtle Franklin	8401 Riverbanks Rd 97527
503-479-1118	
	Fax 503-471-4104

Rates:	**Pvt Bath** 5	**Payment Terms:**
Single	$ 65-130.00	Check
Double	$ 75-150.00	MC/V

Birdwatchers, river runners, fishermen and vagabonds have visited our river retreat; some come for relaxation and pleasure ... some for adventure .... and some to renew their spirit though the scenic solitude of the mighty Rogue River. An oriental garden is the first surprise to await you behind the gated, wood-slat entry. Surrounded by forest, river and sky, the Inn's decor is a rich and varied crossroads of exotic cultures, art and music ranging from the Steinway "B" piano to a cedar and mud sauna shaped like a tepee. Guest room decor includes a Jean Harlow Room, Casablanca Room, Caribbean Dream Suite along with two separate cottages named the Log Cabin and the Zen House - each with period decor and furnishings. Choose the flamingo-color art deco of the Jean Harlow Room; Peruvian carved furniture, tribal carpets of the Casablanca Room; a sunken jacuzzi, Mombassa netting covering the Plantation Canopy queen bed and tropics of the Caribbean Dream Suite; antique-filled Grandma's Room in the Log Cabin or traditional Japanese antiques and furnishings in the Zen House. All rooms includes a hearty full breakfast. Therapeutic massage available by appointment to all guests by Myrtle, innkeeper and owner, a licensed Massage Therapist and member of Assoc of Massage Therapists of America. Prior to her present endeavor as an innkeeper, she worked in the massage staff at the noted Esalen Institute in Big Sur where she taught workshops in music and the healing arts, visualization and Esalen Polarity and Swedish massage techniques. **RESERVATIONS:** One night deposit, 7 day cancel policy for refund. Late arrival by prior arrangement only, check-in 4-7pm, noon check-out **PERMITTED:** Children, drinking, smoking outdoors only **BROCHURE:** Yes **LANGUAGES:** French, Japanese **DISCOUNTS:** Winter (12/1-4/1) 10% less **AIRPORT:** Medford-25 mi [R07FPOR1-11133]

*McCully House Inn	**Jacksonville OR**
Pat Groth/Phil Accetta	240 E California 97530

Oregon

503-899-1942

Rates:	**Pvt Bath** 4	**Payment Terms:**
Single	$ 65.00	Check
Double	$ 75.00	

Classical 1861 Revival home in the center of historic Jacksonville and close to Shakespeare Festival and the Rogue River. Full breakfast included **BROCHURE:** Yes **PERMITTED:** Children, limited smoking [E11ACOR-4349]

**Touvelle House	**Jacksonville OR**
Carolee Casey	455 N Oregon St 97530-9098
800-846-8422 503-899-8938	**Res Times** 8am-10pm

Rates:	**Pvt Bath** 6	**Payment Terms:**
Single	$ 90-95.00	Check
Double	$ 90-95.00	

A grand picturesque home just a few blocks off the famous Main Street of the old Gold Rush town of Jacksonville - guests feel like pioneers after checking into this 1916 Craftsman-style home, to be pampered and spoiled like hotel guests were at the turn-of-the-century. Jacksonville has experienced a rebirth beginning in the 1950's when a few people began restoring the buildings and their homes. Today, over 80 restored buildings are on the *National Historic Register* and *the town has been designated a National Historic Landmark District.* Streets are bustling again with horse-drawn carriages and trolley cars taking travelers past craft and antique shops and the sights. Your hosts have restored their home in keeping with the period and style of the 1900s - and welcome all guests to make themselves feel at home. The common areas include The Great Room, featuring a large-stoned fireplace; The Library, featuring TV and VCR; The Sunroom which consists of almost all windows and the Dining Room, featuring an intricate built-in buffet. Outdoors there are two spacious covered verandas and by the carriage house, there's swimming in the pool and a spa for soaking (comp robes and beach towels are provided). The guest rooms are uniquely furnished and range from The Garden Suite, a floral fantasy in pinks, blues, greens and whites with a queen bed and an antique iron day bed to Granny's Attic, where childhood memories are rekindled with cozy hideaways and

Oregon

angular rooflines. A full breakfast and afternoon appetizers are included. **AIRPORT:** Medford-5 mi **DISCOUNTS:** Corporate Sun-Thursday **RESERVATIONS:** Deposit within 7 days of when reservation is made, 10 day cancel policy for refund less $10 service fee **BROCHURE:** Yes **PERMITTED:** Social drinking **CONFERENCES:** Only when booking entire home, space for groups to twenty [I05FPOR2-4347]

**Brey House "Oceanview" B&B	**Lincoln City OR**
Milt & Shirley Brey	3725 NW Keel Ave 97367
503-994-7123	**Res Times** 9am-7pm

Rooms:	**Pvt Bath** 4	**Payment Terms:**
Single	$ 60-80.00	Check
Double	$ 65-85.00	DC/MC/V

The ocean awaits you just across the street! The never-ending beach, whale watching, beachcombing is just starters for guests staying at the *Brey House.* Famous restaurants abound, along with factory stores and antiquing and famous kite shops. Guests can enjoy one of the four bedrooms, all offering private baths. This Cape Cod-style home built in 1941 is in the heart of Lincoln City. You'll enjoy one of Milt's and Shirley's hearty breakfasts with the ocean looking at you while conversing with the other guests. All rooms have queen size beds, electric blankets, flannel sheets and are beautifully decorated. **AIRPORT:** Portland-90 mi **DISCOUNTS:** Off season **PACKAGES:** Yes, inquire at res time **RESERVATIONS:** Deposit or credit card number required, 72 hr cancel policy for refund **BROCHURE:** Yes **PERMITTED:** Drinking, smoking restricted to certain areas [Z07GPOR2-6342]

**Pine Meadow Inn	**Merlin OR**
Maloy & Nancy Murdock	1000 Crow Rd 97532
503-471-6277	**Res Times** 8am-9pm
	Fax 503-471-6277

Rates:	**Pvt Bath** 3	**Payment Terms:**
Single	$ 95-110.00	Check
Double	$ 95-110.00	

Pine Meadow is a distinctive country retreat on nine acres of secluded meadow and woods, near the gateway to the wild and scenic Rogue River. Our home is styled after midwestern farmhouses, with a wrap-around porch with wicker furniture, a sitting room with fireplace and a dining room with bay windows to capture the morning sun. The French doors open out to the English cutting and herb gardens and a deck with a hot tub under the towering pines. The sitting area near the Koi pond is a favorite place to enjoy the natural beauty surrounding the area. Upstairs

Oregon

are three large bedrooms, well-lit for reading, each with a private full bath, queen size, pillow top mattresses and with window seat and/or sitting area. The Inn is filled with elegant, yet comfortable, turn-of-the-century antiques. Come play on the Rogue River - whitewater rafting, fishing or jet boat trips. Enjoy the nearby Shakespeare Festival, Britt Festival, Historic Jacksonville, the California Redwoods and Crater Lake. Ski Mount Ashland, visit the Oregon Caves or hunt for antiques. If you come just to relax or renew, our country roads are ideal for long walks, jogging and for biking, in a beautiful country setting. *Pine Meadow* is fully air conditioned and we are open year round. We feature healthy breakfasts with seasonal fruits and vegetables from our garden. We invite you to come and enjoy the magnificent Rogue Valley with us. **RESERVATIONS:** One night's deposit per room required within 7 days of booking, 7 day cancel policy for full refund **PERMITTED:** Children 8-up, drinking **BROCHURE:** Yes **AIRPORT:** Medford-40 min [I08GPOR2-20046]

Three Capes B&B	**Oceanside OR**
Ross & Kathy Holloway	1685 Maxwell Mtn Rd 97134
503-842-6126	

Rates:	**Pvt Bath** 2	**Shared Bath** 1	**Payment Terms:**
Single	$ 50.00	$ 45.00	Check
Double	$ 60.00	$ 55.00	

Darling contemporary home nestled in secluded coastal community hillside. You'll enjoy the sandy beaches, sightseeing or watching shore birds and wildlife in the sanctuary. In early Spring, wales will be close enough to see. Continental breakfast weekdays. **BROCHURE:** Yes **PERMITTED:** Children, limited smoking, drinking [E11ACOR-4369]

Home By The Sea	**Port Orford OR**
Brenda & Alan Mitchell	444 Jackson St 97465
503-332-2855	**Res Times** 9am-9pm

Rates:	**Pvt Bath** 2	**Payment Terms:**
Single	$ 60-70.00	Check
Double	$ 60-70.00	DC/MC/V

Home by the Sea is a contemporary owner-built home with beach access

Oregon

and spectacular ocean views from its two guest bedrooms that overlook Historic Battle Rock and it's uncrowded beach in the background. Located away from highway noise, guests are within an easy stroll to fine restaurants, sand beaches and Oregon's only fishing fleet that has to be launched by a crane!! A full breakfast is included with your room rate. **RESERVATIONS:** One night's deposit to confirm reservation, 72 hour cancel policy **BROCHURE:** Yes **PERMITTED:** Limited children and drinking [E06BCOR-4383]

J Palmer House			Portland OR
Mary & Richard Sauter		4314 N Mississippi Ave 97217	
503-284-5893			

Rates:	**Pvt Bath** 2	**Shared Bath** 5	**Payment Terms:**
Single	$ 80-120.00	$ 35-70.00	Check
Double	$ 85-125.00	$ 40-70.00	AE/DISC/MC/V

The *John Palmer House* has been recognized by national TV, newspapers and magazines as **one of the most complete authentic Victorian restorations in the country**. Located in Portland, it offers the convenience of many day trips to mountains, wine country and the Pacific Coast as-well-as the attractions that are part of any big city. The Inn is operated by three generations: Granny at 96 is the oldest; David, the CCA trained chef is twenty-nine. With a need to be creative and inventive, the Innkeepers offer multiple ways to enjoy the home that goes well beyond the B&B. High Tea and Dinners are served with advance reservation. Mystery teas are performed Sundays. Theater Weekends are available. Whether you are planning a relaxing vacation or a once-in-a-lifetime experience, the Inn wants to be there helping serve you. Two suites with private bath and kitchen are available for long-term stays. **RESERVATIONS:** Credit card to guarantee all reservations with a 7 day cancel policy for refund, two-day minimum stay for travel agent reservations **BROCHURE:** Yes **PERMITTED:** Drinking, limited children, limited pets **LANGUAGES:** Sign [Z08GPOR2-4377]

**Yankee Tinker B&B*			Portland OR
Jan & Ralph Wadleigh			
800-TINKER 2 503-649-0932			**Res Times** 9am-5pm

Rates:	**Pvt Bath** 1	**Shared Bath** 2	**Payment Terms:**
Single	$ 65.00		$ 50-56 Check
Double	$ 75.00		AE/DISC/MC/V

Refer to the same listing name under Beaverton, Oregon for a complete description. [M05FPOR2]

Oregon

State House B&B	**Salem OR**
Mike Winsett & Judy Uselman 503-588-1340	2146 State St 97301

Rates:	Pvt Bath 5	Shared Bath 2	Payment Terms:
Single	$ 65.00	$ 50.00	Check
Double	$ 75.00	$ 60.00	MC/V

Snuggled in a natural setting of lawns and mature plantings and on the bank of Mill Creek you'll find animals walking everywhere you turn, including ducks and geese. Originally the 1920's residence of a state politician, it's still filled with the atmosphere of another era. **RESERVATIONS:** Deposit required at res time with refund if canceled 10 days prior to arrival **BROCHURE:** Yes **PERMITTED:** Limited children, smoking [E11ACOR-4385]

Williams House Inn	**The Dalles OR**
Don & Barbara Williams 503-296-2889	608 W 6th St 97058

Rates:	Pvt Bath 2	Shared Bath 3	Payment Terms:
Single	$ 55.00	$ 45.00	Check
Double	$ 65.00	$ 55.00	

At the end of the Oregon Trail is this large Victorian home, registered as a *National Historic Place*, it offers guests hospitality and exciting antique furnishings throughout; clawfoot tubs, four-poster beds, and balconies off each guest room. Continental breakfast included **BROCHURE:** Yes **PERMITTED:** Limited children, limited drinking [E11ACOR-4316]

**Blue Haven Inn*	**Tillamook OR**
Joy & Ray Still 503-842-2265	3025 Gienger Rd 97141 **Res Times** 24 Hrs

Rates:	Pvt Bath 1	Shared Bath 2	Payment Terms:
Single	$ 75.00	$ 50.00	Check
Double	$ 75.00	$ 60.00	

Located on a two-acre parklike setting surrounded by tall evergreens, *Blue Haven Inn* provides guests a peaceful and quite place to "relax and unwind" and assures a restful night's sleep. Built in 1916, your hosts Joy and Ray have lovingly restored and individually decorated each guest room with antiques, limited edition collectibles and modern amenities for a comfortable stay. The Inn has extensive grounds and gardens for the guests to enjoy along with croquet, lawn tennis, a country porch swing,

Oregon

library/game room with a variety of games, books music provided by an old radio or antique gramophone and a VCR for enjoying a movie. Complimentary gourmet breakfasts are served in the formal dining room in a style reminiscent of a more gracious way of dining. Adjacent to the Inn is an "over flow shop" containing antique furnishings, glassware, old sewing machines and claw foot tubs - all for sale. The land of "cheese, trees and ocean breeze", guests can visit the famous Tillamook Cheese Factory, try the excellent fishing, crabbing and clamming at one of the eight rivers and the beautiful ocean nearby. Activities include antiquing, hand gliding, hiking, kite flying, train rides through picturesque settings and winery tours. **DISCOUNTS:** Yes, inquire at res time **RESERVATIONS:** One night's deposit to guarantee, 48 hr cancel notice for refund. Unless by prior arrangement, check-in time is 4-6pm and check-out by 11am **BROCHURE:** Yes **PERMITTED:** Drinking, limited children, limited smoking **AIRPORT:** Portland-75 mi **PACKAGES:** Long term stays, groups; dinner available [R09EPOR2-11135]

Oregon

Albany
FARM MINI BARN
503-928-9089

Ashland
ADAMS COTTAGE
800-345-2570

ARDEN FOREST INN
503-488-1496

ASHLAND GUEST INN
503-488-1508

ASHLANDS MAIN
STREET INN
503-488-0969

AUBURN STREET
COTTAGE
503-482-3004

BAYBERRY INN
503-488-1252

BUCKHORN SPRINGS
503-488-2200

*CHANTICLEER INN
503-482-1919

COACH HOUSE INN
503-482-2257

COLUMBIA HOTEL
503-482-3726

COOLIDGE HOUSE
503-482-4721

COUNTRY WILLOWS
503-488-1590

*COWSLIPS BELLE
503-488-2901

DANIELS ROOST
503-482-0121

EDINBURG LODGE
503-488-1050

FOX HOUSE INN
503-488-1055

*HERSEY HOUSE
B&B
503-482-4563

HIGHLAND ACRES
503-482-2170

IRIS INN
503-488-2286

LAUREL STREET INN
800-541-5485

LITHIA ROSE
LODGING
503-482-1882

MAINSTREET INN
503-488-0696

MCCALL HOUSE
503-482-9296

MORICAL HOUSE
503-482-2254

MT ASHLAND INN
503-482-8707

*NEIL CREEK HOUSE
503-482-6443

OAK HILL COUNTRY
503-482-1554

OAK STREET
STATION
503-482-1726

PARKSIDE
503-482-2320

PINEHURST INN AT
JENNY CREEK
503-488-1002

QUEEN ANNE
503-482-0220

REDWING B&B
503-482-1807

ROMEO INN
503-488-0884

ROYAL CARTER
HOUSE
503-482-5623

STONE HOUSE
503-482-9233

TREONS COUNTRY
HOMESTAY
503-482-0746

WIMER STREET INN
502-488-2319

WINCHESTER INN
503-488-1133

WOODS HOUSE
503-488-1598

Astoria
ASTORIA INN
503-325-8153

COLUMBIA RIVER
503-325-5044

**FRANKLIN
STREET STATION
B&B
800-448-1098

©*Bed & Breakfast Guest Houses & Inns of America, Memphis TN*

Oregon

**GRANDVIEW B&B
800-488-3250

INN-CHANTED B&B

ROSEBRIAR INN B&B
503-375-7427

Baker
POWDER RIVER B&B
503-523-7143

Bandon
CLIFF HARBOR
GUEST HOUSE
503-347-3956

LIGHTHOUSE B&B
503-347-9316

Beaverton
**YANKEE TINKER
503-649-0932

Bend
FAREWELL BEND
B&B
503-382-4374

GAZEBO B&B
503-389-7202

HEIDI HAUS
503-388-0850

HOUSE AT WATERS
EDGE
503-382-1266

LARA HOUSE B&B
503-388-4064

***MIRROR POND
HOUSE**
503-389-1680

Brookings

*CHETCO RIVER INN
800-327-2688

HOLMES SEA COVE
503-469-3025

SEA DREAMER INN
503-469-6629

WARD HOUSE B&B
503-469-5557

Camp Sherman
HOUSE ON THE
METOLIUS
503-595-6620

METOLIUS INN
503-595-6445

METOLIUS RIVER
LODGES
503-595-6290

Cannon Beach
TERN INN B&B
503-436-1528

Cave Junction
OREGON CAVES
CHATEAU
503-592-3400

Cloverdale
HUDSON HOUSE
503-392-3533

SANDLAKE COUNTRY
INN
503-965-6745

Coburg
*WHEELERS B&B
503-344-1366

Coos Bay
CAPTAINS QUARTERS
503-888-6895

THIS OLDE HOUSE
503-267-5224

Corvallis
A BED & BREAKFAST
503-757-7321

HANSON COUNTRY
503-752-2919

HUNTINGTON
MANOR
503-753-3735

MADISON INN B&B
503-757-1274

Cottage Grove
IVANOFFS INN
503-942-3171

LEA HOUSE INN
503-942-0933

Depoe
GRACIES LANDING
INN
800-228-0448

Depoe Bay
*CHANNEL HOUSE
503-765-2140

Elmira
MCGILLIVRAYS LOG
HOME B&B
503-935-3564

Eugene
B&GS B&B
503-343-5739

BACKROADS B&B
503-485-0464

Oregon

****CAMPBELL HOUSE,
A CITY INN**
800-264-2519

CAMPUS COTTAGE
B&B INN
503-342-5346

CHAMBERS HOUSE
503-686-4242

COUNTRY LANE
503-686-1967

GETTYS EMERALD
GARDEN B&B
503-688-6344

GILES GUEST HAUS
503-683-2674

****KJAERS HOUSE IN
THE WOODS B&B**
503-343-3234

***LORANE VALLEY
B&B**
503-686-0241

LYON & THE LAMBE
503-683-3160

MARYELLENS GUEST
HOUSE
503-342-7375

SHELLYS GUEST
HOUSE
503-683-2062

Florence
JOHNSON HOUSE
503-997-8000

Frenchglen
FRENCHGLEN HOTEL
503-493-2565

Gardiner
HOUSE AT
GARDINER BY THE
SEA
503-271-4005

Gates
DRAGOVICH HOUSE
503-897-2157

Gold Beach
BIEN VENUE B&B
503-247-2335

ENDICOTT GARDENS
503-247-6513

*FAIR WINDS B&B
503-247-6753

Grants Pass
AHLF HOUSE B&B
503-474-1381

CLEMENS HOUSE
503-476-5564

HANDMAIDENS INN
503-476-2932

*LAWNRIDGE HOUSE
503-476-8518

PARADISE RANCH
503-479-4333

**PINE MEADOW INN
503-471-6277

**RIVERBANKS INN
503-479-1118

SKY RANCH INN B&B
503-476-9038

WASHINGTON INN
503-476-1131

Halfway
*BIRCH LEAF LODGE
503-742-2990

*CLEAR CREEK FARM
503-742-2238

Hood River
BARKHEINER HOUSE
& ESTATE
503-386-5918

COLUMBIA GORGE
HOTEL
800-826-4027

HACKETT HOUSE
503-386-1014

LAKECLIFF ESTATE
503-386-7000

STATE STREET INN
503-386-1899

Idleyld Park
IDLEYLD PARK
LODGE
503-496-0132

Independence
OUT OF THE BLUE
503-838-3636

Jacksonville
*FARMHOUSE B&B

JACKSONVILLE INN
503-899-1900

LIVINGSTON
MANSION INN
503-899-7107

© *Bed & Breakfast Guest Houses & Inns of America, Memphis TN*

Oregon

*MCCULLY HOUSE INN
503-899-1942

MEADOW LARK B&B
503-899-8963

OLD STAGE INN
800-US STAGE

ORTH HOUSE B&B
503-899-8665

REAMES HOUSE
503-899-8963

**TOUVELLE HOUSE
800-846-8422

Joseph
CHANDLERS BED & TRAIL INN
503-432-9765

WALLOWA LAKE LODGE
503-432-4982

Junction City
BLACK BART B&B
503-998-1904

Kimberly
LANDS END B&B
503-934-2333

Klamath Falls
KLAMATH MANOR
503-883-5459

THOMPSPONS B&B BY THE LAKE
503-882-7938

La Grange
STANGE MANOR
503-963-2400

Lake Oswego
GRAN-MOTHERS HOUSE
503-244-4361

LaPine
BIG BLUE HOUSE B&B
503-536-3879

Leaburg
MARJON B&B
503-896-3145

Lebanon
BOOTH HOUSE B&B
503-256-2954

Lincoln City
**BREY HOUSE "OCEANVIEW" B&B
503-994-7123

PALMER HOUSE
503-994-7932

Madras
MADRAS
503-475-2345

McMinnville
MATTEY HOUSE B&B
503-434-5058

STEIGER HAUS B&B
503-472-0821

YOUNGBERG HILL FARM
503-472-2727

Medford
UNDER THE GREENWOOD TREE
503-776-0000

WAVERLY COTTAGE

503-779-4716

Merlin
MORRISONS LODGE
800-126-1953

**PINE MEADOW INN
503-471-6277

Milton-Freewater
BIRCH TREE MANOR
503-938-6455

Milwaukie
HISTORIC BROETJE HOUSE
503-659-8860

Myrtle Creek
SONKAS SHEEP STATION
503-863-5168

Newberg
LITTLEFIELD HOUSE
503-538-9868

OWL'S VIEW B&B
503-538-6498

SECLUDED B&B
503-538-2635

Newport
OAR HOUSE
503-265-0571

OCEAN HOUSE B&B
503-265-6158

SYLVIA BEACH HOTEL
503-265-5428

North Bend
BAYWOOD B&B
503-756-6348

Oregon

*SHERMAN HOUSE
503-756-3496

Oakland
PRINGLE HOUSE
503-459-5038

Oceanside
*SEA HAVEN INN
503-842-3151

*THREE CAPES B&B
503-842-6126

Oregon City
JAGGER HOUSE
503-657-7820

Pacific City
*PACIFIC VIEW B&B
503-965-6498

Port Orford
GWENDOLYNS B&B
503-332-4373

*HOME BY THE SEA
503-332-2855

Portland
BED & ROSES
503-254-3206

CAPE COD B&B
503-246-1839

CLINKERBRICK
HOUSE
503-281-2533

GENERAL HOOKERS
503-222-4435

GEORGIAN HOUSE
503-281-2250

GREEN GABLES

GUEST HOUSE
503-287-1221

HARTMANS HEARTH
503-281-2182

HERON HOUSE
503-274-1846

HOSTESS HOUSE
503-284-7892

**J PALMER HOUSE
503-284-5893

MAC MASTER HOUSE
503-223-7362

MUMFORD MANOR
503-243-2443

OLD PORTLAND
ESTATE
503-236-6533

PENINSULA GUEST
HOUSE
503-289-9141

PORTLAND GUEST
HOUSE
503-282-1402

PORTLANDS WHITE
HOUSE B&B
503-287-7131

VICTORIAN ROSE
503-223-7673

**YANKEE TINKER
B&B
503-649-0932

Prineville
BALDWIN INN B&B
503-447-5758

Roseburg
HOUSE OF HUNTER
503-672-2335

UMPQUA HOUSE
503-459-4700

WOODS B&B
503-672-2927

Salem
HARBISON HOUSE
503-581-8818

*STATE HOUSE B&B
503-588-1340

Sandy
AUBERGE DES
FLEURS
503-663-9449

WHISPERING FIRS
503-668-4283

Seal Rock
*BLACKBERRY INN
503-563-2259

Seaside
BEACHWOOD B&B
503-738-9585

BOARDING HOUSE
503-738-9055

CHOCOLATES
FOR BREAKFAST
503-738-3622

CUSTER HOUSE
B&B
503-738-7825

GASTONS
BEACHSIDE
503-738-8320

©Bed & Breakfast Guest Houses & Inns of America, Memphis TN

Oregon

GILBERT HOUSE
503-738-9770

RIVERSIDE INN B&B
503-738-8254

SUMMER HOUSE
800-745-2378

VICTORIA B&B
503-738-8449

Shaniko
SHANIKO HISTORIC HOTEL
503-489-3441

Sisters
LAKE CREEK LODGE
503-595-6331

Spray
PIONEER B&B
503-462-3934

Stayton
HORNCROFT
503-769-6287

Steamboat
STEAMBOAT INN
503-496-3495

The Dalles
BIGELOW
503-298-8239

WILLIAMS HOUSE INN
503-296-2889

Tillamook
****BLUE HAVEN INN**
503-842-2265

Vida
MCKENZIE RIVER INN
503-822-6260

Welches
MOUNTAIN SHADOWS
503-622-4746

OLD WELCHES INN
503-622-3754

Westport
KING SALMON LODGE

Wilsonville
WILLOWS B&B
503-638-3722

Wolf Creek
WOLF CREEK TAVERN
503-866-2474

Yachats
ADOBE
503-547-3141

OREGON HOUSE
503-547-3329

*SEA QUEST
503-547-3782

RENITY B&B
503-547-3813

ZIGGURAT
503-547-3925

Yamhill
FLYING M RANCH
503-662-3222

Utah

Castle Valley Inn	Castle Valley UT
Lynn Forbes	424 Amber Lane 84532
800-842-6622 801-259-6012	**Res Times** 7am-9pm

Rates:	**Pvt Bath** 2	**Shared Bath** 4	**Payment Terms:**
Single	$ 50.00	$ 45.00	Check
Double	$ 65.00	$ 55.00	AE/MC/V

Secluded nature's haven for artists and naturalists in beautiful location close to Colorado Canyon River and Matni-La Sal Range. For everyone seeking a tranquil and peaceful setting. Continental plus breakfast is included. Sauna, Roman jet bath, bikes and sitting room **BROCHURE:** Yes **PERMITTED:** Children, limited smoking, drinking, pets [E11ACUT-2765]

Center Street B&B	Logan UT
Clyne & Ann Long	169 E Center St 84321
801-752-3443	

Rates:	**Pvt Bath** 8	**Shared Bath** 2	**Payment Terms:**
Single	$ 35-65.00	$ 35-65.00	Check
Double	$ 35-65.00	$ 35-65.00	

Elegant turn-of-the-century Victorian in the heart of town furnished with period antiques and family heirlooms. Amenities include a canopy water bed, marble jacuzzi with a crystal chandelier extending from a vaulted ceiling. Continental breakfast is included **BROCHURE:** Yes **PERMITTED:** Children 8-up [E11ACUT-2769]

Homestead	Midway UT
Britt Mathwich	700 N Homestead Dr 84049
800-327-7220 801-654-1102	**Res Times** 24 Hrs

Rates:	**Pvt Bath** 92	**Payment Terms:**
Single		Check
Double	$ 59-165.00 EP*	AE/MC/V

Nestled on sixty beautiful acres is this full-service resort dating back to 1886 when the hot mineral water baths attracted travelers. Today, this spectacular natural setting provides its guests with perhaps the broadest

Utah

range of amenities and activities of any small resort in the US! Every outdoor activity is available for every child (of any age) to try and in many instances, world-class level! Ski at Robert Redford's Sundance Resort (nearby), golf Utah's challenging Wasatch Mtn State Park Course with some of the best scenery in all of the West; x-country skiing on miles of groomed trails, snowmobiling adventures, sleigh rides for two or fun-filled rides for twenty pulled by their own Clydesdales or Belgian Draft horses. Today, there are numerous lodging choices (16 buildings) ranging from the Barn House (the largest with 16 rooms) to cottages with just 3 guest rooms, including suites, offering beautifully furnished guest rooms. There's great dining and gracious hospitality whether its a flambe' dish prepared tableside or their "famous" fried chicken. Comprehensive daily programs are offered for children 3-14 year old, making this a perfect family vacation choice ... as well as a special romantic hideaway. *AAA* ♦♦♦♦ ***Rated***, this Country Inn continues to beckon its guests back with its gracious service, a trademark since 1886! **RESERVATIONS:** One night's lodging as deposit or credit card for guarantee; 7 day cancel policy less $10 service fee; is less than 7 days notice for cancellation, one night's deposit is forfeited. **BROCHURE:** Yes **PERMITTED:** Children, drinking, limited smoking **CONFERENCES:** Yes with six meeting rooms and complete A/V equipment. **LANGUAGES:** German, Spanish [R10BCUT-2771]

---

*505 Woodside B&B Inn	Park City UT
801-649-4841	505 Woodside 84060

Rates:	**Pvt Bath** 2	**Payment Terms:**
Single	$ 55.00	Check
Double	$ 55.00	AE/V

Center of historic district offers this restored miner's cabin complete and exact. Antique furnishings and complimentary gourmet dining at breakfast. Hot tub, complimentary wine or tea. **BROCHURE:** Yes **PERMITTED:** Limited children [E11ACUT-2774]

**Old Miner's Lodge	Park City UT
Hugh Daniels/Susan Wynne	615 Woodside Ave 84060-2639
800-648-8068 801-645-8068	**Res Times** 8am-10pm
	Fax 801-645-7420

Rates:	**Pvt Bath** 10	**Payment Terms:**
Single	$ 50-190.00	Check
Double	$ 60-190.00	AE/DISC/MC/V

A lovingly restored 1889 lodge for miners beckons guests who feel more

Utah

like staying with friends than at a hotel! Each guest room is named for a Park City's historic personality and they are restored to the period fullness including down pillows and comforters. A large fireplace-focused living room becomes the gathering place in the evening for guests to enjoy complimentary refreshments. There's a hot tub for revitalizing after a day of skiing or hiking. The Historic Main Street offers guests restaurants, shops and galleries. A hearty country breakfast greets each guest in the morning, including fresh hot coffee, tea and nectars. Skiers will find The Lodge within easy walking distance of the Town Lift servicing Park City Ski Area along with the ability to "ski home" at the end of the day! There's plenty of activities including snowmobiling, hot air ballooning, golf, tennis, hiking, horseback riding. **Share the warmth of yesteryear at The Old Miner's Lodge. RESERVATIONS:** 50% deposit with bal due 30 days prior to arrival, seasonal cancel policy. Deposit required within 7 days of booking. Group rates available. Advise if arriving after 6pm **SEASONAL:** Rates vary **BROCHURE:** Yes **PERMITTED:** Children, drinking; no smoking. **CONFERENCES:** Yes for social and business events [Z07GPUT2-2777]

Old Town Guest House			Park City UT
John & Debbie Lovci			1011 Empire Ave 84060
801-649-2642			**Res Times** 24 Hrs
Rates:	**Pvt Bath** 2	**Shared Bath** 2	**Payment Terms:**
Single	$ 125.00*	$ 95.00*	Check
Double	$ 125.00*	$ 95.00*	

This beautiful *Historical Registered* home is the perfect place for active skiers, hikers and bikers or anyone wishing to escape to the beautiful mountains of Utah. Guests may enjoy all the conveniences of Park City such as Utah's largest ski area and the well-preserved Main Street district which includes over 85 shops, boutiques, galleries and restaurants.This small and charming Inn has three rooms, each furnished country-style with lodge-pole pine furniture and genuine hospitality making it a nice place to come home to after your active day. Guests may enjoy all of the comforts of the family room which has beautiful hardwood floors and the original fireplace. A complimentary full hearty mountain breakfast is served each morning. Your innkeepers, John & Debbie are very active skiers and bikers and are always able to offer suggestions to help you make the most of your stay. Their love for the mountains of Utah is overflowing and will definitely rub off on you. Back country ski tours and Mountain biking tours are available as well as additional meals upon request. To complete your active day, apres ski snacks are served and you're welcomed to sooth any aching muscles in the hot tub under the stars. **AIRPORT:** SLC Airport-30 mi **RESERVATIONS:** 50% deposit required prior to arrival. *Winter rates; Summer rates are $60.00 &

Utah

$45.00 **BROCHURE:** Yes **PERMITTED:** Children, drinking, limited smoking [Z07GPUT2-15277]

| ****Old Miners' Lodge** | **Salt Lake City UT** |

Hugh Daniels/Susan Wynne
800-648-8068   801-645-8068

Res Times 8am-10pm
Fax 801-645-7420

Rates:	**Pvt Bath** 10	**Payment Terms:**
Single	$ 50-190.00	Check
Double	$ 60-190.00	AE/DISC/MC/V

Refer to the same listing name under Park City UT for a complete description. [M03EPUT2-8713]

| ***Saltair B&B** | **Salt Lake City UT** |

Nancy Saxton
801-533-8184

164 S 900 East   84102

Rates:	**Shared Bath** 5	**Payment Terms:**
Single	$ 49.00	Check
Double	$ 49.00	

A lovely 1903 Victorian home restored to its former elegance and filled with antique furnishings and family heirlooms. Listed on the *Utah Historical Register*. Family-style homemade breakfast. **RESERVATIONS:** Station pick-up with prior arrangement **BROCHURE:** Yes **PERMITTED:** Children [E11ACUT-2786]

| ****Mountain Hollow B&B** | **Sandy UT** |

Doug & Kathy Larson
801-942-3428

10209 S Dimple Dell Rd   84092
Res Times 8am-10pm

Rates:	**Pvt Bath** 2	**Shared Bath** 8	**Payment Terms:**
Single	$ 85.00	$ 60.00	Check
Double	$ 150.00	$ 65.00	MC/V

Mountain Hollow is located on a wooded secluded two-acre estate close to the base of Little Cottonwood Canyon. This puts the world-class resorts of Alta, Brighton, Snowbird and Solitude at our doorstep. In the summer there is hiking and mountain biking as well as golf, tennis, swimming and horseback riding nearby. Our rooms are decorated with antique country and victorian furniture, making each comfortable and romantic. After a day of exercise, shopping in metropolitan Salt Lake City, or business, our 10 person hot tub will be welcomed. Located outside under the trees, you

Utah

can count the stars or catch a snowflake while encircled by luxurious warm water. A waterfall and stream on the property provides relaxation while enjoying the ever-present hummingbirds. Our breakfast buffet can be eaten in the dining room or the patio. We feature muffins, croissants, fruits, juices, yogurts and cereals. Complimentary beverages and snacks are always available. After an evening out, our video library will provide entertainment in the upstairs lounge with a cozy fireplace. *Mountain Hollow* is a peaceful, relaxing way to spend your vacation, honeymoon or getaway! **RESERVATIONS:** 50% deposit within 7 days of booking, full payment before arrival-30 days in-season with 30 day cancel notice (11/20-4/15) 15 days other period with 15 day cancel notice, refunds less $30 fee **AIRPORT:** Salt Lake Intl-25 mi **BROCHURE:** Yes **PERMITTED:** Limited children 5-up, limited drinking **CONFERENCES:** Large room with blackboard; dining room seats 24 at tables [Z07GPUT2-6331]

*****Zion House B&B*** — **Springdale UT**
Lillian Baiardi
801-772-3281
801 Zion Park Blvd 84767
Res Times 8am-8pm

Rates:	**Pvt Bath** 1	**Shared Bath** 2	**Payment Terms:**
Single	$ 50.00	$ 40.00	
Double	$ 58.00	$ 50.00	

A contemporary tri-level residence close to three National Parks and National Monuments with beautiful Utah scenery everywhere and activities that include horseback riding, river tubing, Shakespearean Festivals. Full breakfast included. **RESERVATIONS:** One night's deposit to hold room **BROCHURE:** Yes **PERMITTED:** Limited children, limited smoking [E11ACUT-2794]

Utah

Blanding
OLD HOTEL B&B
801-678-2388

Bluff
BLUFF B&B
801-672-2220

CALABRE B&B
801-672-2252

RECAPTURE LODGE
801-672-2281

Castle Valley
*CASTLE VALLEY INN
800-842-6622

Cedar City
MEADEAU VIEW LODGE
801-682-2495

PAXMANS SUMMER HOUSE
801-586-3755

WOODBURY GUEST HOUSE
801-586-6696

Ephraim
EPHRIAM HOMESTEAD
801-283-6367

Heber City
COTTAGE B&B
801-654-2236

Hunstville
TRAPPERS INN

Huntsville
JACKSON FORK INN
801-745-0051

Hurricane
PAH TEMPE HOT SPRINGS B&B
801-635-2879

Kanab
MISS SOPHIES B&B
801-644-5952

NINE GABLES INN
801-644-5079

Liberty
VUE DE VALHALLA B&B
801-745-2558

Loa
ROAD CREEK INN B&B
800-38-TROUT

Logan
BIRCH TREES B&B INN
801-753-1331

BOULEVARD B&B
801-753-6663

*CENTER STREET B&B
801-752-3443

Manti
MANTI HOUSE INN
801-835-0161

YARDLEY B&B INN
801-835-1861

Midway
*HOMESTEAD
800-327-7220

LUKE HOUSE AT MTN SPA RESORT

801-654-0807

SCHNEITTER HOTEL
800-327-7220

Moab
CANYON COUNTRY B&B
800-635-1792

PACK CREEK RANCH
801-259-5505

RON TEZ GUEST HOUSE
800-232-7247

SUNFLOWER HILL B&B
801-259-2974

WESTWOOD GUESTHOUSE
800-526-5690

Monroe
PETERSONS B&B
801-527-4830

Monticello
GRIST MILL INN
801-587-2597

Mount Pleasant
MANSION HOUSE B&B
801-462-3031

Nephi
WHITMORE MANSION
801-623-2047

Ogden
ROGERS REST B&B
801-393-5824

262   ©*Bed & Breakfast Guest Houses & Inns of America, Memphis TN*

Utah

Park City
505 WOODSIDE B&B INN
801-649-4841

ALPINE PROSPECTORS LODGE
801-649-9975

BLUE CHURCH LODGE
801-649-8009

IMPERIAL HOTEL
801-649-1904

****OLD MINERS' LODGE**
800-648-8068

****OLD TOWN GUEST HOUSE**
801-649-2642

*SNOWED INN
800-545-SNOW

*WASHINGTON SCHOOL INN
800-824-1672

Provo
SUNDANCE
801-225-4100

Rockville
BLUE HOUSE B&B
801-772-3867

Saint George
GREENE GATE VILLAGE
801-628-6999

SEVEN WIVES INN
800-484-1084

Salt Lake City
ANTON BOXRUD B&B
801-363-8035

BRIGHAM STREET INN
801-364-4461

DAVES COZY CABIN
801-278-6136

NATIONAL HISTORIC B&B
801-485-3535

****OLD MINERS' LODGE**
800-648-8068

PINECREST B&B INN
800-359-6663

*SALTAIR B&B
801-533-8184

SPRUCES B&B
801-268-8762

WESTMINSTER B&B
801-467-4114

Sandy
****MOUNTAIN HOLLOW B&B**
801-942-3428

QUAIL HILLS B&B
801-942-2858

Springdale
BUMBLEBERRY INN
801-772-3224

HARVEST HOUSE
801-772-3880

UNDER THE EAVES GUEST HOUSE
801-772-3457

*ZION HOUSE B&B
801-772-3281

Tropic
BYRCE POINT B&B
801-679-8629

Vernal
SEELEYS B&B
801-789-0933

Washington

Albatross B&B	Anacortes WA
Barbie & Ken Arasim	5708 Kingsway W 98221
800-484-9507* 206-293 0677	**Res Times** 7:30am-10pm

Rates:	**Pvt Bath** 4	**Payment Terms:**
Single	$ 80.00	Check
Double	$ 85.00	MC/V

The *Albatross* is a Cape Cod-style home constructed in 1927, with a marine orientation. It is adjacent to Skyline Marina, charter boats, restaurants and parks. The rooms are graced with beautiful period wood finish and romantic crystal chandeliers. Original works of art, collectibles and antiques are displayed throughout. We offer king and queen beds with private bath and a full breakfast in our cheery dining room. The common area feature a fireplace, library, TV, VCR, stereo equipment and current publications. Also available are sightseeing cruises aboard our 46 ft sailboat and bicycle rentals. The *Albatross* is near the ferry boats for access to the San Juan Islands and Victoria BC. We provide courtesy transportation to the ferry terminal and local airports. A bus is also available from Seattle's airport to our door. Scenic beauty abounds in Anacortes which is only a 1-1/2 hour drive from Seattle, Vancouver BC and the North Cascade highway pass. Prominent activities include island, mountain and waterway explorations. Your hosts offer warm hospitality, comfortable accommodations and vacation planning suggestions. Maps and tapes of local attractions are available. From the Spring Tulip Festival to the Summer Jazz Festival and the Fall salmon run, Anacortes is an incomparable vacation destination. Warmth and hospitality plus concierge service for your maximum enjoyment. Seasons: May 1 to September 30 peak; Oct 1 to May 26 reduced rates. **AAA ♦♦ Approved** **RESERVATIONS:** Credit card number for one night's deposit, 72 hr cancel policy for full refund, arrival 4pm-6pm. *Code 5840 **SEASONAL:** Rates vary **BROCHURE:** Yes **PERMITTED:** Children, smoking outdoors, drinking, kitchen privileges for your *"catch of the day"*, pets by prior arrangement. **CONFERENCES:** Nearby facilities at Skyline Marine Beach Club and Skyline Cabana **AIRPORT:** Sea-Tac, 100 miles **DISCOUNTS:** Multiple day stay, seniors **PACKAGES:** *Sailboat, Scenic Flights, Golf* [Z07GPWA2-11836]

Outlook Inn On Orcas Island	Eastsound WA
Jeanine & Jamie	Main St 98245

Washington

800-767-9506 206-376-2200

Rates:	Pvt Bath 16	Shared Bath
Single	$ 110-210.00	$ 69.00
Double	$ 110-210.00	$ 69.00

Res Times 8am-10pm
Fax 206-376-2256
Payment Terms:
AE/MC/V

At the sea's edge on Orcas Island, the Gem of the American San Juan Islands, the *Outlook Inn* carries the look of a Nantucket inn from years past. Originally a homesteader's cabin, the Inn was expanded in 1888 to include the local general store, barber shop, jail and guest rooms. Since the turn-of-the-century, when Orcas Island became popular with travelers from Bellingham and Seattle, the *Outlook Inn* has enjoyed a reputation as the travelers *"home away from home."* Today, forty-one tastefully decorated guest rooms offer the vacationer "old" style comfort blended with "new" amenities. Rooms in the Victorian Style have private baths, those in the Old style, share baths conveniently located nearby in the hall. Recently completed Luxury Suites have sunken living areas, broad views of Eastsound Bay, and whirlpool tubs. All rooms have phones, rooms with private baths have televisions. The restaurant at the *Outlook Inn* is open for all meals during the summer season and for breakfast and dinner off-season. Thai, seafood and vegetarian entrees are featured. Drinks are available in a turn-of-the-century brass-railed bar. Off-season rates: Private Bath $64.00, Suites $120.00, Shared Bath $34.00. **RESERVATIONS:** One nights deposit to guarantee, 7 day cancellation policy for refund **SEASONAL:** Rates vary **BROCHURE:** Yes **PERMITTED:** Children, smoking, drinking **CONFERENCES:** Yes, for groups to ninety with full kitchen, bar, chapel **AIRPORT:** Sea-Tac-80 mi; commuter airline 1-mi **DISCOUNTS:** Senior, AAA, Corporate, Government **PACKAGES:** *Bike Tours, Conferences, Weddings* [I08GPWA2-3196]

**Hillside House B&B
Cathy & Dick Robinson
206-378-4730

Friday Harbor WA
365 Carter Ave 98250

Rates:	Pvt Bath 2	Shared Bath 4	Payment Terms:
Single	$ 95.00	$ 65.00*	Check
Double	$ 95.00	$ 65.00	MC/V

This contemporary home is nestled on an acre of woodlands offering a quiet adult and ideal Bed & Breakfast atmosphere. Beautiful views

©Bed & Breakfast Guest Houses & Inns of America, Memphis TN

Washington

abound with open pastures to the north, a panoramic view of the harbor entrance with its ferries and Mount Baker to the east. The home is newly remodeled and offers three guest rooms upstairs, the largest is called "Captains Quarters" with its spacious king size bed private bath and dramatic views. Two other rooms, one with a queen size bed and one with two twin beds, share one bath. All of the rooms have cozy window seats for enjoying the beautiful woodland setting. A complimentary country breakfast includes homemade specialties, eggs right from the hen house, coffee, tea, juices all served in the living room or on the front deck. Telephones are available for guest use - but don't look for a TV here! **RESERVATIONS:** Deposit for one night due 7 days before res date. Full refund if canceled 7 days prior to res date or if the rooms are re-rented. *$25.00 per extra person. **BROCHURE:** Yes **PERMITTED:** Children over 10, smoking outside and no pets. **CONFERENCES:** Perfect for reunions or weddings; can accommodate special group requests [R11CPWA-11632]

**Shumway Mansion	Kirkland WA
Richard & Salli Harris	11410 99 Pl NE 98033
206-823-2303	**Res Times** 8am-10pm

Rates:	**Pvt Bath** 8	**Payment Terms:**
Single	$ 65-95.00	Check
Double	$ 65-95.00	AE/MC/V

Overlook Lake Washington from this twenty-four room Mansion built in 1909-10 that has been completely renovated and restored, using antique period furnishings and including oriental carpeting. Guest rooms are individually decorated, five of which have water views and one with a veranda. Just 25 min from downtown Seattle, Kirkland is the place for good restaurants as well as antique and small shop browsing. Water and snow sports are close at hand. There are two major waterfront parks within two blocks which offer swimming, tennis, bicycling, jogging and nature trails. Three major Washington State wineries are just 15 mins away by car and provide tours and tasting experiences. Compli-

Washington

mentary use of Juanita Bay Athletic Club. Full breakfast and evening snacks included. **RESERVATIONS:** One night's deposit at res time; 7-day cancellation notice for refund; check-in 3-8:00pm-later with advanced notice; check-out 11:00am **BROCHURE:** Yes **PERMITTED:** Children 12-up, smoking outdoors on covered patio **CONFERENCES:** Excellent facilities for business and social events up to 175 persons, including two full floors, large ballroom, outdoor area, gazebo & patios, with catering available [J05FPWA2-3226]

**Log Castle	**Langley WA**
Senator Jack & Norma Metcalf	3273 E Saratoga Rd 98260
306-221-5483	**Res Times** 8am-9pm

Rates:	**Pvt Bath** 4	**Payment Terms:**
Single	$ 80-105.00	Check
Double	$ 80-105.00	MC/V

"One the seven most unusual B&Bs in the USA . . " says *USA Weekend*! Now you can step into this beautiful waterfront log lodge on Whidbey Island near the historic villages of Langley and Coupeville - with your own private and secluded beach with beautiful views of Mt Baker and the snow-topped Cascade Mountains. This lovely home has now become the *Log Castle Bed & Breakfast*, a charming country inn providing gracious accommodations for travelers and those wishing to experience the quiet, peaceful island life. This exciting residence features leaded glass windows, wormwood stairways, turret bedrooms, charming wood-burning stoves, a large grand stone fireplace and fantastic views of Puget Sound and the surrounding mountains. Our guest rooms are named after our four grown daughters. Choose from the Gayle Room with cozy French doors opening to a porch facing the beach, mountains and morning sun; The Marta Suite, complete with porch and hanging swing overlooking the water to the Cascade Mountains; The Lea Room with two large windows overlooking Saratoga Passage to Camano Island and beyond; and perhaps the favorite - The Ann Room with a panoramic view through five large windows. You'll find the lodge warm and inviting and nature inviting you to relax to the sound of gulls while watching for the bald eagles and sea lions who reside here. A complimentary canoe or row boat is available for guests wanting to enjoy the scenery or try their fishing skills. Don't miss the opportunity to stay at this rare Inn when visiting Seattle - Tacoma. A full complimentary breakfast includes

Washington

Norma's legendary homemade bread and hot cinnamon rolls, direct from her oven and is served daily on a large round log table. **AIRPORT** Seattle-Tacoma Intl 50 mi. **RESERVATIONS:** Deposit required at res time refunded if canceled with 7 day notice **SEASONAL:** Closed Christmas **BROCHURE:** Yes **PERMITTED:** Children over 10, limited drinking **CONFERENCES:** Yes, when renting the entire lodge [I04FPWA1-3232]

Pine River Ranch			Leavenworth WA
Mary Ann & Mike Zenk			19668 Hwy 207 98826
509-763-3959			**Res Times** 8am-10pm
Rates:	**Pvt Bath** 6	**Shared Bath** 2	**Payment Terms:**
Single	$ 75-125.00	$ 65.00	Check
Double	$ 75-125.00	$ 65.00	MC/V

Imagine yourself relaxing on an open wrap-around porch looking out at an immense serene valley with breath-taking Cascade Mountain views. It is so easy to get lost in the magic of the *Pine River Ranch*. This historic Ranch was built in the 40's as a state-of-the-art dairy farm; now it is an exceptional Inn. The rooms are spacious and beautifully decorated, some with woodstoves, decks and sunny sitting areas. Two deluxe suites pamper you with romantic seclusion. Enjoy the hosts warm hospitality and attention to every detail during your stay. Fabulous food and soothing hot tubs help top-off any occasion. The Ranch offers hiking, stream fishing, biking and picnicking in the warmer months. Golf, windsurfing, swimming, boating, water skiing, horseback riding and rock climbing are all close-by. When the snow flakes begin to fall, the *Pine River Ranch* becomes a winter wonderland. Strap on your x-country skis and indulge yourself on the Ranch's private groomed trails. Perfectly located in the beautiful Lake Wenatchee Recreational Area, just two hours from Seattle and minutes from the Bavarian Village of Levenworth. Listed in *Northwest Best Places*, member of *AAA, Washington B&B Guild*. **DISCOUNTS:** Extended stays, inquire at res time **AIRPORT:** Seattle Seatac-2 hrs **RESERVATIONS:** One night's deposit required **BROCHURE:** Yes **PERMITTED:** Children, drinking **CONFERENCES:** Small groups and family gatherings [R12EPWA2-16172]

**West Shore Farm B&B*		Lummi Island WA
Carl & Polly Hanson		2781 W Shore Dr 98262
206-758-2600		
Rates:	**Pvt Bath** 2	**Payment Terms:**
Single	$ 75.00	Check
Double	$ 80.00	MC/V

Washington

Guests looking for a quiet and peaceful setting will find this unique octagonal home on an island a fine choice. Polly (librarian) and Carl (an engineer) built their home in 1977 from native materials such as the Alaskan yellow cedar driftwood log center pole and completed the all-wood interior with the help of their artist/craftsman son, Eric. Built into a slope overlooking the northern tip of island, scenic views abound. Privacy is assured by having the guest rooms on a separate level. One guest room, with an eagle motif, features a reading corner with a leather recliner and the other bedroom, with a blue heron motif, offers its own sink/vanity. Furnishings in each room include a table, chairs and a king-size bed. A full breakfast is included with other meals available at added cost and with prior arrangements. Meals are served family-style, next to the viewing windows and a 12-sided free-standing fireplace. Food preparation is natural (mostly home grown and preserved) and gourmet enough to be interesting. Quiet beaches, seabirds, eagles, seals, 18 miles of country roads, spectacular views of the Canadian Mountains will please any nature-lover. For entertainment, Carl, a member of the Bellingham Pipe Band, gladly awaits all requests, with his bagpipe. Everyone will enjoy your warm and charming hosts who have been doing their own version of English Bed & Breakfasts that inspired them while in England. **RESERVATIONS:** $40 deposit per room or first night's amount if longer than one night stay-seventh night free! Deposit refunded only if room is rebooked, less a $5 service fee, 11am check-out, 3pm check-in **BROCHURE:** Yes **PERMITTED:** Children, drinking **AIRPORT:** Bellingham-12 mi; Seattle-100 mi [Z07GPWA2-3250]

**Ann Starrett Mansion	**Port Townsend WA**
Edel & Bob Sokol	744 Clay St 98368
800-321-0644 206-385-3205	**Res Times** 8am-10pm

Rates:	**Pvt Bath** 8	**Shared Bath** 2	**Payment Terms:**
Single	$ 79-145.00	$ 69.00	Check
Double	$ 79-145.00	$ 69.00	AE/MC/V

Situated on the bluff overlooking mountains and Puget Sound sits the lovingly restored *Ann Starrett Mansion Victorian Bed & Breakfast*. It epitomized the heart and soul of historic Port Townsend. Built by George Starrett in 1889 as a wedding present for his wife Ann, the Inn is internationally renown for its classic Victorian architecture, frescoed ceilings and free-hung spiral staircase which leads to a glorified celestial calendar with frescoes depicting the four seasons. On the first day of each season, the sun shines on a ruby-red glass, causing a read beam to point to the appropriate season. The second floor rooms are furnished with period antiques and offer water and mountain views. The Gable Suite commands a view second to none and includes a hot tub. The Carriage House Level features charming rooms with antique brick walls

Washington

and garden views. Breakfasts at the Inn are truly memorable with a menu only a European pastry chef could dream up. The Inn has been featured in numerous publications including *The New York Times, Vancouver Canada Sun, London England Times, Elle Magazine, Conde Naste Traveler and Northwest Best Places*. Come - stay in this *National Historic Landmark - the most photographed house in the Northwest*. **AIRPORT:** Sea-Tac-1-1/2 hrs. **RESERVATIONS:** Full advance deposit at res time, 5 day cancel notice less $10 service fee **BROCHURE:** Yes **PERMITTED:** Children 13-up, limited drinking **CONFERENCES:** Yes, for dining and meetings **LANGUAGES:** German [R02EPWA-3288]

**Bishop Victorian Suites	**Port Townsend WA**
Lloyd & Marlene Cahoon	714 Washington St 98363
800-824-4738 206-385-6122	**Res Times** 8am-10pm

Rates:	**Pvt Bath** 13	**Payment Terms:**
Single	$ 68.00	Check
Double	$ 78-98.00	MC/V

Built by William Bishop in 1890, the three-story Bishop Block Building is a fine example of the award-winning downtown restoration for which Port Townsend is famous. Located in the heart of the National Historic District, the Bishop houses business and professional offices at street level with two stories of exceptional accommodations above. A short climb upstairs and the unsuspecting visitor is transported into Victorian grace and comfort. Spacious apartments have been renovated into guest suites. Each is furnished with vintage pieces reflecting the grandeur and charm of a bygone era. A home away from home, guests enjoy the comfort and luxury of a complete kitchen, living room, one or two bedrooms and a private bath. Views range from Mount Baker, the Cascade Mountains and rugged peaks of the Olympics to the waters or Port Townsend. The downtown location means convenient access to the town's shops and the Whidbey Island ferry. On the bluffs above the Bishop is a rich variety of Victorian homes which make Port Townsend one of the top attractions in the Northwest. **AIRPORT:** Sea Tac Intl-70 mi **DISCOUNTS:** Yes, extended stays **RESERVATIONS:** Deposit required to guarantee reservation **BROCHURE:** Yes **PERMITTED:** Children, pets (with prior approval, drinking, limited smoking **CONFERENCES:** Yes, conference room to 25 persons [R04FPWA2-3278]

**Palace Hotel	**Port Townsend WA**
Ruth & Les Skogman	1004 Water St 98368
800-962-0741 206-385-0773	**Res Times** 8am-10pm

Washington

Rates:	Pvt Bath 12	Shared Bath 3	Payment Terms:
Single	$ 58-100.00	$ 49.00	Check
Double	$ 63-105.00	$ 54.00	AE/DC/MC/V

Beginning in 1889 as a leading hotel, *The Palace Hotel's* colorful past followed the fortunes of Port Townsend which includes a bawdy reputation when it housed Madame Marie and when it was known as **The Palace Of Sweets** during prohibition, until the sheriff intervened. Now listed on the *National Historic Register*, the Palace's exterior has been carefully restored while interior design changes and improvements are ongoing. This stately 100-year old retains its grand Victorian Heritage with accommodations ranging from Continental bedrooms with shared baths to multi-room suites with kitchens and luxurious private baths. Your stay at the Palace includes a complimentary continental breakfast, served at 9am, cable TV, coffee and tea. Today, Port Townsend is a vital, year round city in miniature. It is one of three remaining major Victorian seaports in the country, retaining its turn-of-the-century architecture and whose renaissance, beginning in the early sixties, is continuing to blossom today. **DISCOUNTS:** 10-20% Winter (Oct-May) **AIRPORT:** Seattle Tacoma Intl-2 hrs **PACKAGES:** Lodging package in conjunction with Victoria Clipper Inc, Seattle **RESERVATIONS:** One night deposit or credit card to guarantee, 48 hr cancel policy for refund **BROCHURE:** Yes **PERMITTED:** Children, drinking, smoking rooms available **CONFERENCES:** Suites available for small gatherings [R07FPWA2-3286]

Lilac Lea Christian B&B   **Redmond WA
Chandler & Ruthanne Haight   21008 NE 117th St 98053-5309
206-861-1898

Rates:	Pvt Bath 1	Payment Terms:
Single	$ 65.00	Check
Double	$ 75.00	

Welcome to Redmond Washington, the *Bicycle Capital of the Great Northwest*. Many miles of fine trails are available to the biker as well as hiker or horseback rider. We welcome you to your large (700 square feet), self-contained, antique furnished suited in your own private, squeaky clean woodland cottage. Your suite features private bath, private entrance, queen bed, large desk and study area, TV and phone. An extra room with twin beds is available to those in the same party. A large outside deck and wooded picnic area are available. Your continental breakfast is ready when ever you want and features locally grown farm fresh fruits and berries, gourmet coffee, herbal teas, fresh juice, muffins and cereal. Our home is located 17 miles east of Seattle Center on a secluded private dead-end country road of forested acreage shared with birds, squirrels, chipmunks and deer - in a smoke free and alcohol free

Washington

environment. Your hosts have widely traveled the local area and will provide assistance in planning your activities. Unsuitable for children or pets **RESERVATIONS:** One night deposit, 7 day cancel policy less $20 service fee **SEASONAL:** Rates vary **BROCHURE:** Yes **DISCOUNTS:** *AARP*, Corporate, Off-season, Groups **AIRPORT:** SEA-TAC, Seattle [S03GWA2-8658]

BD Williams House B&B	Seattle WA
Williams Family	1505 4th Ave N 98109
800-880-0810 206-285-0810	**Fax** 206-285-5826

Rates:	**Pvt Bath** 2	**Shared Bath** 3	**Payment Terms:**
Single	$ 85.00	$ 75.00	Check
Double	$ 99.00	$ 83.00	AE/DC/MC/V

Restful night's sleep in the city at the *BD Williams House*. The 1905 home offers stunning mountain, Lake Sound and city views. Renovations uncovered and retained the original woodwork, including the coffered ceiling and lincrusta walls. Parlor and guest rooms are furnished with comfortable antiques. Glassed and open porches overlook gardens on the quiet residential street, yet the Seattle Center attractions and a busy waterfront are nearby. Breakfast served family-style in the light-filled dining room, reflecting the owners own comfortable approach to the daily gathering of guests and is sure to please. **AIRPORT:** Sea Tac-30 mins **DISCOUNTS:** Off-season, extended stays **RESERVATIONS:** Deposit with credit card number for first night rate, check-in 4-6pm **BROCHURE:** Yes **PERMITTED:** Children, drinking, limited smoking **AIRPORT:** SeaTac-15 mi [Z07GPWA2-3088]

*Chambered Nautilus B-B Inn	Seattle WA
Bunny & Bill Hagemeyer	5005 22nd Ave NE 98105
206-522-2536	**Res Times** 7am-10pm
	Fax 206-522-0404

Rates:	**Pvt Bath** 4	**Shared Bath** 2	**Payment Terms:**
Single	$ 75-97.50	$ 69.00	Check
Double	$ 82.50-105.00	$ 79.00	AE/CB/DC/MC/V

A Classic 1915 Georgian Colonial, *Chambered Nautilus Bed & Breakfast* combines the warmth of a spacious country Inn with excellent access to the city's theaters, restaurants and shopping. This gracious Inn is perched on a green and peaceful hill in Seattle's University district, with a fine view of the Cascade Mountains. Downtown Seattle is ten minutes away by car or bus and the Univ of Wash campus is within walking distance. The area is a haven of nature trails and cherished site for walkers, joggers and bicyclists. Featured in many publications, such as

Washington

Innsider, Historic American Inns & Guest Houses, Seattle Best Places & Northwest Best Places, Chambered Nautilus is Seattle's grandest B&B. Four of the comfortable guest rooms have private porches, a thirty foot living room includes a grand piano, and there is a fine mixture of American and English antiques throughout. The inn has two fireplaces and there are fully stocked bookcases in every room. Breakfasts are a diner's delight, featuring specialties of the hosts such as our national-award-winning *Chambered Nautilus Apple Quiche*, homemade biscuits and muffins, fresh fruits and juices, cheese-baked eggs, French toast with homemade syrups and freshly ground coffee. **AIRPORT:** Sea-Tac Intl-25 mins by car **RESERVATIONS:** One night's deposit or credit card; one week cancel notice for refund less $10 bank processing fee for credit issuance. Check-in 4-6pm, other hours by arrangement **SEASONAL:** Rates vary **BROCHURE:** Yes **PERMITTED:** Children 10-up (only one in same room), limited drinking, limited smoking **CONFERENCES:** Yes, up to 25 persons; living room, dining room, porch and catering **LANGUAGES:** German, English [I08GPWA2-3072]

Chelsea Station B&B Inn	Seattle WA
Dick & Marylou Jones	4915 Linden Ave N 98103-6542
800-400-6077 206-547-6077	**Res Times** 10am-7pm

Rates:	**Pvt Bath** 6	**Payment Terms:**
Single	$ 64-99.00	Check
Double	$ 69-104.00	AE/DIS/MC/V

The moment guests enter *Chelsea Station*, they experience the warmth and memories of their favorite **Gramma's House**. Visions of lace curtains at sunny windows and crocheted doilies, a Victrola and an 1898 pump organ are instant reminders of a pleasant past. This elegant 1920 Federal Colonial home is an outstanding example of the bricklayer's art. Nestled in a wooded setting, it welcomes guests to a quiet, private retreat, just eight minutes from the activity of Seattle's attractions. Guests wishing to relax may stroll through four square miles of parkland including Greenlake, Woodland Zoo and the City Rose Gardens; all just across the street. Adventurous guests can take a day trip to Mt St Helenas, Mt Rainier or Hurricane Ridge. Tea and cookies are always available to bring order back to life. Each morning offers a full breakfast of warm conversation and treats such as ginger pancakes with lemon sauce, egg souffles with homemade muffins, or banana french toast with butterscotch-maple

Washington

syrup. The perfect place to restore the human spirit! **DISCOUNTS:** Yes, in off-season **AIRPORT:** Sea Tac-16 mi **PACKAGES:** Yes, inquire at res time **RESERVATIONS:** 50% deposit, 7 day cancel policy with $10 service fee, check-in 4pm-6pm or by appointment. **BROCHURE:** Yes **PERMITTED:** Children over 12, drinking, no smoking or animals of any kind permitted [Z07GPWA2-3073]

| ****Lilac Lea Christian B&B** | **Seattle WA** |

Chandler & Ruthanne Haight
206-861-1898

Rates:	**Pvt Bath** 1		**Payment Terms:**
Single	$ 65.00		Check
Double	$ 75.00		

Refer to the same listing name under Redmond Washington for a complete description. [M03GPWA2-18784]

| ****Swallow's Nest Guest Cottages** | **Seattle WA** |

Bob Keller/Robin Hughes
800-ANY-NEST 206-463-2646   **Res Times** 7am-10pm

Rates:	**Cottages** 5		**Payment Terms:**
Single	$ 50-165.00		Check
Double	$ 50-165.00		AE/DC/MC/V

Refer to the same listing name under Vashon Island WA for a complete description [M07FPWA1-17776]

| ****Tugboat Challenger** | **Seattle WA** |

Jerry & Buff Brown   1001 Fairview Ave N 98109
206-340-1201   **Res Times** 8am-9pm
                                                    Fax 206-621-9208

Rates:	**Pvt Bath** 4	**Shared Bath** 3	**Payment Terms:**
Single	$ 85-125.00	$ 55.00	Check
Double	$ 85-125.00	$ 70.00	AE/DC/MC/V

Bunk & Breakfast in downtown Seattle while listening to the sound of lapping water outside of your porthole window! This authentic west coast tug boat offers guests a one of a kind floating B&B experience from the solarium and granite fireplace to a sunken conversation pit lavishly furnished in mahogany, pine, oak and polished brass. Guests relax before the fireplace and chart imaginary courses around the world! Other amenities include private baths, carpeting, a working bar with compli-

Washington

mentary mixers, VCR and film library, room stereos, phones and fresh cut flowers. Of eight cabins, no two are alike and though the tug is especially popular with newlyweds, many guests are business travelers who find the *Challenger* a home-like retreat in downtown Seattle. For joggers - jogging is permitted (22 laps around the deck is one mile). Sunrise brings freshly brewed coffee and you'll find your captain ready to serve a full comp breakfast including a seafood omelette, grapes, melon, compotes, waffles or pancakes and hot muffins all served on the original white Armorlite china that came with the boat. While surrounded by sleek yachts, sloops and houseboats, guests will find all of downtown Seattle nearby with numerous waterside restaurants, great shops, parks, Seattle Center, the Space Needle, the Center for Wooden Boats and other sights within a short walking distance. The *MV Challenger* has been featured by newspapers, magazines and TV programs across the USA - so don't miss this unique adventure during your trip to the northwest. **DISCOUNTS:** Yes, inquire at res time **AIRPORT:** Seattle/Tacoma-10 mi **RESERVATIONS:** Full deposit at res time with 14 day cancellation notice for refund, less than 14, deposit is not refunded but maybe applied to another date within one year from date of original reservation **BROCHURE:** Yes **PERMITTED:** Drinking, limited children, pets **CONFERENCES:** Unforgettable setting for business and social meetings, parties, dinners and weddings for groups to 24 [I08FPWA1-3082]

**Greywolf Inn	**Sequim WA**
Bill & Peggy Melang	177 Keeler Rd 98382
206-683-5889 206-683-1487	

Rates:	**Pvt Bath** 6	**Payment Terms:**
Single	$ 50-95.00	Check
Double	$ 50-95.00	AE/MC/V

Northwest hospitality with a southern flair welcomes the traveler to *Greywolf Inn*, a quiet, country retreat. Tucked between meadow and forest on a hilltop overlooking Sequim, *Greywolf* provides peaceful seclusion with easy access to the myriad attractions of the Olympic Peninsula: exploring, camping, hiking, bird-watching, fishing, boating and golf. Six comfortable guest rooms are available, each with private bath. The Pamela, with its huge pine canopy bed and family memorabilia, reflects the owner's German heritage. Visions of the Orient surround those who sleep in Nancy's queen canopy bed, while Kimberleigh's room

Washington

exudes the warmth and comfort of the Old South. Glass doors opening onto a broad deck contribute to the French feeling of the Edith Kirk Room. Miss Lillian's cozy hideaway has twin beds and a private entrance from the south deck. The Marguerite, with it's hand-painted king size sleigh bed, is Greywolf's premier accommodation. Together with Miss Lillian, it becomes a two-bedroom, two-bath suite with private entrance and decks. The full breakfast served from 8-9:30 in the French country dining room features random gourmet specialties such as country ham with red-eye gravy or a delicious salmon tart accompanied by fresh fruit, assorted hot rolls and muffins. *Greywolf Inn* has a walking trail winding through five acres of trees, field and stream; broad decks and patios; a library/game room; a sitting/living room with huge fireplace, and interesting hosts who appreciate travel, music and good company. Make *Greywolf Inn* your seat of adventure on the north Olympic Peninsula, America's mythic land. **DISCOUNTS:** Off-season rates available **AIRPORT:** Sea Tac-80 mi; Port Angeles-20 mi **RESERVATIONS:** One night's deposit with 7 day cancel policy for refund, check in 3-6pm, other by prior arrangement **BROCHURE:** Yes **PERMITTED:** Children 12-up, drinking **CONFERENCES:** Limited facilities for meetings [R10DPWA-12576]

**Moore House	**South Cle Elum WA**
Eric & Cindy Sherwood	526 Marie 98943-0629
800 22 TWAIN 509-674-5939	**Res Times** 8am-10pm

Rates:	**Pvt Bath** 6	**Shared Bath** 6	**Payment Terms:**
Single	$ 59-95.00	$ 30-59.00	AE/MC/V
Double	$ 59-95.00	$ 30-59.00	

All aboard! Destination: The Moore House! Relive the grand era of railroading at this unique Inn, formerly a hotel for train crewmen. Built in 1909 and now listed on the *National Register of Historic Places, The Moore House* offers ten guest rooms, plus two genuine cabooses. Antiques, historic photographs, and authentic railroad memorabilia lend a museum-like atmosphere to this comfortable Inn. Bring your family and stay in one of the charming cabooses adjacent to the Inn. Each caboose features a queen size bed plus three twin bunks, private bath, color TV, and sun deck. Or bring your loved one and enjoy the intimacy of the elegant bridal suite with private jacuzzi. A hearty full breakfast is served each morning in the dining room. The *Moore House* is adjacent to Iron Horse State Park, a non-motorized recreation trail, formerly the railroad right-of-way. Located in the foothills of the Cascade Mtns in Central Washington, this beautiful area offers a wonderful variety of outdoor recreation: biking, hiking, golf, horseback riding, river rafting, fishing, snowmobiling, x-country and down hill skiing. Visit historic Cle Elum and Roslyn (known as Cicely, Alaska, in the popular TV series *Northern*

Washington

Exposure). **AIRPORT:** Seattle-Tacoma Intl 90 mins **RESERVATIONS:** One night deposit to confirm res, 7 day cancel policy for refund, check-in after 10:30 pm by prior arrangement only **SEASONAL:** Closed Christmas **BROCHURE:** Yes **PERMITTED:** Children, limited drinking, limited smoking **CONFERENCES:** Yes, ideal location for special business, social meetings, seminars and family get-togethers. Luncheon and dinners available [Z05FPWA1-3094]

**Swallow's Nest Guest Cottages	**Tacoma WA**
Bob Keller/Robin Hughes	
800-ANY-NEST 206-463-2646	**Res Times** 7am-10pm
Rates: **Cottages** 5	**Payment Terms:**
Single $ 50-165.00	Check
Double $ 50-165.00	AE/DIS/MC/V

Refer to the same listing name under Vashon Island WA for a complete description [M07FPWA1-17777]

**Swallow's Nest Guest Cottages	**Vashon Island WA**
Bob Keller/Robin Hughes	6030 SW 248th St 98070
800-ANY-NEST 206-463-2646	**Res Times** 7am-10pm
Rates: **Cottages** 5	**Payment Terms:**
Single $ 50-165.00	Check
Double $ 50-165.00	AE/DIS/MC/V

An idyllic island retreat -- a short boat ride from Seattle, Tacoma or the Olympic Peninsula brings you to the rural, small town safety of Vashon Island with its beaches, boating, views and wildlife. Country cottages near the beach, some with views, vary in size from studios to a two-story Victorian with woodburning stoves that sleeps eight. Each is furnished in a warm and comfortable style with plants, books, rocking or arm chairs and has cooking facilities and TV. Three of the cottages, the *Nest*, (1 bedroom), the *Robin's Nest* (2 bedrooms) and the *Bird Blind* (studio), are one mile from a golf course on a bluff with spectacular views of Puget Sound, Mt Rainier and the Cascades. It is a quiet spot with mature landscaping surrounded by several hundred acres of field and forest. Guests enjoy watching the deer, the birds (eagles,

Washington

hawks, swallows, pileated woodpeckers, gold finches, owls ... 49 species in a week) and the neighbor's 250 goats. *'It would be hard to imagine a more delightful get-away-from-it-all spot than the Nest.* Edson House, a two-story Victorian restoration in the Village of Burton, has views of Quartermaster Harbor and is right across the road from the Marina and Yacht Club. It is furnished with antique oak furniture and colorful oriental carpets, has a full kitchen, and one of it's bathrooms is graced with a 5-1/2 foot clawfooted tub -- ideal for a soak before a luxurious massage by our professional masseuse. Only one block to the beach and good restaurants, it is *perfect for a small group retreat or family reunion.* **RESERVATIONS:** Full deposit in advance, 21 day cancel notice policy for refund; less than 21 day notice. refund only if rebooked. Credit card payment requires additional 5% for service fees **PERMITTED:** Children, drinking, smoking on porches, pets with prior arrangements only **BROCHURE:** Yes **CONFERENCES:** Seminars and retreats in Victorian Living Room, sleeping space for six couples-plus **DISCOUNTS:** Off-season (Oct to May) **AIRPORT:** Seattle-Tacoma, 1 hr by car including ferryboat; Wax Orchards or Vashon Municipal, grass strips on Island, 2-8 mi [I07FPWA1-3103]

** *'37 House*	Yakima WA
Mike Taylor	4002 Englewood Ave 98980
509-965-5537	**Res Times** 8am-10pm

Rates:	**Pvt Bath** 6	**Payment Terms:**
Single	$ 65-120.00	Check
Double	$ 65-120.00	AE/MC/V

Welcome to *The '37 House*, **an Inn of extraordinary elegance completed in 1937 - a Yakima landmark** gracing a scenic 9.5 acre knoll just northwest of the heart of the city. When it became an Inn, great care was taken to preserve its physical grandeur, warmth and gracious hospitality. From the sweeping hardwood staircase, the formal dining room still furnished with many of the original family's possessions, including cherry dining room chairs with hand-woven cushions to the impressive living room with its massive woodburning fireplace ... guests are truly at home. With a total of 7500 sq ft, a variety of accommodations offer king and queen size beds, a suite with two spacious bedrooms and sitting area - each room has its own unique charm - special touches from '37; built-in desks, window seats tucked under sloping eaves, shutter window panes and full-tile baths. Every overnight stay includes a full gourmet breakfast, artfully prepared and served - and of course, arrangements can be made for additional meals and refreshments to be served in your favorite part of the home - or outside in a sun-splashed corner of the English Garden or the Inn's adjoining grounds and tennis court. Individual attention is the hallmark of *The '37 House*. When you return,

Washington

you're greeted by a staff who remembers your preferences in accommodations and food. We purposely keep our own schedule flexible enough to meet the time tables and needs of our guests. ***Inspected and approved by AAA, ABBA* DISCOUNTS:** Corporate **AIRPORT:** 7 miles **RESERVATIONS:** Verifiable credit card for first night's lodging, 24 hour cancel policy for refund **BROCHURE:** Yes **PERMITTED:** Limited children, limited drinking **CONFERENCES:** Perfect for memorable retreats, dinner parties, meetings and other special events hosted by you and carefully orchestrated by *The '37 House* staff [R07FPWA2-14648]

Washington

Acme
RIVER VALLEY B&B
206-595-2686

Anacortes
ADMIRAL'S
HIDEAWAY B&B
206-293-0106

**ALBATROSS B&B
800-484-9507

BURROWS BAY B&B
206-293-4792

CAMPBELL HOUSE
206-293-4910

*CHANNEL HOUSE
206-293-9382

DUTCH TREAT
HOUSE
206-293-8154

HASTY PUDDING
HOUSE
800-368-5588

LOWMAN HOUSE
B&B
206-293-0590

NANTUCKET INN
206-293-6007

OLD BROOK INN
206-293-4768

Anderson Isl
INN AT BURG'S
LANDING
206-884-9185

Ashford
ALEXANDERS
COUNTRY INN
800-654-7615

ASHFORD MANSION
206-569-2739

GROWLY BEAR
206-569-2339

MOUNTAIN
MEADOWS
206-569-2788

WILD BERRY INN

Auburn
BLOMEEN HOUSE
B&B
206-939-3088

Bainbridge Island
BAINBRIDGE HOUSE
206-842-1599

BEACH COTTAGE
206-842-6081

BOMBAY HOUSE
206-842-3926

ROSE COTTAGE
206-842-6248

Bellevue
BELLEVUE B&B
206-453-1048

LIONS B&B
206-455-1018

PETERSEN B&B
206-454-9334

Bellingham
ANDERSON CREEK
LODGE
206-966-2126

BELLINGHAMS
DECANN HOUSE
206-734-9172

CASTLE B&B
206-676-0974

NORTH GARDEN INN
800-922-6414

SCHNAUZER
CROSSING
206-733-0055

SUNRISE BAY B&B
206-647-0376

Bingen
GRAND OLD HOUSE
509-493-2838

Bremerton
WILCOX HOUSE
206-830-4492

Carnation
IDYL INN ON THE
RIVER
206-333-4262

Carson
CARSON HOT
SPRINGS
509-427-8292

Cashmere
CASHMERE
COUNTRY INN
509-782-4212

Cathlamet
CATHLAMET HOTEL
800-446-0454

COUNTRY KEEPER
B&B
206-795-3030

Washington

GALLERY B&B AT
LITTLE CAPE HORN
206-425-7395

Chelan
BRICK HOUSE INN
509-682-4791

EM B&B INN
509-682-4149

MARY KAYS WHALEY
MANSION
509-682-5735

NORTH CASCADES
LODGE
509-682-4711

Chimacum
SUMMER HOUSE
206-732-4017

Clinton
BEACH HOUSE
206-321-4335

*HOME BY THE SEA
B&B
206-221-2964

KITTLESON COVE
206-221-2734

Concrete Birdsview
CASCADE MOUNTAIN
INN
800-826-0015

Coulee City
MAIN STAY
509-632-5687

Coupeville
CAPTAIN WHIDBEY
800-366-4097

COL CROCKETT
FARM
206-466-3207

COLONEL CROCKETT
FARM
206-678-3711

FORT VASEY INN
206-678-8792

*INN AT PENN COVE
800-688-COVE

VICTORIAN HOUSE
206-678-5305

Cusich
RIVER BEND INN
509-445-1476

Darrington
HEMLOCK HILLS
B&B
206-436-1274

Deer Harbor
PALMERS CHART
HOUSE
206-376-4231

Deer Park
LOVES B&B
509-276-6939

East Port Orchard
"REFLECTIONS" A
B&B INN
206-871-5582

Eastsound
BLUE HERON
206-376-2954

GIBSONS NORTH
BEACH INN
206-376-2660

KANGARO HOUSE
206-376-2175

**OUTLOOK INN ON
ORCAS ISL
206-376-2200

ROSARIO RESORT
HOTEL
206-376-2222

TURTLEBACK FARM
206-376-4914

Eatonville
OLD MILL HOUSE
B&B
206-832-6506

Edmonds
HARRISON HOUSE
206-776-4748

HEATHER HOUSE
206-778-7233

HUDGENS HAVEN
206-776-2202

Ellensburg
MURPHY'S COUNTRY
B&B
509-925-7986

Enumclaw
STILLMEADOW B&B
206-825-6381

Everett
KATMAI LODGE

RIDGEWAY HOUSE

Ferndale
ANDERSON HOUSE
206-384-3450

Washington

*HILL TOP B&B
206-384-3619

Forks
MANITOU LODGE B&B
800-374-0483

MILLER TREE INN
206-374-6806

MISTY VALLET INN
206-374-9389

RIVER INN
206-374-6526

Freeland
CLIFF HOUSE
206-321-1566

PILLARS BY THE SEA
206-221-7738

Friday Harbor
BLAIR HOUSE B&B
206-378-5907

DUFFY HOUSE
206-378-5604

FARMHOUSE
206-378-3463

FRIDAY'S
206-378-5848

**HILSIDE HOUSE B&B
206-378-4730

MARIELLA INN & COTTAGES
206-378-6868

MEADOWS
206-378-4004

MOON & SIX PENCE
206-378-4138

OLYMPIC LIGHTS
206-378-3186

SAN JUAN INN
206-378-2070

TOWER HOUSE
206-378-5464

TRUMPETER INN
206-378-3884

TUCKER HOUSE B&B
206-378-2783

WESTWINDS B&B
206-378-5283

WHARFSIDE B&B
206-378-5661

Gig Harbor
HILLSIDE GARDENS B&B
206-851-3965

NO CABBAGES B&B

OLDE GLENCOVE HOTEL
206-884-2835

PARSONAGE
206-851-8654

Glenwood
FLYING L GUEST RANCH
509-364-3488

Gold Bar
BUSH HOUSE
206-363-1244

Goldendale
THREE CREEKS LODGE
509-773-4026

Granger
RINEHOLD CANNERY HOMESTEAD
509-854-2508

Greenbank
GUEST HOUSE B&B
206-678-3115

Hamilton
SMITH HOUSE B&B
206-826-4214

Hoquaim
LYTLE HOUSE B&B
206-533-2320

Ilwacoq
INN AT ILWACO
206-642-8686

KOLA HOUSE B&B
206-642-2819

Index
BUSH HOUSE
206-466-3366

Indianola
INDIANAOLA B&B
206-297-2382

Issaquah
WILDFLOWER
206-392-1196

Kalaloch
KALALOCH LODGE
503-489-3441

Kalama
BLACKBERRY HILL

Washington

206-673-2159

Kettle Falls
MY PARENTS ESTATE

509-738-6220

Kirkland
SHUMWAY MANSION
206-823-2303

La Conner
DOWNEY HOUSE
206-466-3207

HEATHER HOUSE
206-466-4675

HOTEL PLANTER
206-466-4710

KATHYS INN
206-466-3366

LA CONNER COUNTRY INN
206-466-3101

RAINBOW INN
206-466-4578

RIDGEWAY B&B
206-428-8068

Lake Stevens
LAKE SHORES PEONY HOUSE
206-334-1046

Landley
INN AT LANGLEY
206-221-3033

Langley
BLUE HOUSE INN
206-221-8392

CAROLINES COUNTRY COTTAGE
206-221-8709

EAGLES NEST INN
206-321-5331

GALLERY SUITE
206-221-2978

LOG CASTLE
206-221-5483

LONE LAKE COTTAGE
206-321-5325

MAPLE TREE GUEST HOUSE
206-221-2434

ORCHARD
206-221-7880

SARATOGA INN
206-221-7526

THICKENHAM HOUSE
800-874-5009

WHIDBEY HOUSE
206-221-7115

Leavenworth
ALL SEASONS RIVER INN
509-548-1425

BAVARIAN MEADOWS
509-548-4449

BROWNS FARM
509-548-7863

EDEL HAUS PENSION
509-548-4412

HAUS ROHRBACH PENSIONE
509-549-7024

HEAVEN CANT WAIT LODGE
206-881-5350

HOTEL EURPOA
509-548-5221

MORGANS SERENDIPITY
509-548-7722

MOUNTAIN HOME LODGE

OLD BRICK SILO B&B
509-548-4772

PINE RIVER RANCH
509-763-3959

RUN OF THE RIVER B&B
509-548-7171

Long Beach
SCANDINAVIAN GARDENS INN
206-642-8877

Longmire
NATIONAL PARK INN
206-569-2565

Lopez Island
EDENWILD INN
206-468-3238

INN AT SWIFT'S BAY
206-468-3636

INN AT SWIFTS BAY
206-468-3636

Washington

MACKAYE HARBOR
206-468-2253

MAREAN'S BLUE
FJORD CABINS
206-468-2749

Lummi Island
LOGANITA, A VILLA
BY THE SEA
206-758-2651

SHOREBIRD HOUSE
206-758-2177

**WEST SHORE
FARM
206-758-2600

WILLOWS INN
206-758-2620

Lynden
CENTURY HOUSE
401-354-2439

LE COCQ HOUSE
206-354-3032

Maple Falls
YODELER INN
206-599-2156

Maple Valley
MAPLE VALLEY B&B
206-432-1409

Mazawa
MAZAWA COUNTRY
INN
509-996-2681

Montesano
ABEL HOUSE B&B
206-249-6002

SYLVAN HOUSE

206-249-3453

Mount Vernon
WHITE SWAN GUEST
HOUSE
206-445-6805

Moxee City
DESERT ROSE
509-452-2237

Naches
HOPKINSON HOUSE
509-575-0417

Nordland
ECOLOGIC PLACE
206-385-3077

North Bend
APPLE TREE INN
206-888-3572

INN NEW ENGLAND
206-888-3879

Oak Harbor
EARTH SHELTER
206-398-2030

HARBOR POINTE
B&B
206-675-3379

Ocean Shores
OCEAN FRONT
LODGE
206-289-3036

Olalla
OLALLA ORCHARD
206-857-5915

Olympia
BRITTS PLACE
206-264-2764

HARBINGER INN
206-754-0389

PUGET VIEW
GUESTHOUSE
206-459-1676

Orcas
ORCAS HOTEL
206-376-4300

WOODSONG B&B
206-376-2340

Packwood
PACKWOOD HOTEL
206-494-5431

Pateros
AMYS MANOR B&B
509-923-2334

Point Roberts
OLD HOUSE
206-945-5210

Port Angeles
ANNIKENS B&B
206-457-6177

DOMAINE
MADELEINE
206-457-4174

GLEN MAR B&B
206-457-6110

KENNEDY'S B&B
206-457-3628

OUR HOUSE B&B
206-452-6338

TUDOR INN
800-522-5174

Port Hadlock

Washington

PORT HADLOCK INN
800-395-1595

Port Orchard
"REFLECTIONS" A
B&B
206-871-5582

OGLES B&B
206-876-9170

Port Townsend
*ANN
STARRETT MANSION
800-321-0644

ARCADIA COUNTRY
INN
206-385-5245

**BISHOP
VICTORIAN SUITES
800-824-4738

HERITAGE HOUSE
INN
206-385-6800

*HOLLY HILL HOUSE
206-385-5619

JAMES HOUSE
206-385-1238

LINCOLN INN
800-477-4667

LIZZIES VICTORIAN
B&B
206-385-4168

MANRESA CASTLE
206-385-5750

**PALACE HOTEL
800-962-0741

QUIMPER INN
206-385-1060

RAMAGE HOUSE
206-385-1086

RAVENSCROFT INN
206-385-2784

THE CABIN
206-385-5571

TRENHOLM HOUSE
206-385-6059

Poulsbo
MANOR FARM INN
206-779-4628

SOLLIDEN GUEST
HOUSE
206-779-3969

Prescott
COUNTRY LIVING
B&B
509-849-2819

Puyallup
HARTS TAYBERRY
B&B
206-848-4594

Quinault
LAKE QUINAULT
LODGE
206-288-2571

Randle
HAMPTON HOUSE
206-497-2907

Redmond
**LILAC LEA
CHRISTIAN B&B
206-861-1898

Ritzville
PORTICO B&B
206-659-0800

Roche Harbor
ROCHE HARBOR
RESORT
206-378-2155

San Juan Island
HOTEL DE HARO

STATES INN
206-378-6240

Seabeck
SUMMER SONG
206-830-5089

WALTON HOUSE
206-830-4498

Seattle
ALEXIS HOTEL
SEATTLE
206-624-4844

**BD WILLIAMS
HOUSE**
206-385-0810

BEECH TREE
MANOR
206-281-7037

CAPITAL HILL INN
206-323-1955

CAPITOL HILL
HOUSE
206-322-1752

**CHAMBERED
NAUTILUS B-B INN
206-522-2536

**CHELSEA

©Bed & Breakfast Guest Houses & Inns of America, Memphis TN

Washington

STATION B&B INN
206-547-6077

COLLEGE INN GUEST HOUSE
206-633-4441

GASLIGHT INN
206-325-3654

HAINSWORTH HOUSE
206-938-1020

INN AT THE MARKET
800-446-4484

**LILAC LEA CHRISTIAN B&B
206-861-1898

MARIT'S B&B
206-782-7900

*MILDREDS B&B
206-325-6072

PRINCE OF WALES
206-325-9692

QUEEN ANNE HILL B&B
206-284-9779

ROBERTAS B&B
206-329-3326

SALISBURY HOUSE
206-328-8682

SEATTLE B&B
206-784-0539

**SWALLOW'S NEST GUEST COTTAGES
206-463-2646

**TUGBOAT CHALLENGER
206-340-1201

VILLA HEIDELBERG
206-938-3658

Seaview
SHELBURNE INN
206-642-2442

SOU' WESTER LODGE
206-642-2542

Sequim
DIAMOND POINT INN
800-551-2615

GRANNY SANDYS ORCHARD B&B
206-683-5748

**GREYWOLF INN
206-683-5889

GROVELAND COTTAGE
206-683-3565

MARGIES B&B
206-683-7011

Shelton
TWIN RIVER RANCH
206-426-1023

Snohomish
COUNTRYMAN B&B
206-568-9622

COUNTRYMANOR B&B
206-568-8254

EDDYS B&B
206-568-7081

IVERSON
206-568-3825

Snoqualmie
OLD HONEY FARM
206-888-9399

South Cle Elum
**MOORE HOUSE
800 22 TWAIN

Spokane
BLAKELY ESTATE B&B
509-926-9426

DUROCHER HOUSE B&B
509-328-2971

NETHERINGHAM HOUSE
509-838-4363

HILLSIDE HOUSE
509-534-1426

LUCKEYS RESIDENCE
509-624-3627

TOWN & COUNTRY B&B
509-466-7559

WAVERLY PLACE B&B
509-328-1856

Stevenson
HOME VALLEY B&B
509-427-7070

Sunnyside
SUNNYSIDE INN
509-839-5557

Washington

Tacoma
INGES PLACE
206-584-4514

KEENAN HOUSE
206-751-0702

SALLYS BEAR TREE COTTAGE
206-475-3144

SWALLOW'S NEST GUEST COTTAGES
206-563-2646

TRAUDELS HAUS
206-535-4422

Tonasket
ORCHARD COUNTRY INN
509-486-1923

Trout Lake
MIO AMORE PENSIONE
509-395-2264

Vashon Island
OLD TJOMSLAND HOUSE
206-463-5275

RAMBLING ROSE BEACH HOUSE
206-463-5058

SWALLOW'S NEST GUEST COTTAGES
800-ANY-NEST

Walla Walla
GREEN GABLES INN
509-525-5501

REES MANSION
509-529-7845

STONE CREEK INN
509-529-8120

Waterville
TOWER HOUSE B&B
509-745-8320

Wenatchee
FORGET-ME-NOT B&B
800-843-7552

Wheeling
YESTERDAYS LTD B&B

White Salmon
INN OF THE WHITE SALMON
509-493-2335

LLAMA RANCH B&B
509-395-2786

ORCHARD HILL INN
509-493-3024

Winthrop
DAMMANN B&B
509-996-2484

Woodinville
BEAR CREEK INN
206-881-2978

Yakima
'37 HOUSE
509-965-5537

BIRCHFIELD MANOR
504-452-1960

IRISH HOUSE B&B
509-453-5474

MEADOWBROOK B&B

509-248-2387

TUDOR GUEST HOUSE
509-452-8112

©Bed & Breakfast Guest Houses & Inns of America, Memphis TN

Wyoming

*Lockhart B&B Inn	Cody WY
Mark & Cindy Baldwin 307-587-6074	109 W Yellowstone Ave 82414

Rates:　　**Pvt Bath** 6　　　　　　　　　　**Payment Terms:**
Single　　　　$ 45-65.00　　　　　　　　　　　　　　　　Check
Double　　　　　　　　　　　　　　　　　　　　　　　　　MC/V

Residence of western author Caroline Lockhart still offering antique furnishings, western hospitality, and hearty country breakfasts. Close to spectacular flora & fauna. **BROCHURE:** Yes **PERMITTED:** Children 4-up, limited smoking [E11ACWY-5018]

**Parson's Pillow B&B	Cody WY
Lee & Elly Larabee 800-377-2348 307-587-2382	1202 14th St 82414 **Res Times** 24 Hrs

Rates:　　**Pvt Bath** 2　　**Shared Bath** 2　　**Payment Terms:**
Single　　　　$ 70.00　　　　　　$ 60.00　　　　　　　　Check
Double　　　　$ 75.00　　　　　　$ 65.00　　　　　　　　MC/V

Comfort, elegance and the sense of coming home are yours to enjoy as a guest of the *Parson's Pillow B&B*. Antiques and turn-of-the-century lace surround you. Our 1902 former church has been caringly restored so that you might experience home-style hospitality. Choose from four individually decorated rooms with many personal touches. Enjoy a delectable full breakfast with fellow guests in the dining room. The parlour is always available for socializing, reading (peruse the library), a game or two, piano, TV, take a snooze on the front porch, or croquet anyone? We are **Just Boot Steps from Everything** - Buffalo Bill Historical Center with the Plains Indian Museum, Whitney Gallery of Western Art, and Winchester Arms Museum. Browse unique shops and galleries. Experience white-water rafting on the Shoshone, golf, tennis or go western at Cody Night Rodeo. Just off Hwys 14, 16 & 120, *Parson's Pillow B&B* is the natural starting point while visiting northwest Wyoming - *Cody Country*. Just minutes from Buffalo Bill Dam Visitor Center and Reservoir, Sunlight Basin, spectacular Wapiti Valley and Shoshone National Forest on the way to Yellowstone National Park. Always remember, *"It's Alright to Sleep in Our Church"*. **RESERVATIONS:** Full payment in advance of reservation date, 10 day cancel policy for refund;

Wyoming

less than 10 days notice, credit or refund only if rebooked, less $15 service fee **PERMITTED:** Limited children, drinking **BROCHURE:** Yes **DISCOUNTS:** Week stays, less $10 per day **AIRPORT:** Yellowstone Regional Airport-2 mi [R07FPWY1-12580]

Wolf Hotel			**Saratoga WY**
Doug & Kathleen Campbell			101 E Bridge 82331
307-326-5663			
Rates:	**Pvt Bath** 6	**Shared Bath** 12	**Payment Terms:**
Single	$ 32.00 EP	$ 32.00 EP	Check
Double			AE/MC/V

Built as a stage coach stop in c1893, everything is still the same as then!! All the rooms are in the same original condition and *without TV and phones* during your stay. Lunch and dinner available at added cost. **BROCHURE:** Yes **PERMITTED:** Children, smoking and drinking [E11ACWY-5037]

Savery Thoroughbred Ranch			**Savery WY**
Joyce B Saer			PO Box 24 82332
307-383-7840			**Res Times** 24 Hrs
Rates:	**Pvt Bath** 1	**Shared bath** 2	**Payment Terms:**
Single	$ 65-250.00	$ 65-250.00	Check
Double	$ 65-250.00	$ 65-250.00	

Pristine countryside and abundant wildlife at this small and quaint Inn and YL Ranch lodge offers guests a unique and interesting western experience which includes *a taste of the "original west" but with modern amenities* such as a tennis court for keeping fit! A photographer's and wildlife enthusiast's paradise, trips to the Red Desert offers interesting formations, antelope and wild horses. Horseback riding is featured with fly-fishing, creek swimming, cookouts, rodeos and buggy rides at this oasis with its own private landing field for guests who want to fly in! Guests' quarters are furnished with antiques and fireplaces in some suites with an extensive library to choose from for your reading pleasure. Individual luxurious bedrooms offer queen-size beds and oversized beds in converted sheep wagons! All meals are available on the premises which include home grown vegetables, salads, fruits, fish, beef, lamb and poultry all lovingly prepared by your hostess. Your opportunity to unwind in a serene and spectacular setting. **RESERVATIONS:** 25% deposit of entire stay within 10 days of booking; will meet planes at Steamboat Springs Colorado ($40 additional charge) **BROCHURE:** Yes **PERMITTED:** Limited children, pets and drinking **CONFERENCES:** Yes

Wyoming

with advance notice **LANGUAGES:** Spanish, French [E11ACWY-5038]

Heck Of A Hill Homestead	**Wilson WY**
Bill & Mimi Schultes	PO Box 105 83014
307-733-8023	

Rates:	**Pvt Bath** 2	**Shared Bath** 1	**Payment Terms:**
Single			Check
Double	$ 85.00	$ 85.00	

Jackson Hole homestead offering home-grown meals, a variety of farm animals, and fully restored residence furnished with period antiques. Piano, fireplace, steam bath, and sitting room. Dinner available at added cost. **BROCHURE:** Yes **PERMITTED:** Children, pets [E11ACWY-5041]

Teton View B&B	**Wilson WY**
Jane & Tom Neil	2136 Coyote Loop 83014
307-733-7954	**Res Times** 8am-10pm

Rates:	**Pvt Bath** 1	**Shared Bath** 2	**Payment Terms:**
Single	$ 75.00	$ 55.00	Check
Double	$ 80.00	$ 60.00	AE/MC/V

Enjoy the personal touches your hosts offer during your stay in their charming home with spectacular mountain views, large comfortable beds fitted with flannel sheets and comforters just perfect for snuggling in winter and a cozy country decor. Each guest room offers a second-story deck overlooking the Teton Mountain Range where you can enjoy watching soaring hawks, geese in formation or the resident hummingbirds feeding nearby. Conveniently located just 5 miles from Jackson and the ski resort offering year-round activities including sleigh rides in the National Elk Refuge or around town, excellent hunting (elk, deer, antelope, geese), western museums, performing arts, Snake River raft trips, and nightly "shoot-outs" on the town square! The continental breakfast brings homemade pastries and breads, fresh fruit, juices, teas and famous freshly-ground coffee served family-style around a large table in the family dining room. A common lounge for guests includes a small refrigerator, coffee maker, indoor games, books and brochures on the sights around town and even a telescope for viewing the peaks. A washer/dryer are available along with a storage area for hanging your skis and warming your boots. Relax in the hammock, toss a few horseshoes while your children enjoy the swing set. **RESERVATIONS:** 1-2 nights deposit (depending on length of stay) balance due 30 days prior to arrival. Two week cancel policy for refund **BROCHURE:** Yes **PERMITTED:** Children, drinking, smoking outdoors only [R11BPWY-9501]

Wyoming

Big Horn
SPAHNS BIG HORN LODGE
307-674-8150

Buffalo
PARADISE GUEST RANCH
307-684-7876

SOUTH FORK INN
307-684-9609

THIS OLDE HOUSE B&B
307-684-5930

V BAR F CATTLE RANCH
307-758-4382

Casper
BESSEMER BEND B&B
307-265-6819

DURBIN STREET INN
307-577-5774

Cheyanne
DRUMMONDS RANCH
307-634-6042

Cheyenne
ADVENTURES' COUNTRY B&B
307-632-4087

BIT-O-WYO RANCH
307-638-8340

HOWDY PARTNER B&B
307-634-6493

PORCH SWING B&B
307-778-7182

RAINSFORD INN
307-638-BEDS

Cody
BILL CODYS RANCH

GOFF CREEK LODGE
307-587-3753

HIDDEN VALLEY RANCH
307-587-5090

HUNTER PEAK RANCH
307-587-3711

*LOCKHART B&B INN
307-587-6074

**PARSON'S PILLOW
800-377-2348

RIMROCK DUDE RANCH

SHOSHONE LODGE RESORT
307-587-4044

SIGGINS TRIANGLE X RANCH

THE IRMA
800-626-4886

TROUT CREEK INN
307-587-6288

VALLEY RANCH
307-587-4661

WIND CHIMES COTTAGE B&B
307-527-5310

Devils Tower
R PLACE
307-467-5938

Douglas
AKERS RANCH
307-358-3741

*DEER FORKS RANCH
307-358-2033

PELLATZ RANCH
307-358-2380

TWO CREEK RANCH
307-358-3467

Dubois
GEYSER CREEK B&B
307-455-2702

JAKEY'S FORK B&B
307-455-2769

LAZY L&B RANCH

SUNSHINE & SHADOWS B&B
800-472-6241

UNION PASS B&B
307-455-3238

Encampment
*LORRAINE'S B&B HOMESTAY
307-327-5200

PLATTS B&B
307-327-5539

Evanston
PINE GABLES B&B INN
307-789-2069

©Bed & Breakfast Guest Houses & Inns of America, Memphis TN

Wyoming

Evansville
MISKIMINS RANCH
307-265-5725

Gillette
PETTERSEN HAUS
307-686-1030

Glenrock
HOTEL HIGGINS
800-458-0144

OPAL'S B&B
307-436-2626

Guernsey
ANNETTTE'S WHITE HOUSE
307-836-2148

Jackson
MOOSE MEADOWS
307-733-9510

RUSTY PARROT LODGE
307-733-2000

SPRING CREEK RANCH
307-733-8833

SUNDANCE INN
307-733-3444

TWIN MTN RIVER RANCH B&B

WILDFLOWER INN
307-733-4710

Jackson Hole
BUCKRAIL LODGE
307-733-2079

POWDERHORN RANCH

307-733-3845

Lander
COUNTRY FARE B&B
307-332-5906

EDNA'S B&B
307-332-3175

EMPTY NEST B&B
307-332-7516

MCDOUGALL B&B
307-332-3392

MINERS DELIGHT INN
307-332-3513

Laramie
ANNIE MOORE'S GUEST HOUSE
307-721-4177

INN ON IVINSON
307-745-8939

V-BAR GUEST RANCH
800-788-4630

Lusk
WYOMING WHALE RANCH
307-334-3598

Medicine Bow
HIST VIRGINIAN HOTEL

Moose
BUNKHOUSE
307-733-7283

Moran
BOX K RANCH
800-729-1410

FIR CREEK RANCH
307-543-2416

JENNY LAKE LODGE
307-543-2811

Newcastle
4W RANCH
307-746-2815

HORTON HOUSE B&B
800-845-2717

Pinedale
WINDOW ON THE WINDS B&B
307-367-2600

Powell
BAR X RANCH
307-645-3231

Ranchester
MASTERS RANCH
307-655-2386

Rawlins
FERRIS MANSION
307-324-3961

LAMONT INN
307-324-7602

Recluse
TR RANCH
307-736-2250

Riverton
BLUE SPRUCE LODGE

COTTONWOOD RANCH
307-856-3064

HILLCREST MANOR

Wyoming

307-856-6309

Rock River
DODGE CREEK RANCH
307-322-2345

Rock Springs
SHA HOL DEE B&B
307-362-7131

Saratoga
BROOKSONG B&B HOME
307-326-8744

HOOD HOUSE
307-326-5624

SARATOGA INN

SARATOGA SAFARIS B&B

*WOLF HOTEL
307-326-5663

Savery
*SAVERY CREEK THOROUGHBRED RANCH
307-383-7840

Shell
CLUCAS RANCH B&B
307-765-2946

Sheridan
KILBOURNE KASTLE
307-674-8716

Sundance
CANFIELD RANCH
307-283-2062

HAWKEN GUEST RANCH

800-544-4309

Wapiti
ELEPHANT HEAD LODGE
307-587-3980

MOUNTAIN SHADOWS RANCH
307-587-2143

Wheatland
BLACKBIRD INN
307-332-4540

EDWARDS B&B
307-322-3921

MILL IRON SPEAR RANCH
307-322-5940

Wilson
FISH CREEK B&B
307-733-2586

*HECK OF A HILL HOMESTEAD
307-733-8023

HEIDELBERG B&B
307-733-7820

TETON TREE HOUSE
307-733-3233

*TETON VIEW B&B
307-733-7954

©Bed & Breakfast Guest Houses & Inns of America, Memphis TN

Canada

Halliburton House Inn			**Halifax NC**
Dr Bruce Petty			5184 Morris St B3J 1B3
902-420-0658			**Fax** 902-423-2334

Rates:	**Pvt Bath** 30	**Suites**	**Payment Terms:**
Single	$ 100.00 CN	$ 160.00 CN	Check
Double	$ 100.00 CN	$ 160.00 CN	MC/V

Take a memory home with you - *Halliburton House Inn*! Experience the pleasure of stepping into the past by visiting this *Heritage Property*, for an overnight stay or gourmet meal. Halliburton House was build in 1816 as the home of Sir Brenton Halliburton, Chief Justice of the Nova Scotia Supreme Court. From 1885 to 1887, the building served as Dalhousie University Law School. Today, this registered heritage property is Halifax's finest Inn. All of the Inn's thirty comfortable guest rooms are tastefully furnished with period antiques. Each has a private bath, as well as the modern amenities expected by today's guests. Several suites are available, some with fireplaces. Sit in front of a warm crackling fire and relax before dinner in the library. Our restaurant offers a relaxed elegant setting for both lunch and dinner. The *Halliburton* menu specializes in wild game and fresh Atlantic seafood. During the summer months, relax over lunch in the outdoor garden cafe. With its central location and free parking, the Inn is ideally located in the heart of downtown Halifax. *Halliburton House Inn* is known for its high standards, relaxed ambience and excellent service. **DISCOUNTS:** Yes, inquire at res time **RESERVATIONS:** One night's deposit, 24 hr cancel policy **SEASONAL:** Rates vary **BROCHURE:** Yes **PERMITTED:** Children, drinking, limited smoking **CONFERENCES:** Yes, our boardroom seats 25 persons **LANGUAGES:** English, French [I07GPCN2-11793]

Albert House	**Ottawa ON**
John & Cathy Delroy	478 Albert St K1R 5B5
800-267-1982 613-236-4479	**Res Times** 8am-11pm

Canada

Rates:	Pvt Bath 17	Payment Terms:
Single	$ 62-85.00 CN	Tvlrs Check
Double	$ 72-95.00 CN	AE/DC/MC/V

Albert House is a charming Victorian mansion built in 1875 by and for noted Canadian architect, Thomas Seaton Scott who was the Chief Architect for the Ministry of Public Works at that time. Scott oversaw many government projects including the original Customs House and Post Office in downtown Ottawa and part of the Parliament Buildings. Our seventeen guest rooms are individually decorated and all have ensuite facilities, colour cable TV, direct dial phones and air conditioning/individual heat control. Guests can enjoy our famous Albert House full, hot breakfast in the dining room or continental service is available for those who wish to breakfast in their room. A cozy lounge with fireplace provides a pleasant place to chat with other guests or read one of the many periodicals from our large selection. Complimentary tea, coffee, fruit juices are available during the day and evening. Our downtown location allows guests to park their cars and walk to most of Ottawa's attractions, both cultural and recreational. We have two very large but friendly dogs who have become quite well-known and welcome presence at *Albert House*. **DISCOUNTS:** Seasonal weekends **AIRPORT:** Ottawa Intl-7 mi **RESERVATIONS:** One night's deposit or credit card number to guarantee, arrival before 11pm unless prior arrangements have been made **BROCHURE:** Yes **PERMITTED:** Limited children, limited pets, drinking, smoking **LANGUAGES:** English, some French [Z07GPCN2-9185]

**Austrealis Guest House — Ottawa ON
Brian & Carol Waters   35 Marlborough Ave K1N 8E6
613-235-8461   **Res Times** 8am-10pm

Rates:	Pvt Bath 1	Shared Bath 2	Payment Terms:
Single	$ 88.00 CN	$ 35-Up CN	Check
Double	$ 58.00 CN	$ 45-Up CN	

We are the oldest established and still operating Bed & Breakfast in the Ottawa area. Located on a quiet, tree-lined street one block from the Rideau River, with its ducks and swans and Strathcona Park ... but just a twenty minute walk from the Parliament Buildings. This period, architecturally designed house boasts leaded windows, fireplace, oak floors and unique eight foot high stained glass windows overlooking the hall. Our spacious rooms, including a suite and private bathroom, features many of our collectibles from our time living in different parts of the world. The hearty, home-cooked delicious breakfast, with homebaked breads, pastries ensure you will start the day in just the right way. Our Australian and English heritage combined with our time in Canada provide a truly international flavor with a relaxed atmosphere. We are

Canada

located downtown and have off-street parking. In-addition, we provide free pick-up and delivery from/to the bus and train stations for our guests. We speak both English and French. Multiple-winner of the **Ottawa Hospitality Award** and **recommended** by *Newsweek*. We are full members of the Ottawa Tourism and Convention Authority. **RESERVATIONS:** One night's deposit required **PERMITTED:** Children, limited smoking **SEASONAL:** No **BROCHURE:** Yes **LANGUAGES:** English, French **DISCOUNTS:** 10% off-season 11/1-3/1 **PACKAGES:** Yes, with local restaurants [R05FPCN1-9186]

**Burken Guest House		**Toronto ON**
Burke Friedrichkeit & Ken Bosher		322 Palmerston Blvd M6G 2N6
416-920-7842		**Res Times** 10am-7pm
		Fax 416 960-9529
Rates:	**Shared Bath** 8	**Payment Terms:**
Single	$ 45-50.00 CN	Cash
Double	$ 60-65.00 CN	MC/V

Burken Guest House is located in a beautiful residential downtown Toronto neighborhood next to public transportation and where most attractions can be reached within 30 minutes. Our home is well-kept, quiet and accommodates only non-smokers. Four guest rooms on each floor are wonderfully furnished with antiques with European-style bath facilities (washbasins in each room) while sharing the full bath with three others on the same floor. Each room is equipped with a telephone and includes maid service. A continental breakfast is served in the breakfast room or on the outdoor deck in summer. A TV lounge provides relaxation with a generous supply of newspapers and books. Limited free parking is available on the premises. Your hosts are into their tenth successful year of pleasing guests and are members of *FOBBA*, *MTCVA* and the *American B&B Assoc* and many others. Their friendly and capable service will make your visit to Toronto most enjoyable. **DISCOUNTS:** Weekly rates Nov to April **AIRPORT:** Toronto Pearson Intl-15 km. **RESERVATIONS:** Deposit required to guarantee reservation, 48 hr cancel policy **BROCHURE:** Yes **PERMITTED:** Children, drinking. **LANGUAGES:** English, German, French [K07GPCN2-9199]

**Albion Guest House	**Vancouver BC**
Bill Browning	592 W Nineteenth Ave V5Z 1W6

Canada

604-873-2287

Rates:	Pvt Bath 2	Shared Bath 2	Payment Terms:
Single	$ 110.00 CN	$ 66.00 CN	
Double	$ 110.00 CN	$ 99.00 CN	MC/V

On a quiet tree-lined residential street near city hall is the turn-of-the-century character home with five restful rooms and whose beds are covered with thick feather mattresses, fine cotton linens and down-filled duvets. Imagine yourself sitting in the beautiful sitting room with freshly cut flowers, while relaxing in front of the fireplace, sipping complimentary wine or sherry. At the *Albion Guest House*, we serve a sumptuous breakfast in the formal dining room overlooking the flower garden. Later, you may use one of the complimentary bikes to explore Vancouver on your own. Because we're near city hall, Chinatown and Gastown are just a few minutes away along with the Expo Skytrain; you're just a few minutes walk to gambling casinos, restaurants, specialty coffee shops, delicatessens, theatre and Queen Elizabeth Park. A myriad of attractions and activities are available, including boating, parasailing, windsurfing and health clubs. It's just a 30 minute drive to the famous Capilano Suspension Bridge or to Grouse Mountain, a major ski area with panoramic views of Vancouver. **RESERVATIONS:** Deposit is required to guarantee reservation, one week cancel policy for refund **SEASONAL:** No **PERMITTED:** Drinking **BROCHURE:** Yes **LANGUAGES:** French **DISCOUNTS:** Off-season **AIRPORT:** Vancouver-20 min **PACKAGES:** *Romantic* (Bubble bath, Champagne, Candies and fresh cut flowers) [R09FPCN1-17199]

Abigails   **Victoria BC

Catherine Wollner   906 Mc Clure St V8V 3E7

604-388-5363   **Res Times** 7:30am-10pm

Rates:	Pvt Bath 16	Payment Terms:
Single	$ 90-175.00 CN	Check
Double	$ 90-175.00 CN	MC/V

Following in the tradition of European-style Inns, *Abigails* has been marvelously transformed into a small luxurious hotel. Decorated with soft colours, comfortable furnishings, crystal chandeliers and fresh flowers, you will want to guiltlessly pamper yourself in this romantic ambience . . . All guest rooms have private baths and fluffy goose down comforters. Dream before your crackling fire or relax in a jacuzzi or soaking tub before retiring. Join us in the library each late afternoon for a platter of cheese, fresh fruit and a glass of port before you sample some of the best restaurants in Victoria. In the morning you'll awake to the aroma of fresh coffee and our famous Innkeepers full breakfast. Located

Canada

just four blocks east of the city centre, we are within strolling distance of Victoria's specialty shops, floral parks and oceanside delights. Ours is a world of intimate charm and pleasure . . . **RESERVATIONS:** Credit card deposit at res time, 48 hr cancel policy for refund, no check-in after 10pm **SEASONAL:** No **BROCHURE:** Yes **PERMITTED:** Children and limited drinking [R08BCCN-6620]

**Beaconsfield Inn	**Victoria BC**
Hazel Prior	998 Humboldt St V8V 2Z8
604-384-4044	**Res Times** 7:30am-10pm

Rates:	**Pvt Bath** 12	**Payment Terms:**
Single	$ 100-196.00 CN	Check
Double	$ 100-196.00 CN	MC/V

In 1905, during the Edwardian Era, **"the height of the British Empire"**, famous architect Samuel McClure was commissioned by RP Rithet to build the *Beaconsfield* for his daughter, Gertrude, as a wedding gift. A gleaming sun room/conservatory, rich mahogany panelling, period antiques, oil paintings, a book-lined library and a cozy kitchen complete the main floor. The guest rooms have their own names, such as Rosebud, Oscar's (after Oscar Wilde), Willie's, Daisy's and Lillie's (named after Lilly Langtree), both mistresses of Edward VII. Each guest room has a private bathroom, goose down comforter and is luxuriously decorated. Some guest rooms include wood-burning fireplaces, clawfoot tubs or jacuzzi baths. Each afternoon join us in the library for a sherry hour where we serve an assortment of cheese, crackers and fresh fruit. The following morning guests awake to the aroma of our special blend coffee and the Innkeeper's famous full breakfast. Located only a few minutes walk from our specialty shops, Beacon Hill Park and the Inner Harbor. *The Beaconsfield Inn*, an experience that will linger in your memory . . . **RESERVATIONS:** Credit card deposit, 48 hr cancel policy, no check-in after 10pm **SEASONAL:** No **BROCHURE:** Yes **PERMITTED:** Children, limited drinking [Z11CPCN1-6619]

**Rose Cottage B&B	**Victoria BC**
Robert & Shelley Bishop	3059 Washington Ave V9A 1P7
604-381-5985	

Rates:	**Shared Bath** 4	**Payment Terms:**
Single	$ 70-80.00 CN	
Double	$ 70-80.00 CN	MC/V

Victoria's oldest Bed and Breakfast, *Rose Cottage* is a 1912 traditional Victorian home carefully restored to retain all of the **Heritage** features of

Canada

the turn-of-the-century Victoria. *Rose Cottage* has high ceillinged rooms, period furniture, guest parolor in a nautical theme, a large dining room with library and quiet, well-appointed bedrooms. Your hosts, Robert and Shelley, are part of the character of the *Rose Cottage*. We have travelled extensively before settling in Victoria and know the value of a warm welcome for our visitors. Located on a quiet street close to downtown, guests are just a few blocks from the beautiful Gorge Park Waterway. A full course complimentary breakfast includes fresh fruit and muffins. We have lots of inside info about Victoria to make your visit as adventuresome or as relaxing as you wish. **RESERVATIONS:** First night's deposit or credit card number to guarantee reservation **PERMITTED:** Children, drinking **BROCHURE:** Yes **LANGUAGES:** Canadian and American **DISCOUNTS:** Yes **AIRPORT:** Victoria Intl- 10 mi [R07FPCN1-9114]

Blomidon Inn			**Wolfville NS**
*Jim Laceby			127 Main St B0P 1X0
902-542-2291			

Rates:	**Pvt Bath** 25	**Shared Bath** 2	**Payment Terms:**
Single	$ 61-88.00 CN	$ 39.00 CN	AE/MC/V
Double	$ 72-99.00 CN	$ 49.00 CN	**Fax** 902-542-7461

Situated only an hour's drive from Halifax International Airport is this elegant mansion built in the 1870s by Capt Rufus Burgess. Capt Burgess made his fortune in the glorious days of sailing as a shipbuilder and sea captain. Today his home has been beautifully restored offering 27 elegant rooms (many with handmade quilts and four-poster beds) and two dining rooms and parlours, complete with fireplaces. Nestled near the world's highest tides in a micro-climate that enables the Valley to have a worldwide recognition for its apples and grape harvests! Nearby guests find Grande Pre National Park, the setting for Longfellow's *Evangeline*. A continental breakfast is included with other gourmet entrees offered in the restaurant on the premises. **RESERVATIONS:** Deposit required within 14 days of booking, with 48 hr cancel policy **SEASONAL:** No **BROCHURE:** Yes **PERMITTED:** Drinking, [E11BCCN-8785]

Canada

Albert NB
FLORENTINE MANOR
506-882-2271

Allen SK
MOLDENHAUERS B&B
306-257-3578

Alma NB
CAPTAIN'S INN
506-887-2017

Alton ON
HORSESHOE INN
519-927-5779

Amherst NS
AMHERST SHORE INN
902-667-4800

Annapolis Royal NS
BREAD & ROSES
902-532-5727

CHESHIRE CAT
902-532-2100

GARRISON HOUSE
902-532-5750

MILFORD HOUSE
902-532-2617

POPLAR B&B
902-532-7936

QUEEN ANNE INN
902-532-7850

Antigohsih NS
OLD MANSE INN
902-863-5696

Augustine Cover PE

SHORE FARM B&B
902-855-2871

Baie St Paul QE
LA MAISON OTIS
418-435-2255

Bamfield BC
AGUILAR HOUSE
604-728-3323

Bayfield ON
LITTLE INN OF BAYFIELD
519-565-2611

Belfast PE
LINDEN LODGE
902-659-2716

Beresford NB
LES PEUPLIERS
506-546-5271

Blackstock ON
LANDFALL FARM
416-986-5588

Blaine Lake SK
VERESHAGINS COUNTRY B&B
306-497-2782

Bonshaw PE
CHURCHILL FARM
902-675-2481

Bracebridge ON
HOLIDAY HOUSE INN
705-645-2245

Brackley Beach PE
SHAWS COTTAGE
902-672-2022

Bradford ON
COUNTRY GUEST HOME
416-775-3576

Braeside ON
GLENROY FARM
613-432-6248

Brentwood Bay BC
BRENTWOOD BAY B&B
604-652-2012

Bulyea SK
HILLCREST HOTEL
306-725-4874

Caledon East ON
CALEDON INN
416-584-2891

Campbell River BC
APRIL POINT LODGE
604-285-2222

CAMPBELL RIVER LODGE
800-663-7212

DOGWOODS
604-287-4213

Camrose AL
NORDBYE HOUSE
403-672-8131

Canning
1850 HOUSE
902-582-3052

Cap-a-l'Aigle QE
AUBERGE LA PINSONNIERE
418-665-4431

Cape Breton NS
RIVERSIDE INN
902-235-2002

300 ©*Bed & Breakfast Guest Houses & Inns of America, Memphis TN*

Canada

Carleton Place ON
OTTAWA VALLEY
B&B
613-257-7720

Centreville NB
REIDS FARM HOME
506-276-4787

CH Trudel QE
OTTER LAKE HAUS
819-687-2767

Charlevoix QE
LA PINSONNIERE
418-665-4431

Charlottetown PE
JUST FOLKS B&B
902-569-2089

Chemainns BC
GRANTS
604-246-3768

Chester NS
MCNEIL MANOR B&B
902-275-4638

Cobourg ON
NORTHUMBERLAND
HEIGHTS INN
416-372-7500

Coin duBacn-Perce QE
AUBERGE LE COIN
DU BANC
418-645-2907

Collingwood NS
COBEQUID HILLS
COUNTRY INN
902-686-3381

Como QE
WILLOW INN
514-458-7006

Comte de Mantane QE
AUBERGE LA
MARTRE
418-288-5533

Cookstown ON
CHESTNUT INN
705-458-9751

Cornwall PR
OBANLEA TOURIST
HOME
902-566-3067

Corwan PE
CHEZ HOUS B&B
902-566-2779

Cranmore AL
COUGAR CREEK INN
403-678-4751

Cte Matapedia QE
GITE DU PASSANT
418-775-5237

Darthmouth NS
MARTIN HOUSE B&B
902-469-1896

Denman Island BC
DENMAN ISLAND INN
604-335-2688

Digby County NS
HARBOUR VIEW INN
902-245-5686

Downsview ON
SCHWEIZER LODGE
514-538-2123

Duncan BC
NORTH PACIFIC
SPRINGS
604-748-3189

Duncan Island BC
FAIRBURN FARM
604-746-4637

Dunham QE
MAPLEWOOD
514-295-2519

Eagle Creek BC
BRADSHAW'S
LODGE
604-397-2416

Elora ON
PENSTOCK INNS LTD
519-846-5356

Fergus ON
BREADELBANE INN
519-843-4770

Fort Steele BC
WILD HORSE FARM
604-426-6000

Frederickton AL
BACKPORCH B&B
506-454-6875

Gabriola Island BC
SURF LODGE
604-247-9231

Galiano Island BC
HUMMINGBIRD INN
604-539-5472

LA BERENGERIE
609-539-5392

Gaspe Peninsula QE
HOTEL LA
NORMANDIE
418-782-2112

Canada

Gaspesie QE
HENRY HOUSE
418-534-2115

Georgeville QE
GEORGEVILLE
COUNTRY INN
819-843-8683

Gores Landing ON
VICTORIA INN
416-342-3261

Grand Manan Isl NB
SHORECREST
LODGE
506-662-3216

Grand Manan NB
CROSS TREE GUEST
HOUSE
506-662-8663

FERRY WHARF INN
506-662-8588

GRAND HARBOUR
INN
506-662-8681

Granville Ferry NS
BAYBERRY HOUSE
902-532-2272

SHINING TIDES B&B
902-532-2770

Guysborough NS
LIMBSCOMBE
LODGE
902-779-2307

Halfmoon Bay BC
LORD JIM'S HOTEL
604-885-7038

Halifax NS

APPLE BASKET B&B
902-429-3019

****HALLIBURTON
HOUSE INN**
902-420-0658

QUEEN STREET INN
902-422-9828

Hampstead NB
EVELEIGH HOTEL
506-425-9993

Hartland NB
WOODSVIEW II B&B
506-375-4637

Hebron NS
MANOR INN
902-742-2487

Hopewell Cape NB
DUTCH TREAT B&B
506-882-2552

Hornby Island BC
SEA BREEZE INN
604-335-2321

Howick QE
HAZELBRAE FARM
514-825-2390

**Huntington
St Anicet**
LEDUC
514-264-6533

Iona NS
HIGHLAND HEIGHTS
INN

Iroquois ON
CEDARLANE FARM
613-652-4267

Jackson Point ON
BRIARS INN &
COUNTRY CLUB
800-465-2376

Kamourasha QE
GITE DU PASSANT
B&B
418-492-2921

Kelowna BC
BLAIR HOUSE
604-762-5090

GABLES COUNTRY
INN
604-768-4468

Kensington PE
BEACH POINT VIEW
INN
902-836-5260

BLAKENEYS B&B
902-836-3254

MURPHYS SEA VIEW
INN
902-836-5456

SHERWOOD ACRES
902-836-5430

WOODINGTONS
COUNTRY INN
902-836-5518

Kingston ON
PRINCE GEORGE
HOTEL
613-549-5440

Kleena Kleene BC
CHILANKO RESORT
604-553-3625

Knowlton QE

Canada

AUBERGE
LAKETREE
514-243-6604

Ladysmith BC
MANANA LODGE
604-245-2312

YELLOW POINT
LODGE
604-245-7422

Lansdowne ON
IVYLEA INN
613-659-2329

Little York PE
DALVAY BY THE SEA
902 672-2048

Lle d Orleans QE
CHEZ LES DUMAS
418-828-9442

MANOR DE L'ANSE
418-828-2248

London ON
ROSE B&B
519-433-9978

Lousibourg NS
GRETA CROSS B&B
902-733-2833

Lower Bedeque PE
WAUGHS B&B
902-887-2320

Mabou NS
CAPE BRETON
ISLAND FARM
902-945-2077

Mactaquac NB
MACTAQUAC B&B
506-363-3630

Marshfield PE
ROSEVALE FARM
902-894-7821

May River AL
HABOR HOUSE
403-874-2233

Mayne Isl BC
OCEANWOOD
COUNTRY INN
604-539-5074

Mayne Island BC
FERNHILL LODGE
604-539-2544

GINGERBREAD
HOUSE
604-539-3133

Maynooth ON
BEA'S B&B HOUSE
613-338-2239

McKeller ON
INN & TENNIS
CLUB/MANITOU
416-967-3466

Merrickville ON
SAM JAKES INN
613-269-3711

Mill Bay BC
PINELODGE B&B
604-743-4083

Millarville AL
MESA CREEK RANCH
403-931-3573

Millet AL
BROADVIEW FARM
403-387-4963

Minden ON

MINDEN HOUSE
705-286-3263

Mont Tremblant QE
AUBERGE
SAUVIGNON
819-425-2658

CHATEAU
BEAUVALLON
819-425-7275

Montague PE
BRYDONS B&B
902-838-4717

Montreal East QE
LE BRETON
514-52-7273

Montreal ON
*MANOIR AMBROSE

Montreal QE
ARMOR INN
514-285-0894

Morris BC
DEERBANK FARM
204-746-8395

Murray Harbor PE
HARBOURVIEW B&B
902-962-2565

Murray River PE
BAYBERRY CLIFF
INN
902-962-3395

Musquodoboit Harbor NS
CAMELOT
902-889-2198

Nanoose Bay BC
THE LOOKOUT

Canada

604-468-9796

Nanton AL
TIMBERIDGE
HOMESTEAD
403-646-5683

Nelson BC
HERITAGE INN
604-352-5331

Nelson NB
GOVERNOR'S
MANSION
506-622-3036

New Brunswick NB
HAPPY APPLE ACRES

New Hanburg ON
WATERLOT INN
519-662-2020

Newboro ON
STERLING LODGE
613-272-2435

Niagara On Lake ON
ANGEL INN
416-468-3411

KIELY HOUSE
HERITAGE INN
416-468-4588

MOFFAT INN
416-468-4116

OBAN INN
416-468-2165

OLD BANK HOUSE

Nine Mile Creek PE
LAINE ACRES B&B
902-675-2402

Nobel ON
PAINES B&B
705-342-9266

Normandale ON
UNION HOTEL
519-426-5568

North Sydney NS
ANNFIELD TOURIST
MANOR
902-736-8770

North Vancouver BC
**ALBION GUEST
HOUSE
604-873-2287

GROUSE MTN B&B
604-986-9630

HELENS B&B
604-985-4869

LABURNUM
COTTAGE
604-988-4877

PLATTS B&B
604-987-4100

VICTORIAN B&B
604-985-1523

Norwich ON
WILLI-JOY FARM B&B
519-424-2113

Okotoks AL
WILDFLOWER
COUNTRY

Ottawa ON
**ALBERT HOUSE
800-267-1982

**AUSTRALIS GUEST
HOUSE
613-235-8461

BEATRICE LYON
HOUSE
613-236-3904

BLUE SPRUCE B&B
613-236-8521

CARTIER HOUSE INN
613-236-INNS

CONSTANCE HOUSE
613-235-8888

DORAL INN HOTEL
613-230-8055

FLORA HOUSE
613-230-2152

GASTHAUS
SWITZERLAND
613-237-0335

GWENS GUEST
HOUSE
613-737-4129

HAYDON HOUSE
613-230-2697

MCGEES INN

RIDEAU VIEW INN
613-236-9309

WESTMINSTER
GUEST HOUSE
613-729-2707

Owen Sound ON
MOSES SUNSET B&B
519-371-4559

Parson BC

Canada

TALISIN GUEST HOUSE
604-348-2247

Pender Island BC
CORBETT HOUSE
604-629-6305

Penticton BC
ROSE COTTAGE B&B
604-492-3462

Pentifcton BC
TINA'S TUC INN
604-492-3366

Perth ON
PERTH MANOR
519-271-7129

Pictou NS
L'AUBERGE
902-485-6900

Plaster Rock NB
NORTHERN WILDERNESS LODGE
506-356-8327

Plympton NS
WESTWAY INN
902-837-4097

Pointe-Au-Oic QE
AUBERGE DONOHUE
418-665-4377

Port Carling ON
SHERWOOD INN
705-765-3131

Port Dufferin NS
*MARQUIE DUFFERIN SEASIDE INN

Port Renfrerw BC

FEATHERED PADDLE
604-647-5433

Port Severn ON
ARROWWOOD LODGE
705-538-2354

Port Stanley ON
KETTLE CREEK INN
519-782-3388

Port Williams NS
PLANTER'S BARRACKS
902-542-7879

Portneuf QE
EDALE PLACE
418-286-3168

FRANCE BEAULIEU HOUSE
418-336-2724

Pugwash NS
BLUE HERON INN
902-243-2900

Quathiaski Cove BC
TSA-KWA-LUTEN LODGE
800-665-7745

Quebec City QE
AU CHATEAU FLEUR DE LIS
418-694-1884

AU MANOIR STE GENEVIEVE
418-694-1666

AUBERGE DE LA CHOUTTE
418-694-0232

CHATEAU DE LA TERRASSE
418-694-9472

LE CHATEAU DE PIERRE
418-694-0429

MAISON MARIE-ROLLET
418-694-9271

Quyon QE
MEMORYLANE FARM
819-458-2479

Regina SK
TURGEON INTL B&B
306-522-4200

Riverside NB
CAILSWICK BABBLING BROOK
506-882-2079

Rockport ON
AMARYLLIS HOUSEBOAT B&B
613-659-3513

Rossland BC
RAMS HEAD INN
604-362-9577

Rothesay NB
SHADOW LAWN COUNTRY INN
506-847-7539

Sackville NB
MARSHLANDS INN
506-536-0170

Salmon Arm BC
CINDOSA B&B INN
604-832-3342

Canada

SILVER CREEK
GUEST HOUSE
604-832-8870

Salt Spring Isl BC
HASTINGS HOUSE
800-661-9255

Seebe AL
BREWSTERS
KANANASKIS RANCH
403-673-3737

Sooke BC
HARBOUR HOUSE
800-665-7745

Souix Narrows ON
YELLOWBIRD LODGE
807-226-5279

St Andrews NB
PANSY PATCH B&B
506-529-3834

PUFF INN
506-529-4191

SHIRETOWN INN
506-529-8877

St Anne De Mont QE
GITE DU MONT
ALBERT
800-463-0860

St Antoine Tilly QE
AUBERGE MANOIR
DE TILLY
418-886-2407

St Jacobs ON
JACOBSTETTEL
GUEST HOUSE
519-664-2208

St Laurent QE

MAISON SOUS LE
ARBRES
418-828-9442

St Marc Richelieu QE
HANDFIELD INN
514-584-2226

St Roch Aulnaies QE
LELLETIER HOUSE
418-354-2450

*St Sauveur des
Monts QE*
AUBERGE ST-DENIS
514-227-4766

Stanley Bridge PE
CREEKSIDE FARM
B&B
902-886-2713

GULF BREEZE B&B
902-886-2678

Ste Petronille QE
AUBERGE LA
GOELICHE
418-828-2248

Stratford ON
BURNSIDE GUEST
HOME
519-271-7076

SHREWSBURY
MANOR
519-271-8520

STONE MAIDEN INN
519-271-7129

Summerland BC
THREE PINES LODGE
604-494-1661

Summerside PE

SILVER FOX INN
902-436-4033

Sussex NB
ANDERSONS
HOLIDAY FARM
506-433-3786

Sutton QE
AUBERGE
SCHWEIZER
514-538-2129

Tantallon NS
SEABRIGHT B&B
902-823-2987

Tingish PE
HARBOUR LIGHTS
902-882-2479

Tisdale SK
PRAIRIE ACRES B&B
306-873-2272

Tofino BC
CLAYOQUOT LODGE
604-725-3284

Toronto ON
ASHLEIGH
HERITAGE INN
416-535-4000

**BURKEN GUEST
HOUSE
416-920-7842

Treherne MA
BEULAH LAND INN
204-723-2828

Tyne Valley PE
WEST ISLAND INN
902-831-2495

Ucluelet BC

Canada

BURLEYS LODGE
604-726-4444

Upper Stewiacke NS
LANDSDOWN INN
902-671-2749

Val David QE
AUBERGE DU VIEUX FOYER
819-322-2686

PARKERS LODGE
819-322-2026

Vancouver BC
**ALBION GUEST HOUSE
604-873-2287

DIANA'S B&B
604-321-2855

PENNY FARTHING INN
604-739-9002

PILLOW'N PORRIDGE GUEST HOUSE

ROSE GARDEN GUEST INN
604-435-7129

VINCENTS GUEST HOUSE
604-254-7462

WEST END GUEST INN
604-681-2889

Vernon BC
FIVE JUNIPERS B&B
604-549-3615

SCHROTH FARM B&B
604-545-0010

TWIN WILLOWS
604-542-8293

WINDMILL HOUSE B&B
604-549-2804

Victoria BC
**ABIGAILS
604-388-5363

BATTERY STREET B&B
604-385-4623

**BEACONSFIELD INN
604-384-4044

CAPTAINS PALACE INN
604-388-9191

CHERRY BANK HOTEL

CRAIGMYLE B&B
604-595-5411

ELK LAKE LODGE
604-658-8879

HIBERNIA B&B
604-658-5519

HOLLAND HOUSE

OAK BAY BEACH HOTEL
604-598-4556

OXFORD CASTLE INN
604-388-6431

PORTAGE INLET B&B
604-479-4594

*PRIOR HOUSE B&B

**ROSE COTTAGE B&B
604-381-5985

SUNNYMEAD HOUSE

604-658-1414

TOP O' TRIANGLE MTN
604-478-7853

TUCHERK'S B&B
604-658-5531

Victoria By Sea PE
VICTORIA VILLAGE
902-658-2288

Vieux-Quebec QE
AU PETIT HOTEL
418-694-0965

W Vancouver BC
BRAMBLEWYCK BY THE SEA
604-926-3827

Wallace NS
SENATOR GUEST HOUSE
902-257-2417

Waterloo QE
PERRAS
514-539-2983

Wawota SK
PLEASANT VISTA ANGUS FARM
306-739-2915

©Bed & Breakfast Guest Houses & Inns of America, Memphis TN

Canada

Weymouth NS
GILBERTS COVE
FARM
902-837-4505

Whistler BC
DURLACHER HOF
604-932-1924

SABEY HOUSE B&B
604-932-3498

Windermere ON
WINDERMERE
HOUSE
705-769-3611

Winnipeg MA
CHESTNUT B&B
204-772-9788

Wolfville NS
*BLOMIDON INN
902-542-2291

TATTINGSTONE INN
902-542-7696

VICTORIA
HISTORIC INN
902-542-5744

York PE
AMBER LIGHTS B&B
902-894-5868

Youngs Point ON
OLD BRIDGE INN
705-652-8507